Spaces of
Their Own

PUBLIC WORLDS

Edited by Dilip Gaonkar and Benjamin Lee

MAYFAIR MEI-HUI YANG, EDITOR

Spaces of
Their Own

Women's Public Sphere

in Transnational China

PUBLIC WORLDS, VOLUME 4
UNIVERSITY OF MINNESOTA PRESS
MINNEAPOLIS LONDON

Published with assistance from the Margaret S. Harding
Memorial Endowment honoring the first director of the
University of Minnesota Press

The University of Minnesota Press gratefully acknowledges permission to reprint the
following. Chapter 11 originally appeared as "Gender and a Geopolitics of Desire:
The Seduction of Mainland Women in Taiwan and Hong Kong Media," *Signs: Journal of
Women in Culture and Society* 23:2 (winter 1998), used by permission of University of
Chicago Press.

Published by the University of Minnesota Press
111 Third Avenue South, Suite 290
Minneapolis, MN 55401-2520
http://www.upress.umn.edu

Library of Congress Cataloging-in-Publication Data

Spaces of their own : women's public sphere in transnational China /
    Mayfair Mei-hui Yang, editor.
        p.   cm. — (Public worlds ; v. 4)
        Based on a conference on "Mass media, gender, and a Chinese public: Mainland,
    Taiwan, Hong Kong" held in Santa Barbara, Calif., in April 1995.
        Includes bibliographical references (p.   ) and index.
        ISBN 0-8166-3145-X (alk. paper). — ISBN 0-8166-3146-8 (pbk. : alk. paper)
        1. Women—China—Congresses. 2. Women in public life—China—Congresses.
    3. Women in mass media—China—Congresses. 4. Feminism—China—
    Congresses. I. Yang, Mayfair Mei-hui. II. Series.
    HQ1767.S6   1999
    305.4'0951—dc21   98-30875

Printed in the United States of America on acid-free paper

The University of Minnesota is an equal-opportunity educator and employer.

10 09 08 07 06 05 04 03 02 01 00 99   10 9 8 7 6 5 4 3 2 1

Contents

Editor's Acknowledgments

This book emerged from a conference that I organized, "Mass Media, Gender, and a Chinese Public: Mainland, Taiwan, Hong Kong," which was held in Santa Barbara in April 1995. I wish to thank the National Science Foundation, Presidential Young Investigator Award, for support toward this conference, and also the Interdisciplinary Humanities Center at the University of California, Santa Barbara. Thanks are also due for a Rockefeller Fellowship at the Chicago Humanities Institute, University of Chicago in 1996, which provided me with research time, facilities, and a stimulating environment. In addition, I thank the University of California, Santa Barbara's Education Abroad Program for providing funds to bring Dai Jinhua to the campus for a quarter in 1995 as a visiting scholar, and enabling a rich intellectual exchange. I am indebted to Esther Yim for the index work and to Everett Yuehong Zhang for the title idea.

Finally, I wish to thank Benjamin Lee for his support in this project, and the two outside readers of the manuscript for their suggestions, especially Gina Marchetti, whose lengthy and careful review was extremely helpful in revisions. This book would have taken much longer to finish were it not for the help of Everett Zhang, who spent considerable time taking care of our son Kai Keyang Zhang, while also pursuing his own intellectual projects; and my mother, Yu-shu Ou Yang, and Catherine Nesci, who both generously lent a helping hand with the baby in times of need.

Introduction

Mayfair Mei-hui Yang

"Father's time, mother's species," as Joyce put it; and indeed, when evoking the name and destiny of women, one thinks more of the *space* generating and forming the human species than of *time*, becoming or history.
                                                    —Julia Kristeva, "Women's Time"

It is in space, on a worldwide scale, that each idea of "value" acquires or loses its distinctiveness through confrontation with the other values and ideas that it encounters there. . . . Groups, classes or fractions of classes cannot constitute themselves, or recognize one another, as "subjects" unless they generate (or produce) a space. Ideas, representations or values which do not succeed in making their mark on space . . . will lose all pith and become mere signs. . . . whatever is not invested in an appropriated space is stranded. . . . Space's investment—the production of space—has nothing incidental about it: it is a matter of life and death.
                                                    —Henri Lefebvre, *The Production of Space*

In her provocative essay "Women's Time," Julia Kristeva described the challenge that a women's "monumental time," linked to the cyclical reproductive temporality of the life and death of a civilization or the species, could pose to the male time of linear history and nation-state unfolding. Yet it is curious that she thought of *space* as having a female imprint. It would seem that differential gender formations, and therefore struggles of gender, are also found in the production of space. Indeed, in modernity we have witnessed not just the domination of masculine linear temporality, but also what Henri Lefebvre calls "the space of phallic verticality" (1991: 36, 287), found in the male spatial metaphors of state monuments, construction projects, and military parades, encasing the brutality of political power (police, military, bureaucracy), and in the virile erections of capitalist vertical cities around the globe. Far from comfortably embodying space, women in modernity have been multiply displaced and enclosed (Massey 1994) and must mobilize to repossess the space that they have lost, while being poised to occupy and direct new spaces opened up by technological innovation. This book will consider the gender politics of the "public sphere," a new space established in modernity as the space of public discourse and debate, cultural and ideological production, and mass-media representation, which is also basically a masculine space.

The Chinese term *gonggong kongjian* or public space is often used to translate the English term *public sphere*, a translation itself of Jürgen Habermas's German notion of *Öffentlichkeit* (1989), a category of modern society referring to activities of public expression and debate that reflexively feed back into the self-knowledge and restructuring of society. (The Chinese term *gonggong lingyü* [public domain] is also used.) According to Miriam Hansen, the English term implies both a spatial concept of a site for the articulation of social meanings, and the notion of a collective social body of "the public." However, the English term does not possess the German suggestion of openness suggested by the root *offen* (Hansen 1993a: ix). Although the Chinese phrase is found more in intellectual discourse in Taiwan and Hong Kong than in that from the Mainland, new sites of public expression have opened up on the Mainland in the post-Mao era to warrant us applying this notion there. In its Chinese-language usage, *kongjian* means space, in the sense of spaces and sites of expression, and *gonggong* refers to a public collective entity. Even more than the English word *sphere*, the Chinese term emphasizes the spatial dimension and openness, in that *kongjian* suggests two other modern compound words, air (*kongqi*) and outer space (*taikong*). *Air* conveys the sense of an uninhibited breathing space commonly available to everyone. *Outer space* suggests an open vista stretching out indefinitely, a three-dimensional, unoccupied, and unexplored space, which is therefore open to new possibilities. It is especially these senses implied in the Chinese phrase that I would like to emphasize in this book.

This book chronicles the struggles surrounding the coming-into-being of a collective body of women-identified subjects, voices, and visions in different sites of "public sphere" and "public space" across "transnational China" at the turn from the twentieth century to the twenty-first. Embedded in this sentence are four key conceptual dimensions that inform the writing throughout this book. First, the scholars in this book would like to contribute to the spatialization of public sphere theory by departing from the usual site for locating public sphere, the West, and instead examining the different situations of public gender politics in the increasingly integrated entity of what I call "transnational China," comprising mainland China, Taiwan, Hong Kong, and overseas Chinese communities around the world. A second form of spatializing public sphere is in foregrounding the specific sites and media of women's discourse and gender politics, which here include street demonstrations in Taiwan; a women's museum in Zhengzhou, Henan Province; a feminist magazine (*Women Awakening* [*Funu xinzhi*]) and a women's bookstore in Taipei; public meetings and conferences; women's literature in a U.S.-based diasporic Chinese journal (*Today* [*Jintian*]); Hong Kong, Taiwan, and mainland film and television; and even a telephone hot line in Beijing. Third, the essays situate this process of coming-into-being of women in the public sphere in the historical context of Chinese modernity and its impact on gender from the beginning to the end of this century. Fourth, the essays examine the gender politics of public spaces by taking note of the public domination of masculine voices and visions on the one hand, and the struggles to establish women's public spheres on the other. Some of the essays provide critical analyses of reconfigured patriarchies and new forms of masculine domination in public culture, while other essays uncover the ways that male perspectives, though ostensibly making women visible and promoting them, actually in many ways recontain women's power and drown out their voices (Kaplan 1989).[1]

The idea for this book first emerged from my participation in two sets of face-to-face discussions. First, in 1992, while living in Los Angeles, I formed a discussion group of Chinese-speaking professional and diasporic women from the mainland, Taiwan, and Hong Kong, which met about once a month in each other's homes for a potluck dinner. The group included women who were, or were studying to become, filmmakers, film critics, scholars, a lawyer, a librarian, and an international business manager.[2] Discussions were mainly in Mandarin Chinese, and topics often had a personal dimension, including the pressures and misunderstandings of our Chinese families, our childhood, our Chinese or American partners, the freedoms and problems of single professional women, our relations with American society, and comparisons of women's situations in the different Chinese societies we came from.

The second forum was an international conference I organized in April 1995 in Santa Barbara, called "Mass Media, Gender, and a Chinese Public: Mainland, Taiwan, and Hong Kong," which generated several of the articles presented here. The conference gathered together scholars of China and gender studies in the United States[3] and guests from China and Taiwan, such as woman film director Huang Shuqin of Shanghai Film Studio (Dai and Yang 1995); Lee Yuan-chen, feminist scholar and founder of Taiwan's major feminist organization, Women Awakening Foundation; feminist film scholar Dai Jinhua from Beijing University; and Luo Jun, a woman editor of Shanghai's *Wenhui Film Times*. Both gatherings gave me the idea that women from different Chinese backgrounds could (and should) bridge political boundaries to carry on dialogues on women's issues.

Spatializing Chinese Public Spheres

In his book *The Structural Transformation of the Public Sphere* (1989), Jürgen Habermas traces the historical emergence of a public sphere of debate and discussion of cultural and political issues in eighteenth-century Western Europe. Such institutional shifts in early capitalism as the transfer of economic productive activities from the household to the factory, the independence of a bourgeois class from the aristocracy, and the commodification of art, music, literature, and news brought public expression out of the narrow confines of courtly life to the wider circulation of the public. The expansion of the modern state also propelled "private people" to "come together to form a public, . . to compel public authority to legitimate itself before public opinion" (1989: 25). Although the book deals with early modernity and ends in the 1950s, many of the issues it raises concerning the vicissitudes of a sphere of cultural-political discussion perched precariously in between two modern power formations of the state and the capitalist economy are still extremely relevant today in late modernity.

Habermas's work has important spatial implications in that he identified such sites of public sphere as the modern newspaper, the novel, the public library, the concert hall, the opera house, and the salon and coffeehouse as places of independence from the absolutist state. He also examined the shift from aristocratic dwellings to an architecture of privacy in the bourgeois home; from a front public salon to an inner family room and individualized bedrooms separate from servants' quarters (1989: 44–45; Landes 1988: 62). However, lacking a gender analysis, he missed an opportunity for a spatial critique of the male domination of the public sphere and the relegation of women to a modern private domestic sphere. While he discussed the importance of long-distance trade (which crossed city-state and nation-state borders) for the development of newspapers, he still took the nation-state as the basic unit, as when he analyzed the situations in England, France, and Germany separately. While he mourned the collapse of the public sphere in the era of mass media and commodification, he did not examine the novel qualities of the mass media, and how they have a different spatial form from that of the face-to-face interactions and print media form of the classical public sphere.

The categories of gender and race, and the development of modernity in non-Western nation-states, did not figure in Habermas's universalistic construction, nor did he recognize alternative public spheres to the classical bourgeois public. So it has been left to others to flesh out the pluralistic and contestatory process in the history of public sphere. Several scholars have pointed out the difference between a dominant public and such "subaltern publics" as those of peasants in nineteenth-century Germany (Eley 1994), women in the contemporary United States (Fraser 1992), counterculture Basque ethnic youth in Spain (Urla 1995), and new counterpublic social movements in 1970s West Germany (Negt and Kluge 1993). In moving "away from the universalizing ideal of a single public" (Robbins 1993: xii), Houston Baker finds the notion to be "expressive and empowering" for African Americans' collective "self-fashioning" in late twentieth-century America (1994: 9). However, these efforts all address the modern West, and there have been few public sphere inquiries into non-Western experiences of modernity.

What this book hopes to do is to focus on two spatializations of women in the realm of *cultural production* in transnational China. First, the book will examine the positioning of women in domestic or public space in Chinese mass media and public discourse. Here, although figures of women are prevalent, they appear mainly as *objects* of representations by men; women are encoded and excluded from the production of discourse. Second, the book also documents what Lefebvre calls the fugitive "representational spaces" (1991: 33) of women who live a semiclandestine life and try to carve out a larger space for themselves in the male public discursive world.

By introducing public sphere considerations into conceptualizations of both literal and metaphoric space, this book encourages thinking about the space of various kinds of media (both intellectual and popular-culture media) and the transmission of gender representations across space. When we rethink the public sphere in spatial and gender terms, what comes to prominence are the spatial strategies of the now globalized yet differentiated women's movement. Being sensitive to space means that the public sphere will no longer be assumed to operate only within national boundaries, but also *across* national and cultural space. Finally, gender theory highlights issues of gender politics and uncovers the fact that space is often constructed in terms of differential gender domains of power, such as public and domestic spaces, and that the dominant gender images and narratives found in public spheres are constructed from male points of view.

Chinese culture in the world today is composed of the various subcultures, classes, and minorities that are collected into the giant nation-state of mainland China, from whose geographical land mass and ancient cultural heritage emerged many diasporic cultural offshoots, which have planted themselves in new sites around the world. This is a loosely organized global collection of Chinese cultural branches that still share, to varying degrees, some cultural features (one could propose such features as language [although in different dialects] and writing; a work ethic; a family focus; a patriarchal orientation; food practices; entrepreneurial acumen; and so on). Various terms have been proposed for the globally dispersed yet still interconnected nature of Chinese culture around the world today. Tu Wei-ming's notion of *cultural China* is a useful term that describes a common Chinese culture underlying political and territorial separations. Cultural China is first composed of the people of the Chinese core areas (the mainland, Taiwan, Hong Kong, and Singapore); second, of overseas Chinese communities around the world; and third, of non-Chinese people who study or have close interactions with Chinese culture (Tu 1991). In addition, the term *Greater China* was featured in a special issue of *China Quarterly* in December 1993, devoted to analyzing the increasing integration of Chinese peoples in East and Southeast Asia through capitalist investment and trade linkages between mainland China and other economies in the region. In the current development of the mainland, foreign investment comes more from Chinese capitalists in Taiwan, Hong Kong, and Southeast Asia than from the West (Ash and Kueh 1993).

As a neo-Confucian scholar, Tu Wei-ming's "cultural China" is informed by the importance he confers on the cultural and especially the intellectual heritage of the Confucian past as the glue that holds the dispersed cultures together. What he emphasizes is the common experiences of the past, and what he looks for is a cultural revival and renewal of the treasure house of Chinese culture. From a feminist perspective, it is difficult to share this celebration of traditional Chinese culture, especially the long tradition of male scholar–official discourse that is neo-Confucianism. What seems necessary is a more critical approach to the cultural heritage, and a perspective that examines not just the past as a defining feature of what is Chinese, but also new modern elements of Chinese culture, and ongoing contemporary forces that increasingly constitute Chinese subjectivity and cultural practice. The notion of Greater China is a concept that focuses only on the present, on how relations of capitalist economic exchange are more often the integrative forces that give shape to this emergent Chinese entity. However, this term *Greater China* has the problem of being associated with what Aihwa Ong and Don Nonini (1997) have called "triumphalist narratives of Capital" that have emerged out of both the West and Asia, concerning the rapid economic development of East and Southeast Asia.[4] Moreover, it seems to me that by focusing only on capitalist economic relations as an integrative force, *Greater China* overprivileges capitalism as both the driving force and teleology, to the neglect of flows of Chinese culture, people, products, and media whose causes and effects cannot be reduced to being either the products or servants of capitalism. I would like to join the two feminist political economists J. K. Gibson-Graham in refusing "social representations in which everything is part of the same complex and therefore ultimately 'means the same thing' (*e.g.*, capitalist hegemony)" and instead envision the globalization of Chinese culture as a "prolific disarray" of multiple counter- and noncapitalist tendencies and outcomes (1996: ix).

I would like to adopt the term *transnational China* to capture the spatial and geographical extension of Chinese culture across national and political boundaries and to take into account the persistent interconnectedness among these cultural offshoots with each other and with the "Motherland." This interconnectedness can be seen in terms of both the flows of people, goods, and culture across these boundaries as well as the maintenance of a "Chinese identity," still defined as singular even though it is distinctively differentiated according to place. The fact that transnational China can be seen as a very loosely organized entity (more a network than a social organism) in the world today is due both to its being the product of an inherited cultural heritage as well as to the ongoing maintenance, renewal, and reinvention of cultural connections and a Chinese identity through cultural and material flows across political borders. These movements involve not only capitalist investment, trade, and technology transfer but also educational and intellectual exchanges; mass media and not-so-mass-media elite cultural productions; kinship, family, and friendship network dispersals; political counterstate organizations; religious flows; and other movements of emerging Chinese transnational civil societies and public spheres such as feminism.

Although the term *transnational* is employed here, the borders that a Chinese women's public sphere must breach are not just nation-state borders such as those between China and the United States, but also political boundaries of different degrees of porousness, such as those between Hong Kong and the Mainland, and Taiwan and the Mainland, places that in official discourse are supposed to belong to a single nation-state. However, as the essays here will perhaps show, it is much easier to document emerging feminist public spheres *within* each of these places than to claim the existence of a *transnational* Chinese feminist public sphere, which would be tantamount to an act of what Ann Anagnost has called *prolepsis* (1997: 140), "the representation of a future development as if presently existing or accomplished" according to *Webster's Dictionary*. Nevertheless, this act of prolepsis, this imagining of an as-yet-unformed Chinese women's public forum that straddles the political borders laid down by men, cannot be simply dismissed as groundless speculation or complacent indulgence, for as J. L. Austin (1962) has shown, language does not merely represent but also exercises performative power and effects. Proleptic utterances and transmissions not only conjure up a possible future but may help bring it into existence.

Furthermore, the speed of recent developments in the transnational flow of Chinese-language media—such as satellite television transmission, international film festivals, the availability of transportable Chinese cassette tapes, videos, CDs, laser discs, video compact discs (VCDs), and Chinese computer software—accompanied by the rapid development of the Internet, not to mention the old print media of newspapers, magazines, and books, and the increased transnational traveling and migration of Chinese bodies, all suggest that Chinese local, regional, and national public spheres are becoming more connected and integrated through the reception of an increasingly common body of cultural products by dispersed Chinese audiences and readers. This means that the raw materials and technical means for linkages among different Chinese women's public spheres are being laid down, although of course having women take control of such means to further women's projects would be the next step.

This book is also predicated on a *Chinese-language* public space cutting across political and international borders. That is why, although we have an article by Zhang Zhen on mainland women's diasporic literature in the United States and Britain, we have not included the larger body of Chinese American literature and minority discourse in the United States, which is mainly in English. Although there are connections between Chinese and Chinese American culture, the language difference still acts as an important separator between them. This book focuses on Chinese-language public space so that, instead of following the usual anthropological procedure that treats the Other as the periphery or minority of the West, we will take China as the core and treat the West and its Chinese minority as its periphery.

The State at Center Stage

The space of transnational China is an especially rich and complex site for an examination of public sphere in that it has nourished perhaps the oldest living tradition of the state in the world, and it has also witnessed the fastest economic growth rate in the world in recent years and the highest accumulation of capital outside the United States, Western Europe, and Japan. As an arena of public discussion and social self-reflection, the notion of public sphere holds out a promise to resist the "colonization of the life world" by modernity's two-system mechanisms of *the state* and the *capitalist economy* (Cohen and Arato 1992: 525). For Habermas, the life world is a socially integrated and communicatively created civil society that in modernity comes to be increasingly "uncoupled" from and controlled by the two-system integrations that operate through the impersonal media of power and money (1987b: 153–97). Thus the study of gender in modernity must take note of the impact of two hypertrophied institutions, the state and the market economy. In recent years, scholars studying Asia have paid much attention to the conventional understanding of colonization, that is, Western imperialism, especially in the nineteenth century, and not enough attention to this other "colonization of the life world" in the twentieth century, which is both the product of modernity and of national resistance to Western colonialism.

This book's approach differs from other collections dealing with transnational Third World feminist practices that adopt a framework of theorizing Western colonialism and Western transnational capital (Grewal and Kaplan 1994; Mohanty et al. 1991). Public sphere theory here also allows us to take note of local contexts where the state as a mode of production and cultural force is much more ancient and developed than capitalism and has expanded tremendously as a result of modernity and anticolonial efforts. In mainland China, a state mode of production continues to operate alongside transnational joint ventures and private enterprises, especially in the interior.

Public sphere theory, which defines the public sphere against both the state and capitalist economy, is especially relevant to the East Asian context where, even when capitalist economic development takes off (Japan in the 1950s, Hong Kong in the 1960s, Taiwan, Singapore, and South Korea in the 1970s, China in the 1980s), it does so as a process directed and controlled by the state to a much greater degree than in Western economies (Appelbaum and Henderson 1992; Castells 1992). Indeed, the model of East Asian development is especially vexing to both neoclassical economics and dependency theory because of the crucial role of the state. When these state economies have recently sustained high growth rates, won substantial shares of the global economy and capital investment, and built up strong discursive and organizational state structures motivated by nationalistic projects, we can no longer rely on the old anticolonial theoretical frameworks designed to represent poor and weak Third World colonies dependent on the West. Manuel Castells points out that in terms of a deeper state logic there is much more similarity between a *revolutionary state*, such as Maoist China, and *developmental states* in East Asian capitalism. For both kinds of states, "economic development is not a goal but a means" to its nationalist power (Castells 1992: 56–58, 62–66). Thus, an inquiry into women's public sphere in transcultural China must examine the multiple relations that women have with the state, and feminist studies must look for resistance not only to transnational Western capitalist and colonial patriarchies, but also to *national* capitalist and *state* patriarchies, and to male nationalist discourses, as well as emerging male public spheres that call for liberation from the state.

The Cultural Zones of Transnational China

Each of the three main Chinese culture zones discussed in this book presents unique contexts for the emergence of modern women's subjectivity and the struggle for asserting women's public space/public sphere. In mainland China, 1979 marked the beginning of the post-Mao economic reforms. There has been a shift from a totalitarian state formation, in which the social body was submerged within the totalizing body of the state, to a more differentiated social body with the beginnings of civil society, guided by a state that now relies on what Antonio Gramsci described as a more indirect hegemonic form (1971: 12, 55–57). The movement away from a centralized state economy toward a market economy has produced the co-existence of different forms of ownership for cultural production: large state-owned publishers and film studios continue to operate, but semi-private print publishers, film companies, and music companies have formed by fissioning off from or attaching themselves to (or "hanging and leaning on," *guakao*) large state companies. At the same time, transnational corporate investments from overseas Chinese film and music productions, and Japanese, European, and American (Hollywood) companies increasingly flow in, as China becomes connected, in spite of state restrictions, with circuits of globalized media (Yang 1993).

Like early modern Europe and early twentieth-century China, the market economy today has enabled new spaces to emerge for public discourse in urban areas, such as the increased numbers and varieties of newspapers, popular magazines, new academic and literary journals (Wang Shaoguang 1995: 161), private or local collectively owned bookstores, publishing houses that sell their state quotas (*shubao*) to small independent semilegal publishers, salon (*shalong*) discussion groups, small theater performances, new cinema offerings (Berry 1991; Pickowicz 1995), and dramatic developments in electronic media such as innovative programming on radio and television stations (Lull 1991), and cassette, videotape, VCD, and laser disc players (Yang 1997). Through this expanded array of media can be heard new and different voices (although consumerist ones predominate), while new visual images of gender and sexuality displace the old masculinities of revolutionary culture. However, the political devastation of 1989 slowed down the development of an elite intellectual critical public based on print, while expanding a consumer popular culture of electronic mass media (Lee 1993: 174–75).

As my own contribution to this collection shows, during the Maoist era on the Mainland, while making strides in women's education, basic rights, and employment, state feminism was concerned mainly to give women entrance to the public realm of labor, while women's production in the public realm of discourse was denied by the dominance of state discourse and by a state "erasure of gender" (*xingbie muosha*), especially female gender. In the current period of China's entry into global capitalism, at the same time that women are in decline in the public sphere of labor and are being sexualized by a male business and entertainment culture, the heightened awareness of gender difference and discrimination also contributes to the reemergence of women's subjectivity.

In Taiwan, capitalism exploited women's, especially young women's, labor power, but the state also had a major role in renewing patriarchal arrangements. The Kuomintang government sought to counter the radical social changes on the Mainland by undertaking to preserve Confucian culture, which included traditional domestic roles for women. While the state gave the private familial spheres wider scope than on the mainland, the public sphere was severely curtailed by Martial Law (1948–87), which censored all publications, limited the number and contents of newspapers, banned public meetings, assemblies, strikes, and marches, prohibited the formation of nongovernmental organizations, and controlled the state-run television stations (Ku 1989: 12; Chun 1994, 1996). Thus, Martial Law severely hampered the development of the women's movement, as seen when Lu Hsiu-lien, a pioneering feminist activist in the 1970s, had her book banned because it was thought that feminism was tantamount to advocating "sexual emancipation" and "promiscuity and group marriage" (Ku 1989: 16). As in the rest of East Asia, economic development in Taiwan has also produced a powerful male state and business culture that patronizes women's erotic and sexual services,[6] often with the implicit consent of the state, which collects taxes from the sex industry (Cheng and Hsiung 1992: 244–49).

With the end of Martial Law in Taiwan in 1987, public expression has gone much further than on the Mainland in openly challenging the ruling Kuomintang Party and its cultural hegemony. The switch to export-oriented economic growth in the 1970s, the rapid expansion of small- and medium-sized enterprises, and the increasing demands for autonomy by Taiwan businesses operating in the global economy cut into the state-controlled economy and the party-state's authoritarian military rule, paving the way for the upsurge of social movements and civil protests in Taiwan in the 1980s and '90s (Gold 1986: 97–121, 128–31; Hsiao 1992: 58). Such social movements as those of consumers, conservation, aboriginal rights, women, students, labor, farmers, human rights, nonhomeowners, and antinuclear activists all mounted street demonstrations and, as government censorship eased, expressed their opposition through the mass media (Hsiao 1992).

Since Taiwan did not enjoy a strong state feminism as on the Mainland, an independent women's movement in Taiwan had to struggle from outside the state to fight for many of the things granted to women overnight by the Communist Party on the Mainland, such as basic legal rights for women to work after marriage or pregancy, to inherit property, to be given fair divorce settlements by husbands, to have political participation, and to be protected from being sold into prostitution. At the same time, opportunities to organize women's nongovernmental organizations (NGOs), to publish feminist magazines, to develop a strong women's culture and solidarity and a feminist discourse openly critical of male institutions were greater than on the mainland, especially after the end of martial law in 1987 in Taiwan. As a feminist leader, Lee Yuan-chen gives us an inside look at the practical and organizational dimensions of the Women's Awakening Foundation. She outlines its strategies for getting women's issues into the public space, through mass demonstrations in the streets, and by pressuring newspapers, magazines, and finally, television to report and discuss women's issues (fig. 1).

Whereas Taiwan has experienced a recent opening of the window of public space and expects to continue critical public expression on social issues, Hong Kong presents a different picture. As Rey Chow has pointed out, Hong Kong's 1997 postcoloniality presents an anomalous situation where the release from one sort of imperialist rule does not lead to independence but an ambivalent encounter with one's origins, in this case, a powerful modern state with its own imperialist tradition (1992). Unlike Taiwan, Hong Kong's public sphere trajectory can be traced as a movement from partial closure (when the colonial government imposed censorship and a capitalist culture commodified the media) to an opening up in the decolonization process (1984–1997), and then to a new closure with the return to the "Motherland" in 1997.

Hong Kong's difficulties in forming and maintaining a public sphere of critical discussion stem from several situations. As a marginal Chinese community not under the tutelage of either the Kuomintang or the Communists, Hong Kong could publish many materials not permitted either on the Mainland or in Taiwan (Lee 1995: 77). However, the colonial state also curbed any signs of anticolonial sentiment, especially after the anti-British riots of 1967 (Li Cheuk-to 1994: 165). In the period of 1967–84, a strong capitalist economy and a British colonial state that avoided direct political intervention produced an apolitical popular and media culture, which closely approximates Theodor Adorno and Max Horkheimer's notion of a capitalist "culture industry" (in Chun 1996). This was a situation of the absence of public sphere not so much because of the state but because of the strength of capitalist culture. Ackbar Abbas has also written of Hong Kong as a "culture of disappearance," where under British colonialism the stateless residents had a peculiar lack of place and identity, due to the nature of a port city that serves as a transit point for migrants from China to other places (1997). In addition, since colonialism blocked the expression of political activism, the colony's population turned their energies to economic pursuits, and this culture of economic self-interest has also been detrimental to a public sphere. Following Paul Virilio, Abbas also

Figure 1. A Taipei street outside National Taiwan University, with a sign pointing to the Women's Bookstore. Photograph by Mayfair Mei-hui Yang.

suggests that the "speed" of a culture of media saturation alters people's experience of space so that it becomes abstract, dominated by signs and images that dispel memory, history, and presence. Such a lack of a sense of place would lead to a peculiar paralysis of Hong Kong's public sphere, for although public spheres can spread transnationally, and increasingly do so in the process of globalization, a sense of place is often crucial for the initial establishment of a public sphere.

It is therefore not surprising that Hong Kong's public sphere entered a period of efflorescence after the 1984 Sino-British Joint Declaration to return Hong Kong to mainland Chinese sovereignty in 1997. In this fourteen-year period of decolonization, large segments of Hong Kong people were suddenly confronted with a question of identity, and many moved to differentiate their identities from the larger Chinese state identity descending from the North. As I was to discover at the International Conference on Cultural Criticism: Public Sphere and Public Cultures, held in Hong Kong in 1993, where most of the Hong Kong papers were presented in the Cantonese dialect despite the presence of mainland and American scholars, language politics became an important component of this resistance identity.[7] Thus a sort of public sphere of antistate cultural localism emerged in Hong Kong in the years preceding 1997, whose traces can be found also in popular culture. The chapter by Shu-mei Shih

Figure 2. A public rally organized by the Hong Kong Federation of Women's Centers in preparation for the United Nations Women's Congress in Beijing, 1995. Photograph courtesy of Hong Kong Federation of Women's Centers.

analyzes the deployment of women in this new Hong Kong discourse of resistance to mainland hegemony, a discourse that like many critical discourses in the public sphere is a masculine one.

The beginnings of the Hong Kong women's movement also coincides with this period of colonial relaxation of controls on public sphere and local identity formation. Before the mid-1980s, there were no local feminist women's organizations, only some "expatriate" or British groups that were not integrated with Cantonese-speaking communities (Choi 1995). Since the mid-1980s, many young feminist groups have emerged with close links to grassroots activities and causes, such as protests and demonstrations, the lesbian movement, the democratic front in party politics, and working-class women's issues. All of these groups "regard[ed] 1997 as the major threat to the space for women which they have fought for in the public agenda" (Choi 1995: 98). It will be interesting to see whether, in the aftermath of 1997, there will be an absorption of these grassroots feminist organizations by official feminism, or a new expanded role for these independent feminist groups in addressing the situation of women in the rest of China (fig. 2).

It is in the context of a search for an independent Hong Kong identity that New Wave cinema emerged in the late 1970s, bringing with it the films of its only woman director, Ann Hui. As Elaine Ho's article in this collection shows, Ann Hui's films are preoccupied with a dual pursuit of identity: first, a gender identity of woman caught in between the patriarchal past (and present) of Chinese tradition and the alienating masculine world of modernity; and second, an ethnic identity of Hong Kong as a pawn between Western capitalism and the "juggernaut of empire" associated with the mainland.

Modernity: A Historical Perspective

In a special 1993 issue of the journal *Modern China*, there is another discussion of public sphere by historians of late imperial China. While the debate as to whether a public sphere was emerging in late imperial China, even before the full impact of the West was felt, is fascinating and useful, the terms of this debate also seem problematical. First, it is puzzling that this debate among historians is couched in synchronic terms, that is, whether a Western category of analysis fits a Chinese social structure, so that the historical rupture of modernity that Chinese culture experienced in the twentieth century is not addresssed. If the application of Habermas's notion of public sphere to Ming and Qing dynasty China has laid studies such as William Rowe's open to charges of imposing Western categories onto Chinese patterns (Rowe 1990; 1993: 139–41), I think the same could not be said of public sphere inquiries into twentieth-century China. In the seventeenth, eighteenth, and even nineteenth centuries, traditional culture was much more intact in China and continuous with the past. Outside structures did not penetrate deeply and so did not alter traditional culture's fundamental core. Therefore, importing a foreign mode of analysis to late imperial China has more chance of doing violence to native Chinese cultural logic or social patterning. In contrast, China in the twentieth century has seen the revolutionary tearing down of old institutions and cultural reasoning (Yang 1996a), as well as the deeper penetration of outside logic through transnational circuits of media, migration, commodity production, trade, and even warfare.

Whereas Mary Rankin (1993) has pointed out that public opinion among late imperial gentry was not even national, but strictly local and rural until the commercial press in the last decades of the nineteenth century, by the twentieth century the transnational flows of modernity into China included such discourses as evolutionism, Marxism, nationalism, fascism, democracy, and feminism, altering the native social order so that it becomes appropriate to consider questions of public sphere in modern

China. Thus, while both the late imperial and modern Chinese states are much more involved in all forms of social organization than in the modern West (Wakeman 1993), rather than conclude that a public sphere cannot be found in China, it seems to me that a more pressing question is what are the special constraints and possibilities for a public sphere under such conditions? In other words, the experience of modernity in China means that it is no longer a question of whether a Western category fits traditional Chinese culture, but how a modern global category would work itself out in the particular modernity of China.[8]

Second, the discussions in *Modern China* are limited by a narrow conception of public sphere theory. They are mainly concerned with a descriptive empirical project of establishing whether or not late imperial or contemporary China had or has a public sphere, a question that does invite charges of measuring China against a Western standard. They miss the performative, utopian, emancipatory, and critical dimensions of public sphere theory. To invoke the public sphere is to call for an examination of the ways by which public spheres can establish and maintain their independence from three institutional forces that dominate modern societies: the logic and interests of the state, the market, and evolving forms of patriarchal kinship and family modalities. To look for a particular historical public sphere is a performative act that contributes to bringing it into existence. At the same time, one must keep in mind the utopian aspects of this endeavor, since no public sphere has yet lived up to its ideals of democratic representation and engagement. It must be remembered that in the West, the public sphere is not historically stable, as it has been subjected, especially in advanced capitalism, to incursions and a steady shrinking of its emancipatory possibilities by the commodification of culture. Therefore, a public sphere in the West cannot be reduced to a list of features with which Chinese counterparts either fit or do not fit, but it must be treated as an ongoing process and struggle that is also endangered in the very locus where the concept originated.

Third, these studies of public sphere in China remain uncritical of the masculinist, universalist, bourgeois, and nostalgic assumptions of Habermas and have not incorporated recent critiques of Habermas (as well as his own recent reflections) (Habermas 1992). No consideration is given to the gender dimension of public sphere, and there is no critique of the male power exercised by the gentry class. An important feature of modernity in China is left out: the entrance of women into public life and discourse. Lacking also is a critical perspective on gentry activities, and an accounting of other discourses that competed with gentry positions in the public sphere.[9] Indeed, modern social movements that countered mainstream gentry by way of print media, such as the movements of nationalism, youth, and feminism in early twentieth-century China, should be viewed as challenges, not only to dynastic power but also to male gentry power in a dynamic new public sphere.

Forces of modernity begun in the twentieth century—such as the influx of women workers into urban factories and wage labor; the participation of women in anticolonial, nationalist, and military struggles against Western and Japanese imperialism; and the opening of modern education to women—have greatly multiplied the social roles available to women beyond the past domestic sphere roles of "wives, concubines, and maids" (Watson 1991). The gender discourses of late imperial China introjected a ritual spatial code of "inner" (*nei*) household space for women and "outer" (*wai*) space for men, charged women with being the media for patrilineal continuity, while configuring the realm of state and empire as patriarchal family writ large, with the emperor and his officials as paternal authorities. Through successive waves, modernist discourses of nationalism, individualism, gender equality, revolution, and capitalist consumerism irrevocably altered the contours of Chinese gender discourse. In 1920s and '30s Shanghai films, "woman" often symbolized either the allure of individual sexual freedom or a social corruption that needed to be controlled (Zhang Yingjin 1994). In the nationalistic war years of the 1930s, she signified the raped and wounded nation and rallied men to save the Motherland (Liu 1994). The female figure in revolutionary drama of the Maoist era in the 1960s and '70s celebrated socialism's liberation of the oppressed and stood for the gratitude of the masses for the generosity of the party (Meng 1993). Meanwhile, the figure of woman in Taiwan and Hong Kong became both a commerical object propelling what Gilles Deleuze and Félix Guattari call "the desiring economy" of capitalism and an anchor in the new private domestic sphere of the bourgeois family (1983).

The contemporary situation in mainland China, Taiwan, and Hong Kong is quite different from the history of the West in that the two periods of public sphere (early capitalism's birth of public sphere and advanced capitalism's eclipse of the public sphere) are conflated into a *single* period of simultaneous birth and death in East Asia. In the Habermasian narrative, as capitalism moved into its advanced phase in the twentieth century, the public sphere suffered at the hands of the very commodity economy that had brought it into existence: exchange value started to determine and overtake artistic and political values in the very content and substance of public culture. The strong consumer orientation of mass culture and the

overriding concern for sales led to the blunting of the critical edge of public discourse, indeed, even the packaging and predigestion of cultural products to make them "consumption-ready." Thus, culture became "a commodity not only in form but also in content" (Habermas 1989: 166). For
Habermas and the Frankfurt School (Horkheimer and Adorno 1968), mass
culture and the electronic media no longer question and reformulate society,
because they now only serve as leisure and entertainment. As a latecomer
to industrialization and capitalist economy, capitalism in transnational
China today is often more organized, rationalized, and sophisticated than
the early Western capitalism of the eighteenth century, so that while a critical public sphere can develop by carving out spaces from modern state
control, it is immediately subjected to the encroachments of commodity
logic, which blunts oppositional sentiments in favor of maximizing consumption. This process is illustrated by Tze-lan Deborah Sang in this volume when she shows how the Taiwan commercial mass media feed on
emergent lesbian oppositional voices. No sooner has political relaxation
started to produce public lesbian voices than the forces of the commodification of art and news have eroticized and sensationalized them for voyeuristic consumption and economic returns.

mass culture is not critical

Sites and Media: Public Culture in Transnational China Today

In modernity, cultural and social reproduction, including the construction
of gender, is increasingly "disembedded" from the localities of face-to-face
interactions and takes place in the mass media, which span time and space
(Giddens 1990) In his classic essay, Walter Benjamin noted that the art of
mechanical reproduction (printing and photography, then radio and film)
brings about a radical break from the past because this new process takes
the art object out of its traditional ritual and religious context and inserts it
into its multiple viewers' own surroundings (1968). The effect of the "disembedding" of the art object from its original context means that in each
new instance of its reproduction (involving editing, cutting, dubbing,
framing, and so on), and in each moment of its reception in different contexts, the art object becomes activated, and the possibilities for the revision of its meaning are multiplied and politicized (Enzensberger 1986:
121). Perhaps due to this decontextualizing effect of media, modern gender forms, like art that has lost its "aura" of authenticity, have been partially
released from their traditional moorings in kinship and ritual and have attained a certain independence and revisability. This independence is only
relative, however, since with the decline of religion and kinship the mass

Benjamin

independence is limited

media have been dominated by new institutional forces, such as the state and market, that try to define and deploy gender forms for their own purposes. On the other hand, while the mass media enable the spread of new forms of power, they have also been the site of oppositional movements that struggle to employ the media for their countermessages. Thus mass culture is invested with tremendous power for social control as well as social change and has become a contested space where visions of society are proffered, gain acceptance, get institutionalized, and are in turn challenged by oppositional discourses.

In contrast to Habermas's dismissal of electronic media, Oskar Negt and Alexander Kluge seek to directly confront the new "industrialized public sphere of production" that has overlaid and displaced the classical bourgeois public of elite letters. With its consciousness industry, advertising, and depictions of the daily experience of work, home, and consumption, this new sphere incorporates the private, familial, and sexual realms (Negt and Kluge 1993: 13). Whereas the classical public subscribes to an "artisanal mode of production," this new sphere operates at a more highly organized level of financial investment, production, and technology. Whereas the classical public was admired by Habermas for its "rationality," the linear and abstract disembodied logic of print media has given way in the new public sphere to a communicational order based on visual "fantasy,"[10] emotional identification, and desiring sexuality. In the fascinating documentary *Yang and Yin: Gender in the Chinese Cinema*, film director Stanley Kwan illustrates how sexuality is so developed in this new public sphere in Hong Kong and Taiwan films that it often departs from the normative tracks of heterosexuality and enters into the realm of exploratory sexualities, such as the gender switching of actress Brigitte Lin (Lin Qingxia) in director Tsui Hark's films.

Thus, Negt and Kluge do not foreclose the possibility that "new forms . . . of experience, new modes of expression, self-reflection, and intersubjectivity might emerge from the same cultural technologies that were destroying the old" (Hansen 1993a: xviii). Indeed, they argue that the trouble with intellectual critiques of television is that they are carried out in the medium of the classical public sphere, which is print. For Negt and Kluge, we "can only influence a mass medium through a counter-mass medium" such as television (Liebman 1988b: 40; Negt and Kluge 1993: 127). To this end, they have been engaged in film production and television programming (Liebman 1988a, 1988b). In keeping with this spirit, this book, an artifact of print media, does have a video counterpart to reach out to a wider audience. I have made a fifty-minute documentary called "Through Chinese Women's Eyes," that provides a visual accompaniment to my essay in this collection.[11] Through interviews with women of different walks of life in Shanghai and Beijing and through archival footage of the Cultural Revolution era, the film documents the changes urban women have experienced from the Maoist era of state feminism and masculinization of women to the current commercialized era of their commodification and sexualization.

In mainland China, the increased commercial underpinning of cultural production means that the media no longer depend on state funding and therefore convey more diverse voices, some of which diverge from the former monologue of state propaganda (Yang 1993; 1997). The standardized, "ungendered" viewing subject of the classical socialist Chinese film, noted by Chris Berry, where the camera was rarely aligned with individual characters, has given way to the positioning of different types of viewing subjects who are gendered (Berry 1994). Transnational financing and media connections have enabled a male counterstate filmic public sphere of Fifth Generation films to be produced and disseminated around the globe.[12] A pattern has emerged, called "foreign sales converted to domestic sales" (*waixiao zhuan neixiao*), whereby some mainland media personages and products gain fame and are "packaged" (*baozhuang*) abroad and then are sold back to the domestic market, such as the heavy-metal rock band Tang Dynasty and their Taiwan distributor (Shih 1995).

For Dai Jinhua in this volume, overseas capitalist forces have dislodged structures of state feminism, so that much of the cultural production of the 1980s and '90s, both intellectual and popular, has been taken up with a reconstruction of masculine narratives. Many recent films and novels are narratives of father-son conflict, where readers/viewers identify with the son's generation and attempt to overthrow the patriarchal father. These narratives often stamp linear progressive history with a male gender imprint and construct the eternity and immobility of the land and tradition as feminine. Toward the former there is affirmation, while the latter evinces an ambivalent attitude of nostalgic longing and contempt. Reflecting a symptom of injured Chinese masculinity in its recent reencounter with the West, male filmmakers like Zhang Yimou and Chen Kaige have started to address a Western audience by assuming the feminine position vis-à-vis the West. In their films they erase Chinese male subjectivity in order to present Chinese culture as an exoticized, Orientalized, feminine Other for the Western male gaze.

The economic reforms and transnational financing on the Mainland have also enabled independent filmmakers producing a small critical counterpublic according to the small-scale entrepreneurial mode of production of early capitalism favored by Kluge (Liebman 1988b: 24–25), such as the work of independent filmmakers Zhang Yuan and Wu Ming,[13] and rock musician Cui Jian (Jones 1992). However, they are a tiny drop in a vast sea of big state and big business productions from abroad. They are threatened by these two forces at every turn, by state censorship and confiscation, and by a selling out to capitalist and commercial interests.

It was also in the 1980s that an interrupted tradition of women's writing reappeared in mainland China, and a new gender and feminist consciousness diverging from state feminism developed in women's literature, as shown in the articles by Dai Jinhua, Lisa Rofel, and myself in this book. Ironically, this occurred just as China witnessed a shrinking of the reading public. The recent decline of intellectuals as "the articulators of new subjectivity" in mainland China (Lee 1993: 176) is probably related to the declining influence of print and literature as electronic media become more sophisticated and enticing in their entertainment appeal. Referring to the Frankfurt School, Kluge remarks in an interview, "It is old-fashioned to assume as they did in the 1930's that these struggles will be determined in the streets when there is a mass medium in every house that acts as a kind of window. Against such a power to convince millions through television, all conventional means are powerless" (in Liebman 1988b: 40). Two essays in this collection, those by Brownell and Erwin, show how this most powerful medium, television, is dominated by masculinist voices, against which the voices of women's literature are barely audible in China today.

Focusing on female athletes as symbols of the nation in Olympic sports, Susan Brownell's article examines the emergence of a new "popular nationalism" in mainland China, which is not always allied with state discourse but retains the implicit male orientation of state discourse and state feminism. This popular nationalism is what is specific to public sphere emergence in China and many other postcolonial societies. An interesting feature of this new popular nationalism is that it often comes to be expressed and emotionally felt in a transnational context, such as the television coverage of Olympic sports. In addition, it stems from a wounded masculinity and national pride seeking to repair themselves through a deployment of female symbols (Brownell 1995), which at the same time erase female gender and subjectivity.

As an American woman playing a lead character in a Shanghai television drama, Kathleen Erwin had ample opportunities to observe firsthand how the narrative she was a part of served to reconfigure Chinese masculine nationalism in a more internationalist reformist vein. In this particular reconstruction of the new Chinese international family, Chinese women are written out of the story in order to foreground the sexual desirability of Chinese men for Western white women, thus assuaging the cultural, racial, and sexual anxieties of Chinese nationalist masculinity as it enters into deeper economic and political competition with the masculinized West.

In her history of the Taiwan women's movement, Lee Yuan-chen in this volume would agree with Negt and Kluge's assessment of the power and centrality of television. However, her article also counters their statement that street struggles are unimportant. She shows that the *street* as a public space to broadcast women's points of view cannot be dismissed. In the early stages of the Taiwan women's movement in the 1970s and early '80s, when it was ignored by the mainstream media of the major newspapers, magazines, and television, it *had to* resort to occupying the streets through marches and public sit-ins. Similarly, media theorist Jean Baudrillard contested Hans M. Enzensberger's criticism of the Left for its anachronistic and bourgeois fear and contempt for the electronic mass media (1986: 102). Instead, Baudrillard celebrated such things as hand-painted placards, silk-screen posters, and direct speech in the streets. Unlike mass media, street speeches are "given and returned, spoken and answered, mobile in the same space and time, reciprocal and antagonistic. The street is . . . the alternative and subversive form of the mass media, since it isn't, like the latter, an objectified support for answerless messages, a transmission system at a distance" (Baudrillard 1986: 134).

Despite their differences, both Baudrillard and Enzensberger emphasized public participation in the production and response to the media. In the heady revolutionary days of the 1970s in Europe, Enzensberger optimistically proclaimed that a social movement can accomplish a reversal of media hegemony and transform it from a medium of one-sided transmission to one of multidirectional communication (1986). This conviction of the subversive power of media was countered by Baudrillard's pessimistic conclusion that the very form of the medium was based on a nonreciprocal model, so that neither tinkering with the content of media nor taking over the ownership of the media would make a difference (1986). One must either dismantle the current technical form of media or find an alternative form that would allow simultaneous receipt and return of messages.

Virginia Cornue's study of the Beijing Women's Hotline offers a glimpse of how women's public space can be expanded through the unique properties of another medium, the telephone. Unlike other mass media that create a separation between active producer and passive recipient, the telephone answers Baudrillard's call for a medium that allows for simultaneous transmission and response. Cornue describes how this telephone hot line airs out women's issues and addresses the personal, romantic, and marital concerns of women's private sphere in an anonymous but public way. Cornue was struck not by "culture shock" in her fieldwork but by the "shock of familiarity," of hearing women's voices responding to crisis calls about women's sexuality, divorce, childbirth, domestic violence, and sexual harrassment, just as in her years of feminist activism in the United States. She had to grasp the underlying difference of a Chinese feminism that continues to be connected to state feminism, even as it observes superficial similarities with American feminism. However, she found the telephone hot line fell short of establishing a women's public sphere in that the anonymity and geographical isolation of callers and hot-line respondents prevent the construction of a women's community.

Toward a Transnational Chinese Women's Public Sphere

In the history of the modern West, the public sphere was created not only by differentiating itself from the state, but also by separating itself from the family, when "commodity exchange burst out of the confines of household economy" (Habermas 1989: 28). In the shift from a feudal manorial economy to a capitalist one, the economy moved out from the household to the market, and the public sphere was created by the privatization and enclosure of the bourgeois conjugal family. Thus capitalism put an end to extended families, radically reduced kinship's role in economic and political realms, and compartmentalized kinship into the nuclear family and domestic sphere. The new extrakinship realm was then divided into the private market economy, the state, and a public sphere that defined itself against the domestic sphere.

Feminist scholars have pointed out the discrepancy between the ideals of the public sphere and their actual historical practice in the West. Women were excluded from such public places as coffeehouses, public associations, and the political public sphere of parties and voting (Landes 1988; Fraser 1992). The absence of women in the public and political realm cannot be explained as merely the persistence of archaic patriarchies but also as the result of a modern reconfiguring of gendered domains (Eley 1994: 312–13). Therefore, in the history of the West, feminism did not emerge as a result of the liberation of the public sphere from the absolutist state in the eighteenth century, but from a *later* development in the nineteenth century (Ryan 1992; Landes 1988), which was a reaction to the growth of a masculinist public sphere that excluded women.

In applying the notion of a gendered public-private split to a Chinese cultural setting, we must be careful to maintain a historical perspective. At the beginning of Western feminist anthropology in the 1970s, the opposition of "public and domestic spheres" was first made by Michelle Rosaldo (1974), who contended that women in all cultures were subordinated because they were relegated to the domestic sphere and shut out of the public sphere. It was later pointed out that this opposition stems from the particular Western legacy of the privatized Victorian bourgeois family (Rosaldo 1980; Lamphere 1993: 71) and does not fit tribal societies where the lines between family and a larger public are indistinct (Leacock 1978).[14] Similarly for premodern China, the divisions between public and domestic and between public and private may not be appropriate to a social formation where the kinship order and the state were inextricably intertwined, and where each spoke in the discourse of the other so that there was no sharp separation but a continuity between them. State Confucianism was predicated on promoting filial piety and familistic principles, and lineage organizations usually reinforced state ideology and prepared some of their male members to serve in state bureaucracy. Francesca Bray has also shown how the Chinese inner (nei) and outer (wai) realms did not correspond with a modern oppositional binary of public and private spheres, in that up through the Song dynasty and through much of the Ming virtually all textile weaving was women's work in rural peasant and manorial households, whose products were used as household tax payments or sold as income-earning commodities in the "outer" world, imparting a great degree of social status to women (1997: 205, 237, 261, 263).

Yet, if we focus on the modern period, this notion becomes important and relevant, as forces for reform called for an end to women's bound feet, which came to be seen as a cruel way of restricting women to the domestic sphere. Male exclusivism in the external world of the imperial examination system, the bureaucracy, property inheritance, lineage management, and merchant trade all became the target of the early twentieth-century women's movement in China, which fought for women's right to education, work, and political participation (Ono 1989; Jing Shenghong 1995).

The Maoist era of the 1950s through '70s is also a period where a public-domestic division was not marked. The state sought to expand a politicized public sphere to encompass the whole of social life, and the private and domestic spheres were whittled down. The state also came to "governmentalize" (Foucault 1991) family and kinship relations by regulating the age of marriage and choice of marriage partner, by evaluating model Five Virtues Families (wu hao jiating), and by deploying families as units of

biopower?

mutual surveillance. Work units and local party cells organized unpaid "voluntary labor" on Sundays and holidays and during intense political movements, so that family time was often organized by the state (Wang Shaoguang 1995: 152). The state's policy of inducting women into the public labor force eroded the divide between public and domestic spheres, thus improving women's position. However, the system of state housing assignments and housing shortages perpetuated the patrilineal preference for sons, patrilocal residence, and stem families (Davis 1993). State housing offices and work units tended to assign new housing units to men on the basis of seniority.

It is in the post-Mao era of economic reform and the retreat of the state from direct involvement in many domains of activity that the division between the public and domestic spheres becomes relevant in China. Despite the state's one-child policy in 1979, we can discern a growing private enclosure of domestic space (Wang 1995). Such recent developments in urban space as the private ownership of housing, the switch from a six-day to a five-day workweek, the importance of television viewing in domestic space, the consumer desires for home appliances whipped up by an advertising industry (with its images of middle-class housewives), and the return of a portion of the female workforce to the home have all enhanced the private domestic space and gendered it female. Much like postsocialist Eastern Europe (Funk and Mueller 1993), there is a historical irony that as the possibilities for creating a public sphere independent of the state increase opportunities for many mainland women are shrinking. What makes mainland China and Eastern Europe different from the West is that the return of women to the domestic sphere, both in society as well as in media representations,[15] is occurring *after* a period of having women in the public sphere.

In Hong Kong, studies have shown that industrialization has not automatically improved women's position but, like early modern Europe, has reformulated the traditional public-domestic divide in modern guise so that women do the vast majority of housework and many aspire to the middle-class images of a nurturing female homemaker in a privatized nuclear family purveyed in advertisements (Ng 1995). Taiwan provides an interesting case of a political discourse and legal system that perpetuate the old patriarchal moral discourse of state-kinship continuity, so that an important agenda of the women's movement there was to change the family law favoring paternal lines in cases of marital property, inheritance, choice of residence, child custody, and so forth (Ku 1989: 19). However, along with Hong Kong, a new model of domestic sphere is also offered in Taiwan's consumer culture and media: the image of housewives in privatized modern nuclear families encroaches on the traditional female domestic sphere based on vertical lines of paternal descent.

At the same time, we must also take into account other modern forces such as mass media, which work to transect this binary division of public and domestic. Television, an important aspect of urban life in all three Chinese contexts, both strengthens and weakens the domestic sphere. On the one hand, it gathers the family as the primary form of its audience, but on the other hand, in its family soap operas, its talk shows, and news reporting, it also broadcasts endless representations of private domestic life to a general public. This making public of a private domestic sphere can have the effect of opening up the private to public discussion and debate (which occur both inside and outside the medium), so that gender relations within the home are brought to public reflection and revision. Thus, television is an important medium that interpenetrates public and domestic spheres and can also serve as a facilitator (although usually not an arena) for the public sphere.

In Section II, several essays show the emergence and struggles of a Chinese women's public sphere in different media and public spaces. Tze-lan Deborah Sang's essay examines the way that the consumer economy in Taiwan has both enabled the emergence of a lesbian movement in the 1990s and also tries to defuse its oppositional elements in the drive to incorporate this new lesbian discursive terrain as another exotic space to promote consumer interest. Although the mass media and market economy have been crucial to the development of lesbian identity, there is a distinction between alternative small-scale lesbian media and the mainstream media. It is also in the pages of the feminist journal *Awakening* that the tensions and differences between the heterosexual and lesbian feminist movements in Taiwan are expressed, even while the two movements try to maintain an overall alliance.

On the mainland in the post-Mao era, there are not as many women's organizations outside the structures of the state, nor is there any open confrontation by women's groups with the state. However, new ways of articulating women's collective identity and women's issues have emerged in the 1980s and '90s. An innovative type of space for a women's public sphere is the public site of a museum. Lisa Rofel's article is a discussion of the first Women's Museum in China (and perhaps the world), which was founded a few years ago in the provincial city of Zhengzhou, Henan Province, through the efforts of Li Xiaojiang, a Chinese feminist whose work also appears in this volume. Rofel examines the museum collection of

Han and minority women's clothing, quilts made by women, women's cosmetic and cooking artifacts, among other things, as a public sphere site for the construction of women's identity. In comparing this museum with Western anthropology museums, she finds that it differs significantly from the Western project of constructing the Other and arraying it in subordination to the West. Rather, the Chinese women's museum resembles more the politics of subjectivity of lesbian and gay history archives, which give voice and visibility to a collective nascent and embattled self.

For Dai Jinhua, the lack of a clear feminist perspective in mainland public discourse is due to a number of factors. Since feminist discourse was for a long time tied in with state discourse, many women confuse one with the other and reject both. The emergence of women's voices, especially in women's autobiographical novels, is a salutary development. Many women writers boldly describe the inner world of women's psyche and reveal the depths of female sexual desire. However, these voices are immediately contained, redirected, and commercialized to appeal to a male voyeuristic readership.

Habermas's notion of public sphere took the nation-state as the natural unit of its operations, and he neglected the transnational dimensions of public life that were perhaps already there in early capitalism. Various authors have noted how in the late twentieth century, advanced capitalism shifts to a new intensity of globalized production and communication, shrinking real time and space, and unleashing diverse cultural flows that transect nation-state boundaries (Appadurai 1996; Harvey 1989; Gupta and Ferguson 1997). As the space of transnational China becomes more economically integrated within itself and more outwardly expanding, media and popular culture have also become traveling cultures across this same terrain. Not only is Hong Kong, Taiwan, and American popular culture being exported to mainland China (Gold 1995; Zha 1995), but Chinese Fifth Generation films, Hong Kong New Wave and popular action films, and even a Beijing five-woman rock band called Cobra have been exported to the United States.[16] In this transnational flow of Chinese bodies, culture, media, and money across political and national borders, can a transnational Chinese women's public sphere emerge?

Lee Yuan-chen devotes a section of her article to showing the transnational connections that her Women's Awakening Foundation in Taiwan has forged with women activists in the Mainland, Hong Kong, the United States, and other places. Her foundation has published several mainland feminist works, such as those of Dai Jinhua and Meng Yue, Li Xiaojiang, as well as the recently discovered traditional "women's script" written by peasant women in southern Hunan Province. At the same time, there are serious obstacles in the construction of a women's public sphere across Chinese political borders due to the tense nationalist and separatist politics in the area, as evidenced in their foundation's not being granted visas by the mainland government to attend the Women NGO Conference in Beijing in 1995 (Walden 1995).

The article by Shu-mei Shih deals with a growing border crossing: the "traffic in women" from mainland China to Taiwan and Hong Kong. Shih discusses the Taiwan and Hong Kong media's treatment of mainland women who serve as prostitutes, mistresses or concubines, wives, and even surrogate mothers for men in Taiwan and Hong Kong. Seen in the light of the larger history of conflict between the political entities of the Mainland and Taiwan, the sexualization of mainland women in a masculinist media discourse is an assertion of Taiwan's economic power and also a compensatory move in light of Taiwan's political and military vulnerability vis-à-vis the Mainland. In Hong Kong's case, images of mainland women in films are deployed in negotiating the fear, ambivalence, and sense of superiority that Hong Kong people feel toward their powerful new master. These political and economic disparities lead Shih to the conclusion that a transnational Chinese women's public sphere has not and cannot develop, despite increased economic exchange, due to the world of male nationalist politics.

This sentiment is also implied in the essay by Li Xiaojiang, which shows the obstacles to a shared women's public sphere between Chinese and Western women. In an age of increasing contact between China and the West, Chinese women are being exposed to more Western feminist discourse. For Li, this means that Chinese women must choose carefully which discourse they employ for addressing their own situation in China because the historical experiences of Chinese women are very different from those of Western women. She provides a very useful list of Western feminist phrases that will have a different interpretation and be of questionable relevance in a Chinese context.

In contrast, Zhang Zhen's article on diasporic mainland women's literature suggests a better outlook for a transnational Chinese women's public sphere, in print media at least. Through an analysis of the works of several educated women writers residing in the West and writing in Chinese in the exile journal *Today* (*Jintian*), she shows how their gender and feminist consciousness has sharpened in their years abroad. Their immigrant experiences and exposure to a different dominant culture and a different language enable them to put into perspective the nationalist male narratives and "male historical linear time" of their homeland, while freeing them to experiment in a new female-centered language. Although this journal has a small circulation and is officially banned from distribution in the Mainland, issues are still smuggled in, its contributors and readers include Chinese residing in the Mainland or abroad, and its editorial board is scattered in several cities around the world. Thus, these are the possible beginnings of a transnational Chinese women's public sphere.

Whether or not a transnational Chinese women's public space has developed is not the main question of this book, but it is certainly a hoped-for future possibility. What this book is concerned with is exploring the historical conditions for the emergence of women's identity movements and the creation of women's public space across different Chinese spaces. The essays here seek to give a sense of the obstacles and difficulties entailed in this ongoing process, and to show how each particular cultural context might require a different set of strategies. As to whether this volume will actually contribute to building this transnational Chinese women's public space, that will have to wait for this book's Chinese translation. For now, the book will have to be satisfied with its task of introducing the varied situations of Chinese women's public discourse to an English-reading public.

NOTES

1 See Ann E. Kaplan's astute analysis of how the mainland film *Girl from Hunan*, although appearing to be a pro-woman film, at the same time deprives women of subjectivity and agency (1989).

2 Members included Emily Liu, Meng Yue, Wang Chaohua, Ming Fengying, Sun Hong, Fu Hsiu-ling, Zhang Lihui, Shu-mei Shih, Chen Yan, Zhang Xiwen, Yeh Yue-yu, and Esther Yau.

3 They included Constance Penley, Lisa Rofel, Carrie Waara, Sheldon Lu, Mingyan Lai, Ming Fengying, Lydia Liu, Susan Brownell, Shu-mei Shih, Shirley Lim, and myself. Other Chinese participants included writer A Cheng, film director Peng Xiaolian, and former cinematographer Chen Yan.

4 The edited volume from Ong and Nonini (1997) deals with the cultural and social changes in the Pacific Rim brought on by transnational Chinese capital.

5 Aihwa Ong has shown that women and feminism in Asia must be understood in terms of their embeddedness in a "moral economy" and discourse of the nation-state (Ong 1996).

6 See Anne Allison's discussion of Japanese male business culture and its commercialization of women's sexual services as both the product and safety valve of an embattled Japanese corporate masculinity that brutalizes men (1994).

7 It should, however, be noted that pragmatic considerations of doing business with the Mainland have also led to the rise of Mandarin usage in Hong Kong in recent years.

8 As Prasenjit Duara has pointed out, it is no longer a question of "*if at all*, but of *how and when*" modern European categories become relevant to modern China (1995b: 147). In addition, in her inquiry into modern Chinese print journalism in the first years of the twentieth century, Joan Judge notes the particular discursive and institutional differences from the emergence of modern Western print publics. Most important for this book is the fact that "whereas the development of the public sphere in Europe was premised on the existence of civil society, in China it was the organs of publicity that served as the impetus for the creation of the institutional infrastructure that constitutes a civil society" (1996: 11–12). Furthermore, whereas in Europe it was the *economic* forces of commercialization and bourgeois society that produced a public sphere, in China the development of a print public was tied up with a *political* project to reform the decrepit dynastic order.

9 In early modern China, what is strikingly different from the trajectory of the modern West is that although the gentry landowning class may have started to organize a public sphere, the subsequent Communist Revolution meant that they did so as a declining rather than ascendant class like the European bourgeoisie. Also different from the West is the fact that the modern state in China and Taiwan was able to close up the public sphere.

10 See Heidi Schlupmann for a perceptive critique of Kluge. She applauds Kluge for developing a sophisticated notion of the productive force of "fantasy" in mass media, which is contained and prevented from serving as a "mediating force between the drive structure, consciousness, and the external world" (1990: 76). However, Kluge does not address the emancipatory possibilities of women's fantasy through the media but defines female only in terms of motherhood.

11 This documentary video is available through the distributor, Women Make Movies in New York City (212-925-0606; fax, 212-925-2052; e-mail, orders@wmm.com). The video was shown at a transnational forum of women's public sphere—the Creteil Women's International Film Festival in Paris, sponsored by the French Ministry of Culture in April 1998.

12 The term *Fifth Generation films* refers to those made by the fifth generation of film directors in China's film history, who attended film school after the end of the Cultural Revolution. These directors include Zhang Yimou, Chen Kaige, Tian Zhuangzhuang, and Li Shaohong.

13 Zhang Yuan is an independent filmmaker who financed his 1990 film *Mother* (*muqin*) independently of both the state and outside capital. He also made *Beijing Bastards* (*Beijing zazhong*) about rock-and-roll nihilistic urban youth. Wu Ming (a pseudonym) made the underground film *Frozen* (*Jidu Hanleng*), about an alienated youth who explores death through performance art.

14 Eleanor Leacock writes of the Iroquois longhouse economy, which was managed by women: "'Household management' was itself the management of the 'public economy'" (1978: 253).

15 The popular TV melodrama *Yearning* (*Kewang*) in 1990 depicted the progressive retreat and physical demobilization of the self-sacrificing lead female character Liu Huifang to the domestic sphere. She ends up paralyzed by an accident.

16 *New York Times*, August 31, 1996, 16.

PART I

The Political Economy of Gender and Feminism

1

From Gender Erasure to Gender Difference:

State Feminism, Consumer Sexuality, and

Women's Public Sphere in China

Both the Cultural Revolution and commercialized society today are based on male power. In this respect, they are the same. The difference is that during the Cultural Revolution, men wanted women to become masculinized. In commercial society, however, men want women to become feminized. Both periods are men telling us what to do, so in terms of male power, they are basically equivalent.

> —Huang Shuqin, "A Conversation with Huang Shuqin"

The road of Chinese woman's liberation is different from that of Western woman's liberation because the [Chinese woman] has a different reality and past. For her, "equality of men and women" was once a mythical trap, and "equal pay for equal work" was all but forced upon her. Gender difference is not a concept to be discarded or abandoned, but a necessary path through which she must pass.

> —Meng Yue and Dai Jinhua, *Emerging from the Horizon of History*

The mechanisms that historically liberated female desire and subjectivity from domestic seclusion were the same that de-substantialized that experience for the cause of consumption.

> —Miriam Hansen, Special Issue on Female Spectators,
> *Camera Obscura*, no. 20–21

≈ 35 ≈

What historical forces have led reflective Chinese women to assume feminist subject-positions, which diverge from both the Maoist state subject and from the new consumer nationalist subject under construction in market socialism?[1] By exploring the vicissitudes of the category of gender in modern China, and its relationship with the modern state and market economy, this article will try to delineate the historical conditions surrounding the emergence of a women's public sphere in China today.

More specifically, what is suggested here is that existing approaches in feminist theory, whether postcolonial approaches to Third World women or postmodern feminist exhortations to transform Western society into a postgender order, cannot fully take into account the historically specific situation of women and feminism in contemporary China. The former approach generally focuses on the two-pronged brutal forces of Western colonialism and capitalism and neglects the influence of new nationalist state structures on women (Mohanty et al. 1991; Grewal and Kaplan 1994). The latter approach seeks to deconstruct gender as a category of identity and analysis, to problematize its taken-for-granted links with sexed bodies, and to incorporate other indices of difference, such as class, ethnicity, and race (Alcoff 1994; Moore 1994; Flax 1987). What is put forth in this essay is that the modern category of gender in China is a fragile formation and that its emergence was so overshadowed by the project of nation building that it did not develop into a category of affirmative self-identity for a women's movement led by women themselves. Furthermore, in the Maoist era, gender was not intertwined with modern discourses of sexuality[2] in a sustained way until the 1980s, the effect of which is yet to be fully understood. Thus, Chinese feminism today may be caught up in a historical juncture that requires *reconstructing* binary gender, rather than a *deconstruction* of gender, as advocated at this historical moment in a West where modern sexual differentiation and gender identity have well-established and hegemonic histories.

The women's movements in early twentieth-century China and other Third World countries were tied in with nationalist movements resisting Western (and Japanese) imperialism (Ono 1989; Beahan 1981; Jing 1995; Jayawardena 1986; Gilmartin 1995). However, on the threshold of the twenty-first century, Chinese feminism today is sprouting from the soil of a more confident sovereign state, which threw out the Westerners and has entered the global capitalist economy on its own terms. Thus, China shows much more clearly than other postcolonial situations that a truly *post*colonial feminist approach must take into account not only the legacy of Western domination but also the effects on gender systems made by the nationalist resistance to the West, that is, the relationship between gender and the newly independent states. Feminism in China today differs both from Western feminism as well as other Third World situations in that it is emerging from a "state feminism" administered by the Chinese Communist Party (CCP). This means that Chinese feminism will remain linked to state feminism, and at the same time, it may also develop critical discourses surrounding this link.

State Feminism and Gender Erasure

The term *state feminism* has been applied to Scandinavia and Egypt in the 1960s to refer to a system of state support of women that includes employing women in the state sector, making women's reproduction a public rather than a private concern (maternity leave, day care), and instituting progressive state laws that guarantee women's equality with men (Hatem 1992). States in state socialist orders took a much more proactive role than other types of states in championing women's liberation, by decreasing gender difference in the media and weakening the traditional family structure in order to replace family patriarchy with a new state patriarchy (Verdery 1994).[3]

Both in the Chinese Constitution (1954) and the Marriage Law (1950), women's equal rights in the political, economic, cultural/educational, social, and familial realms are explicitly upheld (*Hunan* 1987: 113). The Marriage Law did away with polygyny, arranged marriages, child-adoption marriage, prostitution, the buying and selling of women, and other overt abuses from the past against women. Other laws guarantee women's rights to paid maternity leave, to equal pay and inheritance, and to light work assignments with no night shifts during the last three months of pregnancy, while prohibiting violence against women by family members and divorce initiated by the husband during the wife's pregnancy. In 1983, rape, abduction and selling of women, and incitement to prostitution became crimes liable to capital punishment (*Hunan* 1987: 114–16). In terms of legal statutes at least, China may be better than the United States, since the Equal Rights Amendment to include a gender provision in the U.S. Constitution never passed, despite heavy lobbying by American feminists.

Friedrich Engels's work *Origin of the Family, Private Property and the State* (1975) had a tremendous impact on gender and family relations in socialist China. Engels argued that the enlargement of the male-controlled realm of social production outside the family led to the devaluation of the household and of women's work, which was no longer for the group as a whole but only for their families. His solution was for women to leave the domestic scene and enter into the public arena of social production. During the Great Leap Forward (1958–61), great waves of urban Chinese women entered the ranks of waged labor. Small neighborhood factories and shops were formed to provide employment for women, and child care was to a certain extent socialized, so that many working-class women today look back with nostalgia to the 1950s when they were rescued from poverty (Rofel 1994a; Andors 1983). Women were also admitted into higher education and professional occupations, and affirmative action quotas helped women to become cadres in state administration.

The Communist Party also created a state bureaucracy of women at the national level called the Women's Federation (*Fulian*), which has branch organizations at each local level. *Fulian* mediates family conflicts and divorce procedures, sees to women's health and birth needs, rewards model families, and intervenes to protect women in cases of unfair work demands by work units, inheritance disputes, and domestic violence. In the post-Mao period, two new tasks of *Fulian* are (1) to implement the birth control policy by monitoring women's menstrual flows and IUD insertions, and upholding state limits on births for each family, and (2) to help those women who lose their jobs in the new market economy. Thus state feminism is integrated into the biopolitical and eugenic projects of the state to control population growth and raise the "quality" (*suzhi*), both physical and cultural, of the population (Yang 1994b: 177–86; Anagnost 1997: 117–37).

Michelle Rosaldo has argued that "women's status will be lowest in those societies where there is a firm differentiation between domestic and public spheres of activity" (1974: 36). As in Eastern Europe and the former Soviet Union (Meyer 1985; Lampland 1989), Chinese state feminism in the Maoist period collapsed the boundary between public and domestic spheres, brought women out into the world of work, and socialized reproduction. The state also diminished patriarchal family power to a certain extent through replacing family units with collective units as the basic unit of production and accounting. These three changes meant that, as in Eastern Europe, the state "broke open the nuclear [and extended] family" and altered the relation between gendered domestic and public spheres (Verdery 1994: 232).

However, women's entrance into the world of men has not resulted in full equality with men; indeed, one problem may lie in this very discourse of equality. Contrary to Rosaldo's and Engels's expectations that collapsing the divide between domestic and public spheres would liberate women, many Chinese feminists find that women's liberation remains unfulfilled.

The fragility of state feminism can be seen in the rapidity and ease with which a more overt patriarchal culture has reasserted itself with the return to a privatized economy and transnational capital in the post-Mao era. Despite the real measures taken by the state on women's behalf, what is it that led one observer to call Chinese women's liberation a "revolution postponed" (Wolf 1985)?

What is needed to understand the vicissitudes of women's social position and of Chinese feminism is a historical genealogy tracing the changing categories of women in modern China. An impressive first step in tracing these changing categories was taken by Tani Barlow (1994b), who charts the transformations in the construction of Chinese women from late imperial "kin-inflected" gender categories, to their insertion in the early twentieth century into a new colonial biological and sexual binarism of essentialized physiologies of "women" (*nüxing*), and then to the Maoist state category of "woman" (*funü*), which was subordinated to the dominant categories of class and state biopolitical designs for reproduction. However, when Barlow states that "no positivity, no universal woman independent of man could exist under the terms of the Victorian sex binary" (1994b: 267), it should be noted that the same could also be said of the late imperial kin-inflected category of woman, where women were always defined in terms of their roles vis-à-vis fathers, husbands, and sons.

In hindsight, after several decades of state feminism, it would seem that there are emancipatory aspects to a discourse of sexual difference in a Chinese context.[4] In a patrilineal kinship mode of power where women were divided by class, kinship statuses, and affiliation to male familial groupings, a new sexual binarism served to introduce into discourse women as a collective subject, set in opposition to men. Lydia Liu has shown how the introduction into written Chinese of the feminine third-person pronoun *ta* with a female radical "participated in a larger gendering process under way since the turn of the 20th century" and enabled deictic relationships of gender in which it was possible for men and women to speak to and about each other, thus opening gender power relationships to be expressed and explored in a new language (Liu 1995a: 38). May Fourth women's literature, especially women's literature of the self, also provided a public space for women to construct, explore, and strengthen their personal subjectivity as women (Lydia Liu 1991; Larson 1993).

It is significant that the importation of a new sexual binary historically coincided with the emergence of a women's movement in early twentieth-century China. In considering why the male-female binary based on a gendered, sexualized, and psychologized self did not go further toward feminist liberation, it is not sufficient to rely on an *epistemological* critique of this binary's limitations as a modernist universalist trope. We need also to take into account the larger *historical* context in which a powerful nationalism and later statism were able to appropriate or colonize this still nascent category of *nuxing* as gendered self. In socialist state feminism, which does not emphasize the male-female binary, it has been difficult for women to assert independence from a male state machinery, since the very category of "woman" in opposition to men is no longer salient. This historical dimension is important in understanding why in post-Mao China, after four decades of state feminist discourse, there should be a resurgence of interest among women in women's literature of the May Fourth period, and a desire to reconnect with an interrupted tradition (Meng and Dai 1988; Li Ziyun 1994).

From the very beginning, the imported *nuxing* category of women was deployed in Chinese masculinist and nationalist concerns of building nation and state to save China from its shameful weakness in the world. For Liang Qichao, women's education would allow women to support themselves so that they would no longer be parasites on men and sap the strength of the nation (Ono 1989: 26–28). Two of the reasons for Kang Youwei's "Memorial Requesting a Ban on the Binding of Women's Feet" were to increase the nation's hereditary racial and military strength (Ono 1989: 33). The liberation of women was always tied in with the liberation of the nation, so that the former was a means to the ends of the latter struggle. This legacy of the linking of women's liberation with the needs of the nation and state was to continue and expand in the Maoist era, so that the latter came to submerge the needs of women and women's concerns were endlessly deferred in favor of projects of nation building. Although I do not take binary genders as either starting points or end points of history, it is still important to acknowledge that the historical decline of binary genders in Maoist China had an adverse impact on the trajectory of feminism.

GENDER ERASURE, DESEXUALIZATION, AND
THE MASCULINIZATION OF WOMEN'S BODIES

When I first started doing fieldwork in Beijing in the early 1980s, I was struck by the lack of response to my questions concerning the gender dimension of giving and receiving gifts and favors in "the art of social relationships" or *guanxixue* (Yang 1994b). To my questions about gender differences, people would frown, scratch their heads, and think for a long time before responding. Both men and women often reacted as if it were the first time that they had thought of differences between women and men.

What is remarkable about Maoist China, especially during the Cultural Revolution, is what many educated urban Chinese call "the erasure of gender and sexuality" (*xingbie muosha*) in public space. Of course, gender difference was not completely erased. The terms *male* and *female* remained in use in everyday parlance; state discourse deployed the category of women in its discussion of women's liberation; and traditional prejudices and discriminations against women continued in less overt ways. However, in many social situations, gender became an unmarked and neutralized category, its role as a vessel of self-identity was greatly diminished, and it lost its significance for gender politics, which was replaced by class politics.

Dress and personal style were important sites for state gender erasure, which reached an extreme form in the unisex dress code during the Cultural Revolution (1966–76). Han Lina, a woman factory worker in Shanghai, was seventeen when the Cultural Revolution broke out. She remembers going to have her hair cut short with her mother. "Women wore olive green army clothes, with PLA cap, or they wore blue or grey clothes with baggy pants just like men, so from behind, you couldn't tell they were girls. If a Red Guard saw anyone who was dressed in 'bourgeois style'—dresses too short, blouse too revealing, high heels, or permed hair—he would forcibly cut your hair or your dress on the spot," she said. In the dominant language of class at that time, to look feminine was to look "bourgeois" (*zichan jieji*), while a revolutionary image could only be coarse and manly (fig. 1).

Another woman factory worker, Gu Liqin, remembers that back then she and her classmates wanted to wear loose-fitting blouses with sleeves, so they would not show their bare arms, and bulky jackets to hide their breasts. "Large breasts looked very ugly (*hen nankan*) to us, especially when you bent your body backwards. But now the size and shape of breasts are considered part of feminine beauty," said Gu, shaking her head at the tremendous changes she has seen. A woman doctor in her fifties, and a Taiwan soap opera fan, Kang Xiujin declared, "During the Cultural Revolution, you only felt like a woman when you gave birth; at other times you don't exist as a woman." It was only when she became pregnant and her body swelled up that the category of gender intruded on her self-identity and all who saw the physical markers of her sex. Otherwise, gender, especially female gender, was culturally invisible.

Now a writer, Lin Ruihong was sent down to work in the countryside during the Cultural Revolution. She remembers that the urban girls were "masculinized" (*nanxinghua*) in their rural area when cadres in charge of "sent-down youth" could not understand why girls would not work in the

Figure 1. Red Guard girls perform the Loyalty Dance during the Cultural Revolution.

rice paddies at certain times of the month, and the girls were too embarrassed to explain. The male cadres demanded, "What do you mean, you can't go down into the fields right now?" Lin said to me with a shudder, "Can you imagine girls with menstrual flow, being forced to immerse their bodies in the cold water?" Traditional Chinese medical notions of women's health specify that when women menstruate, they should not expose their bodies to cold and wet substances. Lin thought male cadres had no inkling of women's special bodily needs, and that is why many sent-down girls developed women-specific illnesses.

In Maoist China, the state presided over the erasure of gender in the public discursive and visual realm of the mass media and didactic art in posters and magazines. A perusal of the covers of the magazine *Chinese Women* (*Zhongguo funu*) between 1958 and 1966 shows women dressed in plain working clothes engaged in various forms of physical labor, especially agricultural, industrial, and military (Feng 1992). Images of women doing difficult men's work such as oil drilling, suspension from electric high-tension wires, and coal mining crystallized into the model figure of "iron maidens" (*tiegu-niang*), which was to be derided in the 1980s as "unnatural" for women (Honig and Hershatter 1988: 24–26).[5] While these state feminist portrayals of women avoided traditional stereotypes of weak and passive women or images as sexual objects in capitalist societies, they also made invisible two aspects of gender domination in the state socialist order. First, since women (and men) were seldom portrayed engaging in housework, the reality of the exhausting "double load" where women had to struggle with both wage work as well as unpaid housework was not addressed. Second, the gender hierarchy in the sexual division of labor where men continued to occupy higher level decision-making positions was also obscured by the visibility of women at work outside the home (Dölling 1993: 170), and by the lack of images of women working in the company of men in a gender hierarchy.

In the Maoist era, socialist narratives in novels, drama, radio, and film portrayed the liberation of female subjects from the economic exploitation of "feudalism" and "family patriarchy" by the Communist Party (Dai 1995b). This central theme can be found in the revolutionary "model opera" (*yangban xi*) *Red Detachment of Women*, which later became a film directed by Xie Jin (1961) and also a ballet made into a film during the Cultural Revolution (1970). Wu Qinghua, a poor peasant woman, and others like her are saved by a handsome party representative (*dang daibiao*) when he recruits them to serve in a women's regiment of the Communist forces. The peasant women soon lose their feminine gender characteristics that had so oppressed them and adopt the fierce persona of revolutionary soldiers. The playing down of the love and sexual attraction between Wu Qinghua and the party representative, of which a faint suggestion is still to be found in Xie Jin's film, allows her to rechannel her libidinal energies from him to the larger male object of cathexis that he represents: the party and the nation-state. Wu's unruly female individuality is disciplined when she seeks personal revenge on the wicked landlord who had persecuted her without first obtaining permission from party leaders. Only when she is made to recognize her mistake in acting on her own is she domesticated and integrated into the masculine state machinery.

The improvement of Wu Qinghua's position from female peasant to degendered soldier obscures the fact that although the women's regiment is given guns to kill men, it is also led by men who train them, lead them in battle, and transmit directives to them from higher male levels. This gender hierarchy is portrayed in one scene of Xie Jin's film where the various women's regiments gather together in a rally and rows of women respectfully listen to the authoritative and inspiring speech given by the party representative. However, it is difficult for the audience to "see" a gender hierarchy because these women have lost their gender identity in their transformation to soldiers just like men.[6]

In a perceptive essay, feminist scholar Meng Yue brings to light the process of desexualization and defeminization in successive versions of *The White-Haired Woman* (*Baimao nü*), another Maoist model opera. There is a "gradual erasure of Xi-er's [the female protagonist's] body and her sexual situation" (1993: 121). In the original 1940s opera version, after Xi-er is raped by the evil landlord, she uses her pregnant body to demonstrate his crime and condemn the hated old society. In the film version of the same story, her pregnant condition is indicated in dialogue but not shown in the frame. By the time of the later ballet version, the scenes of pregnancy and childbirth are erased altogether. In still later versions, Xi-er does not even get raped but becomes a virgin mother. What the story achieves is the displacement of the theme of male sexual domination by the only kind of conflict and domination recognized by official discourse, the political struggle between revolutionary classes and capitalist-feudal forces.

What often got erased were not only women's bodies and female gender but also sexual desire itself, through a combined process of repression and an emptying out of public discourse on sex.[7] Revolutionary asceticism imprinted young people's aspirations with lofty ideals of nation building, so that love and sexuality were relegated to petty personal matters of a sordid and lowly nature. Such was the case with Song Lian, now a forty-year-old professional woman who never married, because in her youth she was, in her retrospective account, so busy carrying out campaigns against whomever the leadership condemned that she did not have time to think of love or sex. During the Cultural Revolution, many young people developed an abhorrence to notions of love or sex, and any suggestion of sexual liaisons outside of marriage was severely punished (Li Yinghe 1997). This situation was different from Michel Foucault's refutation of the "repressive hypothesis" (1990), where he showed how a vociferous Victorian discourse repressing sexuality actually incited sexual desire. In China, the frequent stories of urban people's sexual ignorance in that period suggest that rather than a proliferation or incitement, there was a *dearth* of both public and private discussion of sex during the Cultural Revolution.[8]

In the Maoist period, the only difference that was important was that which was produced in state political classifications of "class" categories (Billeter 1985), so that other differences were smoothed over, such as those based on religion, ethnicity, region, kinship distance, age, and gender. Collective identifications other than class and nation were discouraged, as were identities or groups that were inclusive of several classes. Thus, gender relations in China in this period were not so much transformed as gender itself declined as a salient category of discourse, and the desexualization of gender contributes to this decline. The key to answering the question of why, despite state feminism's discourse of gender equality and the weakening of the separation between gendered domestic and public spheres, women's liberation remains incomplete and fragile, may be this very decline of gender salience.

These examples of the erasure of feminine gender suggest that we ask a different question from the usual question of how the state shapes gender and sexuality, which puts the state *outside* gender and sexuality. Instead, we need to ask, "What gender is the state?"[9] This is not simply a question of personnel, of who represents the state or who carries out state functions, as in Katherine Verdery's account of Nicolae Ceauşescu's Romania as a patriarchal socialist family in which the bureaucracy, heavy industry, army, and police were predominantly male, while women occupied the lower levels of bureaucracy (education, health care, and culture) (1994: 233). In the same way that Evelyn Fox Keller brought attention to the gender of science (1987) by analyzing the gendered structure of its knowledge rather than the gender of scientists, we need to get at the deeper underlying masculine structure of the logic, mode of organization, and telos of different states. Since women can often participate as agents of male discourse, what becomes important is the construction of gendered state discourse, rather than the gender of its agents.

As an increasing body of feminist writings show, states and the nationalism they promote have an overall masculine character (Peterson 1992; Sutton 1995; Enloe 1998; Brown 1992; Lydia Liu 1994; Afshar 1987). Asking about the gendered cultural logic of state institutions does not mean essentializing masculinity or the state, because there are divergent historical and cultural constructions of state masculinities. For example, U.S. nuclear defense discourse is based on a language of masculine competition in sexual virility and "equipment," where disarmament is likened to "emasculation" and missiles are "penetrators" (Cohn 1987). The Serbian state policy of rape as a strategy of war is the expression of a collective masculinist heterosexual impulse linked with deep-seated principles of state territorial sovereignty, which takes the form in wartime of the extreme misogyny of the violent possession of the enemy's women (Borneman 1998). Both these male sexual discourses and practices of statism differ from the patriarchy of Singaporean "state fatherhood," a curious melding of scientific eugenics with a Confucian familism that demands that Chinese educated women fulfill their reproductive duties to the state (Heng and Devan 1992). In Maoist Chinese state discourse, there is no obsession with male virility, but we find a desexualized narrative of a family-state of degendered revolutionary subjects led by a wise father.[10]

In noting the hidden male point of reference behind Mao's slogan "Everything male comrades can do, female comrades can do also," Dai

Jinhua suggests that the ostensibly gender-neutral language of state discourse actually assimilates female gender to the male (1995a). Thus, the discourse of "equality" takes male gender as the standard to which women must conform. Female difference is suppressed and sameness is promoted, that is, being like men. As Zillah Eisenstein says of both liberal and socialist state feminism,

> Difference(s) is assumed to mean inequality because there is a silent referent: a woman's body is *not* like a man's, she is less than man. In order to be equal she must be the same. Homogeneity becomes the standard and individuality a problem. . . . Individuality, difference(s), and the female body [must] transform the meaning of sex equality. [Feminism] must be specified in more than economic and legal terms. (1989: 335)

Thus, state processes erased more of feminine gender than masculine and at the same time took away the language that could articulate the disappearance of women.

The Chinese imperial state seldom came into contact with women directly but worked through the patriarchy of family and kinship modes of power, which it promoted in state Confucianism, through its rewards to virtuous and chaste widows (Elvin 1984; Carlitz 1994), and its scriptural praises of exemplary women (*lienü*) in history. The socialist state exerted gender power directly by penetrating down to the level of locality and family, displacing old gender norms, and directly confronting traditional patriarchy in state discourse. Through its concerted efforts to eliminate lineages and weaken the patriarchal family, the socialist state reduced the authority of male kin, weakened the divide that separated women from the public, and came to administer women's labor and reproduction directly and transform them into loyal state subjects. This process achieved a systematic integration and direct absorption of women into a male state apparatus.[11] In extending state emancipation and protection to Chinese women, state feminism brought women into public life as never before. However, Chinese women achieved mainly an entry into the public domain of production, not into the production of public discourse, which was reserved for the state. Thus, although state discourse granted women a central position, its very language also undermined women's self-identity and gender consciousness, which could serve as a basis for building a women's discourse and women's community.

Recent research has shown that there is in modern Western discourse since the eighteenth century an inordinate emphasis on the sexual dimorphic nature of the human body, which in turn has produced a personal identity whose core is a gendered identity (Moore 1994: 37; Herdt 1994). The discovery of this distinctive modern Western obsession with essentialized sexual difference grounded in the body (Martin 1987) has been accompanied by an intellectual movement to problematize the categories of gender (Ortner 1996) and to critique the naturalized binary gender order and move toward a postgender order. This movement can be found in the interest in "third genders" (Herdt 1994) such as European hermaphrodites (Barbin 1980), Indian hijras (Nanda 1990), and native American berdache (Whitehead 1981; Roscoe 1991), and in Donna Haraway's classic formulation of the "cyborg" as the transcendence of a naturalized sexual binary through the constructedness of organic-machinic formations (1991).

However, although the uncovering of this hegemonic essentialized binary was accomplished through a meticulous historical excavation, the subsequent move to demolish this modern Western binary has often been couched in ahistorical and universalistic terms. That is to say, there has been little consideration of alternative historical contexts of the emergence and dismantling of gender binaries. In the case of China, the reconstruction of women's identity in the 1980s and '90s and the extrication of feminism from its imprisonment in state discourse have required a "strategic use of [the] essentialism" (Spivak 1988b: 13) of the gender binary, which itself has not been historically stable or firmly rooted in China.[12]

Commodification and the Coding of Gender Difference and Sexuality

In the current economic reforms and market economy, the figure of sexualized woman has returned in mass-media representation. Her face is no longer plain and flat but glamorous and made-up, her hair is no longer woven into braids, and her figure is no longer hidden under baggy army pants but increasingly revealed under low-cut tops, translucent chiffons, and short shorts. She appears ubiquitously in public and private places: on giant billboards selling everything from cookware to computers, on posters and calendars hanging in living rooms and dormitories, on the covers of magazines at bookstands, in television commercials, in fashion shows as models, and in new films that adopt a more modest version of the sex-and-violence formula imported from abroad (fig. 2). Images of white women are also presented, with less clothes on than her Chinese counterpart, their voluptuous bodies draped across manly motorcycles and sports cars, expressing a complex racial and sexual attitude on the part of the male Chinese viewer.[13] In a study of images of women in 120 Chinese television

Figure 2. Woman as commodity image in a Shanghai subway station. Photograph by Li Weimin.

commercials in Kunming, Beth Notar found that the figure of young women predominated in most ads, outnumbering all categories of men, and older women and children (1994: 30). In most of the commercials displaying both women and men, it was the young woman who was objectified, playing a passive role of being gazed on or waiting for her businessman husband to come home from the office. In only two ads did women return the male gaze or was the gaze of the camera constructed from a woman's point of view.

Tang Lifei is a Shanghai woman writer and media hostess in her forties who has lived through the political vicissitudes of gender in both Maoist and reform eras. She embodies the contradictions and curious amalgamations of two different gender orders. Like other women in her generation who came to maturity in the Cultural Revolution, she believes she is a "middle-sex person" (*zhongxingren*), or someone without a marked gender, because she does not know how to "express the softness of [her] femininity." She first started putting on makeup around 1986, while younger people in their twenties started a few years earlier. To my query as to how she felt when she first put on makeup, she said her strongest feeling was that she did not want others to know she did, so she applied it very lightly. This transition was difficult because she was making a "fundamental transformation of positional stance" (*genben lichang de zhuanyi*), from that of identifying with the proletariat to participating in bourgeois culture and becoming a woman. For Tang during the Cultural Revolution, "It was another kind of murder of human nature, of women's nature. You could not express your soft and pliable [*wenrou*] side. If you did, you were called 'petty bourgeois.' You had to be manly to join the ranks of the proletariat." Today, she feels different after she has put on makeup. She is used to being rough and loud, but after applying makeup, she feels she should restrain herself from expressing the manly side of herself and behave in keeping with her looks. Makeup has allowed her to discover her feminine side, and she felt a pleasurable thrill when men would turn around to look at her walking down the street in makeup and elegant clothes.

The complex situation and transformation of Chinese women are revealed here in Tang's statements. Her hesitation and discomfort about first applying makeup is the radical transformation in subjectivity and self-positioning she is undergoing. From a genderless person she will come to regard herself as a woman, a possibility at once liberating and disturbing. Liberation is in being able to recover that lost side of herself, the soft and gentle side, that had been declared self-indulgent and off-limits. Still carrying the remnants of the Maoist order in which gender was thought of in class terms, she feels a certain guilt about replacing her proletarian masculinity and defecting to the bourgeois feminine side. Once she has gotten used to her new persona, she begins to enjoy the male desire and admiration she can elicit. In this new identity as a beautiful woman, a different gender structure emerges in her, where a male structure no longer overpowers and displaces female subjectivity; now it defines the female by encouraging her to evaluate herself in her reflection in the male. Thus, her subjectivity is gauged by the pleasure she can produce in the male. This new construction of woman has a definite material dimension, as it is both product as well as driving force of the new market economy. The makeup, clothing, and fashion industries have become crucial components of the Chinese economy, and integral to the media and consumer industries.

Training classes and self-help classes for women have sprung up in the 1990s in Chinese cities. For a fee, they teach women to be more feminine, and to realize their women's identity and roles. Younger women often take classes called "Culture and Etiquette Training" (*wenhua liyike*) and middle-aged women take classes called "Home Management" (*jiazheng ke*), which teach them the psychological balance and practical skills needed to be good mothers and housewives. I interviewed twenty-two-year-old Kang Hualan in Shanghai, who had taken the first kind of class. Over a month-long period, she learned the following skills: how to speak graciously and skillfully in Mandarin; how to have self-confidence; how to smile win-somely; how to apply makeup and be up-to-date in fashion; how to con-duct business negotiations; how to act out roles; how to appreciate music, art, film, and television; how to socialize at public banquets; and how to put on a dinner for guests at home. Graduates of these courses will have an edge in finding jobs as hotel or restaurant hostesses or in filling the new gendered occupational category of "public relations ladies" (*gongguan xiaojie*) for business firms. Chosen for their beauty, poise, and social grace, these women will have duties ranging from opening doors in large department stores to taking business clients out to dinner and evening entertainment and softening them up as targets for business transactions. Beautiful women are increasingly deployed by economic enterprises to be their public face. One middle-aged woman accountant who has been part of a managerial staff for many years at a large Shanghai restaurant recounted with bitter-ness how, after the state-owned restaurant was sold to a Hong Kong Chin-ese, the new ownership moved the middle-aged women from the front space of the restaurant to the dirty back space of the kitchen and rear office cells and replaced them with young twenty-year-old women dressed in tight body-clinging Chinese dresses (*qipao*) with high, revealing leg slits.

Here it is clear that the new consumer culture is based on a fundamen-tal gender bifurcation, and the exaggeration and celebration of gender dif-ference and sexuality. However, this bifurcation of gender is also an asym-metrical construction, so that there is the knowing and controlling male gaze and the female object of contemplation and desire. As Laura Mulvey shows, in this new patriarchal structure "woman . . . stands . . . as signifier for the male other" (1986: 199). That is to say, it is not so much that the meaning of woman is expressed through sexual difference, as the meaning of woman *comes to be* sexual difference. In this sexual economy, women are invested (literally and economically) with the quality of "to-be-looked-at-ness," and their function is to provide a contrastive background against which male subjectivity is foregrounded and brought into sharper relief. The effect of making women palpably visible is to make viewers identify with the subject-position of the male eye. In this way, male subjectivity and its power are made invisible, as in the Maoist gender order, but this invisibility is not based on an erasure or blurring of genders but depends on the hypervisibility of the female image.

What is astonishing is the rapidity of the return of gender differentia-tion, the ascendancy of the male gaze, and masculine sexuality's domina-tion of a public sphere partially vacated by the state. After a hiatus of four decades in the Maoist era, the male gaze returned again in the 1980s, along with consumer culture from Hong Kong, Taiwan, Japan, and the United States, foregrounding male sexuality and subjectivity, and positioning women as the expressive means for operationalizing an active male desire.[14]

Most Marxist feminist approaches to gender subordination address the exploitation of female labor, such as unpaid housework and an underpaid reserve army of female workers needed to balance out unpredictable economic fluctuations. Capitalism commodifies more than women's labor: it directly commodifies the bodies, sexualities, and images of women. In large cities like Shanghai today, there are innumerable places of "soft" sexual servicing of men by women. Some night clubs and karaoke bars have what are called "handwashing rooms" (xishoujian), where men can use their hands to touch and stroke the waitresses, and in a few high-class karaoke bars there is even "kneeling service" (guishi fuwu), where the waitresses bear drinks on their knees to the mostly male guests. This is supposed to move their customers to slip money down their low necklines. A Taiwanese businessman told me the practice of kneeling service probably came to China from Taiwan, which in turn probably learned it from Japan. The recent phenomena of "chartered sister" (baomei) (women promised to a man in exchange for money) and "golden canary" (jinsi que) (mistresses or second wives of wealthy men who set up a second household unbeknownst to the first wife) look like new versions of traditional polygynous marital arrangements. Women have also entered into prostitution, from peasant women working along long-distance truck routes and in train station hotels, to college students and working-class women who sell themselves to rich overseas Chinese and Westerners in luxury hotels.

REASCENDANT MASCULINITY

In the post-Mao period, we can detect not just the refeminization of women, but also the new masculinization of men. Several urban men I spoke with used the term castration (yange) to describe the situation of men in Maoist society. In the "old society" before Liberation, they said, men could go out into the world and gain economic and political power, but in the "new society" they were stuck in socialist work units earning the same meager wages as women. The party kept constant watch over them, dampening their personal ambition and preventing them from standing up and saying what was on their minds. That is why today's men lack "initiative" (zhudongxing), "boldness" (danliang), "vision" (yanjie), and "creativity" (chuangzaoxing). Zhang Xian, a male Shanghai playwright, thought that men in his society today cannot be assertive and cannot provide for their families. He was certain that an American "cowboy-type individualist" in

China would sooner or later run afoul of the state and be put into prison. Wang Shengming, a male cadre in his fifties, said to me, "The Communist Party has mounted so many political campaigns and 'struggled' so many people that now you get men who do not have masculinity [*meiyou nanzihan qizhi*]. Men have become timid and obedient. They even fear their wives."

In the realm of post-Mao literature and film, there has been an abundance of portrayals of raw masculinity in heroic characters by such writers as Jia Pingwa and Zhang Xianliang, and in many "Western" films (*xibupian*) of the rugged Northwest peasant culture coming out of the revived Xi'an Film Studios. Critics based in the West like Wang Yeujin (1991) and Zhang Yingjin (1990) find in the celebration of the male body in the film *Red Sorghum*, for example, a life-affirming remasculinization of language and ethos and an oppositional political allegory that challenges the sterile artificialities of state discourse. Others have been critical of the new masculinities. Zhong Xueping (1994) shows how in Zhang Xianliang's novel *Half of Man Is Woman* the hero, a prisoner who becomes impotent, regains his masculinity and political and sexual potency with the help of women, but only to abandon them later. Women in Zhang's novels serve merely to facilitate men's recovery of their masculinities. The film *The Raft-Rowers*, whose premiere at Xi'an Film Studios I attended in 1992, contains a recurring theme of women posing as threats to male bonding. The peaceful life of a close-knit band of poor, male river-raft transporters is destroyed when a woman fleeing a bandit gang arrives on the scene. By becoming the object of desire for two "sworn brothers," she breaks up their friendship and turns them into rivals. Although the ending was redeemed by having the raft-rowers break their age-old rule against accepting female members, the thrust of the film was on male bonding and the solidarity of a male community.[15]

THE DECLINE OF STATE FEMINISM

Throughout the 1980s and '90s, urban women, especially working-class women, have been departing the arena of public labor or experiencing a lowering of their work positions. In cities across China, there is the phenomenon of "stepping-down women workers" (*xiagang nügong*), where factory women are relieved of their work or are pressured to take early retirement. With the market economy and enterprise autonomy, many state-owned factories have scaled down their operations and personnel in order to become more competitive. Other factories sell their operations to overseas investors who demand less personnel, and women are usually the first to go. In their focus on profitability, the newly empowered, largely male managerial force is not particularly sympathetic to the plight of women and the larger social issues of gender equity. College and professional women also face new forms of discrimination. College and professional schools' entrance score requirements are often higher for women than for men, "to balance out the gender ratio." After graduation, women often find it difficult to secure employment because many enterprises and government offices refuse to hire women.[16] The severe employment situation has given Chinese feminists such as Li Xiaojiang strong reservations about the economic reforms (Li 1988a: 210–11). Yet at the same time, women's setbacks in market society pointed out a more complex problem that had been obscured in the Maoist era. Li explains that formerly, when both men and women were equally poor and there was no competition, the system hid women's problems from view, so that such issues as the low levels of women's education and abilities, and women's double burden of work and home were not brought out into the open (Li 1988a). There were those who thought women's difficulties in the market economy were due to internal psychological obstacles that made women "unable . . . to compete because of low self-esteem, and a desire to sacrifice themselves for their families," and there were those who thought the problems were due to sexual discrimination in society (Rosen 1994). Thus, we can see that state feminism, which changed the gender division of labor, often did so without making a lasting impact on gender culture and psychology.

In the 1980s, there were recurrent calls in the print media for the return of women to household labor, especially by male economists (*Hunan* 1987: 162). The various arguments put forward included the claim that this would free up room for the millions of (male) unemployed. A second argument was that this would solve the problems of weariness and household neglect that plagued families with two working parents. A third claim was based on concerns for economic efficiency and profits: female employees were said to overtax an enterprise's leave-of-absence time, and welfare and maternity benefits. There was also the concern that working women caused the neglect of children's upbringing and education, and a reduction in breast-feeding mothers, leading to market-supply problems in cow's milk. A final reason was unabashedly in defense of male privilege: as husbands' leisure time was taken over by housework, this would lead to disharmony in the family. State organs such as the powerful Propaganda Ministry of the Politburo and the Labor Ministry have maintained the principle of women in public labor, and the Women's Federation lobbied vigorously in public editorials against these proposals (*Hunan* 1987: 161–62).

A recent example calling for an end to state feminism can be found in a 1995 book by Zheng Yefu called *On Paying a Price* (*Daijia lun*), which borrows the authority of Western anthropology and American free-market ideology to condemn state feminism for "prematurely" distorting a "natural" situation of gender inequality in China: "Through aiding the weak and suppressing the strong, a huge administrative force has interfered with and damaged the normal division of labor between the strong and the weak in the family. It has even made the weak think that they are not weak, and made the strong lose their rightful self-confidence" (Zheng 1995: 69). Zheng blames socialism's "generous gift" (*enxi*) to women for men's inability to discover their own strength, and for their progressive "feminization" as they become entrapped in the home. He hails the new "sexual discrimination" (*xingbie qishi*) against women in China by the market as a "rectification" of past distortions in state planning (1995: 72).

Such opposition to state feminism runs parallel to a similar development in Eastern Europe, where a male dissident discourse of "anti-politics" emerged to counter the intrusive Stalinist state (Goven 1993). This discourse celebrated the family as the last refuge of society against the state, and the traditional nurturing role of women in the family to support their men's resistance against the state. There is an antifeminist thrust to this movement, which sees an alliance between the state and liberated women to destroy the family (hence, civil society) through women's employment and the domestication of men.

New Openings in Women's Public Space

The economic reforms of the 1980s and '90s have brought new conditions to China, which have both opened up and closed off public spaces for women. Media images of women have been diversified from the heroic revolutionaries of the model operas (Mao 1989). First, the "virtuous wife, good mother" (*xianqi liangmu*) image of a sweet domestic woman was first showcased in 1990 in the self-sacrificing character of Liu Huifang in the television soap opera *Yearnings* and the popular Taiwan film *Mother, Love Me Again* (Rofel 1994b, Mayfair Yang 1993). This image has also been deployed in television commercials for products such as Love-Your-Wife brand (*Aiqi pai*) washing machines ("If you love her, you will buy this"). Second, there is the figure of the abused and humiliated woman who is the victim of male sexual aggression. Her body can be found in lurid photographs in tabloid news magazines (*xiaobao*) and novels of violence in small bookstands on city streets, as rape, murder, and battery victims, women captured and sold by criminal rings, and so on. Despite the ostensible condemnation of these acts and their thinly disguised police report format, this image has significant commercial appeal to its male consumers. A third image of women is the capable but personally unfulfilled "strong woman" (nü qiangren), who forges ahead in career but has an unhappy family life. This image is always presented negatively: she does not know how to be a real woman, she neglects her family and children, and she fiercely dominates her husband. A fourth female symbol harbors an ambiguous message. This is the figure of the "immoral woman" (fandaode xing) who is often the "cold-blooded woman assassin" and "sexy spy" found in police and spy novels, films, and television shows. Although she is a sexual object for men, she also exhibits an active sex drive and violates traditional women's decorum and sexual taboos. Whereas in Maoist era films sexually alluring women were usually counterrevolutionary, the new "immoral woman" is someone with a complex motivation that needs to be understood, as in the 1990 film, Miss Anli (Anli xiaojie).

The wealth of new journals, magazines, and radio and television talk shows in post-Mao China no longer just report the latest party meeting and industrial and agricultural production figures. Instead, these commercialized media have developed a keen interest in matters of everyday life, the domestic sphere, and questions of love, marriage, and sexuality, offering many opportunities for the public discussion of women's issues. Along with the introduction of new media images of women, the media have also presented public debates and criticisms of such images as Liu Huifang in the television drama Yearnings and the "strong woman" (Yang 1996b). These discussions suggest the beginnings of a women's public sphere of gender self-reflection.

At the same time, the decline of state funding for Women's Federation activities and affirmative action for women in public positions means that a social gender discrimination against women has returned in the market economy. For example, according to three women film directors in Shanghai, now that they must compete with male directors in obtaining commercial investment in films, many female film directors are unable to find financing for their films because they do not cater to a male-oriented commercial film culture. There is a historical irony in the fact that in the Maoist era, when more women participated in cultural production, they did not create a women's public sphere, but now that a space is increasingly being carved out from the state for a public sphere, many women encounter difficulties of entry.

In 1920, Lu Yin, one of China's earliest feminists, asked in a speech, "Why is it necessary that women's own problems should be solved by others, who are not women? Why is it that the pain and suffering of women are not felt by women themselves? Women also have brains, we also have four limbs and five senses, so why don't women feel anything? That we must rely on men to do everything, this is unthinkable" (Lu 1985: 3). At that time, many of the prominent figures in the feminist movement in China were men speaking on behalf of oppressed womanhood. This was due perhaps not only to the thoroughness of women's oppression under the old system, which made it difficult for women to emerge as vocal agents in the public sphere, but also to the deep imbrication of early feminism in the nationalist movement, where male nationalists saw women's oppression as a national shame and sought to liberate women in order to strengthen the nation and recover its prestige.

Seventy-five years later, Lu Yin's concerns were echoed in a different way by Song Lian, a middle-aged professional woman, who said to me,

> One big difference between our women's equality and that in Western societies is that the latter was wrested and struggled for with blood and sweat, so it is more treasured and appreciated by Western women. It's not like that for Chinese women, because it was handed down to us all of a sudden by administrative fiat. Therefore, many Chinese women are not subjectively ready for equality.

It is difficult to know how to interpret such a statement, which seemingly affirms the superiority of Western feminism. Certainly, it need not be taken as an assertion that the particular trajectory of Western feminism is the only universal form that should be adopted for all histories. Chinese feminism arose out of a colonial situation and anticolonial nationalism, which Western feminism did not encounter, thus feminism in China must work with and address this particular legacy. Furthermore, the support of such a powerful centralized state has given certain advantages to Chinese women not enjoyed by Western women. While at the present moment there is a sentiment that what is needed is a struggle of women's *self*-liberation and a collective gender identity movement (a change in subjective consciousness from within that revolution from above could not give), it does not mean that Western feminism is the only model. As the next section and Li Xiaojiang's article in this collection will show, even as Chinese feminism in the reform period is becoming more independent of the state, it also assumes several unique forms.

By *independent women's voices,* I do not mean that these feminists have mounted an oppositional movement against the state nor that they always occupy positions outside the state. These voices diverge from the general tenor of state feminism, which assumes that the liberation of women is already a fait accompli and that women continue to be well served by the state. However, most of these women speak largely from positions within the state; many of them are scholars employed by state-run universities or re-search institutes, or are Women's Federation cadres and researchers. Even women writers and novelists who increasingly derive their income from the print market are often still attached to state organs such as the Writers Association or Cultural Federation. What I am referring to is a turning from within certain segments of the state, as women intellectuals and professionals use their state positions to support feminist activities not ini-tiated by the state and speak of feminist concerns, without at the same time furthering the ends of the party.

One distinctive feature of an emerging feminist public sphere in China is that, unlike the male oppositional public sphere, it does not wish to drastically roll back the state. Since the economic reforms, the loss of jobs by women, and the humiliations brought by a commercialized male sexu-ality, the state has become the sole institution that can defend women's equality in the face of the relentless logic of the market. Another reason is a political and strategic one: open confrontation with the state would be counterproductive to expanding feminist inquiry and discussion.[17]

At the same time, however, these new feminist outlooks also seek to disengage themselves from the restrictions and orthodoxies of state femi-nism. In an early work of the new feminism, Li Xiaojiang laid out three "taboo" areas of inquiry in state orthodoxy that had to be overcome in the "women's studies" she was founding in China: sex, class, and feminism (1988a: 31–33). These three taboos not only reveal the theoretical and dis-cursive obstacles that an alternative feminism emerging out of state femi-nism had to face but also provide us with three more distinctive features of a new Chinese feminist discourse. By *sex,* Li meant biological/physiological differences of sex rather than sexualities. For Li, the dominant way of thinking in the Maoist period presented male and female as only social products without considering biological differences. According to Li, social constructionism may have seemed to promote gender equality, but it actually increased the burden on women by denying women's bodily differences, so that forcing them into certain types of physical labor ruined women's health and created painful role conflicts between women's mothering role and work (Li 1988a: 31).

Here a second distinctiveness of Chinese women's historical situation can be seen in how the new feminism reverses the temporal order found in both Western second-wave and Taiwanese feminisms. Whereas a major thrust of Western feminism has been to critique essentialism and to escape the "biology is destiny" ideology, Li is critiquing Marxist social constructionism for its neglect of biological differences. What is oppressive for Li and many other Chinese feminists is not that women have been made to symbolize the body, "sexual difference," or maternal nurturing qualities (Flax 1987), but that a social discourse has rendered women invisible (Dai 1995a), suppressed their gender, and denied them specificity and difference from men. In other words, for Li Xiaojiang, and also in a different, less essentialist way for Meng Yue and Dai Jinhua (1988), the important task at hand is to awaken gender identity in women, and a convenient and visible basis from which to claim this identity is bodily difference and the physiological and psychological experiences that are particular to women.[18]

A third distinctive feature of independent feminist voices lies in the effort to retrieve gender as a salient category from what in the Maoist era had become the hegemonic discourse of "class." Li Xiaojiang asserted that gender cannot be collapsed into class but is an independent category transcending class; proletarian women cannot represent all of women's existence in history but are only a particular part of history. In seeing class as a barrier to women's consciousness, Li shows how the situation of Chinese feminism is quite different from the historical experience of feminism in the West. Li had to fight for a public space from which women could speak and construct their gender identity against a backdrop of state discourse, which spoke in the name of the peasant and working classes. In the United States, both first- and second-wave feminisms were dominated by white middle-class women until the 1970s, when they encountered challenges from multiculturalism and women of color, who pointed out feminism's restricted class and racial standpoint (Sandoval 1991; hooks 1984; Fraser 1997). In China today, intellectual women have barely begun to make incursions into a powerful male state discourse and into a new male oppositional public sphere. At this point, they have yet to incur feminist challenges from peasant and working-class women, and the working classes have yet to create their own public sphere and differentiate their collective voices from that of the state.

By addressing the taboo of "feminism" (nüquan zhuyi), Li sought to forestall the easy dismissal of women's studies in China as Western or "bourgeois," which would close off Chinese women from engagement with ongoing transnational feminist discussions. However, in recent years Li Xiaojiang has spoken out against the easy adoption of Western feminism, whose conceptions are not always relevant to Chinese women's situations (see her essay in this collection). For her, Chinese women are quite capable of finding solutions to their own problems. Like the Japanese feminist Chizuko Ueno, she believes that East Asian feminism must make the family and domestic sphere much more integral to its movement than Western feminism has (Ueno 1997). Here we can see that a fourth feature of independent feminism in contemporary China is its ambivalent and sometimes tense relationship with both nationalism and transnationalism.

What Julia Kristeva saw as the first two generations of women's movement in the modern West is quite relevant to the Chinese feminist experience. In her essay "Women's Time" she portrayed the early women's movement as an attempt to "gain a place in linear time as the time of project and history," when women sought to participate in male time, which was deeply rooted in the phenomenon of the nation-state (1986: 193). Enlightenment egalitarianism and universalism, which can be found in both Western socialism and East European state socialism, set up an identity between the two sexes as the only way to liberate the "second sex" (1986: 195). This blurring of genders for the sake of equality was also put into operation in socialist China, resulting in a loss of gender consciousness. For Kristeva, the younger generation of feminists "refuse linear time and distrust politics as the realm of the male," are "interested in the specificity of female psychology, and . . . seek to give a language to the intrasubjective and corporeal experiences left mute by culture in the past" (1986: 194). In China today, a new generation of women is also now expanding their consciousness through exploring these very themes. Yet just as they thematize gender difference, the market and consumer culture have already started to appropriate it for its own ends.

MARKET ECONOMY AND A FEMINIST PUBLIC SPHERE

The market economy has provided the conditions for the emergence of a women's public sphere in the mass media, and a smaller feminist public sphere whose locus is mainly to be found in print media. At the same time, the market economy also ensures that these spheres are delimited and contained by a male-oriented commercial culture. Li Xiaojiang's inaugural feminist book *Explorations of Eve* was published in 1988 in a special series on women by Henan Publishing Company, which also included Meng Yue and Dai Jinhua's pathbreaking feminist literary criticism, *Emerging from the Horizon of History* (1988). In her introduction, Li also touched on the Chinese translation of two important Western feminist texts that influenced her and a generation of urban women in the 1980s: Simone de Beauvoir's *The Second Sex* and Betty Friedan's *The Feminine Mystique*. All of these works were published in the post-Mao era, when new publishing outlets expanded publication opportunities. Yet at the same time, the feminist public sphere also cannot survive in the pure book market, where best-sellers are often male pornographic novels (Jia 1993; Zha 1995); it must seek shelter in state institutions such as universities, research institutes, and Women's Federations, where about thirty women's studies research and educational programs have sprung up around the country (Li and Zhang 1994).

Feminist writer Xu Kun (1995) discusses the process by which an authoritative collection of literature, titled *Red Opium Poppies*, by twenty-two contemporary Chinese women writers came to be assembled on the occasion of the Fourth UN Women's Conference in Beijing in 1995. This was a significant step, for "in a society dominated by male-centered discourse, it is very difficult for women to win a space to exercise their rights to their own discourse" (Xu 1995: 8). However, instead of rejoicing at the book-signing ceremony where thousands of fans clamored to get a peek at their favorite authors, Xu started to reconsider the event. As hordes of fans in search of autographs descended on the scene, and the television news cameras rolled, as journalists took notes, and the Xinhua Bookstore manager gleefully announced that three thousand books were sold that afternoon for a total of forty thousand yuan, Xu could only wonder to herself, "Since when did our gender become so marketable and command such charismatic appeal?" It was the market that had carved out a space from state discourse and state control of the publishing industry, enabling women to disseminate their own voices in public; however, this same market was also run by men. The book series was under the general editorship of none other than the authoritative writer-official Wang Meng, and men ran the publishing house, bookstore, and news media, which were packaging the women in a way designed to maximize the market for their books. Thus, this feminist reflection on women's public sphere shows how the market is at once an enabling and constraining device for women.

THE REGIME OF SEXUALITY AND WOMEN'S BODIES AND PLEASURES

Meng Yue and Dai Jinhua observed that the gender imagery of Maoist "revolutionary model operas" was predicated on the father-daughter relationship rather than a man-woman relationship (1988: 268). What a father-daughter relationship does is to activate the incest taboo, so that romantic interest and sexuality between man and woman are suppressed, while the intergenerational subordination of the daughter to the paternal party is foregrounded. In contrast, contemporary mass consumer culture plays up the dyad of male and female, where the female is not a daughter but a sexualized woman in dynamic attraction and sexual tension with the male.[19]

This consumer culture that is pervading Chinese cities, especially on the eastern seaboard, provides a vivid testimonial to Gilles Deleuze and Félix Guattari's assertion that capitalist production and desiring production of the libido are one and the same process: "The conjunction of the decoded flows in the capitalist machine tends to liberate the free figures of a universal subjective libido. . . . The discovery of an activity of production . . . in capitalism is the identical discovery of both political economy and psychoanalysis" (1983: 302). Such industries as makeup, clothing, fashion, popular music, and a great deal of the print and electronic mass media industries are direct productions of sexuality, and all of them are propelled by advertising that relies on sexual images. Thus, mass consumer culture works with a key dimension of gender construction, sexuality, which Gayle Rubin, in an interview with Judith Butler, declared was a lacuna in Marxist theory:

> Marxism, no matter how modified, seemed unable to fully grasp the issues of gender difference and the oppression of women. . . . I was one of many who finally concluded that one could only go so far within a Marxist paradigm and that while it was useful, it had limitations with regard to gender and sex. (Rubin 1994: 63)

Similarly, for Kristeva, state feminism in Eastern Europe had met three feminist demands: economic, political, and professional equality. However, a fourth equality, sexual equality for women, which implies permissiveness in sexual relations, including homosexuality, has been suppressed "for reasons of state" (Kristeva 1986: 196). Mass consumer culture supplies this missing ingredient in state feminism: the power of sexuality in reconstructing gender. The potential that this new sexual culture harbors for a women's movement is infusing women with an active female desire so that feminism can rely less on the protection of a paternal state.

There are signs that a new consciousness of sexuality has begun to inform a feminist discourse, so that it no longer relies on the protection of a paternal state but on an assertion of women's sexual rights and sexual desire. In an early piece on feminine sexuality, Pan Suiming (1987), a male feminist, uses evolutionist discourse to argue that since women have evolved erogenous zones that have nothing to do with the reproductive organs, women were therefore not designed solely as instruments for giving birth, but also as people to enjoy the pleasures of sex. And since women have evolved a different pacing and path to sexual arousal from those of men, human sexual culture is therefore not only one in which women must satisfy men, but where women can also ask men to adapt to women's sexuality. In the evolution to agricultural society, there was a great decline in women's sexuality as women's bodies were commodified in marriage exchange so that men could buy a monopoly on sexual access to a woman, while women were denied any reciprocal rights to take the active role in sex. The challenge in modernity is for women to regain their lost sexual assertiveness and correct the tragedy of history, which is also a tragedy for men because they have been denied the experience of women's sexual pleasure. For Pan, the restoration of women's sexual rights forms the precondition for their other social rights.

Pan's evolutionist approach to women's sexuality is part of an increasing body of institutional discourses found in medical science, in biology and psychology, and in self-help sex-education and marriage counseling handbooks, which have discovered sex in the post-Mao era and seek to liberate and regulate it. All of these discourses of sex are also linked up with both the biopolitical state project of population control (Anagnost 1997) and the marketing strategies of global capitalism. Thus Foucault's thesis on the modern deployment of sexuality in the historic shift from a "society of blood and death" to one of the "management of life" (1990), which could not quite capture the Maoist combination of sexual repression without an incitement to sexual discourse, seems to be much more relevant to post-Mao China. In this new formation of state biopower and market normalization and masculinization of sexuality, "we must not think that by saying yes to [women's] sex, one says no to power" (Foucault 1990: 157). For Chinese women to merely embrace a notion of true liberated female sex would be to fall into the very strategies of this new deployment of sexuality and power. Yet even as Foucault was suspicious of the notion of a unitary sex of human nature that society must set free, he also called for a "tactical reversal" of sexuality's very mechanisms, through an exploration of the multiplicity and resistances of "bodies and pleasures" (1990: 157).

In women's literature of the 1980s and '90s, there has been a proliferation of women's exploration of their bodies and pleasures (see Dai, this volume). Breaking with the established Chinese convention of a moralistic treatment of sexual desire and passion, and with an emerging pattern of male writers who deploy a discourse of (male) sexual liberation to address the politics of the nation-state, the works of the woman writer Wang Anyi explore the complexities, pleasures, and trials of women's sexual experiences and foreground women's gender subjectivity (Wang 1986a, 1986b). Instead of portraying women as objects of male passion, Wang's novels present the point of view of women and explore the emotional and subjective experience of women taking the sexual initiative and violating moral taboos of premarital and extramarital sex.

However, this women's public sphere in print is but a trickle compared to the tidal wave of masculine heterosexual desire produced in both intellectual film and literature,[20] as well as in the mass media and popular culture. This gender asymmetry in desiring production means that female sexuality and desire in China, which could strengthen women's active engagement with the world, remain for the most part submerged. Despite the difficulties of seeing and experiencing female sexuality amid the masculine media, recent feminist theories of female spectatorship suggest that Laura Mulvey's thesis of the male gaze was too "totalizing" and that a female audience can assume an active subject position in their consumption of popular culture (Bergstrom and Doane 1990; Hansen 1990b; Williams 1989).[21] Since the market economy and consumer culture are predicated on an economy of desiring subjects, the raw materials for reconstructing women's psychology, culture, and sexuality are there. What is needed is both a revolution in female modes of spectatorship as women watch mass-media productions of masculine desire and an expansion of women's production of desire.

This essay has attempted to present the larger historical conditions and social forces that have begun to produce a new kind of feminist awakening in contemporary China. State feminism did much to release Chinese women from traditional kinship patriarchy, but although women were catapulted into the public sphere of labor and politics, the feminist agenda was forgotten with the decline of gender salience and women's transformation into state subjects in a new masculine state order. While sharing the production of traditional female passivity and self-sacrifice more evenly with men (the state demanded self-sacrifice of everyone to the nation), state feminism also made it difficult to sustain a critical gender perspective and feminist discourse mounted by women themselves, issuing from their own lived experiences. The new market economy harbors retrograde forces that would return some women to the domestic sphere, position women in lower-level jobs, and subjugate women to male desire. At the same time, the logic of such desiring production also holds out a possibility of releasing female desire, which would work on a neglected area of state feminism: women's culture, psychology, sexuality, and discourse. Poised uneasily in between the two powerful masculine forces of the state and the market, the tender sprouts of a Chinese feminist public sphere must rely on them both so that state feminism can be deployed to counter the retrograde elements of market culture and economy, while the latter can be used to carve out more discursive space from the state. Thus Chinese feminism must play off one force against the other, while at the same time widening the space for itself.

NOTES

I wish to acknowledge the National Science Foundation for funding this research, and the Chicago Humanities Institute, University of Chicago, for allowing me the time to write. I also appreciate the input I received when I presented this paper at the Gender and Society Workshop, University of Chicago; Center for Chinese Studies, UCLA; Anthropology and Sociology Institute at National Tsinghua University in Taiwan; Women's Research Program, National Taiwan University; the American Anthropological Association meetings in 1997; and the anthropology department at the University of California, Irvine. Thanks also to valuable discussions and comments from Lisa Wedeen, Huang Shuqin, Shu-mei Shih, Lydia Liu, Miriam Hansen, Nivedita Menom, Lisa Rofel, Louisa Schein, Aihwa Ong, Gail Hershatter, Victoria Bernal, Susan Greenhalgh, Joan Judge, and Allen Chun. Special thanks to Dai Jinhua, who has been inspiring and encouraging.

1 The focus is on urban areas, especially Shanghai and Beijing, where I conducted fieldwork and interviews with thirty women of different occupations in 1993 and 1995. About fifteen hours of these interviews were videotaped as raw footage for my documentary "Through Chinese Women's Eyes" (1997).

2 Harriet Evans (1995) documents how a state normalizing medical discourse of sexuality and gender operated briefly in the 1950s and '60s. However, gender was not interwoven with a commercial or oppositional (in the sense of alternative sexual practices) discourse of sexuality until the 1980s, which continued what was started in urban areas in the 1920s.

3 For works on women in contexts of state socialism, see Wolchik and Meyer 1985, and Kruks, Rapp, and Young 1989. For recent works on changes for women in the postsocialist era in Eastern Europe, see Funk and Mueller 1993, and the 1994 special issue of *East European Politics and Societies* (Gal 1994, Verdery 1994).

4 It is not clear why notions of sexual difference from men necessarily leads to "notions of female passivity, biological inferiority, intellectual inability, organic sexuality, and social absence" (Barlow 1994b: 267), since the works of French psychoanalytic feminist theory do not derive these conclusions from women's different physiology (Irigaray 1985).

5 Before 1989, the East German magazine *Für Dich* also portrayed women as working or reproductive bodies, and depictions of sexuality were extremely rare (Dölling 1993).

6 There is a difference between this scene in Xie Jin's 1961 film, and the 1970 ballet version rendered into film, expressing different periods in state feminism. In Xie's film, the male party representative is slightly elevated above all the assembled women, but in the Cultural Revolution version, he is at the same level, and the assembled soldiers, both male and female, all bow down before the great red sun, a symbol of the higher authority of Mao. The more severe egalitarianism and gender blurring of the latter version perhaps reflect the influence of Jiang Qing, Mao's wife, who headed cultural production in the Cultural Revolution.

7 Harriet Evans notes the remarkable silence of official discourse (which was the only public discourse) on sex during this time (1995: 365).

8 Stories of sexual ignorance during the Cultural Revolution abound in my interviews, such as the one about couples who thought impregnation came from sperm flying like atomic particles from one bed to another. See also the interviews by Chinese sociologist Li Yinhe (1997).

9 In the zany spirit of Deleuze and Guattari, Kenneth Dean and Brian Massumi also ask, "Is the state neuter?" For them the state embodies the masculine despotic desire for mastery, control, order, and subjugation: "The state apparatus is not a neuter instrument. It is gendered: masculine. State desire is by nature patriarchal" (1992: 83).

10 In the *Diary of Lei Feng*, the hero has several dreams in which Chairman Mao appears "like a kind father" to stroke his head, and he is filled with gratitude and loyalty to this paternal saviour of China (Lei 1968: 7, 8; Yang 1994b: 258–59).

11 Wendy Brown's question is relevant in China: "How might the abstractness, the ostensible neutrality, and the lack of a body and face in the [state], help to . . . [inhibit] or [dilute] women's consciousness of their situation qua women, thereby circumscribing prospects of substantive feminist political change? (1992: 11–12).

12 To be sure, traditional Chinese culture did operate with a loose gender binary, as there was severe discrimination against women, especially from the Song dynasty onward. However, this binary did not have the same totalizing, universalistic, and rigid essentialism that modern biology introduced into the Western binary. It was counterbalanced by other equally important categories of social status, age, generation, kinship positioning, and the flexibility and situational construction of yin-yang principles (see Barlow 1994b). It would seem, then, that neither traditional gender constructions nor the gender erasure of Maoism were able to keep the gender binary stable and prominent enough to build a collective women's gender identity that was *for* itself rather than *in* itself.

13 See Louisa Schein 1994, for a discussion of how in the post-Mao era, a new form of masculine heterosexual Chinese nationalism is being constructed by an Occidentalism of images of the sexualized bodies of white women on the one hand, and an internal Orientalism of images of minority women on the other.

14 John Hay shows that Chinese literary and artistic traditions abound with male appreciation of female bodies, although these bodies were not nudes, but socially defined by ornament and clothing (1994). Peter Brooks suggests that the Western male gaze may be a recent product of modernity. He notes that although the female nude was present in the artistic repertoires of both Classical and Renaissance traditions, it was the male body and male nudes that predominated and were considered the public body. It was not until the mid-eighteenth century that the female nude

was established as the "erotic object of specifically gendered spectatorship," while the male nude was subjected to censorship (1993: 16–19).

15 Jia Pingwa's short story "Human Extremities" also uses the theme of women breaking up a sworn bond of brotherhood (Louie 1991).

16 A middle-aged woman textile worker from Shanghai said that women workers in her factory are demoralized by the prospect of being ejected into a merciless market where their only possibility of earning income is the demeaning work of street peddling. In her factory, there are now virtually no Shanghainese workers younger than thirty-five, because her factory has hired fresh young female recruits from rural areas. This new rural force enjoys none of the workers' benefits that they used to enjoy, such as pensions or paid maternity or sick leaves, because they are now classified as temporary "contract laborers" (*hetong gong*). Nor are the plights of professional women much better. In 1992 in Shanghai, nine senior women engineers launched a formal collective protest against their forced retirement at the age of fifty-five. All of the engineers older than fifty-five who were kept on with a special contract appointment were men (Rosen 1994; Ge Shannan 1992).

17 For example, many women writers do not call themselves "feminist" (*nüxing zhuyi* or *nüquan zhuyi*), in order to distance themselves from Western feminism (Li and Zhang 1994: 148) and to forestall opposition from the state or mainstream culture.

18 There is a generational difference between Li Xiaojiang and Meng Yue and Dai Jinhua. Li remains attached to a Marxist humanist discourse and adheres to the importance of marriage and family in addition to career for a woman's identity. For her, "Every normal [*zhenchang*] woman hopes for a perfect romantic life, the emotional depth of a mother, and the social respect gained from having an independent character. . . . To miss out on any of these would result in a tremendous absence or gap [*quehuo*] in her being" (1988a: 132–33). For Meng and Dai, gender difference does not need to be fixed or anchored in biological makeup.

19 See my discussion of the narcissistic dynamic between self and love object in karaoke singing and popular music in China (Yang 1997).

20 This is seen in cultural productions such as the films of Zhang Yimou, which feature the male desiring gaze on the face and body of the actress Gong Li; the best-selling pornographic novel *Abandoned Capital* (*Feidu*) by Jia Pingwa (1993), which recounts the sexual escapades of a dissolute man with countless women (Zha 1995: 129–64); and the film *The Sun-Splashed Days* (*Yangguang canlan de rizi*) directed by Jiang Wen, a nostalgic reverie on the Cultural Revolution as experienced by an adolescent boy coming to sexual maturity.

21 Miriam Hansen traces a fleeting moment in early Western cinema, before the crystallization of the classical Hollywood form, when the screen catered to a female gaze, as seen in Rudolf Valentino films and a heavyweight boxing match in 1897 where women made up 60 percent of the audience (Hansen 1990b). Linda Williams argues forcefully that even as masculinist a film genre as pornography can make sex more "democratic" because such films make women's pleasure visible (1989).

Mama, Love Me Again (Mama zai ai wo yici). (Taiwan) 1989.

Miss Anli (Anli xiaojie). Directed by Qin Zhiyu, Beijing Film Studio, 1990.

The Raft-Rowers (Fazi ke). Directed by Zhang Zi-en, Xi'an Film Studio, 1992.

Red Detachment of Women (Hongse niangzijun). Directed by Xie Jin, Shanghai Film Studio, 1961.

Red Detachment of Women (Hongse niangzijun). Film version of ballet, Beijing Film Studio, Red Detachment of Women Production Group, 1970.

Red Sorghum (Hong Gao liang). Directed by Zhang Yimou, Xi'an Film Studio, 1988.

The Sun-Splashed Days (Yangguan canlan de rizi). Directed by Jiang Wen, 1995.

White-Haired Woman (Baimao nü). Directed by Wang Bin, Shui Hua, Beijing Film Studio, 1950.

White-Haired Woman (Baimao nü). Film version of ballet, Shanghai Film Studio, White-Haired Woman Production Group, 1972.

Yearnings (Ke Wang). Directed by Lu Xiaowei, Beijing Television Arts Center, 1990.

Virginia Cornue

Practicing NGOness and Relating Women's Space

Publicly: The Women's Hotline and the State

Start with a Shock of Recognition . . .

In a sparely furnished, concrete-walled office, a woman is hunched over a white push-button speakerphone—listening. "Uh, uh, eh, eh, eh, uh, uh," she subvocalizes comforting sounds to the caller. The caller also is a woman. She is crying and her voice sounds thin and tight. Words are constricted in her throat. A black portable radio-recorder is clicked on to tape the conversation. Another woman leans close, attending to the interaction over static on the line while she writes case notes. It is hour two of their four-hour evening volunteer shift, and the calls are roughly twenty minutes long and are coming with less than a minute break in between. In brief pauses that punctuate the emotional intensity of many calls, the women in the room straighten their backs, shift on their straight-backed wooden chairs, and chat softly while sipping tea and quietly slipping cookies from crinkly cellophane wrappers.

Sexuality, sexual harassment, and extramarital affairs have been the major topics this pale winter afternoon. About five calls have come in so far; perhaps ten more will come. That is an average number. A few calls have been from the far western border of the country, one from the south; most come from big cities, many from Beijing. That is where we are sitting:

the Chinese counselor, the Chinese case-record keeper, and the American anthropologist chatting between calls, November 1992, at the Women's Hotline (*Funü Rexian*). There in one of the five rooms rented by the Women's Research Institute (WRI) from a middle school just off Dian Men Dong Dajie north of the Forbidden City in the east district of the city, we are comparing notes on women's hot lines and on issues raised by callers. We are figuring how widespread nationally and globally the problems are. We are discussing what have been and might be personal, national, and global responses to problems affecting primarily women, and what might be done in our respective countries and globally after the Nongovernment Organization (NGO) Forum on Women[1] and the UN Decade Fourth World Conference on Women coming up in 1995.

The Shock of "Familiarity"

I begin in this somewhat impressionistic way to describe my first visit to the Women's Hotline just ten weeks after the hot line opened in September 1992. My ensuing assessment of the hot line and its parent organization, the Women's Research Institute (founded in 1988), is set against nearly two decades of professional experience cofounding and/or directing a number of local and national American women's organizations. My work in New York and New Jersey entailed a mix of advocacy, service, policy development, and management. Among the many positions I had working either as volunteer activist or paid staff, I served as director of the National Organization for Women-NYC, cofounder of the National Network of Women's Funds, and director of Newark Emergency Services for Families. I began full-time doctoral studies in 1989.

My shock, therefore, was not due to the differences I encountered but, rather, to my surprise that physical, social, and administrative forms and problems could seem so similar. These similarities or "familiarity shock" posed a starting point for situating Chinese women's NGOs, and particularly the Women's Hotline, in the debates on civil society, public sphere, and public space in China and globally.

Benjamin Lee has suggested, drawing on Benedict Anderson (1991), that new forms of publicness are helpful "in being able 'to think the nation'" (1993: 167). One such new form developing in China during my time in the field was the "cultural feminism" that Linda Alcoff (1994: 98) identifies in Western Europe and America. Alcoff theorizes cultural feminism as a set of discourses and practices, which relies on a particular moral and ethical framework concerning women and their roles and positions in society. Extending her argument, cultural feminism can be seen as composed of structures of feeling (Schein 1997b), essences of being (Belenky et al. 1986), critiques of theories of universality (Moore 1994), cognition (Gilligan 1982), and other behaviors, social patterns, and organizational forms that mark differentiated notions of "women." Often these are counterpoised against equivalent or dichotomous and oppositional feelings, essences, modes, and hierarchies of masculinities. These cartologies of gender subsequently map the borders of analysis, discourses, practices, and/or struggle. Most often they describe a public-private divide that has at times shepherded "women" into the private and awarded "men" the public and that (in the West) cultural feminism contests and reworks. Indeed, cultural feminism draws its strength and organizing power (in the West) from a critical stance that challenges the current map of gender spaces, even while it reinforces "new" but still differentiated notions of women and men.

On a larger scale, global formations and transformations in the late twentieth century have been marked by multiple international flows (Appadurai 1991a) including NGO forms such as Oxfam and Planned Parenthood International. Western-inflected cultural feminisms have also spread around the globe to encounter indigenous forms by means of such international disseminators as the United Nations World Conference on Women, which commenced in Mexico City in 1977.[2]

In China the post-Mao era of *gaige kaifang* (reform and opening) also has seen the emergence of local cultural feminism. New practices, forms, identities, and discourses have emerged consolidating from current sharply gendered notions of women and women's issues and specific social responses to the questions raised by accentuated, asymmetrically ordered differences between men and women in the late Deng era of market reform. Do these new forms/responses then work the way that Western theory suggests? Does Chinese cultural feminism give rise to the sorts of contestatory discourses and practices common in Western forms? Do new organizations mark a women's public space as they commonly do globally? How do Chinese women's NGOs stand in relation to the state? Are they constitutive of civil society/public sphere in China as they are internationally?

I argue that Chinese women's NGOs are constitutive of a fragile women's space and simultaneously subvert a contestative sphere emblematic of Western forms and theories of public sphere and civil society. Chinese women's NGOs function in a blended relationship with the state to valorize the moral economy of emancipation while aiding volunteers and consumers of the Hotline's services to adjust to the new market economy.

No study treats the recent development of nongovernmental women's organizations and/or their relation to the debates on public sphere and civil society. Indeed, scholars cannot agree whether in China there is (or has ever been) a sphere that might be called "public," as Louisa Schein (1992) has noted.[3] As Mayfair Yang points out in the introduction to this volume, studies of Chinese civil society and public sphere have "altogether left out . . . the entrance of women into public life and discourse."

Herein I ask in China, what is a (women's) NGO, and how do organizations and the state interrelate? I bring these themes together in order to better assess public sphere and cultural feminism theory. I investigate the Women's Research Institute, China's first nongovernment research institute for women, and its project organization, the Women's Hotline, China's first nationwide hot line for women and men.

Marking a Transnation Space for "Women"?

Breaking new social ground, the Women's Research Institute and the Women's Hotline (WH) were founded in 1988 and 1992, respectively, due to problems women faced from economic restructuring in the post-Mao era (Cornue 1995). Wang Xingjuan, cofounder and director of WRI and WH, stated at the opening ceremonies for the WRI:

> Intense social competition . . . [leads us] to have no choice but to recognize that our sisters who are independent enough to successfully adapt to the overwhelming challenges in the face of the competitive market are only a faction of those who are struggling to survive. Reality tells us that achieving complete liberation is still a challenging and arduous task. Therefore, what the WRI strives towards is to help women gain their own rights, to develop their own abilities, and to not only adapt to, but also succeed in the face of the rapidly developing society. In summary, initiating women's own awakening is the demand of our time; it is also the principle of the Women's Research Institute (WRI 1995: 2–3).

Approximately fifty to sixty scholar/activists and professionals[4] concerned with women's issues (*funü wenti*) form the collaborative association, WRI, and conducted during my research periods in 1992, 1994–1996, large-scale, nationwide research projects. The WRI founded the Women's Hotline (1992) to serve China nationally, based on the results of one study. A second national line for expert advice opened in 1993; a third general line was added in 1994. The WH operated as a project of WRI out of the institute's offices and was supervised by WRI staff; altogether, approximately one hundred married or divorced volunteers worked four hours every two to three months. Together, the three lines provided sixty hours of service weekly. The Specialists' Hotline (*Zhuanjia rexian*) advised on more complex questions of health, sex, legal issues, employment issues, and women's issues that could not be answered by the more general women's hot line. Volunteers to the specialists' hot line were women and a few men with particular expertise in certain fields—medicine, psychology, sexuality, law, employment, and so on. The WRI administered the WH with five paid staff: director Wang Xingjuan, an administrative vice director, and three support staff, one of whom dispensed biscuits and tea, volunteer transportation stipends, and locked up at 8 P.M.—the end of hotline hours.

The WH was supported by funds that Wang Xingjuan and volunteers raised largely from the United States, including the American Friends Service, Global Fund for Women, Ford Foundation, and UN Development Program. The WRI and its project organizations (the WH and the Beijing Weekend Social Club) functioned under the explicit oversight of the Chinese Academy of Managerial Science (CAMS) and the dimly seen oversight of the All-China Women's Federation (*Fulian*), the Chinese Communist Party's feminine public face. The WRI operated outside of the *danwei* (work unit system). During my research periods, the relationship between *Fulian* (CCP) and WRI was much more opaque than that between WRI and CAMS, although the NGO Forum and the UN Conference on Women opened a unique window.

The "Re-Cognition of Familiarity" as Method

Here I insert a discussion of liberal humanistic dreams of civil society to caution against the projection that a partial women's space signaled by the development of specific forms such as WRI and WH might inevitably result in a women's sphere and contribute to a Western-style civil society. As Nicholas Garnham has noted, "'Left' cultural romanticism sees all grassroots as resistance" (1992: 373), and resistance or opposition is a necessity to current public sphere theory. It is well, then, to explore how familiar-seeming data may contribute to such a viewpoint by naturalizing the researcher's feeling and cognitive "commonplace." The seductiveness of the obvious may potentially blind scholars such that the observing eye skips over what appears to be known. As cultural products flow transnationally along telecommunication lines at an ever-increasing rate, the risk of not seeing also increases.

Because transnational flows, in part generated by the very telecommunications technology focused on in this paper, yield apparent resemblances, I thematize another experience not often dealt with in anthropology: familiarity shock. It is an anthropological given that the ethnographer enters the field experiencing a shock of difference (*culture shock*, a term credited to R. Benedict) that gradually gives way to relative familiarity and understanding (Anderson 1990; Bowen 1964; Geertz 1973; Golde 1986: 11). The emotional result of nonrecognition (culture shock) theoretically tunes the ethnographer's perceptive skills; signs and symbols become more familiar and blunt the initial edge of difference while mutual understanding and acceptance grows.

On one level, the sense of familiarity I felt was enchanting, stimulating an almost unconscious "felt" fantasy of global utopian feminism, to include China—a global women's space, a global women's sphere, the ultimate civil society—even as I knew that such a dream was naught but a dream. Personal and professional skepticism served as an antidote to ostensible likenesses enabling me to flag these recognitions for further scrutiny. What seemed utterly familiar soon gave way to myriad textured details of difference, as well as points of connection, overlap, and mutual familiarity.[5]

Similarities in form, purpose, and function that seemed so familiar obscured fundamental state-organization relations. One of the most striking and simple differences is the very meaning of the term *nongovernment organization*. In China, a women's NGO is considered to be nongovernmental because it does not receive state funding, but it is subject to varying degrees of state intervention. In noncommunist countries, NGOs are largely separate from state intervention, whether or not they receive state funds (Cornue 1995). Glossed in English as NGO, women's organizations, such as WRI and WH, are known in Chinese as *minjian*. Yang notes, that in China "the sphere of minjian refers to a realm of people-to-people relationships which is non-governmental or separate from formal bureaucratic channels" (1994b: 288). While I agree that *minjian* organizations are nongovernmental, my data show that women's NGOs particularly operate in a blended relationship with the state and are not always free of formal bureaucratic channels. These dissimilarities go to the heart of organization-state relations and contradict much of public space, public sphere, and civil society theory.

Yang suggests (in this volume) that state feminism, which I call the women's face of the Chinese Communist Party, is weakening in the reform era. My fieldwork suggests that state feminism is not retreating but is assuming new forms and, more important, new relationships. While it is no longer as explicitly tied in with the Women's Federation as in previous decades, many of the basic assumptions about what constitutes women's emancipation obtain for the state and for most women's NGOs with which I am familiar.

The Women's Hotline and Public Sphere Theory

Since the seminal study by Jürgen Habermas (1984) on the connection of modes of communication to the development of civil society and ensuing critiques of Habermas, such as Craig Calhoun's edited volume (1994) or volume 5 of *Public Culture* (1993), the notion of communication has been a key analytical construct. For my study, I extend this notion to its precursive necessity, relatedness, a point to which I will return shortly. Habermas predicated his theory of civil society on print modes of communication and decried the development of technology as destructive of civil society. Yang has found technology to be efficacious in the development of new forms of public spheres and has extended Habermasian theory to new visual technologies. In doing so, she has laid out an excellent review and critique of Habermas and his critics. I refer the reader to her review in this volume rather than reiterating what she has analyzed so well.

Telecommunications technology in contemporary China has originated new forms of communications based on coaxial cable and fiber optics. These forms include telephone hot lines (*rexian*), faxes (*chuan zhen*), and e-mail (*dian zi xin jian*), which have yet to be probed for their contributions to civil society/public sphere development and theory.[6] This chapter focuses on telephones and hot lines.

A telephone hot line is an auditory communicative form, contingent on one anonymous caller to one counselor. Communication can travel over great distances and necessitates the creation of some type of formal structure, which callers can access from multiple sites by depending on the fixity of the hot line. Unlike faxes and e-mail, which may be impersonal and anonymous, a hot line is distinctly personal and often a highly emotional transaction that relies on a disembodied vocal and emotive "fleshiness." Neither Habermas nor his critics have analyzed telephone hot lines, the associational qualities of hot lines, or the public uses to which data from hot lines are put; nor has the notion of relatedness and hot lines been found in the literature.

Second, few scholars have centered their research on contemporary nongovernmental Chinese organizations addressing women's problems. Cecilia Chan and Nelson Chow have produced the only full study that approximates this topic with their general survey of contemporary Chinese welfare systems development (1992; see also Shue 1994 for a preliminary survey of Chinese philanthropic NGOs). Their study does not specifically treat nongovernmental organizations and only tangentially mentions women and women's organizations. This paper, then, aims to fill the lacunae revealed in this review of the literature.

Recalling my earlier discussion of "left romanticism" and resistance, I initiate the term *NGOness* in an elucidative gesture to suggest that organizational structures, forms, relations, and operational methods of local women's organizations in China and NGOs in general, are not stable, transparent, or uniform transnational entities, although there are similar, even overlapping, characteristics. Rather, they are sets of practices through which individuals enact relations and through which varying logics in Pierre Bourdieu's sense are reinforced (1990). These relations produce particular cognitive and social effects, which can be called a "space," and like any cultural production this space is shaped by local circumstances, not the least of which are political and legal constraints. An examination of women's "public" space in China, therefore, entails particularizing aspects of cultural feminism produced by differing actors (individuals, organizations, literary forms, and the like) such as the WRI and the WH, which interpret "women" as a category. As an actor producing discourses to fill the empty category of women, the WH, for example, enters into a relationship with callers that channels the voices of women (and men) from all over China and produces a particular women's discourse from interpretations of raw data.

I wish to draw together the entrance of women into public life and telephone hot lines with the notion of relating. This notion is at the core of concepts underpinning public sphere theories and as such is useful to "think the various aspects of a hot line." A telephone hot line depends on access of callers to telephones; on interactions between caller and counselor; on the connection of staff and volunteers to form an association; and on the production of reports and statistics from a typology of problems and demographics. Data reports are publicized through print and electronic media and (sometimes) are employed by governing bodies to formulate policy or used by civil groups as foundational evidence for contestory public discourse. The Women's Hotline in Beijing performs all these functions, except the last item.

Caller anonymity is central to the content of problems and the connection of issue discourses to the *scribing* of public consciousness,[7] but the hegemonic constraints within which both NGOs and the women's discourse they produce operate also tell us something about Chinese women's NGOs in the global women's sphere and in the contemporary Chinese nationalistic context.

Telephones, Women's Consciousness, and Women's Personal Public Space

The Chinese idiom—family scandal should be kept inside (*jia chou bu wai yang*)—points to an extraordinary shift in cultural practices. Through the Women's Hotline, women from all over China speak publicly about what have historically been private concerns and use new telecommunications technology to voice their unmonitored concerns directly to the capital: Who is gaining access to this technology and what are they calling about?

Personal access to telephones is relatively recent in Chinese history. "Long distance telegraph services in China originated in 1881," as did the "first local telephone network in Shanghai" (Hook 1991: 51). By 1987 there "were approximately 10,000,000 telephones in China . . . less than one phone per 100" (Sivin et al. 1988: 177). In 1952 there were 3,777 1,800-medium coaxial cable carriers; by 1985 those had grown to 37,551 long-distance channels (*Encyclopedia of New China* 1987: 404). In the 1990s widespread wiring has made possible the development of hot lines. The Post and Telecommunications Ministry reported that in Beijing, from 1992 to 1995, the number of private telephones grew from 171,070 to 900,000, while cellular phones grew 11,333 to 76,578 in 1994. (Cell phone figures for 1995 were not available.) Nationwide, private telephones grew from 4,944,204 in 1992 to 5,384,847 in 1994.[8] Orange and turquoise telephone booths installed in 1995 now dot the road verges in Beijing, especially in the Haidian district.

Sidewalk public telephone kiosks are relatively common in cities all over China. Callers stand streetside at a kiosk window where one or two desk phones sit on a shelf. Calls are audible to personnel staffing the kiosks, and others within hearing range wait impatiently; lack of privacy obviates sensitive or lengthy calls. The few new enclosed telephone booths offer a measure of privacy to which most callers to the Women's Hotline or other women's hot lines do not have access.[9] Upscale hotels have so-called public lobby telephones, which most ordinary citizens might not be comfortable with or might be barred from using.

The expense of long-distance telephone calls was another factor limiting access. In 1995, a three-minute call from Beijing to Guangzhou cost about sixty yuan, representing about 12 percent of an average state worker's monthly salary. With the relative low density of private telephones nationwide, it is likely that many callers availed themselves of workplace phones.[10] Wang Xingjuan concurred with this analysis. Sixty percent of hot-line calls were placed from Beijing and other large cities in the first year of operation; by the second year the ratio had shifted in favor of mid-size cities, and a few calls began coming from the countryside as well. Nationwide publicity had been effective, facilitated by the rapid spread of telecommunications.

Women accounted for about 80 percent of all calls to the Women's Hotline and the Specialists' Hotline. The two hot lines had until February 28, 1994, delivered 554 days of service and responded to 7,323 calls for help. After only six months of service the Specialists' Hotline had received calls from "29 provinces in China, including Heilongjiang, Xinjiang, Hainan Dao and Zhejiang provinces" (WRI n.d.: 45). Sixty to 70 percent of the calls were from women younger than thirty, 20 percent from those aged thirty-one to fifty, and only 10 percent from those older than fifty. About 90 percent were at least senior high school graduates or held a higher education certificate. Most callers were workers, cadres, or intellectuals; only a smattering of farmers, students, and soldiers called. Only a small percent of divorced, remarried, or widowed people called; more than 50 percent of the women and men who called were married (WRI 1994a: 4–7).

What did callers from all over China hear when their calls were answered? "Hello. This is the hot line for women. Welcome to be our first friend" (WRI 1995: 21) were the words spoken by Ding Juan, first volunteer counselor at the hot line and research associate of *Fulian's* Women's Studies Institute. As volunteers answered calls with kindness and warmth, they and WRI staff also were acutely aware that "callers' questions mirror . . . problems plaguing contemporary Chinese women" (WRI 1994a: 1).

The following statistics drawn from a Hotline report show why women (and men—20 percent) called the hot line. About 46.6 percent of calls from 1992 to 1994 concerned marriage and love. Questions pertaining to women's and children health accounted for 16.7 percent; 9.1 percent of callers asked about sex; general information, work, psychological, and law questions totaled 26.5 percent. Sexual harassment calls accounted for 1.2 percent. Women far outweighed men in their concerns about marriage and love, and more men called to ask about sex problems or pleasures. Of a total 1,670 calls pertaining to love and marriage, women asked 85.4 percent and men asked 15.08 percent of the questions, while men asked 67.7 percent of all questions about sex and women asked 32.3 percent (WRI 1994b).

What is striking about these differences is not that women concerned themselves more about love and marriage than men given the cultural insistence on women and marriage, but that so many women concerned themselves with questions of love and sexuality, since from the 1950s on the CCP "promulgated a stiffly antibody, antiflesh, and antisexuality attitude" (Zha 1995: 139). An almost equal number of calls concerning love (697) were made as on the subject of marriage (729). Looking at numbers of calls made on the topic of sex suggests a different picture when compared with percentages. Of a total 328 calls about sex, women made 106, while men made 222. So even though men made twice the number of calls about sex than women made, overall relatively few calls were made when compared with the next biggest category, love, for which a total of 848 calls were placed. Unmarried people asked about love, married people asked about marriage and health problems, and remarried people asked about difficult relations with their new families.

In the 1980s, love and sex delineated aspects of a public feminized personal that marked a historical and philosophical moment of renewed debates on the nature of subjectivity (Lin et al. 1996). The right of women to love and be loved and their right to sexual expression (Li 1994b: 7–8) saturated the new women's literature, such as Zhang Jie's *Love Must Not Be Forgotten* (1986), that burst forth. Hotline callers' concerns about love and sexuality mirrored on the national level what I found on the microlevel at the Beijing Weekend Club (*Beijing Zhoumo julebu*), WRI's second organizational project. There, single, divorced, and never married women and men struggled with issues of sexuality and love (Cornue, Boyle, and Gilmartin 1998), as did twentysomething migrants to Shenzhen (Clark forthcoming).

Women aged thirty-one to forty with questions pertaining to marriage and law expressed a different aspect of the love-sex question. They called because their husbands had taken "the third one" (*di san zhe*, the third one inserted into the marriage, i.e., taking a lover) and were asking their wives for divorces. Abuse entered into the picture when wives refused these requests and husbands tried to "persuade" them to divorce. Of 460 calls pertaining to marriages in crisis, 252 stemmed from the husband's love affair with another woman. Inharmonious sex accounted for only twenty calls, the wife in love with another man totaled only fifty calls, while bad relations between the wife and husband numbered seventy-four calls.

Callers' (and club members') concerns therefore were consistent with a growing women's consciousness articulated in literature and other public media (Croll 1995: 173). This subjectivity was inflected with a publicly expressed domesticized individual personal that was distinctly interpersonal and gendered. This personal stood in sharp contrast to the "renunciation of individual sovereignty" (Esmein 1973: 328) and the "erasure of gender"

(Yang, this volume) characterizing public revolutionary culture. Nancy Fraser's critique of Habermas calls our attention to the relegation of women and associated concerns to the domestic or private sphere as a necessary opposition against which to create a male public sphere (1989). Elsewhere she argues for a "multiplicity of publics" that would expose the limitations occurring from labeling some concerns "private" (1992). Privatizing some concerns renders them invisible to potential advocates who might contest the forces that exclude the issues from public debate.

[My reading of her proposal is thus: women's formerly "private" concerns that have been brought public alter and augment the existing public sphere and allow for contestatory action to transform society in a form more beneficial to women.]Women's emancipation from limiting strictures is strengthened. Though the Women's Hotline brings women's unmonitored, untutored voices from afar by telephone to the capital and magnifies individual women's personal voices and concerns in a public "women's" discourse or space, Fraser's theory is only partially applicable. Let me sketch how I think a public space for women differs from a public women's sphere in China.

The process of calling a hot line sets in motion nondiscursive practices in the Bourdieuian sense of habituation (1990: 81–97) that scribes a new space for women. Enacting calling and counseling, enacting listening and telling, enacting communicating private matters anonymously over the telephone are new forms of relating and subjectivity that contribute to the creation of this new public space for women. News of the Hotline spreads by way of media and print, engaging more women (and some men) in new practices that bring into the open previously private concerns. Women's public space is broadened and further explicitness is given to Chinese cultural feminism, but how does a space for women differ from a sphere?

Public sphere theory calculates "at least three analytically distinct things" as Fraser schematizes. In the Habermasian sense the public sphere is a "theatre . . . in which political participation is enacted through the medium of talk. It is the space in which citizens deliberate about their common affairs, and hence an institutionalized arena conceptually distinct from the state; it is a site for the production and circulation of discourses that can in principle be critical of the state" (Fraser 1992: 110). Three distinctions are key: here, political participation is grounded in an institutional arena that can produce potentially critical stances toward the state. Let us examine how the discourses of "common affairs" that callers share through the WH differ from the institutionalized disciplinary regimes within which counselors work.

The parameters of WRI philosophy guide the terms of counseling as laid out by the mission of the WRI, which aims at encouraging women's self-esteem, self-reliance, independence, and effectiveness—direct adoption of *Fulian's* national four selves' project. *Fulian's* project reveals the socialist national ideology written into the notion *qi lai* (stand up, also the title of the PRC's national anthem) and also particularizes it as the state's ideological frame for contemporary women: emancipated women stand up. In effect, this is the state's national identity project writ small and, written even smaller, is inserted into the counseling offered to women nationwide through the Hotline. Statist emancipatory rhetoric infuses advice and points of view of counselors. Thus, in the case of the WH and other hot lines dedicated to rectification of women's problems the practice of confession and ideological reeducation (*sixiang gongzuo*) is suggested rather than development of an institutional arena for critical debate. Paradoxically, these new practices inscribe another set of social practices, which decenters both the family and the family writ large in the guise of the government and also displaces the *danwei* (work unit), which itself had replaced the family in the postliberation period. Here lies a tantalizing aspect of WRI/WH cultural feminism and a tantalizing, potential avenue for the development of a women's sphere.

A new "woman-only" relational and cultural space is created as callers are lifted out of their social positionalities while they speak anonymously to "warm-hearted," faceless, disembodied women counselors, who nonetheless are trained in particular points of view. A new women's "family," minus parents, husbands, and child, is created in the intimacy of the interaction.[11] Advice not only upholds the socialist logic of liberation but also contradictorily at times reinforces "traditional" notions of femininity and masculinity. One woman was advised to feed her sexually disinterested husband more meat to increase his yang vitality. Another counselor told her caller to adjust to her husband's lover by thinking of her child's needs. Cooking and self-sacrifice were long important aspects of feudal femininity; I argue that even these "reactionary" counselings are statist discourses of economic modernity, which rely on gender asymmetry to function effectively.

Tani Barlow notes that gendered difference has underwritten the modernist projects of many states. In China, as the state lost control over its original politicized mass woman/*funü* (1994b: 277), a new project of gaining control over individual sexually differentiated woman/*nüxing* was under way. Leaders of the Hotline/WRI/Beijing Weekend Social Club, as did most volunteers, embraced not only the concept of *nüxing* but also the concept

of *xingbie*—that is, sex difference that added gendered psychological difference to essential biological difference for *nüxing*. These were rooted in
biological distinctions linked to gendered sex roles and women's special
characteristics. Counselors endorsed women's "adjustment" to the requirements of the new economy in order to ease their psychological distress.
Even as women accessed the public phone lines to reach the Women's
Hotline, counselors aided their adjustment to the rigors of the new market
economy by upholding newly gendered hierarchies. Yet because they were
"revolutionary" women, they believed and worked for women's emancipation and decried the forces distressing women.

Philosophical and institutional links with and "management" by *Fulian*,
the Chinese Academy of Managerial Science, and even by the Central
Committee of the CCP argue for an NGO women's space closely tied
to the national modernist identity project and against an independent
women's sphere. What is less clear is how individual women are affected
by their new practice of linking with supportive, nonkin women, since
there is no way of measuring or interrogating how new practices and discourses marking a "women's" space impinge on individual women.

(Differing) Feminism(s) and the Women's Hotline
in a Possible Chinese Public Sphere

Differences in definitions of *Women* as a social category and how those definitions play out in the public arena are the foundational ideas that underwrite a public sphere for women in their everyday lives. Yet not just any
definition of *Women* will underpin notions of feminism. At the heart of any
debate over feminism and *Women* are three ideas: where women are located
socially, where women are located relationally, and who decides where
women are located. Feminisms generally argue that women should (at
least) have the option to emerge from the domestic, the option (at least) to
be on a par with men, and the option to decide for themselves. Women,
then, figure in most debates between feminisms and conservatisms tugged
between public and private; ranging over, equal with, or under stable Men
as a social category; and silent/silenced or unconscious to awakening and
speaking out. Feminisms are predicated on the option for the emergence
of Women, and therefore women, into the public as conscious, speaking
subjects.

The *trope of feminism*, however, is a term invoked by both activist scholars
in China and the West with a taken-for-granted/we-know-what-we-mean

essentialism that is remarkable given the reams of paper that have been produced criticizing (Western) "feminists," "feminism," and "feminist organizations" (Spivak 1988a; Mohanty 1988; Rofel 1994a; Chow 1991). (Undifferentiated) feminism has historically been suspect as part of Western bourgeois ideology in the Chinese socialist context. Thus Chinese workers for women use feminology/women's studies—*funüxue* or *nüxingxue* (Li 1994a: 148)—to indicate work by, for, or with (mostly) women to enhance women's lives. In a series of letters from 1992–1994 between Wang Xingjuan and me, as I negotiated my fieldwork access with her and not through a *danwei*, we debated the way in which Western feminisms were represented in China. Lao Wang asserted that in China "women did not hate men" (November 1993). I replied that in America in general feminists worked to dispel social conditioning and barriers, and it was those who detracted from feminists who represented them as man-haters.

Chinese activists thus disavowed themselves of terminology that inscribed women's NGOs as separate from state discourses. Privately to me as well as publicly, Wang Xingjuan rejected the terms for *feminist* (*nannüpingdengzhuyi*, or man woman equalityism, and *nüquanzhuyi*, or women's rights-ism). She did so less from a position of carving out a separate space from which, under the guise of doublespeak, the WRI and the Women's Hotline could mount opposition to the state. Rather, her sense was that her organizations were carrying out the incomplete agenda of (socialist) women's emancipation, and her feminism (*nüxingxue*) was consonant with state feminism. I call attention to this philosophical problematic precisely because the content of calls articulated by women through the Hotline, as well as of data drawn from studies and personal interviews, overlaps in category with problems identified elsewhere globally through (feminist) women's organizational channels.[12] Yet correspondence in topical content belies the political and philosophical parameters incongruent with the spaces and spheres of cultural feminisms in noncommunist nations.

Yang holds that one nonstate feminism in China is defined as women contesting "men telling women what to do" (Dai and Yang 1995). I judge that this feminism is fairly consonant with state feminism and it, too, is not oppositional but, rather, is synchronous with underlying assumptions of state feminism that imagined a new nation grounded on *nannüpingdeng* glossed as woman and man equality. Conceptually, it forms the backdrop for the current term *nüxingxue*. Efforts of women to *qilai* (to stand up and achieve men's level) while contestive of generalized male power are not pointedly directed at the state. Unlike Huang Shiqing (interviewed by Dai Jinhua and Mayfair Yang 1995) and other women intellectuals in (easily broken) rhizomatic networks (Yang 1994b) who have developed a women's group consciousness, many callers to the WH spoke about their personal problems without constructing a subjectivity that was linked firmly to any aspect of Chinese cultural feminism. Most callers to the Hotline did not identify "men telling women what to do" as their major concern; only WRI and some Hotline personnel analyzed this problematic as a lack of the callers' consciousness as women.

Feminisms, in their varying Chinese forms—state, nonstate, and NGO—are predicated on the awakening of real women's consciousness linked with the personal or subjective (*zhutixing*) materialized from universal society in the post-Mao era (Lin, Rosemont, and Ames 1996: 733). Thus a space of Chinese cultural feminism, instead of a public women's sphere, turns not on contestation but, rather, on how "Women as an issue" (Li 1994a: 5) has marked the public personal:

> Women as an issue, has posed a challenge—a challenge to the rights, already won, that are threatening to revert to traditional ways; a challenge to the thousands of years to that tradition; and a challenge to the new tradition of "sexual sameness" which has predominated in social relations in China for the last forty years. Making "Women" an issue and confronting these challenges has opened a new page in the Chinese women's liberation movement—the awakening of group consciousness.

Consciousness raising was thus aimed toward developing women's group identity and was a major goal of state, nonstate, and NGO feminisms in contemporary China. The category Women (*nüxing*) could be a prize to be won, if varying contenders were pouring different definitions into this category. If, on the ground, NGOs, nonstate feminists, and state feminism were articulating entirely different definitions of *nüxing* and were actively debating and vying over the meaning, status, and roles of women, a vibrant women's public sphere to underwrite a (Western-style) civil society could be born. But neither radically different definitions of *nüxing* nor feminisms are being discussed in China. Women's leaders such as Huang Qizao, vice director of Fulian, and Kang Ling, vice director of the Children and Teenager's Fund and standing committee member of *Fulian* both told me, "*Nüxing* can do everything in this time." [Other ordinary women articulated similar sentiments: women could be or do whatever they wished and were no longer bound by rigid, unitary (state-produced) definitions of femininity or masculinity.]

Consequently, what was being maneuvered and strategized was not what should "women" mean or do, or even how women's emancipation should be achieved, but who would achieve women's emancipation. What emerged, then, was not so much a debate over values or goals but a competition over public recognition and trust of the institutional entity that would engineer women's emancipation.[13] A socialist, emancipatory vision—influenced in part by women's activities in other parts of the world—remained important for women scholars and activists in Beijing and across China involved with women's NGOs. Their vision served as a driving force to counteract latent influences of the "socialist monologue," as Yang has termed it (in this volume) Transnational feminist visions reworked and merged with or contrasted against the local China context served to particularize Chinese cultural feminism and enabled women to articulate their personal concerns in the new vocabulary of contemporary *nüxingxue*—one discourse of cultural feminism—which as I have argued, encompassed state feminism and nonstate feminisms.

Close state oversight and edginess, then, flowed less from contestatory activities and ideologies that constructed a women's public sphere in which to ground a civil society rivaling the state than from the reality that NGOs were new and relatively unpredictable forms in China—women's NGOs were among the newest. Further, because women's emancipation underpinned the moral legitimacy upholding the political power of the party, state officials could not afford to let women's NGOs stray far from their poised grasp. Yet it would be a mistake to assume that because NGOs existed at all and exercised some self-defined and generated activities, that they desired to oppose state control, whether tightly or loosely exercised. I found no evidence to suggest that organizations desired a contestatory relationship with state power. By contrast, I found much evidence that NGOs were covetous of state resources in order to more easily achieve emancipatory goals officially articulated through state policy, such as the Constitution and the Women's and Family Law promulgated in 1991. Wang Xingjuan often complained of the arduousness of fund-raising. When in a humorous mood, she called herself a "high class beggar" (Ford Foundation 1995: 11), and when frustrated and worried about making ends meet or impatient to expand her programs, she complained to me that her *guanxi* was not strong enough to secure state funds.

NGOs adjusted to state constraints and sought state resources, but women calling from all over the nation were not so readily managed for the state's advantage. The relative security provided by anonymity safeguarded them from direct state intervention and allowed for revelation of intimate and personal troubles women felt they could not reveal in their private lives or the relative privacy of workplace relationships. The hot line paradoxically became a public private space for women. According to civil society/public sphere theory as reviewed by Yang (in this volume), communicative structures and public space for discursive formation are the preconditions for a public sphere. The space mapped by and the communicative structures provided by the hot line seem to meet the criteria necessary to form a women's public sphere. I draw on the work of public sphere theorists Mary P. Ryan and Nancy Fraser and historian Nancy Cott to differentiate the case in China.

Ryan neatly dissects Habermas's theory, which posits a male public foregrounded against a female (re)domesticized private, in her study of nineteenth-century American life (1992: 259–60) to show how the deliberate exclusion of women enabled the construction of the public. The nineteenth-century public was a male domain dependent on an exclusively female private/domestic domain, with the former speaking to state structures for themselves and on behalf of women. Economic restructuring in China has increased pressure especially on urban women to return home and step down a now vertical employment ladder (Croll 1995: 117–24). Redomestication has been positioned not against a male public sphere but, rather, set firmly against an increasingly male-inflected productive sphere. "Habermas's construction of the public sphere . . . freed politics from the iron grip of the state" (Ryan 1992: 261) and allowed a space for women contesting domestication to voice their cares. In China, the economy has been set free to an extent, but politics is still firmly in the grasp of the state—politics has not become a neutral object, detached from party control and open to vociferous debate: Chinese women cannot make politics their own to contest state control. Finally, Ryan makes the point that "not only could women find access to a [public] sphere, once there, [they] seemed to be promised a hearing whatever their concerns" (261). Telecommunications technology has allowed for individual private concerns to be heard, which have added to a public space for women but cannot generate a women's public sphere distinct from the state, because of state-organization relations.

[margin note: lack of autonomy of orgs from gov.]

Both Ryan (1992) and Cott (1987: 85) make the case that feminists and workers on behalf of women began the project of cultural feminism in late nineteenth-century America by creating nonstate organizations as sites of new publics from which to articulate their concerns. Here is a tantalizing similarity to the current China case. Feminists did seize the moment opened by the state (Schell 1985) to create nongovernment organizations to research women's problems. As Hou Zhijin, a volunteer to the Hotline stated, "After we have done these researches we thought about why we did these research. What could we do for women" (1996: 1). State constraints on the license of voluntary associations' scope and organizational missions congruent with state aims, however, warrant a conclusion that women's NGOs ally and overlap with the formal socialist project of women's emancipation and adjustment to the new economy.

I suggest a new form called a statist public sphere in which women's NGOs function in a blended relationship with the state. This relationship may mirror earlier forms of social organization and may point to a Chinese particularity.[14] While Chinese women's NGOs may not conform to organizational or public sphere theory in other parts of the world, state buttressing does allow for women's discursive space that contests masculinist powers,[15] so that the *minjian*/NGO institutional arena may uphold the state within the current political context.

Conclusion

The apex of egalitarian moral virtue and political legitimacy of the state/Chinese Communist Party in its triumph over the Kuomintang was gained in part through the differing positions that "women" and women played in each party (Sui 1981: 15–60). After more than three decades of political ideological campaigns, suffering, and hardship, the CCP lost moral legitimacy due to its own excesses in the name of that same equality that brought the CCP to power, and turned its attention to economic reform in what Jane Jianying Zha calls "a slow, soft, messy meltdown of the old structure" (1995: 11). Unlike other former socialist states in Eastern Europe and the former Soviet Union, the Chinese Communist Party "stays on to guide and control the reform process" (Zha 1995: 10). Now more than ever it needs women's organizations, and particularly those beyond its formal public women's face (*Fulian*), to do its moral and economic reform work for it.

Recent nonstate groups, such as the WRI or the Hotline, or university-based programs such as women's studies programs, publicly viewed as products of the period of reform rather than the state, are not besmirched by the excesses of the past, as is Fulian, but neither are they entirely independently created (Li 1995). Paradoxically these groups need the political face (weight) of the state as leverage to accomplish and legitimate their programs to combat deep-rooted cultural and political prejudice as well as snowballing discriminatory market forces. These blended or interactive agendas speak to a much more nuanced relationship between new organizations and the state than unmistakable distance, militant contestation, or open opposition. As such, they contradict theories articulated by Habermas (1984) that opposition and contestation are essential elements of civil society, public sphere, and public space; and they contradict the theories of Habermas's critics who make similar assertions in the specificity of China.

When compared transnationally, Chinese women's NGOs did not perform the function of state contestation that many groups elsewhere do.[16] Yet with all the dissimilarities I have detailed in this brief study, there persisted a mutual recognition that I shared with staff and volunteers at the WRI and WH (as well as many other women's NGOs that I visited). Emotionally we shared a passion for understanding women's roles in the world, in our countries, and in each other's countries. We—hundreds of volunteers, staff, and associates of the WRI and WH and other women's NGOs and I—shared a passion for "doing something" to improve women's condition.

Elizabeth Janeway calls "doing something" (1980) power. Antonio Gramsci (cited in Williams 1973) and Michel Foucault (1979) discuss power in terms of oppositional and dominance-configured relationships that are characterized by varying the degree of agency to the degree of hegemonic constraint, the former allowing for some individual agency and the latter allowing for virtually none. Janeway approaches the question of agency from an entirely different angle and supposes that collective effort has a dynamic and potentially cumulative effect individually, organizationally, and socially.

Janeway's insights coincide with comments of Li Xiaojiang that the collective agenda of individual women's self-awareness and self-development is the liberatory project of modern Chinese women (1994a). Li and other women in contemporary China extend their power by "doing something": creating organizational structures, conducting research, telephoning the hot line, writing about "women" and volunteering in nonstate structures. All these acts have a dynamic effect, which has mapped a discursive and structural women's cultural space in the late-twentieth-century evocation of cultural feminism.[17] The state's hegemonic project, by contrast, is to legitimate the party in its modernist economic project for which politically it needs the emancipatory moral high ground. Women's organizations can carry out the incomplete agenda of liberation, which gave the CCP its moral legitimacy in the first place.

Feudal society, Japanese invasion forces, and the Kuomintang engendered profound hatred because they were rapists, to use Friedman's sense of the word (1995: 149–87), literally or figuratively violating women. On the imaginative level they violated "women," which symbolically stood for the nation in the world's eyes. The CCP captured moral and political (high) ground through upright behavior, indeed by promising to emancipate women from the violations they suffered and bring them into society as full and equal, albeit productive, citizens. The CCP further promised a strengthened nation impervious to penetration or violation from any aggressor by transforming weak "women" and women into stalwart, unitary, national citizens (Meng Yue 1993).

If women's organizations—and here I include Fulian, women's studies groups, and "independent" organizations such as the WRI, the Hotline, and newer organizations such as the Mobile School project of People's University's Women's Center and a self-funded battered women's shelter set up privately in Wuhan in the winter of 1995–96—are successful in achieving what party politics could not accomplish, and if the CCP can maintain its close embrace, then the party is strengthened in its endeavor to create a moral, stable society that offsets the difficulties raised by the market economy. Imaginatively, the nation can achieve what early revolutionaries promised.

Contemporary Chinese cultural feminism, which blends organizational forms—NGOs, Fulian, university women's studies programs, and "independent" feminists—has as one gossamer thread the Women's Hotline. In the weaving of this fabric of meaning, produced by new discourses and practices of women, a women's public space of great fragility is being netted together. Yet it is never far from and certainly must abide by certain state boundaries and principles. Its makers do not appear or want to be far from the state, nor am I sure they should be; for however limiting the state is for women, it is still the major author and articulator of their right to be equal. Ironically, it is their best protection against the market (the state's economic face) and resurgent traditionalism, even while it severely constrains the incipient buds of public space they are growing.

Speaking into this fragile public space, callers are allowed by the anonymity of the Hotline to move beyond the limitations of family, neighborhood, and *danwei* and access a trans-China, if not a global community. The very isolation of callers, however, undercuts the building of a robust and authoritative "public" community following a critiqued Habermasian model. What must happen for a nonstatist public women's sphere to develop is that the collective results of calls must somehow find their way back into the awareness of the callers so that they perceive their problems as collective social problems of Women rather than just as personal ones. Currently, there is no such mechanism for those outside of local Women's Federations or the sparse scattering of recent NGOs.

Without the means of linking individual women to groups locally, nationally, or internationally as active participants in cultural feminism, as one informant put it, "Women's mind liberation will take a very long time."

NOTES

1 *NGO* is a United Nations term, which means nongovernmental organization. Wang Xingjuan, cofounder and director of WRI and the Hotline, used the term *minjian* (people-to-people organization) on material printed in Chinese. In printed English versions of organizational material, the term *NGO* was used. When speaking Chinese and English, she used the English term *NGO*.

2 One aspect of my field research, which was conducted from August 1994 to January 1996, entailed participating in more than eight of the fifty-five "prep coms" (preparatory conferences) held in the years before the NGO Forum and the UN Conference. All Chinese participants to the world meetings were required to attend these prep coms. Of those I attended, I often was cast as the *laowai* (foreign friend). During the world meetings (glossed *Funu Da Kaihui* or grand women's congregation), I traced the activities of informants as a fellow participant in the NGO Forum and an observer at the UN Fourth World Conference on Women. All informants understood the two conferences as aspects of one big meeting.

3 For an extended discussion of this point, please see Schein's work on gender politics and the post-Mao era (1997a).

4 These numbers are my best estimates based on observation over four years. They are also gleaned from conversations, annual reports, and grant proposals.

5 Outside of China one cultural feminism envisioned a global feminism constructed on women's human rights and emancipation. This discourse was certainly a key element at work in the visioning of the NGO Forum and the Fourth World Conference on Women. I offer the suggestion that such is the case in the academy as well. It is the (sometimes unarticulated) desire that drives much research, women's studies programs, passion for gender studies, and other organizing efforts. Rather than ignore or renounce this desire, I propose that scholars and activists embrace and make explicit the feelings and visionary desire that nourish the growth and development of scholarship or actions to enhance women's and men's lives precisely as a relational bridge across the differences that sensitive scholarship reveals.

6 Faxes and e-mail are beginning to be available to a broader Chinese community. In 1994 two American professors carried on a regular e-mail conversation from China to America. American embassy officials expressed surprise and stated that it was the first time they had heard of e-mail being used. By the summer of 1995, China Net was operating. In the summer of 1996, I conducted research by e-mail, interviewing an informant. Faxes have been employed since at least 1989. Students organized at Tiananmen Square using faxes to communicate internationally. Rumors were circulating in 1995 that all e-mail users would be required to register and would be monitored. During the final revision of this chapter in June 1997, I received an e-mail notice about a new online magazine, *The Tunnel*. The magazine was written in Beijing and looped through global networks in such a way as to protect recipients and authors by evading registration requirements, which had been instituted. In the months prior to editing this manuscript, I learned that Beijing had a cybercafe.

7 I employ the woodworking term *scribing* to suggest the process whereby the articulation of particular problems forms a raised profile against which public consciousness is drawn, outlined, and reformed.

8 A research assistant collected data directly from the ministry using his *guanxi* (relationships forged through mutual obligation) and reporting skills learned from Ron Hollander, Fulbright Professor to the China School of Journalism. The ministry declined to give me information. These data have not previously been published to the best of my knowledge.

9 The first hot line for women in China was opened in Shanghai in cooperation with the Shanghai Women's Federation and is sponsored by a local sanitary napkin manufacturer. It opened in the early 1990s and its callers are strictly local. The Jinglun Jiating Zhongxin (Jinglun Family Center) opened a national hot line specifically for abused women in October 1994. This hot line was not anonymous and worked with unions and work units to mediate violence. In 1996, Huang Heng Yu, volunteer director of the WH, traveled several times to other cities, Shandong and Tianjin, to facilitate the opening of local hot lines. Hot lines sprang up all over China. In 1994 even the government got into the act with a corruption hot line for citizens to inform on corrupt officials.

10 At the time this research was conducted, the U.S. exchange rate was approximately $8.10 to one yuan. At this writing, Chinese currency is still soft and does not trade on the global financial market. Also, Chinese currency was unified in 1994. The two-tiered system was abolished in January 1994. Previously, Chinese nationals were supposed to use the RMB (*Renminbi*) and foreigners the FEC (Foreign Exchange currency). The lesser value of the RMB had generated a thriving street-corner black market. As late as January 1996, hopeful traders still plied the sidewalks in front of Friendship Stores openly seeking gullible tourists as customers for the now worthless FEC. Additionally, the RMB also lost value with currency unification. During my initial research trip in 1991 the U.S. dollar traded approximately one to five RMB. Inflation caused a hardship for those on fixed state salaries.

11 Callers sometimes name their counselors sister. It is impossible not to reinscribe status dissimilarity between women to some degree, since deploying the word *sister* in Chinese automatically creates a relationship pungent with meaning and rank. A woman can either be an older sister, *jiejie*, or a younger one, *meimei*. Callers, if they label the transaction in familial linguistic code, routinely name counselors *jiejie*. The notion of (equal) sisterhood held so dear to Western feminist notions is an unachievable project short of inventing Chinese neologisms.

12 In addition to the issues I have talked about previously, violence against women began to be discussed in 1995, in part, I believe as a result of the emphasis of the NGO Forum and the UN Conference. A striking omission from WH calls were the infinitesimal number of calls pertaining to rape. Yet many Western women professors told me that women students routinely sought them out for assistance after being raped.

13 Thanks to Liu Xiaodong for this observation.

14 Several presenters at the 1996 annual Association for Asian Studies meeting concurred with this point and suggested historical congruency with preliberation China.

15 My thanks to Louisa Schein for pointing out this connection.

16 The results of a fifty-organization world survey I conducted at the UN conference

showed that 100 percent of the thirty organizations that responded defined an NGO as being entirely independent of state control, even if one group stated that it received "funds from the government." Other groups stated that NGOs are "the voice of the people" (as opposed to the state's voice through the people), "formed of volunteers," "for the welfare of the people," "to build public space," and to function as "the watchdog of the government" (Cornue 1995).

17 Cultural feminism is not a stable construct. Rather, I hope to suggest that notions of "women" that are produced by feminisms scribe or mark the "shape" of relatively cohesive historically situated identities—individual, group, and societal—that have recognizable features transnationally and globally. It is on the social level that cultural feminism develops. It is in the minds of individuals that cultural feminism is felt. It is from their altered beliefs and practices that cultural feminism emerges.

PART II

Expanding

Women's Space

and Building

a Women's

Public Sphere

Lee Yuan-chen

(Translated by
Mayfair Mei-hui Yang and
Everett Yuehong Zhang)

3

How the Feminist Movement Won Media Space

in Taiwan: Observations by a Feminist Activist

Lee Yuan-chen is a founder of the Women's Awakening Journal *in Taiwan, which became a foremost nongovernmental organization for feminist activism there. She also teaches Chinese literature at Tamkang University near Taipei. In this essay she gives her personal historical account of how the Taiwan feminist movement struggled to put feminist issues in the public space of the mass media.*

The Early Period

After three hundred years of Han Chinese domination during the Ming (1368–1644) and Qing (1644–1911) dynasties, what was established in Taiwan was a society that honors men and devalues women.[1] Between 1900 and 1915 (Wu 1988), the Japanese colonialists, who had ruled over Taiwan since China's loss of the Sino-Japanese War in 1895, launched an anti-foot-binding movement in Taiwan. In the condescending manner typical of colonialists, they paved the way for integrating Chinese women into the labor force to serve the Japanese colonial government. Han women in Taiwan were able to gain the liberation of their bodies as an unintended consequence of these political changes. Between 1920 and 1945, the Han Chinese in Taiwan gave up their militant resistance against the Japanese and began their cultural enlightenment movement in line with trends in modernist thinking in Japan and China. Progressive-minded men and women expressed their ideas in such journals as *Taiwan Youth, Taiwan Magazine,* and *Taiwan People's Daily,* advocating such things as equality of men and women, women's right to receive education, marriage based on love, women's participation in social activities, the prohibition of selling daughters, and the abolition of polygyny. Women's associations such as the Chang-hua Women's Support Association and Chu-luo Women's Development Association appeared around 1925. Although each lasted for only one year or less, these associations had an influence on the formation of women's reading groups later. Yet the issue of women's participation in politics was not raised, because under the rule of colonialism even the movement aiming at establishing a parliament of Taiwanese men failed (C. Yang 1993: 2–17), so, naturally, it was even more impossible to have women's political participation.

The period after the GMD (Guomindang or Kuomintang) government moved to Taiwan in 1949 was a time when Taiwan also enjoyed the fruits of the global and Chinese women's movements, such as improvements in women's social status in education, legislation, marriage, employment, and participation in political affairs. Although Taiwanese men found many faults with the Chiang Kai-shek (Jiang Jieshi) dictatorship, they did not criticize it on its women's policy for they thought that women's social status was already very much improved. The reality, however, was that, although women did enjoy some basic rights, they were not making any significant progress, because under Chiang Kai-shek the official women's organizations such as the Women's Association and the Women Workers Union had advocated the retrograde idea of bringing order to the family so as to repay the kindness of the nation. It was not until Lu Hsiu-lien, a woman intellectual who grew up in the post-World War II period, began in 1971 to criticize gender inequality in Taiwan in newspapers (Ku 1989: 110) and initiated the New Women's Movement that things really started to change. She won the support of many open-minded men and women for her view that "women must strive to be human before they can be women" and "women must not be confined to the kitchen, but must realize their talents." However, in the conservative atmosphere of the times, her views were regarded as too radical. After 1978 Lu Hsiu-lien became more concerned with the movement of democracy and was put in jail because of the Beautiful Island Incident (*Meili dao shijian*) in Kaohsiung in 1979.[2] Thus, the New Women's Movement was brought to a halt.

The Establishment of the Women's Awakening Journal

Although activists of diverse social and political causes suffered a tremendous setback after the Beautiful Island Incident in 1979 and the *Beautiful Island* magazine was closed down, new political magazines kept on sprouting up in 1980 and 1981, like bamboo shoots after a spring rain. The publishers kept up their resistance to GMD government control and censorship, daring to publish again and again each time they were prohibited from doing so. Through the efforts of these magazines, the quota of Central Parliament representatives was increased at the end of 1980, which led to the election of some members of families who had suffered from political persecutions, as representatives to the Legislative Yuan.

Disappointed that the women's movement did not have anyone to continue the struggle and worried about missing the great opportunity of social change that was presenting itself in Taiwan, I started the *Women's Awakening Journal* in February 1982. The inaugural issue was forty to fifty pages, and it was unable to compete with the other political magazines and well-designed glossy women's fashion magazines at the newsstands. We had learned from other oppositional movements how to get around the restrictions of the government's Public Association Law,[3] by using the medium of a legally registered journal to gather new recruits and earn material income to reattract the membership that was lost after Lu Hsiu-lien's imprisonment. After one year of publication, it became clear to us that just relying on this small journal, with a readership of only six hundred, would mean that our social influence and our public voices would be terribly small and weak. So with a core group of ten activists, we applied to the Asia Foundation, an American grant organization, for funding and to *China Times* newspaper's column "Life" for matching funds.

The following year our journal sponsored the March 8, 1983, Women's Week. At this event, the major attraction was the Women's Abortion Consultation Clinic. We also sponsored lectures and seminars on all kinds of topics concerning women such as legal issues, politics, how to start a business, housewife life, and mutual education across the genders. In the evenings we showed a total of eight feminist films, including *Brothers and Sisters, Cry without a Sound*, and *Women Workers of the Rearguard*. The theme of this activity was set as "The Potential of Women and the Development of Women," rather than notions of "feminism," "women's movement," or "new feminism," out of fear that, still in the shadow of the Beautiful Island Incident, women would worry about the reaction from the government and would stay away. We made use of the occasion of the International

Day of Women (on March 8) to take advantage of the media's regular coverage of this holiday to advertise the Women's Week activities in the newspapers, and to make known to the mass of readers the existence of our Women's Awakening group. After this event, we also organized other activities such as publicizing our *Report of a Survey of Sexual Harrassment* in articles such as "The Year of Protecting Women" in 1984; the "Housewives' Re-education Campaign in 1985," where many mothers' reading groups and housewives' development groups were spawned; and the "1986 Dialogue between the Sexes," which was designed to produce the "new male" and which has not yet succeeded.

Although Taiwan society was more liberal in the 1980s than in 1970s, ordinary women still rejected the message of gender equality and anti-patriarchy from Women's Awakening. I knew that out in society many divorced women suffered both personal crisis and social discrimination, and many widows who had lost their husbands due to sudden or accidental death had difficulties coping. I therefore helped set up the Taipei Women's Development Association and the Taipei Late Sunrise Association, in order to help these women find psychological support from each other. Although they were not the types to struggle for their rights, at least they could socialize and develop themselves through these organizations. Some women formed the Progressive Women's Alliance, joining male democratic activists in pushing the GMD into the direction of democracy. Similarly, many housewives formed the Housewives' Alliance, articulating their concern with the environment and their children's education. Although those women's associations did not demand gender equality, the fact that they were all women's organizations meant that they were on good terms with Women's Awakening and shared some of our outlooks.

All these developments meant that the media could no longer ignore the growth in women's organizations (J. Jiang 1994: 7). The 1986 protest organized by the Housewives' Alliance against McDonald's for the high price of their hamburgers was immediately noticed by the media. In fact, activities concerning the environment and education spearheaded by the Housewives' Alliance all attracted more media attention than those of Women's Awakening. Furthermore, the protest by the Progressive Women's Alliance of the dictatorial policies and violations of human rights by the GMD government attracted more public attention than Women's Awakening. While their protests were ignored by the mainstream newspapers such as *China Times, United Daily News*, and the three television stations, they still received more coverage by the nonmainstream media, such as oppositional political magazines. We were able to gain mainstream media attention only when we made a quick response to the government's policies toward women, such as the time we organized a petition drive for the right of abortion in 1984, in which a dozen women were summoned to the Legislative Yuan to attest to the right of all women, regardless of marriage status, to an abortion. Yet many issues raised by our group, such as problems with the Dipo contraceptive needle (we felt that the government agencies did not disclose enough reliable medical data on the procedure), the lack of women at all levels of government, and the problem of serious gender inequities in the Kinship Section of the Civil Code, were passed over by the mainstream media. Only women's magazines reported these initiatives, and they did not bother to mention our Women's Awakening group.

The Strategy behind the Demonstration to Rescue Child Prostitutes in 1987

In the 1960s during the Vietnam War, Taiwan became one of the major vacation centers for American servicemen. Pei-t'ou in Taipei had the dubious international reputation of being a "paradise for men." Through the magazine *Hsia Ch'ao* and the efforts of Catholic nuns of the Boundless Charity Women's Employment Center of Taipei, I came into contact with about thirty child prostitutes, ages twelve to seventeen. Working with them twice a week as a voluntary instructor, I discovered that the problem of prostitution, especially child prostitution, was very serious in Taiwan. Therefore, together with Su Ch'ing-li, editor-in-chief of *Hsia Ch'ao* magazine, and folk singer Yang Tsu-chun, we organized a Green Grass Charity Concert to raise money in support of vocational training and psychological instruction at the employment center. The Taipei Bureau of Social Issues, the Police Bureau, and members of the legislature were invited to discuss the possibility of establishing halfway houses and women's vocational schools, but the discussion produced no results. Although reporters from major newspapers, magazines, and television stations attended this public discussion, except for *Women Magazine*, none of the mass media ended up carrying any story on this event. At the Asian Churches Women's Conference, the theme was "Asia's Tough Question: Tourism and Prostitution." Liao Pi-ying, a member of the Women's Affairs Section of the Senior Christian Association, reported on her investigation of the serious problem of child prostitution in Taipei's Hua-hsi Street neighborhood. Her presentation also received no media interest (Lee 1986: 6). It would seem that the GMD government was willing to sacrifice the lives of young girl prostitutes in order to maintain the lucrative tourism industry, and the mass media were complicit in this by helping to cover up the problem.

Afterward, Liao Pi-ying proposed that we organize a demonstration called A Demonstration to Rescue Child Prostitutes. She wanted to mobilize the Taiwan Human Rights Promotion Association, aboriginal rights groups,[4] religious organizations, and political dissidents to put collective pressure on the GMD government and challenge the cover-up of the mass media. I liked the idea, but I was worried that if the *Women's Awakening Journal* was unable to mobilize enough women to participate, then the demonstration would lose its original guiding theme of a women's issue, and the whole affair might turn into a mere anti-GMD political activity. So we organizers tried to ensure that the focus of the demonstration remained on the issues of women and would not be diluted by other issues. In a joint effort with the major political male oppositional political organizations, this demonstration was successful in gaining the attention of the government and of society to the problem of child prostitution. Although this was the first women's demonstration in the history of post–World War II Taiwan, the three major television stations did not cover it, but quite a few mainstream newspapers ran stories along with photos of this event. The media were still basically apathetic toward women activists and their oppositional efforts against patriarchy.

In spite of the general indifference of the media, our banner stating "Prostitutes Must Enjoy Basic Human Rights" caught the attention of many photographers, so that pictures of marchers holding this banner were run over and over again in popular magazines, including the *China Times Weekly*, shortly after the event, and it is still favored by the print media today when the topic of child prostitution comes up. After this demonstration we organized the Taiwan Women's Rescue Association (currently a foundation) and continued to investigate cases of child prostitution and to hold meetings and publicize the situation in newspapers. In addition to the inquiries made by representatives in the Legislative Yuan, our efforts resulted in the government setting up a special task force and even allocating money to the task of rescuing child prostitutes.

In February 1987, *China Forum Magazine* and *Minsheng News* sponsored a symposium called Women Intellectuals and Taiwan's Development. Ku Yen-ling of Chiao-t'ung University presented her paper "Feminist Consciousness and the Development of the Feminist Movement," in which she praised Lu Hsiu-lien and Women's Awakening, affirmed the significance of the feminist movement, and discussed its neglect by the media. Subsequently, Ch'en Yi-chen, editor of the supplementary page of *China Times*, published a special issue under the title "From the Kitchen to the Streets: Our Nation's Feminist Organizations Pass a Milestone." Supplementary pages of mainstream newpapers were influential back then when martial law and the censorship of the press were in effect. After this special issue, men could no longer shamelessly declare that "Taiwan does not have any women's problems." As a result of an increase in our resources and membership, *Women's Awakening Journal* expanded and became Women's Awakening Foundation. This change enabled the news media to refer to the name of our foundation in their coverage from then on, as they no longer had to suppress our name as a profit-making institution.

After this breakthrough in media coverage, what was impressed on us was the effectiveness of taking to the streets in order to call attention to issues of feminism. After the lifting of Martial Law in July 1987, all sorts of street demonstrations flourished, such as the peasant movement, the worker's movement, and the student movement. On August 3, 1987, in cooperation with the Housewives' Alliance, we organized a demonstration at the Sun Yat-sen Memorial to protest the firing of a pregnant thirty-year-old female receptionist. We also held a public discussion calling for the end of the annual competition for Miss China, and presented a short satiric skit, "The First Mr. Taipei Beauty Pageant." All these activities were covered by the newspapers and on the radio, and we also got opportunities on television to debate with men who were in favor of holding beauty pageants. Since then, as long as an event was sponsored by our foundation, and regardless of whether or not it was on Women's Day, we could get the announcements out or a report published in the Women or Family sections of major newspapers like *China Times*, whose women reporters were now quite sympathetic to us. As for television news, stories about our activities appeared quite often on the eight o'clock news in the morning, the noontime news, and on the news at midnight.

The Social Effectiveness of "Public Hearings"

On January 1, 1988, the government removed their controls on the press, so that new newspapers were permitted to form and existing ones were allowed to increase their page lengths. In the following two years, the press entered into a sort of Warring States Period[5] in which it was quite easy for all sorts of different political and social movements to be reported by different newspapers. At the same time, however, since mainstream newspapers such as *United Daily News* and *China Times* increased their pages from four to six, or from eight to twelve or more (J. Jiang 1994: 4–6), stories about women in the pages of the Women or Family sections began to face the danger of losing their influence if they were put on the last pages.

In 1988 Women's Awakening Foundation became the largest women's political activist organization, and it became permissible for people to openly talk about a feminist movement and feminism. Yet as a foundation, the official regulations did not allow us to expand the size of our leadership and membership,[6] so it was difficult to increase our influence at the grassroots level. We had to change our strategy for promoting women's interests by monitoring the decision making of the government, particularly through influencing the legislation process. Between 1987 and 1988 the foundation began to be concerned with problems of professional women. Lawyer You Mei-nu, then trustee of the foundation, led several younger lawyers in drafting the Law of Equal Opportunity of Employment, aiming first at improving the current Labor Law, which was indifferent to female workers in the service industries. Eventually, the aim was to replace it altogether with a new comprehensive labor law free of gender discrimination in all aspects, ranging from employment and promotion, to women's rights, to job security in pregnancy, and maternity leave for childbirth and child rearing.

In 1989 we invited members of the Legislative Yuan and scholars to attend a public hearing on this draft Labor Law and persuaded them to present it as a bill at the legislative meetings. We anticipated opposition from patriarchal capitalists and many of the legislators, who were mainly of the male bourgeoisie. Fortunately, by this time the Democratic Progressive Party (*Minjindang* or DPP) had come into existence,[7] so that getting this bill presented and debated in the Legislative Yuan was not a problem, although it will be much more difficult to get it passed. The hearing of this bill in the Legislative Yuan and its debate easily caught the attention of the media, and we had many opportunities to present our bill to a wide audience. We were reported on page 3, 5, or 7 of newspapers, and on the noon or midnight news on television. Since this bill was controversial and had the novelty of being put forth by a women's organization, the television talk show *Public Square*, anchored by Li T'ao of China Television, devoted some time to discussing issues of equal-employment opportunities for women. As a result, issues previously considered merely women's personal matters (pregnancy, childbirth, child rearing) were now discussed and debated as social and public issues. Yet we still have a long way to go before we can get the bill passed.

After the establishment of the Democratic Progressive Party, and the visibility of the social movements of peasants, students, workers, aborigines, and women, Taiwan society and the government had reached a common understanding of the necessity of democratic elections. Although women's associations were not yet influential enough to produce their own political candidates for election, they did exercise their rights to assess all candidates' political goals. They were often able to get their criticisms and assessments of candidates on page 3 of newspapers. In the 1990s, Women's Awakening Foundation and other women's associations have been able to work with legislative bodies to hold hearings on issues such as the protection of child prostitutes and compensation for so-called comfort women who suffered in World War II. We held many public hearings on such topics as "Sexual Harassment in the Workplace," "AIDS from Women's Point of View," "The Case of the Rape of the Secretary," and the "Single Women Regulation," a rule in the finance and banking industry to fire pregnant women. This series of hearings was covered by print media and even by the seven o'clock television news in the evening. Although the media's point of view did not exactly coincide with those of feminists, at least this kind of hearing provided a good opportunity for women's associations to express their own opinions to the public without being upstaged by legislators' voices. These events showed the growing authority that women's associations were commanding in their public appearances.

Adapting to Current Issues and Making Organizational Connections

The ultimate goal of the feminist movement is to turn women's issues into public policies, but in this goal, pressure groups badly need the support of the mass media and public opinion. In traditional patriarchy, society as well as the media always regarded women's issues as "nonpublic issues" and criticized the feminist movement for being indifferent to important affairs of the nation. In our eight years of experience we have mainly adhered to direct feminist issues, but in dealing with other public issues such as democracy, environmental protection, labor, and AIDS, we have sought to imprint them with a feminist perspective. In participating in the Oppose the Formation of a Military Cabinet demonstration in 1990, we highlighted the theme of women's opposition to power mongering. On April 26, 1991, we joined the Housewives' Alliance in forming the antinuclear brigade in the demonstration to oppose the government's plan to build a fourth nuclear power plant. On December 12, 1993, we formed the Little Red Hat Brigade in the Labor Legislation Demonstration, in order to call attention to pregnant women's loss of jobs in the banking and service industry.

In 1994, due to our policy of adapting to current public issues and establishing effective communication among different women's associations, several feminist issues were aired in the public media. The first one was the case of Teng Ju-wen's murder of her husband, which had already been covered in the media the year before. Several female lawyers (You Mei-nu and T'u Hsiu-jui from the foundation, Ts'ai Ming-hua of the DPP, and Wan Ju-hsuan of the New Women's Federation) all connected with and consulted each other and got involved in this case. They defended Teng in court and argued that the cause of the tragedy was not Teng but her husband who physically abused her. In the press conference after the defense in the court, the attorneys raised the issue of marital violence in a media interview and expressed dissatisfaction with the court for announcing that Teng's sentence would be reduced because Teng had turned herself in. The women lawyers stressed publicly that the abuse that Teng had suffered should be the reason for the sentence reduction. In this case, the various newspapers and other media started relying on news sources from women's groups and even incorporated some feminist viewpoints (A. Jiang 1994). Several women's associations took advantage of newly instituted Public Debate Forum sections in such newspapers as *United Daily News, China Times,* and *Independent Evening News* to write articles discussing marital violence from a feminist perspective (A. Jiang 1994). The strong voice of women's associations and the public discussions in the newspapers on marital violence not only catapulted the story onto the seven o'clock news on television but also influenced the final sentencing. The sentence was eventually reduced from five and a half years to three years with a bail of NT$30,000. The defendant was also permitted to regain custody of her two children. As a result of this development, our foundation was allotted funds by the Interior Ministry to research and prepare a Law on Stopping Marital Violence. Women's groups adapted to current issues of the time and made use of the U.S. case of Lorena Bobbitt, who was acquitted of castrating her husband in a moment of panic after years of sexual abuse, to further the cause of reducing Teng's sentence.

The second case was the sexual assault of a female student by a teacher at Taiwan Normal University. This case was exposed to the public by *China Times* on March 19, 1994, and led to the resignation of Professor Li. The president of the university accepted the resignation on the grounds that Li had violated the faculty ethical code and then requested that the parents of the student come to bring the student home. Disappointed with the university administration's handling of this affair, particularly with the unfair treatment of the student in being sent home, the Association of Women Faculty and Staff and woman legislator Ye Chu-lan held a public hearing, Uncovering the Truth of Sexual Violence on Campus, in the

Legislative Yuan. Meanwhile, female students presented a list of "seven sexual monsters" in the Department of Chinese Literature at Normal University and demanded an investigation. On April 15 the victim made a presentation revealing the details of the sexual attack. Eleven newspapers covered this event intensively. Women's associations became the second most important source of the news, after female students and female university people (Lin 1994a). Since this sexual persecution occurred between two people who were familiar with each other (Luo 1994), we worried that people influenced by patriarchal ideology might easily think of it as merely a case of "love between student and teacher" and thus overlook the message that feminists were trying to convey of female students' rights to receive education and to control their own bodies. Therefore, feminist associations and women's studies students of several universities held anti-sexual-harassment demonstrations, to which the media gave ample coverage.[8] So, in striving for women's own space in the public sphere, feminist associations must unite female scholars, female legislators, and assembly-women in battling patriarchal attitudes.

In addition to the Law of Equal Opportunity of Employment, feminist associations are most concerned with the revision of the Kinship Section of the Civil Code, which was propounded as long ago as 1920 and came into effect in 1936. Because the feminist associations in 1985 were not strong enough, they did not have any say over the revisions to the Kinship Section carried out that year. Therefore, in key articles such as "Marital Property," "Child Custody of Divorced Couples," "Family Names of Children," "Residence of Husband and Wife," and "The Execution of Children's Kinship Rights," the revised Civil Code that was announced on June 3, 1985, did not reflect any idea of gender equality.

The high divorce rate in Taiwan (1.41 per thousand married couples in 1992) ranks it first in Asian countries, therefore, many women suffer from the problems brought on by divorce.[9] Women generally have a hard time getting a job after divorce due to discrimination, and they suffer from unfair legislation. Shih Chi-ch'ing, founder of the Late Sunrise Association, put woman lawyer You Mei-nu in charge of leading a group of young lawyers to revise the Civil Code. In cooperation with the foundation she made a tour around Taiwan, lecturing on legal issues and raising funds for this project. The first hearing for the revision of the Kinship Section of the Civil Code was held at Taiwan University and attracted an enthusiastic army of reporters, scholars, professionals of judicial affairs, and legislators and representatives. Among them were about two hundred women. The media covered this event very well the next day. After several more public hearings, the first draft of a new Kinship Section of the Civil Code was ready, and work was started to assemble a brigade of women to spearhead activities to pass the revised section. Members of the Late Sunrise Association went to local neighborhoods to explain the proposed changes. On March 6, 1994, Women's Awakening and Late Sunrise Association together organized a Civil Code Informational Event in the New Park in Taipei. This event attracted more than a thousand supporters from the onlookers, and it was reported by the media. We will continue to hold public hearings, distribute videotapes of lectures on the legal significance of the proposed changes, and reach out to the public, as we wait for an opportune moment to send this proposal to the Legislative Yuan to get it passed.

Due to the media coverage, many women began to use the civil law consultation hot line set up in August by the Awakening Foundation, and many women volunteers also offered to help work the phones. Female lawyer Luo Yin-hsueh and female legislator Hsieh Ch'i-ta began to work with us, inquiring into Article 1089 of the Civil Code and bringing it and its unfair gender bias to public attention. According to this article, if parents disagree on how to execute the children's rights, then the father has the right to decide on matters for the children. Obviously, it is against Article 7 of the Constitution, which ensures equality of men and women, and against item 5 under Article 9 of the Amendment to the Constitution, which calls for ending gender discrimination. They brought this question to the Supreme Court Justice, asking for an explanation.

Taking advantage of the occasion of the inquiry of the nominee to the sixth Supreme Court Justice seat being held in the Second National Assembly, we made the announcement that "women have questions to ask the nominee for Supreme Court Justice." We reminded the public that a Supreme Court Justice must have an awareness of issues of gender equality. On August 15 the coalition of feminist associations put forward the document "Ten Questions We Women Want to Ask the Justice." On August 18, we started the action of Women Test the Supreme Court Justice on Grass Mountain. Grass Mountain was where the official inquiry would be held at the Chung-shan Hotel. We demonstrated and shouted slogans outside the meeting hall. National Assembly members of both the GMD and DPP met with us. On September 23, in his public speech, the outgoing Supreme Justice said, "Article 1089 of the Civil Code, regarding the father's preferential right, is unconstitutional." His statement was reported in the front pages of the three major evening newspapers as well as in their daily editions. This illustrates the fact that if we incorporate our activities into domestic news events, then it will be easier for feminist views to catch the

Figure 1. Inside the Women's Bookstore in Taipei. Left to right: Mayfair Mei-hui Yang, Lee Yuan-chen, and Cheng Chih-hui.

media's attention, and that if the news event is politically or economically significant, then the chance for the story to be put on the front pages of newspapers increases.[10] Later, on September 27, 1996, the Legislative Yuan passed an amendment that granted equal rights to both parents in the custody of their children.

Due to the difficulties of our funding, Women's Awakening has found it hard to sustain the continued publication of works on women's culture. Helped by Su Ch'ien-ling and Cheng Chih-hui, and many other sisters' participation, we were able to open the Women's Bookstore (*Nu Shu Tian*) near National Taiwan University in 1994. The bookstore started with the goal of selling books on women in Chinese and other foreign languages, and later we developed plans to publish our own selection of books. Cheng Chih-hui has been an important personage in the publishing effort of the Taiwan women's movement in the 1980s and 1990s. Along with Ku Yen-ling, she is a major mover in Taiwan's women's studies. She has been in charge of the business and managerial work of selling women's books in our bookstore (fig. 1).

Transnational Sisterly Exchanges and Mutual Support

After the Second World War, Taiwan's international status and relations were tremendously influenced by the United States. In the seven or eight years of the establishment of Women's Awakening Foundation, we have also often accepted the financial assistance of the American-based Asia Foundation and, in addition, have engaged in exchanges with American women's groups, such as visiting the well-known National Organization of Women (NOW). In 1989, our foundation invited Columbia University political science professor Ethel Klein to talk on the topic of "Women's Political Participation," and in 1995 we invited a famous American women's movement leader of the 1970s, Jo Freeman, to Taiwan to discuss "Women's Movement and Politics." We have also received development funds for AIDS education provided by the American Women's Global Fund and sent representatives to San Francisco to learn about AIDS prevention for women. Needless to say, after the mid-1980s, a large number of graduates from our universities' foreign language departments have gone to study in American universities, thus being exposed to a diversity of American feminist thinking and women's studies issues, and they have returned to participate in and strengthen the Taiwanese women's movement.

Besides its close contacts with the United States, the Women's Awakening Foundation has also since 1985 had close ties with the New Women's Support Association established in Hong Kong in 1984. Li Yen-fang, the general editor of our *Women's Awakening* journal, visited the association in Hong Kong in 1986, as well as other women's groups, and gathered a great deal of information on the situation of women in Hong Kong. She was especially impressed that, besides publishing the frank and polemical book *Views of Women*, the association has also published a *Women's Handbook* of very useful basic knowledge of women's needs in everyday life, reflecting a closer understanding of women at the grassroots level than possessed by Women's Awakening. In 1987, Wu Chia-li, *Women's Awakening* journal chief-of-staff, again visited Hong Kong's New Women's Support Association, resulting in the organizing of a joint conference between our foundation and their association held in Taiwan in 1988, called "Comparisons between the Women's Movements of Hong Kong and Taiwan." We found out that in between the 1970s and '80s, the Hong Kong women's movement managed to pass the Statute Abolishing Male Polygamy and a law on the legalization of abortion, while also carrying on campaigns against rape, and campaigns promoting "equal pay for equal work" and women's right to maternity leaves, as well as working for victims of marital abuse. We were especially envious that in 1986 they pressured the government to pass a law forbidding the use of violence in the home because up to the present, the Taiwanese government still has no law against husbands beating their wives.

Since the New Women's Support Association published their *Women's Flow* journal for only two years, they admire the fact that we have been able to support *Women's Awakening* journal for twelve years. In the ranks of the support association, there are a few men, who in the course of the conference and in private discussion all revealed a perspective of true gender equality. This may be due to the fact that they are also social movement activists, and so they are able to support women because they share the same vantage point as those of low social status. This sort of honest and sincere attitude is much more progressive than the standpoints on women's issues of most male social activists in Taiwan. Although progressive men in Taiwan pay lip service to the idea of gender equality, their inner hearts and their actions are actually conflicted, and there are virtually no men in Taiwan who directly work for the women's movement.

Since Hong Kong had been a colony of the United Kingdom and has been made into a major international and Westernized commercial port, its access to diverse information from around the world was achieved earlier than in Taiwan. However, its colonial status and return to the Mainland in 1997 have also meant that political participation by the mass of the people has also been suppressed, resulting in a situation where ordinary people (especially women) do not concern themselves with the connections between public issues and the play of politics. In addition, the traditional patriarchal Chinese view of "men operating in the external world, women operating in the domestic world" has also shaped a situation whereby Hong Kong women easily support the idea of women enjoying social welfare help but have trouble understanding the deeper insight that it is traditional patriarchal values that are the major reasons behind the denial of their rights.

In 1981, policy makers on the Chinese mainland started their birth control program. *Women's Awakening* journal reported on this program in 1983 and expressed our concerns about the incidents of female infanticide. At the 1989 Conference on the Study of Gender in Chinese Society sponsored by and held November 9–11 at the Chinese University of Hong Kong, Ku Yen-ling, director of Women's Awakening Foundation, made the acquaintance of Li Xiaojiang, the head of Zhengzhou University's Women's Studies Center. This acquaintance resulted in Women's Awakening sending three representatives to mainland China to attend the following year's (1990) Conference on Chinese Women's Social Participation and Development held at Zhengzhou University on March 19–21. Besides Professor Ku Yen-ling, Women's Awakening Foundation trustee member and director of the Publishing Department, Cheng Chih-hui, and Awakening Foundation advisor Chen Ling-fang all enthusiastically attended this conference and took the opportunity to travel around the mainland. Upon their return, they have written many reports of the situation of Mainland women in the pages of our journal.

In 1986, Cheng Chih-hui learned from an English-language newspaper that a special women's system of writing had been discovered in rural Hunan Province. A few days later, Taiwan's *Min Sheng Pao* newspaper also reported on the "women's script" (*nushu*) in Jiang Yong County, Hunan Province. When she attended the Zhengzhou conference, she also met Gong Zhebing, a mainland scholar of the South Central Minorities Institute who was studying the women's script. Their discussion made her realize that it was imperative to mount a rescue operation of these valuable resources. The script had received international recognition among women's studies and philological circles around the world, but in the Mainland there was no existing plan to bring them together into a systematic, edited publication. After her return to Taiwan, she vociferously persuaded Awakening Foundation to publish the volume *Women's Script*. This book is the world's first book devoted to a script written and used by women—the independent creation of Chinese women of the ancient Xiang and Chu cultures. The script is like embroidery and pictograph, and the contents of the writing not only celebrate the play of human happiness and tragedy but also reveal the water-like flow of sisterly emotional friendships and includes a female rewriting of traditional mythology and folk tales. It is a valuable source of study for anthropology, women's studies, art history, and aesthetics. For all these reasons, we sisters at Women's Awakening, with our limited material resources and personnel, worked hard to put out one thousand copies of *Women's Script* in a luxury edition and two thousand copies in a standard edition. After its 1991 publication, it not only made waves in Taiwan's cultural, academic, and media circles but also attracted international attention. Thus its publication was an example of Chinese sisters linking hands across the straits in a joint effort to disseminate "the most truthful inner voice of women."

In April 1992, the Awakening Foundation also published Li Xiaojiang's *Women, a Distant and Beautiful Legend*. We also had Cheng Chih-hui take copies of my own book edited by her, *Liberate Love and Beauty*, and a book translated by her, *The Liberation of Men*, to bookstores in China to sell. Furthermore, Cheng Chih-hui recommended to China Times Publishing Company the book *Emerging from the Horizon of History: Modern Chinese Women's Literature* (1988) by mainland women authors Meng Yue and Dai Jinhua and persuaded them to republish it in Taiwan in 1993. Cheng Chih-hui also had me write an introduction to this book in *Chen P'ing T'uo-tu,* a journal she edits (February 1994). This book is the first in Taiwan's publishing history to employ a "women's discourse" perspective to systematically present and analyze the works of modern Chinese women novelists, and it has become an important resource in Taiwan for the feminist study of women's literature.

In 1895, Taiwan came under Japanese colonial rule, and since 1949 it has come under Guomindang rule and been engaged in tense relations with the Chinese Communist Party, resulting in the separation of the two shores for almost a hundred years. As a consequence, my knowledge of mainland women is only superficial. In addition, in 1995, due to the animosities between the governments on both sides of the straits, members of Women's Awakening were put into a position where we could not go as free agents to Beijing and Huairou to attend the important UN Fourth World Women's Congress and the NGO Forum on Women.[11] Therefore, we seldom have an opportunity to get to know our sisters in the Mainland at a deeper level. Honestly speaking, before the opening up of China in 1979, we feminists in Taiwan always thought that mainland women's positions were higher than those of European, American, and Japanese women (except Northern Europe), and that the situation of Hong Kong and Taiwan women was not even in that league. Now we still believe that mainland women enjoy a relatively equal status in the Chinese Constitution and in the Kinship Civil Code. Chinese women are far better off than Hong Kong and Taiwanese women in employment rates and rates of political participation, and in many cities they enjoy very good maternity leave provisions and child-care facilities, incurring the admiration of women in the capitalist societies of Hong Kong and Taiwan. However, from diverse information sources, we also have found out that Chinese women have been released from the patriarchy of feudal familial groups, only to be caught up in the power of a patriarchal state. Furthermore, due to political authoritarianism, both men and women are unable to express different points of view freely. A more recent trend is that with the capitalist commercial penetration of China, Chinese women are again encountering sexual discrimination in employment, and in the areas of sexual traffic and population control leading to female infanticide, they are reencountering the poisonous destructiveness of gender discrimination. This brings them more into alignment with the situation in Taiwan and Hong Kong. It is probably the case that Chinese women must, on the one hand, preserve the equal status they had gained under the Communist political system, and on the other hand, under this wave of commercialism and openness, they also need to look for opportunities to form different kinds of independent small groups and think of ways to punch innumerable small holes into the great wall of patriarchy and political authoritarianism. This approach would be similar to the women's groups of the social movements of the 1980s in Taiwan. Although this approach cannot achieve the immediate overthrow of the authoritarian and patriarchal state, it will gradually cause it to change character, so that different interests of the people (especially women's diverse interests) can emerge on their own initiative. All social and cultural changes in the world are not achieved overnight but are the accumulations and repetitions of oppositional movements.

Besides the contact between Women's Awakening and their sisters in the United States, Hong Kong, and mainland China, we have also met with Japanese, Filipino, South Korean, Singaporean, and Indian sisters. These transnational exchanges have not only been extremely beneficial to Women's Awakening but have also spurred on the Taiwan women's movement to incorporate a wealth of feminist insights from around the world into its work in Taiwan society.

A Retrospective and Prospective View

It was not until the 1990s that mass communication studies in Taiwan academies began to face the fact that the mass media do not report on reality but construct it. The feminist movement in Taiwan serves as a good case example of the distinction between media reality and social reality. In two articles, Professor Ong Hsiu-ch'I (Ong Xiuqi) (1994a, 1994b) of the Journalism Institute of Political University has pointed out that only 526 news stories had to do with the feminist movement in the twenty-nine-year period of 1961 to 1990, compared to 696 stories on the labor movement within a period of only six and a half years. This discrepancy shows the media neglect of the feminist movement. In addition, she found that 60.38 percent of news stories concerning women depicted women's roles as remaining unchanged, and they did nothing to promote women's consciousness. She also pointed out that all journalism or communication departments in universities, except the Department of Broadcasting of the National Arts School, had more female students than male students, but among faculty, men far outnumbered women. Likewise, there were more men than women reporters and media personnel throughout the profession. Moreover, women accounted for an even smaller percentage of managers at all levels. This illustrates that women have much less opportunities to make use of the media. No wonder there were so few representations of women's problems or of the feminist movement; instead, we have seen the trivializing of women's issues in the media.

Ong's study also shows that in the case of the movement to revise the Civil Code, demonstrations and street protests were the most effective strategies in using the media. The second most effective strategy was to persuade the National Assembly to work toward revision of the Civil Code, and the demand that the Supreme Court Justice explain the discrepancy between the Civil Code and the Constitution. Next in effectiveness were public initiatives of all kinds, such as hearings, press conferences, symposiums, and so forth. This shows that dynamic outdoor actions were more likely to attract media attention than indoor and static events. It was also pointed out that the media tended to react to events in terms of the power hierarchy of the society. For example, the meeting with the Supreme Court Justice attracted more attention than other feminist organized events, since women's organizations are regarded as low in social power.

In another study, associate professor Lin Fang-mei of the journalism department of Political University pointed out that more recently, in 1994, the media have increased the coverage of feminism and women because of the greater involvement of feminist associations (Lin 1994b). In her two papers on the case of sexual harassment at Taiwan Normal University, she discussed the construction of the news and the operation of their "regime of truth." According to her, although feminist associations created an intense public interest in this media case, the construction of the news and the interpretations of the events were so framed by the ideology of patriarchy and the regime of truth that they actually strengthened unequal gender relations. Feminist associations still have a long way to go before a new regime of truth in accordance with the principle of equality is built up in the public sphere.

If the Taiwan women's movement is to continue expressing its viewpoints in the mass media, it is not enough to hold marches and demonstrations in the streets, or to hold public hearing meetings and press conferences. Feminist associations must also make an effort to expand themselves and attract more members. For example, Women's Awakening Foundation formed a Taipei Branch Association in April 1995, thus establishing an alliance with the Tai-chung City Women's Awakening Branch and the Kao-hsiung City Branch. It is hoped that as the association branches increase their members at the grassroots level, they will be able to have more power to wield in the democractic elections of Taiwan in the future. Besides the importance of mutual support and interactions among different women's groups within Taiwan and with international women's groups, we should especially see the importance of mutual support and interactions with mainland and Hong Kong women's groups, so that we may start to construct a pan-Chinese women's space.

NOTES

1 The names of persons and places in Taiwan are romanized in both the Wade-Giles and pinyin systems in the text of this article, but the publications of Taiwan authors cited here are listed according to the pinyin spelling of their names in the bibliography, unless they have already used the Wade-Giles spelling in English-language publications.

2 In the Beautiful Island Incident, Taiwan was still under Martial Law. In response to antigovernment sentiments published in the political oppositional magazine *Beautiful Island*, the GMD cracked down on a political demonstration and imprisoned the leaders.

3 This law refers to a GMD regulation during the period of Martial Law called the Law Regarding People's Associations during the Period of Mobilization and Chaos, which strictly forbade the people to form associations. After martial law, this law was relaxed, but associations still needed to be monitored by the government.

4 [Many child prostitutes in Taiwan were/are aborigines. Trans.]

5 [The Warring States was a period of disunity and warfare at the end of the ancient Eastern Zhou dynasty in the fourth and third centuries BCE, when many philosophical schools of thought flourished because there was no centralized power to control and unify them. Trans.]

6 The regulations on foundations limit the number of board members to only fifteen and trustees to only three, unlike public associations, which can undergo unlimited expansion of members.

7 The Democratic Progressive Party, the main oppositional party to the GMD, was founded on September 28, 1986.

8 In 1988, Po Lan-chih, a woman student at Taiwan University and a member of Women's Awakening, organized the first Women's Study Society at the university and also started the *New Voice of Women* magazine, devoted to the problems of Taiwan women workers. By 1990, four out of five Taiwan college campuses had feminist organizations, which displaced the conservative Women's Federations already in existence. These are the seeds of a new generation of the women's movement, and they also include the appearance in 1990 of lesbian women's organizations and issues.

9 *China Times*, March 26, 1993, 5.

10 In the December 1, 1994, issue of *China Times*, the news of women's groups chastising candidate for governor Chu Kao-chen for his inappropriate cussing "Fuck your mother" was reported on page 2. On February 25, 1989, when Chu Kao-chen got into an altercation with female GMD legislator Wu Teh-mei, I also criticized him for using this sexist cursing, but I defended his contributions to the democratic movement, and this news made it to the front page of *Independent Evening News*. It would seem that only if we connect with famous news figures will the women's movement make it to the front page, and this shows our weakness.

11 [Here Lee Yuan-chen is alluding to the fact that Women's Awakening members were

made by the mainland Chinese government to understand that they would only be permitted to go to China if they declared themselves to be representing Chinese and not Taiwan women. Perhaps because they did not concede this, they were never issued visas by the Chinese government, except Cheng Chih-hui, who had been late in her paperwork and so had not applied as part of Women's Awakening Foundation. See Walden 1995. Trans.]

4

Museum as Women's Space:

Displays of Gender in Post-Mao China

With the decline of socialism in the 1980s and '90s, public culture in China evinces a hopeful as well as angst-ridden self-reflexivity about the future state of the nation. Economic, political, and cultural transformations provide a complex and paradoxical context for contemplating vital questions of subjectivity and identity in relation to fundamental institutional shifts. One finds the mercuric development of capitalism by way of the "socialist market economy" accompanied by the continued power of a state organized by the Communist Party. "Actually existing" Maoism has surely come to an end, but traces of nostalgia for Maoist ideals—and kitsch for an idealistic youth lost in the Cultural Revolution—surreptitiously castigate the current regime. An emergent bourgeoisie jostles with a stratum of intellectuals who yearn to reestablish their elite position vis-à-vis the state. Finally, a virulent nationalism pervades public discourse in equal measure as China has abandoned Maoist politics of unequivocal rejection of the West and entered forthright into a global capitalist economy.

A recurrent question echoes everywhere: what constitutes the identity of China, now that the progressive, heroic story of socialism has slithered into the dust? This question pervades both elite and popular culture, from controversial novels among Beijing intellectuals to mass-media soap operas to internationally acclaimed films. Most striking is the way in which this question articulates itself through representations of gender and sexuality. As feminist scholars of China have argued, the overarching role of class difference in providing the foundation of subjectivity and power during the Maoist era obscured ongoing dynamics of gendered relations of dominance and inequality (Meng and Dai 1988; Gilmartin et al. 1994; Li Xiaojiang 1990; Lydia Liu 1991; Yang this volume). Protocols of official feminism, Tani Barlow has argued, constructed a Maoist woman whose liberated femininity was put to the service of state interests (1994b).

Post-Mao China, as the articles in this volume attest, has witnessed an explosion of discussion about gender difference (see Barlow 1994a). Much of this public discourse about gender is a critique of the socialist state and the means and mode of reaching modernity. This discussion can be found not simply among Chinese feminists, who nonetheless provide the most articulate critical analyses of this phenomenon. To the contrary, visual media and literature that grapple with the aggressive, if sometimes uncertain, masculinity of their protagonists dominate post-Mao public culture. The stories they tell represent explicit, assertive masculine desire as a more meaningful alternative to state politics but also as the means by which to challenge state power (Hershatter 1996; Rofel 1994b; Zhong 1994). Women in these narratives are the objects and the ground for male agency or the subject-position of victimization, which the male author ultimately identifies with and occupies (Dai 1995a). These forms of sexualized public culture provide a post-Mao masculinist discourse with which an emergent nonstate feminism must contend.

One can discern in these public debates about gender and sexuality what I have elsewhere called an allegory of postsocialism (Rofel forthcoming). This allegory tells a story of how communism repressed human nature, and for that reason—because such repression was bound to be impossible—communism failed. Maoist notions of women's liberation through transgressions of gendered divisions in labor are portrayed, in this allegory, as a transgression, rather, of innate femininity. Maoism deferred China's ability to reach modernity, so this allegory goes, by impeding Chinese people's ability to express their natural humanity that all along lay beneath the cultural politics of socialism. This allegory is an emancipatory story. It holds out the promise that people can unshackle their innate human self by emancipating themselves from the socialist state. To the extent that the state recedes, people will be free to "have" their human natures.

The pervasiveness of this allegory means that gender and sexuality will be at the heart of any emergent "public sphere" in China. A discussion of the concept of the public sphere in relation to China has been well re-hearsed by Mayfair Yang in the introduction to this volume. Here, I simply wish to add three points. One is that the public-private division under-lying the concept of the public sphere will necessarily have a distinctive dynamic in contemporary China. Maoist discourses of women's liberation made the question of femininity a public matter inextricable from politics. In the post-Mao era, even as femininity has been identified with a domes-tic realm, the political need to oppose the state involves a critique of state gender politics. Thus, efforts to create a public realm separate from the state necessarily entail a public discourse on gender. Second, while the public sphere might usefully indicate a means for extracting social life from state power, the pervasiveness of debates about gender in multiple public sites indicates that this public sphere will continue to operate in conjunction with power rather than apart from or outside of it. We might usefully remember Michel Foucault's injunctions about power—that it is not merely repressive but constitutive of knowledge, truth, and subjectivity (Foucault 1990). Chinese feminists have been tracing the contours of these complex forms of productive power.

Third, we must move beyond artificially drawing the boundaries of the public sphere within the boundaries of the nation-state. If it ever resided within these boundaries in Western Europe—and one could usefully ques-tion that assumption as well by examining the effects of colonialism on European publics—contemporary transformations in transnational capital-ism have eviscerated those borders for all practical purposes. Thus, the alle-gory of postsocialism in China draws its strength, in part, from the way in which China's public culture, especially film, has exploded into trans-national networks of cultural production. There is a process of cultural accumulation one sees here that wends its way through representations of "Chineseness," national identity, and, most important, masculinity. The exploration of masculinity, the themes that suture questions of masculine identity and national identity dominate those cultural productions that have also garnered the most capital investment. They speak in one direction to the desires of many in China to move beyond Maoism, including its state-defined feminism, and in the other direction toward a transnational public that, like earlier nation-state publics, has configured itself on a division be-tween the masculine public and the feminine private. Thus, when one fo-cuses on a feminist project in China, as I will do in this essay, it is too easy to ignore this transnational masculinity in favor of an argument that might replicate the localization of such a project. But it is the localization effects of the masculinization of transnational space that I ask you to keep in mind as

I turn to the women's museum. This transnational context—applauding audiences in the United States and Europe as well as in other Asian countries—allows the allegory of postsocialism to appear as a "natural" description of reality rather than a just-so story, while the masculinist heroics of this allegory join with other male backlashes against feminism elsewhere.

Feminist cultural productions in China thus struggle with multiple contexts: state feminism, nonstate gender politics dominated by the equation of a masculine self with the humanist self, and a transnational network of cultural communication that tends to marginalize their critiques. Conversely, precisely because of the history of feminism in China, Chinese feminist theories and practice of gender identity have a visible effect that cannot be ignored. One particularly striking and creative attempt to make gender visible is the women's museum, created by Li Xiaojiang and located in Zhengzhou in Henan Province. The museum theorizes gender by putting it on display. It creates gender identities by encouraging a visual performance of them. And it offers a productive tension between the assumption that gender difference is natural and the notion that it is culturally constructed. It thus at once reinforces and disrupts the postsocialist allegory of gendered human nature. I turn, then, to the women's museum.

The Women's Museum

Li Xiaojiang, the founder of the women's museum, is one of the most controversial feminists to emerge on the contemporary landscape. Li is a professor of Western literature at Henan University in Zhengzhou.[1] She is a prolific and outspoken author, who early on made possible the publication of a series on feminism through the Henan People's Press.[2] She has publicly ridiculed the national Women's Federation in Beijing for colonizing the category of woman in the name of the state, lacking a feminist theory based in gender identity and difference, and failing to find the courage to fight against new forms of subordination that women face as a result of the economic reforms (Li 1988b). The national Women's Federation, in turn, has virtually made Li Xiaojiang a persona non grata at their national forums. Yet even as she theorizes gender identity in contradistinction to the official version of feminism, Li has not completely abandoned a Marxist analysis of the structural constraints that women face. For this reason, she is sometimes portrayed as a paradoxical figure—a radical feminist who is "mainstream." Li is also controversial among feminists who, like her, have moved away from state feminism. Her analyses of women as a social category in Chinese history lead her to reject Western feminism as a measure of Chinese women's progress—and, at times, to reject diasporic Chinese feminists who study and write about feminism in the United States.[3] Li has encouraged and fostered younger feminists under her direction, while some have also accused her of failing to engage in a collective feminist dialogue.

Li Xiaojiang's ability to act as a lightning rod of controversy comes in part from her location in Zhengzhou. Zhengzhou, seventeen hours from Beijing by train, is a dusty, polluted industrial city on the North China plain, where the dry winds seep down and catch the loess sands in people's throats. Virtually nothing in this city has been turned into a tourist attraction. Multinational capital from Hong Kong and Taiwan, however, has scented the cheap, desperate labor that exists here and has begun to move in. But the women's museum stands in an indirect relation to these regimes of flexible accumulation. While Li Xiaojiang has received Ford Foundation funds for a multiprovincial project on women's history, she has not managed to attract funding for the women's museum. Zhengzhou is a seemingly marginal site from which to theorize feminism—the more prominent voices emerge from Beijing and Shanghai. This marginality paradoxically fosters Li's ability to challenge orthodoxy. Yet this ability in turn is supported by the fact that Li comes from a prominent local family—her father is the former president of Zhengzhou University.

Before my visit to the women's museum in the summer of 1993, rumor of its existence had already reached the United States. The commentary it generated among feminists in China indicated that it was one significant practice among many in the early 1990s that brought the burgeoning field of feminist studies into existence. Before the visit, however, I was leery. The promotional literature on the museum describes one of its purposes to be the initiation of a "women's cultural anthropology" through the collection of cultural relics used by women. This statement resonated uncomfortably with anthropological critiques of museums as sites that fix otherness, imply the death of living colonial subjects, and re-create racist stereotypes (Clifford 1988; Haraway 1985). I anticipated a museum that would essentialize a folk culture of women, a museum that would be representational—that is, purport to provide images that merely reflected reality—rather than interpretive or deconstructive. The women's museum, however, challenges ethnographic critiques of the "museumizing" of culture. It does so by way of the materiality of its location and in the performativity of its displays of gender. As I eventually came to understand, the term *museum,* though used in the Chinese designation as well, is somewhat of a misnomer. It produces a misrecognition of what occurs in the space of the museum. What actually occurs is an activist construction of the social category of woman.

Let us begin with its location. The site of the women's museum is fraught with irony, for it is installed on the grounds of the Henan Women's Federation school for training women cadres. I should add that the provincial Women's Federations do not always follow to the letter the positions of its national umbrella organization. Thus Li Xiaojiang is on good terms with the local Women's Federation. The Henan federation school has been on the verge of collapse for some time due to lack of interest. Women do not see a future for themselves in becoming party cadres and representing the state. One can envision the school, then, as a site of the socialist state in decay. It recalls Walter Benjamin's notion of allegory as a tale of history in ruins. In his study of German Baroque drama (1977), Benjamin argued that the allegorical qualities of Baroque drama addressed the immanence of history as torment. It did so through hieroglyphs, both linguistic and emblematic, that served as multilayered icons of human cruelty that leads to ruin. The women's museum literally writes over socialist history by occupying a full wing of the school's central building. It writes another allegory over this material history by reinscribing postsocialist feminist politics where state feminism once resided. Smadar Lavie (1990), reinterpreting Benjamin in an ethnography about the Middle East, has taught us that allegory addresses the paradoxes of political domination. The women's museum, far from offering fixity of representation, engages an ironic politics of space. It builds feminism from within the ashes of the socialist ruins, even as the layerings of this history indicate that what exactly will come out of those ruins is a matter of persistent political struggle.

Li Xiaojiang led me on a tour of the museum. The museum's four large rooms hold a dense variety of objects that Li weaves into a story about women's culture. The first room we enter is filled with quilts that Li has managed to gather from families in rural areas throughout Henan and neighboring provinces. Women's quilts. The quintessential icon of women's culture. The sort of icon that could be associated with a cultural feminism that celebrates and naturalizes femininity. But as one moves closer to the quilts, their historical detail belies this familiar critique. These quilts have a politically distinctive quality: rather than displaying abstract designs, they are filled with large political slogans that have been woven into them. There is a quilt made in the 1940s that reads, "Down with the Japanese devils." The one from the 1950s exhorts its user to "Resist U.S. aggression and aid Korea." The Cultural Revolution quilt instructs, "Follow the highest directive: Serve the people," while the late 1970s quilt directs us to "Become civilized, gain knowledge, study science." Finally, in the most recent quilt, made in the late 1980s, we contemplate love: "The spring has arrived with the peach blossoms." These slogan-laden quilts cannot be incorporated into an ahistorical narrative of feminine culture across the ages. They are rooted too firmly in a history of socialist politics. They move from the Anti-Japanese War and the anti-imperialism of the early years of the socialist state to the "mass" politics of the Cultural Revolution and the subsequent rejection of Maoism. The invocation of science and love—the dual ideological frameworks of post-Mao China—succinctly captures the dramatic transformations of the past decade. These quilts thus cannot be relegated to a "domestic" realm that is bounded and separate from a "public" one. Nor can they construct an essential femininity. A women's culture, perhaps, but one that is necessarily entangled with the state.

The next room marks a sharp contrast with the first: the room is filled with brightly colored paper-cuts highly stylized in the form of naive realism. Political slogans have disappeared in what appear to be unaffected portraits of women's daily life. Yet these are not the portraits of an Everywoman. Li Xiaojiang explains that these paper-cuts are the artwork of one Ku Shulan, who has gained national fame as the "scissor-cutting lady." They tell her life story, which Li Xiaojiang expands into a story about women's oppression and women's creativity. "She ate much bitterness," Li says, echoing the narrative form of socialist stories about class oppression. But this story shoves class aside. "Her husband beat her constantly." In her pain and loneliness, and because she did not know how to write, Li continues, Ku Shulan poured out her bitter story in little cuttings. Little, indeed. Upon closer inspection, one finds that each figure is a pasted montage of myriad, infinitesimally tiny pieces the size of a teardrop: the figure of a woman alone, dragging a pail of water; a woman alone, with paper tears trailing down her face; a woman sending her child off to school.

This exhibit makes "women's complaints" public. It circulates a discourse on women's lack of power, marginal status, and silence through an artful expression. By reenacting scenes that mark the aftermath of daily oppression, the art and its public display dislodge some of the constraints on women's speech. Such a public display makes women's bodies, affect, and desire visible. Feminist discourse in the United States argues that women are always associated with their bodies and emotions, that these make women and racial minorities visible in the public sphere, simultaneously allowing the abstract invisibility of the male body (Morrison 1992; Pateman 1989b; Ryan 1990). In China, by contrast, post-Mao feminists decry the invisibility of women's bodies, at least those bodily experiences that are distinct from labor. They argue that this invisibility keeps women tied to an outmoded state feminism. It also makes it impossible for women to speak about new forms of devaluation they experience. This exhibit of a cutout life literally cuts out the female body in order to highlight its presence and affect, to make it unmistakably visible. Displayed in a women's museum, it participates in constructing a femaleness that women will recognize but also be led to interpret as distinctive from the Maoist political imaginary of woman—a femaleness developed on its own terms and in its own cultural representations.

The following room swerves from the pictorial to the textual. The artifacts here are precious examples of "the women's script" (*nüshu*). The women's script has garnered much lively intellectual interest from feminists and nonfeminists, linguists and social historians alike. It appears to be a unique example of a phonetically based writing system, written only by women to other women and only in one small rural area of Hunan Province.[4] The women's script served before the socialist revolution as the means by which young women created nonkin social ties—girlhood couples and sworn sisterhoods. The conventionalized poems written in the women's script—often meant to be sung—express lasting attachments and lament the loss of one's coupled friend to marriage (Silber 1994). As a sociotextual phenomenon, the women's script was a language of communication the men did not share. Yet it was not clandestine; the girlhood couples and sworn sisterhoods could also be the means by which a woman's marriage was arranged. The antipathy toward marriage they often express was both culturally appropriate as well as an articulate depiction of unhappiness.

The museum room is filled with the striking black fans on which these poems were written, as well as the books they have recently been collected in to preserve them from the suppression that occurred with the socialist regime. Pictures of the two surviving writers of the script, elderly women in their nineties, also grace the walls. But this exhibit does not tell a strident story of resistance to patriarchy. Little in the exhibit hints at laments about marriage; the writing itself is the focus. The display tells, rather, a celebratory story of recovering the strands of women's creativity from under socialism.

The last two rooms of the museum address women's reproduction and minority women. Black figurines, in the shape of a uterus or a penis and uterus together, lie chastely side by side in a glass casing. They are meant to serve as fertility symbols. Li Xiaojiang interprets these figurines as deriving from early worship of the fertility goddess, Nüwa. The video that accompanies this display recaptures the early importance of female goddesses as well as the contemporary significance of Nüwa. We see multitudes of women and men entering the cave in the southwest where Nüwa's spirit is said to reside, praying to her for the gift of life.

The final room displays so-called minority women's lives through their "typical" costumes. It holds the various colorful costumes of women from the Hmong and Dai groups of China. Wedding outfits, everyday costumes, waist belts, aprons, and multicolored caps with tassels adorn the walls. Their presence in the museum is meant to signal an inclusiveness among women in China that breaks down the rigid binary that divides designated minority peoples from the Han majority. In the museum, they represent heterogeneity. Yet exhibiting minority women in this fashion separates them off from the general category of woman produced in the rest of the museum. Their use as a sign of heterogeneity serves to highlight their distinctiveness from the Han majority. Here, then, the women's museum jostles uneasily with differences within the category of Chinese women. The gaze structured in this last exhibit is that of Han women examining otherness. Minority women are made to stand for the difference that allows Han women to remain the unmarked norm.

Gender Performativity

Mimesis and alterity rift through the women's museum. The exhibits do not merely reflect a reality of women's lives in Chinese society. They mimic an imaginary of women that resides in the Chinese feminist imagination. Returning to the image of the ruins of socialism, one could argue that this mimicry is produced with the implicit alterity of state feminism as the unexhibited background. Postcolonial theories intimate the decentering potential of mimesis: the emulation of the colonizer by the colonized is never an exact replica, nor can it ever be an exact replica, for the dominated subject must also always stand for difference (Bhabha 1994; Taussig 1993). Thus, mimesis unexpectedly throws the project of domination into a skewed trajectory. Anna Tsing (1993), in a recent ethnography on Southeast Asia, has argued that gender is at the heart of mimetic practices.[5] Women imitating male political power, in her descriptions, subtly subvert the serious intentions of that power. By turning these theories of mimesis slightly, one can begin to discern that the mimesis involved in the women's museum does not, with the important exception of minority women, produce the alterity of the other but, rather, constructs the self: women making the category of women visible for other women.[6] Yet this self-mimicry also subverts the "Maoist woman" of state feminism. A politics of subjectivity is at work here that resembles the cultural productions of marginalized peoples in the United States rather than anthropological museums of natives. One thinks, for example, of the numerous theatrical and artistic endeavors of lesbians and gay men to produce an image of the self that one can live by that also mocks dominant gender norms.

Indeed, queer theory, rather than anthropological critiques of museums, might enable better insight into the radical potential in the women's museum. Queer theorists have effectively argued that gender is nothing more or less than an arbitrary performance. Theories of gender performativity have arisen out of lesbian and gay communities in the United States because these communities have developed a remarkable self-reflexivity about transgressive behaviors that have marginalized them as abject or perverse but that simultaneously offer them enormous liberatory potential. Drag queen performances, transvestism, butch-femme relationships, and transsexuality have been extended in theory and practice to reveal the lack of ontological substance in sexual identities and therefore the contingent fabrication of gender. In an early ethnographic formulation, the anthropologist Esther Newton (1972) studied gay men who were theatrical drag performers. After following them in their lives both on and off stage, Newton concluded that it was not at all clear when these men were performing gender and when they were not. For they performed as "men" in public life off the stage with the same amount of artifice they used in their performances as "women" in the night clubs. Therefore, Newton argued, they implicitly subverted the belief that gender identity was "inside" the person while the "outside" was mere artifice, instead demonstrating that the "substance" of gender lay in the performance itself.

Philosopher Judith Butler (1993) has extended Newton's insights to go beyond both the cultural determinism and the naturalism she finds in much gender theory. Butler argues that gender is constituted not in a Durkheimian manner, by a static set of norms or by impersonal forces lodged in social institutions, but in reiterative practices in speech, writing, and bodily activities that "cite" powerful discursive norms that both produce and constrain gender identity. Far from a matter of free will, however, these performative practices are compelled by the compulsory nature of normative demands for identification. These include, but are not limited to, threats of exclusion and abjection. Thus, gendered subjects find themselves compelled by a matrix of power relations to continuously produce their gender identities by assimilating to a heterosexual symbolic. This is a process that, over time, produces the effect of a fixed boundary between the feminine and masculine but also, because of its very reiterative process, opens up instabilities in the construction of gender. Such a notion of performativity also disrupts the sex/gender binary, in which *sex* is said to represent the natural basis on which the cultural norms of gender are imprinted. In American culture, where gender and sexuality mirror one another (e.g., an "effeminate" man is assumed to be a homosexual), gender performativity produces both the sexed body and the gendered identity.

Through this lens, one might begin to appreciate that the women's museum in China fixes a category "woman," but only to hold it in place long enough to enable women who come to the museum to perform their gender in the mirror of its production in the collection. The category of woman has proven to be elusive and wildly transitory in the post-Mao social imaginary. By fabricating it in a museum—as opposed to, say, a theater performance—Li Xiaojiang facilitates women's ability to hold on to the images even after leaving the museum. For these images do not have the total ephemerality of a performance; their fixity in the museum creates enough of a sense that the images might last for women to grasp them firmly. She thus creates a political tool for women to challenge state feminism as well as the new forms of devaluing women ushered in with economic reform.

The museum gathers meaning from but also challenges the allegory of postsocialism. The exhibits assume a social category, woman, has a relevant and expressive cultural existence, that quilts, paper-cut images, and fertility symbols meaningfully belong together as demonstrative of "women's" creativity. Yet the museum's performative aspect implicitly draws attention to the constructedness of gender and to the need for those who have experienced social life as women to transgress, through a display of gender, the norms of state feminism.

Gender Politics

Li Xiaojiang's women's museum participates in a larger discursive field of women's studies in post-Mao China. This field is multiply positioned in a number of intersecting political border zones from which it reconstructs the meaning and significance of Chinese women as a social category. It places woman alongside other subject-positions that have little to do with the socialist class subject but that dominate the social horizon today: the official "socialist with Chinese characteristics" subject, who sits comfortably if somewhat unstably in the interstices between capitalism and socialism; the Chinese cultural subject, popular among intellectuals but ignored by the state, who seeks the reasons for China's imagined backwardness or simply basic character in cultural roots; and the intellectual humanist subject, who complains of being thwarted by the state in his abilities to express his panhuman desires. Women's studies in China laces through and crosses over the boundaries of this post-Mao discursive landscape. Therein lies the heart of its excitement and complexity. It depends on but also destabilizes critical cultural borders of difference that proliferate in China: the socialist state versus the oppositional humanist subject; the difference between women and men; and the constitution of China in terms of the West. The women's museum, as part of women's studies, does not construct social life in these stark oppositions. It does not choose one or the other of these binary terms. Rather, it speaks to the state but not as a male humanist; it challenges the naturalization of gender difference and, finally, replaces the China-West opposition with a concern about differences within China.

As an outspoken and controversial feminist scholar, Li Xiaojiang effectively intervenes into the naturalization of power by both the state and male intellectuals who place themselves in opposition to the state. Through both her museum and her writings, she calls into question the imagined visions of modernity that infuse so much of the self-conscious sense of lack and need for development pervasive in China. Her performative construction of gender in the women's museum also reflects her refusal of "the West" as a measure of Chinese women's progress.

Rather than create a unified vision of China, Li Xiaojiang is committed to tracing its contentious boundaries, concerned about whether women will even be full subjects of the nation. The women's museum, in this respect, is one part of a larger project enumerated in her prolific writings. In her writings, Li Xiaojiang appears to be making a deceptively simple argument: she insists that the past dozen years of economic reform have turned back the tide of women's liberation in China (1988b, 1990). Economic reform is a decisive rejection of Maoist socialism; it is dedicated to catapulting China into the wealth and power of Western nations. It revolves around increasing enterprise productivity, decollectivization of landholdings down to individual household units, and free-market distribution. It depends on inequality.

Li Xiaojiang argues that one inequality that is most crucial to economic reform is that between men and women (1988b). She baldly states that the road down which Chinese society is heading is in exactly the opposite direction from the road women need to be traveling. Li Xiaojiang does not deny the need for China to develop economically. Indeed, she embraces assumptions of progress. But she finds that it is not coincidental that problems for women have appeared at the same time that economic reform has taken off. These problems, she argues, are the method that "society" uses to resolve certain "social problems," such as labor surplus and the need to increase labor productivity. Women are the cornerstone of economic development—so much so that their problems are no longer seen as socially significant. They have literally become *women's* problems. These include pressures to increase rural productivity that have led to the removal of women from production and their return to the home; women in urban industries being forced to take overly long maternity leaves with lowered benefits; young women in cities composing the overwhelming majority of the surplus unemployed; women college graduates finding themselves turned away from jobs that meet their capabilities; and the decrease in women's participation in government.

Li Xiaojiang readily admits there is no necessary relation between economic development and women's liberation. Given China's need for a high level of economic competitiveness and an increase in economic efficiency, coupled with women's double burdens, she agrees that women's experiences of reform not only do not constitute a social problem, but they are the effective solution to social problems—from the standpoint of society. But from the position of women themselves, economic reform has been counter to women's needs and to the ability of women to develop their full potential as contributors to the Chinese nation.

Women's liberation was a real moment in China's recent socialist past. When Li Xiaojiang makes this assertion, she by no means assumes that "women's liberation" is an ontological state, something that, since it once occurred, infuses the dialectic of history forever more. Instead, she argues that at the present time, the old theory that socialism liberates women, parroted over and over again, has been exhausted:

> We used to recognize that "Women's liberation is the entrance of women into society." . . . This certainly is a premise of women's liberation, but . . . women entering society is not the same as women's liberation. . . . Class liberation is not the same as women's liberation. . . . Men's and women's equality is not the same as women's liberation. . . . The development of the productive forces is not the same as women's liberation. . . . What is women's liberation? Simply, it is women's freedom and full development. . . . It is the affirmation of every human being's social value and the value of their very existence. (1988b)

The most important way for women to reach this, according to Li Xiaojiang, is for them to come to consciousness of themselves as a social group.

Deceptively simple, as I said a moment ago. But within this project is a subversion that unsettles the conventional cultural oppositions in China. The most radical aspect of this project is to bring women into existence as a collective social category. The women's museum is the visual strategy supporting this project. For Li Xiaojiang, to speak of women as a socio-logical category is profoundly unsettling for state power.

But if Li Xiaojiang seems to position herself in opposition to the state, she moves unstably across the border of state power versus oppositional intellectual. The latter has configured himself as an unmarked humanist in-dividual, with traces of Confucian overtones. He is someone who has had his fill of collective identities and social struggles over inequality. His ar-gument for democracy is in the name of talented individuals who deserve to succeed to state power in place of the Communist Party because that is what intellectuals do best. Like the party, then, he too embraces in-equality. And he embraces the West, because it is the land of humanism and because Western humanism is the space of resistance to the state.

The East-West border and the Orientalism that grows along it has al-ways occupied a key place in China. "The West" has in turn stood as the imperialist enemy, the source of wealth and technology, and the home of diasporic Chinese intellectuals. It is the space of resistance because the state has deemed it so. We know that resistance never stands outside of power. Both party cadres and humanist intellectuals agree that the East-West divide is a critical one. Senior government leaders use the opposition to praise China, while masculinist intellectuals use it to castigate China. One version of this opposition is a virtual negation of China's entire past, going back four hundred years, a lament about the wrong turns it took that led it away from becoming a world power (see, e.g., the controversial tele-vision series *River Elegy*; see also Su and Wang 1991).

It is this overlapping set of politics on the border that Li Xiaojiang destabilizes. By moving across the state-oppositional intellectual bound-ary, she simultaneously destabilizes the East-West Orientalism of this op-position. The destabilization occurs through her marking a third border: that of sexual difference. She has created that border as much as it has cre-ated her. She has marked it, brought it into visibility. It is a powerful place from which she rejects incorporation into the unitary identities of the state, humanist Man, and Western modern woman. Neither state cadres nor masculinist intellectuals can claim her while she stands on that border. Neither discourse they produce accepts women as social subjects. And the resulting political analysis that Li Xiaojiang has developed in theorizing the position of women also sits unstably within the Chinese body politic. For she rejects the statist revolutionary nongendered woman. And she rejects the state's version of economic reform with its embrace of all necessary inequalities. But she also needs to retain a collectivist, structural approach to social life. She theorizes women as a collective category, not as a number of discrete individuals. And the experiences of this group occur through the economic structures of social life, not through their unique problems. She therefore refuses the humanist embrace of unique desires and talents, for this is precisely the argument that leaves women in the space of nowhere, or "elsewhere." And they refuse her, because any discussion of women's liberation smacks of the Maoist politics that hounded intellectuals for thirty years. Finally, she turns to China's history rather than the West for a sense of possibilities (not just negations).

"The West," then, is not the space of imagined possibilities for Li Xiaojiang. The kinds of masculinist politics it brings to China operate counter to her desire to theorize women into existence. And Western feminism is equally useless for her project. For Li Xiaojiang, Western feminism is a struggle for rights, for equality. These, she points out, Chinese women have long had since the socialist revolution. They have not led to liberation.

The destabilization of the East-West border zone in China might lead one to think of Li Xiaojiang as a postcolonial subject. But she is certainly not the postcolonial of an Achille Mbembe, with his banality, vulgarity, and self-consuming violence. Nor is she the postcolonial of a Homi Bhabha, with his ambivalent disarticulation of colonial representations through the mimicry of colonial subjects. Nor, finally, the postcolonial of Gayatri Spivak (1987), for whom the history of the Third World never stands outside colonial epistemic violence. Li Xiaojiang, I would argue, is not a postcolonial subject at all. Her struggle is an engagement not with Western colonialism but with the representational and practical powers of state socialism. In this struggle, she highlights the importance of subjectivity and identity to the project of constructing public spaces that might foster political discourse not wholly dominated by the state. She reminds us, too, that engendering this space could lead to liberation or oppression. But ignoring gender can only pick up where the state has left off.

NOTES
1 Li has since moved to the Kaifeng campus of Henan University.
2 This series, *Funü Yanjiu Congshu*, includes Li and Tan 1991a, Li and Tan 1991b, Li 1988a, Meng and Dai 1988, Lü and Zheng 1990, Xie 1991.
3 I want to emphasize that Li is not merely a "local" feminist who has not had the opportunity to or who refuses to engage with feminism in the West. She has traveled and spoken at numerous conferences in the United States, Canada, Mexico, and

Europe. At one conference I co-organized at Harvard in 1992, Li argued vociferously with Chinese feminists studying in the United States about the usefulness of Western feminism for China. To read her own explication of these debates, see her 1996 work *Tiaozhan yü Huiying* (Challenge and response).

4 This province is to the south of Henan Province, where the women's museum is located.

5 Taussig, Bhabha, Tsing, and others have revitalized the concepts of mimesis and alterity, turning them back against their Enlightenment origins. Earlier ideas of mimesis as a symptom of realism, as an endeavor to craft an exact replica of the social world, have been reconceptualized by these authors in a poststructuralist manner to signal actions and representations of similitude that, in attempting to copy the original, end up subverting it, or making the copy more "original" than the original, or exposing the provisional and strategic constructions of subjects and objects and the orders of power involved in those constructions. Mimesis, in their theories, depends on a relation between a knower and its object, or a relation of alterity, of making a thing or person into an "other." Taussig draws from the Frankfurt School, Bhabha from psychoanalytic theory, and Tsing from postcolonial, minority discourse and feminist theories; all of them emphasize the importance of colonialism in the dynamics of mimesis and alterity. They all use concepts of mimesis and alterity, then, to conceptualize dynamics of domination and its possible subversions.

6 One finds alterity, by contrast, in museums, for example, constructed by colonizers to display the native peoples they have conquered, or in history museums that produce replicas of the quaint "traditions" of "our forefathers" that reassure us about our modernity. Here, the women's museum, with the exception of the room on minority women, does not display a set of contrasts against which the subject gazing on the exhibit can be reassured about the essential and essentially correct nature of her subjectivity.

5

Tze-lan Deborah Sang

Feminism's Double: Lesbian Activism

in the Mediated Public Sphere of Taiwan

Since martial law was lifted in Taiwan in October 1987, government censorship and regulation of print, television, film, and radio have relaxed on many fronts. Meanwhile, demonstrations and similar public gatherings became legal. Homosexuality, among other issues, came to occupy a prominent place in the new public territory of representability, debate, and activism. A new movement of female resistance, distinguished to some extent from the traditional women's movement, has arisen in Taiwan's public sphere: lesbian activism (*nü tongzhi yundong*). Through a variety of discursive practices ranging from academic theorizing and community magazine publishing to novelistic writing, lesbians—at times in coalition with gay activists but mostly independently—engage in the project of self-definition, challenging rigid modern classifications and stereotypes of female homoerotic feelings, practices, and relationships.

Taiwanese lesbians' search for identity and community through public communication is a counterhegemonic discourse on multiple levels. In the most apparent sense, it is an example of what Michel Foucault has called "a reverse discourse," in which "homosexuality began to speak in its own behalf, to demand that its legitimacy and 'naturality' be acknowledged, often in the same vocabulary, using the same categories by which it was medically disqualified" (1990: 101). Many of the popular stereotypes in Taiwan concerning female same-sex love originated in late nineteenth- and early twentieth-century European male-authored medical literature on sex, which sought to catalog sexual perversions and described same-sex desire, including that between women, in terms of a minority of people's pathology, psychological abnormality, and gender confusion. These stereotypes have acquired global significance due to the hegemony of Western science and popular culture in this century. Recent Taiwanese lesbian activist publications engage in battle with the sensationalist but politically conservative mass media, which on the one hand propagate stereotypes and on the other pry into and capitalize on the eroticism of a formative urban lesbian scene. Lesbian activist discourse also disrupts traditional Confucian family values. Many lesbians must exile themselves from the patriarchal family in order to find the space to be themselves. Insofar as lesbian activism is a female counterhegemonic practice that defies a complex combination of patriarchal control over women's gender and sexuality, it has an intimate link to feminism. The connection between the two "women's movements" in Taiwan deserves a close inspection. Overall, Taiwanese lesbian activist discourse is ineluctably indebted to contemporary feminist and lesbian/gay theory, activism, and art from the West. Modernization, from the introduction of Western homophobia to the borrowing of its counterdiscourse on a large scale, has come full circle. What may be new is a viable, productive lesbian identity that Chinese women have never before been free to choose.

To elucidate the relationship between lesbian activism and feminism in Taiwan, it is essential that the disgrace of lesbianism in Taiwan be exposed as a recent historical construct rather than a long-standing Chinese cultural legacy or a universal given of the a priori order. The intensified stigmatization of lesbianism that took place first in advanced capitalist countries in the West and later in developing Chinese societies can be meaningfully analyzed as a modality of male defense. In an age in which wage labor and urbanization expanded, upper- and middle-class women entered the workforce, and patriarchal kinship lost considerable control over women. For fear of women's autonomy and separatism, anxious males invented a new system of sexual ethics that theorized the naturalness of heterosexuality as *sexuality* for women, that is, as women's desire, pleasure, and identity rather than as women's duty. This system cast lesbian desire as a perversity. The notion helps maintain patriarchal control over women by dividing women and punishing those who form their primary relations with women rather than with men.

Therefore, the recent emergence of Taiwanese lesbian voices and activism in the mass media, alternative publishing, campus meetings, street demonstrations, and so on does not simply mean the political struggle of a sexual minority for public space and legitimacy. It has important significance as a feminist practice. Indeed, many lesbians in Taiwan are feminists, and many dedicated participants in feminist organizations are lesbians. The overlap and tension between a fledgling lesbian identity politics and an already powerful women's movement in the Taiwan public sphere have recently surfaced into a heated debate. The question of whether feminism can be a multifarious practice with dissimilar agendas that does not erase the specificity of lesbians will no doubt continue to inform the future discussion, coalition, and separation among lesbians and feminists.

As lesbian activists enter the Taiwan public sphere to advance a radical critique of the supremacy of the patriarchal nuclear family and to demand public legitimacy for lesbianism, they cannot afford to neglect the fact that one of the major characteristics of the public sphere in capitalist societies is that it is mediated, and that face-to-face communication has come to play a limited role. Unlike mainland China, where the recent conversion from communism to a capitalist market economy is associated with the opening up of a public sphere of private people, Taiwan is a mature capitalist society in which the mass media threaten to collapse both the public and the intimate spheres into media effects.[1] Jürgen Habermas champions the public sphere of budding capitalism but is extremely critical of the public sphere of advanced capitalism. For him, the advanced capitalist mass media, hand in hand with parliamentary politics, hinder rather than encourage society's critical, rational thinking: "Critical publicity is replaced by manipulative publicity" (Habermas 1989: 177–78). The capitalist mass media have also been described in bleak terms by Jean Baudrillard, who believes that the masses are trained to consume rather than respond, and that media simulacra have replaced reality.[2] These bleak pictures do not describe the entire relationship between the mass media and audience in Taiwan, but they point out inherent dangers in the communication structure.

Lesbian activism faces the possibility that the capitalist mass media monopolize communication, reproduce dominant values and ideology, and distort the public sphere. Although face-to-face communication in the public, such as lectures, group discussions, street demonstrations, guerrilla theater, public hearing, and debate in the legislature are possible in present-day Taiwan, and although in recent years lesbians and feminists have created many such events, they realize that the mass media (TV, radio, film, newspapers, and commercial magazines) are crucial fields of social warfare, in that the mass media reach or constitute a much wider public beyond those physically participating in demonstrations, speeches, performances, and discussions. In recent years, feminist and gay/lesbian activities and agendas have succeeded in attracting some media attention. However, preoccupied with profit making and aiming at creating the greatest possible consumption value, the mass media may use radicalism to spice up their otherwise relaxing, ready-for-use content, without ever genuinely embracing radicalism. On the contrary, gender and sexuality constantly run the risk of being turned into sensationalism by the media. Therefore, in terms of mediated communication, lesbian activists and feminists presently rely considerably on low-cost alternative publishing (such as lesbian or feminist magazines and books) and the alternative electronic media (represented by the Internet) to promote critical discourse. At the very least, a prosperous capitalist economy combined with a democratizing government has ensured that it is not difficult for radical groups in Taiwan to raise a minimum capital for the production and distribution of their opinion, even though their product may not make any profit on the market.[3]

The public sphere in Taiwan has become a site of contestation between different discourses: scientific normalization, patriarchal family values, sensationalism, feminist and queer academic theories, and the liberatory self-representation of a new imagined community of lesbians. These discourses serve multiple and dissimilar functions: consumption, leisure, profit, control, information, scholarship, provocation, dissension, and identity formation. In this terrain, lesbian self-representation is the category that has the most difficulty making appearance in the present public sphere. Since the mass media is inhospitable to radicalism and unworthy of trust, most lesbians choose to publish their self-representations in lesbian and feminist magazines, whose circulation is limited. Moreover, due to the fact that revealing one's homosexual identity to family, acquaintances, and strangers in Taiwan still causes predictable and unforeseeable adverse consequences, lesbian authors use substitute names (pseudonyms or group names) for self-protection. In other words, lesbian self-representations have entered the public sphere, but they are often contained there in a few pockets or islands of critical space.

Nevertheless, there are signs warranting optimism about the future growth and vitality of a critical lesbian-feminist public sphere in Taiwan and even the transnational Chinese community. One cheering example is that, while the commercial mass media in Taiwan have been difficult for feminists and lesbian activists to appropriate without getting corrupted by them, the Internet as a new public medium and forum has proved to be remarkably useful in supporting nonprofit feminist and antihomophobic publishing, and open, well-circulated discussion that simultaneously safeguards privacy. The technological development to decentralize mass communication in the postmodern era greatly contributes to the proliferation of lifestyles, and vice versa.

A Historical Perspective on the Phobia about Lesbianism in Contemporary Taiwan

Unlike in the modern period, lesbianism was shrouded in an ambiguous reticence in the male-centered public discourse of late imperial China. In stark contrast to male homoeroticism, erotic love among women made scant appearance in male writings (Xiaomingxiong 1984; Hinsch 1990). When it did surface, it was figured as the insignificant, the laughable, the naughty, and, on rare occasions, the anomalous (Sang 1996). Basically, it was dismissed as a gray zone of amorality rather than demonized as a vice. Lesbian practices were not an object for moral admonition. Confucian tenets of female chastity were obsessed exclusively with female-male congress, and adultery and promiscuity by definition involved males. In a similar fashion, legal codes (whether traditional or modern) did not criminalize lesbian behavior, nor did they mention lesbian desire in any other way.[4] The complete absence of lesbianism from traditional Chinese moral and legal codes suggests that female-female eroticism did not constitute a significant source of anxiety for males. Literature further shows that men often treated female homoeroticism not with punitive prohibition but with trivialization. In fiction, drama, autobiography, and miscellaneous notes, late imperial male authors who touched on women's sexual love were in general so phallocentric as not to acknowledge lesbian eroticism as sex. Typically, female-female affection enjoyed legitimacy as sisterhood, and female-female intercourse was viewed as a secondary, substitutive practice that by no means excluded conventional marriage. The mutual longings and pleasures among women were rendered harmless by the male polygamous imagination, which demanded that they either enhance or collaborate with male desire for female bodies.[5] Even in gay male writings, lesbianism was subsumed under male homoeroticism and deemed inferior (Vitiello 1994: 173). It is only when certain women committed themselves to other women *and* resisted men that women's love was portrayed by male writers as extraordinary and strange, and such odd women were repri-

manded, exorcised, or banished from the human community through a variety of writing strategies (Sang 1996: 29–88).

In the twentieth century, late imperial Chinese phallocentric, dismis-
sive views of female same-sex eroticism underwent dramatic transformation. Because of the massive Westernization of China on many fronts,
which included the movement of women's liberation, lesbian desire in
modern Chinese public discourse acquired the status of the sexual, and at
the same time that of depravity. The term *homosexuality* was first translated
from late nineteenth- and early twentieth-century European sexology—
often mediated through Japanese sources—into Chinese during the 1910s
and '20s (Sang 1996: 89–142). From the very beginning the category's fascination and usefulness for Republican Chinese intellectuals largely lay in
its ability to place the passion between women with the passion between
men under a common rubric, and to make female same-sex love a tangible,
substantive entity open to description and evaluation. In urban journals on
women's issues and sex education pamphlets, Republican Chinese intellectuals depended on such medical neologisms as "female homosexuality"
(*nüzi de tongxing'ai*), "sexual inversion" (*qingyu zhi diandao*), "abnormality"
(*yichang*), and "perversion" (*biantai*) for talking about women's, especially
middle-class New Women's, autonomous sexuality, such as female students
and teachers' passionate friendships in schools.[6] Inherent in the modern
authoritarian project initiated by European doctors such as Richard Krafft-
Ebing and Havelock Ellis, which later was adopted by Republican Chinese
intellectuals who were mostly male, was the attempt to grasp, contain, and
regulate female sexuality by conceptual means in the face of women's
growing access to education and professions, as well as their increasing
economic independence from the patriarchal family.[7] In other words, lesbian desire did not become men's anxiety and fear in China until some
women were gaining the recognition as persons with integrity—as indi-
viduated *grown-ups* just as men were. Prior to women's gaining male recognition of their demand and potential for independence, women's sex meant
nothing but the miming games of child-like slaves in bondage, women's
romantic love the commiseration among slaves.

Republican male intellectuals who accepted the perversion (*biantai*)
theory of women's homosexuality include famous ones such as Zhou
Zuoren, Chen Dongyuan, and Pan Guangdan. Chen Dongyuan apparently associated the threat of lesbianism with independent career women of
the modern style. He complained in 1927: "There is a group of female
teachers in my school who have often made me wonder if they have organized a 'Refuse-to-Marry Party' [*bu jia dang*]. I think they are like that

because they have acquired intimate same-sex friends [*tongxing de nüyou*]"
(Chen 1927). In Chen's seminal work, *A History of the Lives of Chinese Women*
(*Zhongguo funü shenghuo shi*), after describing women's same-sex unions in
Canton, he adds: "It is against nature if women refuse to marry men because of same-sex love [*tongxinglian*]; it's extremely detrimental to women's
health. Ever since [women's] means of livelihood changed in modern
times, more and more women past the marriageable age indulge in same-
sex love. It is a serious problem" (Chen 1928: 300).

During the 1920s and early '30s it became common knowledge among
the educated urban Chinese class that women's "same-sex love" (*tongxing
lian'ai, tongxing ai, tongxing lian*) was a psychological or sexual perversion according to "modern science."[8] The medical division between normality
and aberration categorically relegates women's same-sex desire to a defec-
tive and morbid status. As a form of control, "sexual psychology" is more
insidious than moralism and much more expansive in its grip than legislative criminalization. And beginning in the Republican period, "sexual science" established itself as the chief rationale for the discrimination against
female homoeroticism in modern Chinese culture.[9] During the Republican
period, two views of female homosexuality became popular in urban
Chinese print media and medical sources, largely due to the influence of
Havelock Ellis. Ellis attributes women's same-sex desire to the inversion of
gender: "The chief characteristic of the sexually inverted woman is a certain degree of masculinity."[10] Operating with a rigid, conservative definition of sexual difference, prescribing what either femininity or masculinity
is, this theory of sexual inversion conflates erotic object choice with gender identity. Being phallocentric, Ellis regards all desire for women as masculine.[11] Meanwhile, like other specialists in his time, Ellis believes that
many female homoerotic feelings, behavior, and relations are "pseudo"
homosexuality. Above all, he asserts that girls' romantic friendships prevalent in all-female schools—incidentally, a matter of grave concern for
Republican Chinese intellectuals—are nonserious sexual play. According
to him, since most girls do not lack femininity, their desires are not really
inverted. In love with their own sex, school girls are merely exercising
their sentimental and occasionally sexual faculties in rehearsal for opposite-
sex love later in life.[12] A typical response to Ellis's theory came from Pan
Guangdan, one of Ellis's Chinese translators. For Pan as well as many other
Republican intellectuals, "same-sex love" or "homosexuality" is an intersubjective relation the possibility of which is widespread among the population, rather than a peculiar essence localized in a small number of individuals. Pan is convinced that, although same-sex love is prevalent in

women's schools, most schoolgirls change their minds upon graduation. They willingly follow the path of heterosexual marriage and family life (Pan 1946: 325–26).

After 1949, the Republican Chinese discourse on homosexuality was largely erased from the public arena in mainland China. Literature and the arts avoided the topic of homosexuality for several decades, for there is practically no artistic representations touching on it from the 1950s, '60s, and '70s. During the Cultural Revolution, homosexuality was criticized as "counterrevolutionary" behavior and capitalist corruption, which was not unlike Chinese communists' criticism of male-female "romantic love." Communist China's official dictionary of the modern Chinese language, first published in 1973, includes the Republican neologism for homosexuality, *tongxing lian'ai*, tersely defined as "the love relationship that takes place between men or between women, a form of psychological perversion" (*Xiandai Hanyu Cidian* 1973: 1029). However, details of outdated medical theories of homosexuality as gender inversion and psychic pathology did not resurface into urban popular consciousness until a multitude of publications about sex emerged in the 1980s and '90s, the era of China's reintroduction of a capitalist economy and Western culture.[13]

Meanwhile in post-1949 Taiwan, similar to the situation in Hong Kong, the Western discourse on homosexuality as a sexual abnormality continued to flourish. In addition to recycling ideas from Republican and Japanese adaptations of early European sexology, Taiwan also received current Western opinions on the issue through psychiatry and the mass media (including both journalism and dramatic representations). If we look at Taiwanese fiction in the 1970s and '80s, we encounter clear articulations of a social prohibition against women's homoeroticism and depictions of the lesbian as a distinctive sexual minority. In novels such as Guo Lianghui's *Beyond Two Kinds* (1978) and Xuan Xiaofo's *Outside the Circle* (1990), we find characters discriminating against lesbians as psychobiological perverts, the stereotype of the monstrous, mannish lesbian, secret lesbian circles, lesbian violence, and lesbian tragedies. In other words, due to the continuous influence of modern medicine and popular culture from the West, the notion of female homosexuality as a character trait of only a minority of women, with the connotations of "perversion" and "gender reversal," took hold in Taiwan.

Lesbian Activism and Feminism

It is against a pervasive grid of modern medical stigmatization superimposed on traditional dismissal that lesbian activism arose in Taiwan's public sphere.

Its symbolic beginning can be marked as 1990, when the first Taiwanese lesbian group, called Between Us (*Women zhijian*), formed and announced its inauguration to the public.[14] Since 1990, fresh, revisionist articulations of women's romantic, erotic bonds have become an important political project. Equally important, the negative stereotype of a monstrous, unfeminine lesbian body is being resignified in the urban lesbian bar, reclaimed and celebrated by butch/femme (*ti-po*) lesbians as a sign against an oppressive ideology of gender—that is, a set of limiting definitions of female roles, which must be challenged and opposed.[15] Moreover, the negative discourse about a minority of women pathologically attracted to their own sex is being transformed, much like the word *queer* in the West, into a building block for founding a distinctive, empowering collective lesbian identity.

Since the Taiwan mass media "discovered" lesbians in 1990, they have largely imagined lesbianism as a "sexual perversion" parallel to male homosexuality. In addition, Western queer activism and the notion of sexual orientation have also encouraged Taiwan lesbians and gay males to form a queer political front across the gender divide. This wave of concerted queer activism is commonly called *tongzhi yundong*. Feeling that "the homosexual" (*tongxinglian*)—the medial category that originated from sexual psychology—is almost beyond positive resignification and reclaiming, lesbian and gay activists in Taiwan and Hong Kong have in recent years appropriated the term *comrade* or *cadre* (*tongzhi*) as the common denominator for people with same-sex sexual preference. Many lesbians and gays prefer the new term to sexological taxonomy, for they believe that, wrested from twentieth-century Chinese political history, *tongzhi* is capable of suggesting the elements of choice and political activism in sexual identity.

Certainly, many lesbians consider themselves allies with gay males as citizens of a queer nation. For instance, lesbian and gay activists in Taiwan have jointly claimed the May Festival (*Duanwu jie*) traditionally dedicated to Qu Yuan's memory to be Gay and Lesbian Awakening Day (GLAD).[16] The ancient poet and politician Qu Yuan wrote deeply affectionate and sorrowful poems upon his king's change of heart, comparing himself to beauties and fragrant plants, before drowning himself in the Miluo River. Orthodox Chinese hermeneutics never encouraged any interpretation of the homoeroticism inherent in Qu Yuan's writings but, rather, emphasized that the writings are metaphorical and that Qu Yuan's sentiments are purely patriotic, even though there exists in fact no reliable historical record on Qu Yuan the person. By celebrating GLAD, lesbians join gay male activists in reclaiming queer history against the grains of conventional, straight mentality, carousing for queer pride.

On the other hand, some Taiwanese lesbians and feminists have explored lesbianism as a specifically *female* counterhegemonic practice. As such, lesbianism is mapped in close linkage to feminism. In this section of the paper, I intend to look at how a fledgling lesbian identity politics has been positioned in relation to the stronger, more established women's movement in Taiwan. This will not only enrich our understanding of the extent to which feminism dares to take a militant and anti-institutional stance in Taiwan's public sphere. It will also illuminate how lesbianism as a category has been created and signified as a form of feminism.

A review of the past may put the intricate relationship between feminism and lesbian activism in present-day Taiwan in perspective. On the basis of my earlier reconstruction of the history in which lesbianism became stigmatized in twentieth-century Chinese discourse, I argue that the pleasurable physical interchange among women had always been known to men in China, but it did not take on the meanings of abnormality and depravity until Chinese men saw it against the background of the women's independence movement, that is, feminism. In itself, the reputed connection between lesbianism and feminism is more than a male paranoid fantasy.[17] It has significant validity in modern Chinese history. Like their counterparts in the West, the first middle-class New Women in China transposed traditional forms of female bonding in the inner domestic sphere to the semipublic or public arenas. They depended heavily on sisterhood in their pursuit of intellectual, professional careers in society and fulfilling emotional lives outside the patriarchal family. Many of them formed committed, amorous companionships with female friends. Although no biographical documentation has ever been done, female pairing and cohabitation are easily found among the female teachers in May Fourth fiction.[18] To what extent these New Women's romantic unions were sexual was no doubt a matter of individual variation. Nevertheless, the discussion and fictional representation in the 1910s and 1920s made it clear that not only did Chinese men suspect sexual relations among New Women, but some New Women were also frank about the sexual experimentation in New Women's same-sex relations. Ding Ling's novella *Summer Break* (1928) is an explicit example.

Fundamentally, because traditional Chinese culture did not idealize women as naturally frigid and without sexual "heat" as Victorian England did, when the theory of female homosexuality was introduced to China in the 1910s and '20s, intellectuals of both genders were not shocked but, rather, readily affirmed that many women, even of the respectable class, could desire their female friends physically. Sadly enough, believing that the possibility of homoerotic desire was widespread among women did not lead Chinese intellectuals to discredit the new theory that it was unnatural. The Chinese response to sexology easily entertained the gap between what women can want and what women should want. The reason for such discrepancy has to be sought in the fact that men played a hegemonic role in deciding what women should want. Indeed, since there existed no religious taboo on same-sex intimacy in China, lesbianism could not become demonic in public opinion unless men perceived it as challenging male-female gender hierarchy and male sexual access to women.

Republican Chinese male intellectuals saw the main threat of female homoeroticism in those women who at once appropriated male privileges (public career and active sexuality) and fended off male claims to their bodies. A similar threatening figure combining female homoeroticism and female revolt was theorized by European male doctors as the unfeminine, congenital female sexual invert, the embodiment of an incomplete, pathological masculinity. The masculine lesbian persona was then used to stigmatize and discredit feminists in general. Since not all feminists engage in homoerotic practices, or think of their own qualities in terms of masculinity, it follows that many feminists have tried to distance themselves from lesbianism, now a pathology and gender inversion by public definition. It is sad that although romantic female friendship has always been an integral dynamic to some women's antipatriarchal alliance since the beginning of the women's movement or earlier, male science has stereotyped and stigmatized lesbianism to such an extent that it is despised by many women and censored even within feminist organizations.

The marginalization of and hostility toward lesbians in feminist groups have occurred in many places in the United States and Europe in the 1960s, '70s, and even '80s (Wilton 1995: 87–109; Rosenfeld 1988: 457–66). A similar pattern is playing itself out in contemporary Taiwan. The similarity across space and time may indicate that patriarchy and women's resistance often involve the same structural dynamics around the issue of female sexuality in different cultures. On the other hand, the similarity may also mean that Taiwan, as a developed capitalist society, is highly Westernized in its cultural forms, such as medicine, academic theory, and the popular media. Its cultural assimilation of the West is in positive relation to its integration into the global capitalist system. Discourses first developed in advanced Western capitalist societies such as homophobic sexual science, feminism(s), and gay/lesbian activism are reproducing themselves in contention with one another in Taiwan.

There has been no lack of feminist theories advocating women's gender transgression and sexual freedom in Taiwan. Many feminists denounce the male conspiracy of regulatory theories of female sexuality, and they talk about lesbian sex as a liberated use of the female body. Yet in actual political programming, even feminists in the most radical women's organization have questioned the legitimacy of lesbian agendas in the women's movement. For these feminists, lesbianism is the orientation of a particular minority, and the issues that arise from such particularism cannot be prioritized in the women's movement. Moreover, for fear of contracting ill repute, these feminists wish to set up a boundary between their cause and lesbianism. They argue that the rights of lesbians should be advocated by all-lesbian, or lesbian and gay activist groups, and that a feminist organization may play at best a secondary, supporting role.[19]

This reasoning has surfaced in many forms. One of the forms it assumes is the argument that feminists should not speak for lesbians; lesbians should be the subject of enunciation on lesbian issues. Inherent in this argument, however, is a dichotomous division between lesbians and feminists, as if feminists could not be lesbians, or lesbians could not be feminists. It neglects the fact that at present many dedicated activists in Taiwanese women's organizations are lesbians, but for many years they have been working for women's rights with the implicit understanding that they must erase their own specific needs and visions as lesbians.

Who are lesbians? Are they self-assertive, defiant, and women-loving women who, nonetheless, do not qualify as feminists? Is same-sex desire dispensable to women's alliance? Is same-sex desire something few women have experienced or can relate to? Who can patrol the borders of feminism? Is it all right for lesbians to march for heterosexual women's rights under the flag of feminism, but not vice versa?

A recent series of discussions, "Exploding Feminism," published in the journal of the most active feminist organization in Taiwan, the Awakening Foundation, exposes the fact that homophobia and heterosexual privilege are common within the Taiwanese feminist constituency as well as in the society abroad.[20] Currently, lesbian feminists are among the most dedicated feminists at the Awakening Foundation, and yet by a silent consensus that presumes heterosexuality and celibacy as the only respectable practices for feminists, lesbian feminists are forced to closet their sexual preference from others in the organization as well as when facing the public. Similarly, lesbian agendas—such as the legalization of lesbian marriage, adoption of children, in vitro fertilization, nondiscrimination in the workplace, or the promotion of homoeroticism as a valuable sexual and emotional resource for all women—are either marginalized or nonexistent in the women's movement.[21] The debate exposes that heterosexism is everywhere, even in feminism, which has been critical of male sexual violence and supremacy in male-female sexuality. The debate is significant not only because it explores different ideological and political orientations among feminists and seriously asks whether feminism in Taiwan can be a pluralistic, democratic practice with multiple agendas in the future. More important, the discussion represents serious collective feminist thinking on the implications of lesbianism for the women's movement as a whole. Certain opinions voiced during the debate maintain that lesbianism resides at the heart of feminism, rather than on the periphery, for the first time in Taiwan's public sphere.[22] These reflections are possible because the traditional agenda of the women's movement in Taiwan—equal rights between men and women in the public realm—has already entered the mainstream (Hu 1995a: 14). Thus it is high time that feminists challenge the technology of gender on a deeper level: the structuring of gender norms through sexuality.

The debate was ostensibly ignited by Yuxuan Aji, editor of the lesbian magazine *Girlfriend*. In an article published simultaneously in *Girlfriend* and *Women's Awakening Journal* in February 1995, Yuxuan attacks the Awakening Foundation for reinforcing compulsory heterosexuality and neglecting lesbian and gay human rights:

> Even the most progressive feminist organizations in Taiwan have not tried to challenge the existent structure of the family. They merely pursue through legislature the "equality between the sexes" as classified by the heterosexual system. . . . In their proposal for revising the marriage law, they continue to define marriage as between a man and a woman. (Yuxuan 1995a: 16–17)

In response to Yuxuan's criticism, in July 1995 *Women's Awakening* put out a special issue on the relationship between feminism and lesbian activism titled "Heterosexuality/Homosexuality: Both/Neither." However, tension had long been pent up in the Awakening Foundation itself. These differences exploded in the next five issues of *Women's Awakening*.

In its initial response to Yuxuan Aji, the Awakening Foundation defends itself by claiming that it is just as dedicated to challenging conventional family values as lesbian or gay activists are:

When we were pushing the civil law movement, what we did was more than demanding that the legal codes [on marriage and family] be revised. . . . We promoted the notions that divorce is not one's fault, that adultery should be decriminalized, that domestic labor deserves pay, and that women's choice not to marry should be affirmed. We hoped to deconstruct and redefine marriage and family. . . .

We hoped to open up women's space in marriage and to create women's possibilities outside marriage. Marriage will become one of women's choices, rather than the single, required path. (Xinzhi gongzuoshi 1995: 10–12)

Meanwhile, the same issue of *Women's Awakening* published four other essays reflecting on the relation between lesbian activism and feminism. The first is a translation of the influential manifesto "The Woman-Identified Woman" by Radicalesbians of the United States in 1970. The following statement by Radicalesbians, in particular, is highlighted by the editor of *Women's Awakening*:

As long as the label "dyke" can be used to frighten women into a less militant stand, keep her separate from her sisters, keep her from giving primacy to anything other than men and family—then to that extent she is controlled by the male culture. Until women see in each other the possibility of primal commitment which includes sexual love, they will be denying themselves the love and value they readily accord to men, thus affirming their second-class status. (Radicalesbians 1988: 19)

In her own article, *Women's Awakening* editor Hu Shuwen concurs with Radicalesbians:

Equality between the two sexes—I am awfully tired of this phrase. What feminism and the women's movement want to change is not just the power relation between men and women; we must give more thought and heart to women themselves, that is, reflect on what kind of "same-sex" relationship women want to create. . . .

The opposition between heterosexuality and homosexuality, or the difference between good women and bad women, is defined by male hegemony. Women are defined by the kind of relationship they . . . have with (heterosexual) men. If we do not challenge this kind of classification, as well as the violence and oppression it creates, women's power will be subject to the division and erosion by the logic of heterosexual patriarchy, and the women's movement will have no way of being more than a tamed movement of "good women." (Hu 1995a: 13–16)

Taking the division between "heterosexual women" and "homosexual women" to be the product of male supremacy and oppression, Hu Shuwen urges all feminists to take same-sex relations more seriously and face the challenge that lesbian activism poses. In another article, by contrast, the author Zhang Xiaohong, an influential heterosexual feminist who has been very popular with the mass media, is primarily concerned with how the feminist and the lesbian activist can "see each other in tension" and "form coalition on specific issues." As Gu Mingjun, another feminist, in a later article criticizes Zhang, what feminists need to face first is the lesbian closet in the feminist camp:

> For some reason, the article "Seeing" [by Zhang Xiaohong] seems to forget that lesbianism may be one kind of feminism, and feminism may be one kind of lesbianism. The possibility of coalition or mutual seeing does not have to be abstract, or like a mutually beneficial foreign relation. On the contrary, it can mean the abolishment of policing and the concrete "coming out" in one's own territory. . . . Why is feminism presumed "heterosexual a priori"? . . . Rather than seeing *others*, . . feminists should first see the possibility of further liberating gender within the feminist camp itself. (Gu 1995: 11, emphasis mine)

According to Gu Mingjun, a homophobic ambiance has led lesbian feminists in the Awakening feminist group to keep silent on both their sexual identities and their disagreement with the agendas and strategies that the women's movement presents in public. She believes this has led to a kind of "alienation" (*yi hua*). In a later roundtable discussion, feminists Hu Shuwen, Gu Mingjun, Wang Ping, Zhang Juanfen, Ji Xin, Su Qianling, and Ding Naifei reached the consensus that the women's movement needs lesbian feminists, and that the women's movement must do more for lesbians and have more lesbian perspectives. Meanwhile, Zhang Xiaohong raised the objection that if there is not a large enough number of lesbians in the feminist collective, the advocacy of lesbian rights by the women's movement will be "hollow" without appropriate subjectivity. To Zhang's assumption that feminists are primarily heterosexual, Hu Shuwen wrote a severe response:

> Perhaps, for "heterosexual feminists" there is an unbridgeable gap between lesbianism and heterosexuality. Therefore, when the women's movement begins to face and practice lesbian activism, they think it is probably just a "gesture" on the part of "heterosexual" (what an assumption!) women out of "moral anxiety. . . ."

When we are actively thinking about and promoting a women's movement with a lesbian perspective, we have already come out. You keep worrying that this will be a hollow movement, that it will be a phantasm movement without a subject. You do not know that, the subject has already faced you, but you do not see it. (Hu 1995b: 14)

Hu Shuwen argues that Zhang Xiaohong unthinkingly takes her own orientation and outlook to be representative of feminism. Zhang has not realized that what is happening is precisely that lesbians are demanding to rearrange the power hierarchy in the women's movement. The women's movement does not belong to heterosexual women alone. Hu further implies that there exists a broad lesbian spectrum in the women's movement. By the very act of practicing lesbian activism, she and some other feminists have already claimed lesbian identification. Lesbian identification is either already inside or is growing out of committed feminism. Clearly, Zhang Xiaohong's assumption that heterosexuality is the default position for feminists neglects the fact that for women the predominance of heterosexuality has never been just a matter of desire. It is implicated in the unequal distribution of power and economic resources between men and women. Feminists, of all people, as critics of male domination should not overlook the elements of choice and political resistance in lesbian identities.

As "women's bonding," the continuum and rupture between feminism and lesbianism are captured by the following story that Yuxuan Aji tells about herself, as once an active participant in feminist organizations including the Awakening Foundation, but who has since felt alienated and now dedicates her energy to the lesbian group Between Us. She addresses the confession to her onetime sister feminists:

Isn't it strange? While we were advocating the ideas that women should identify with women and that women should love women, I fell in love with a real woman of flesh and blood, but I did not become a heroine as a consequence. Instead, I automatically withdrew from you and disappeared. When I turned from a "progressive heterosexual woman" into someone who practices lesbian eroticism and claims lesbian identification, the gigantic stigma of homosexuality became a fate I could not dodge. Feminism and Western queer theory at best have kept me from drowning. I must find my way to survive, with other lesbians. (Yuxuan 1995b: 16–18)

Lesbianism may be simply an intense, concrete form of women's alliance, which feminists advocate, but this logical realization or consummation of women's alliance has been made a disgrace. Homophobia inserts a violent rift between homosociality and homosexuality, feminism and lesbianism. As Yuxuan trespasses on embodied love, she finds feminism in Taiwan no longer her home. It is the split, not the continuum, between lesbianism and feminism that requires explanation.

Yuxuan believes that "in theory, lesbian activism can and must be integrated with the feminist movement." But given the homophobic atmosphere in the women's movement in reality, there has to be a lesbian movement separate from the women's movement. Lesbians must build their own collective identity and politics:

> Although lesbians are subject to the oppression of the male-female gender hierarchy, for them that oppression is not as pressing as the oppression of sexual orientation. Moreover, some lesbians (especially Ts [tomboy or butch lesbians]) resist female identity. They have always fought against the institutional violence of heterosexuality with their individual bodies. They do not identify as women as defined by the heterosexual institution. It is difficult for these lesbians to subscribe to feminism's principle that women identify with women. . . .
>
> Although the lesbian movement . . . does not call itself feminism, as lesbians grope for the ways women may love each other and treat each other equally, another kind of feminism is growing out of the subjectivity of lesbians. (Yuxuan 1995b: 18)

On the one hand, Yuxuan upholds "sexual orientation" as a fundamental category of difference that sets lesbians apart from other women. On the other, Yuxun does not deny that "feminism" can be redefined and reinvented by lesbians. Nevertheless, as Yuxuan's overall position privileges the experience of those lesbians who do not identify with the women's movement as it exists, she underplays the fact that there are many other lesbians for whom feminism is an important part of their lives and who would try to transform the women's movement from within. Indeed, the recent effort that Awakening feminists made toward challenging the homophobia in the feminist camp represents a different antihomophobic tactic—that is, rather than reify a minority sexual identity, they seek to deconstruct the classification and particularization that established female homoeroticism as a localized phenomenon in the first place.

While feminists debate whether lesbianism is internal to themselves, for lesbians "feminism or not" has also been a source of disagreement. Besides what Yuxuan points out about Ts, at Taida Lambda (the Society for the Study of Lesbian Culture at National Taiwan University), for example, some lesbians have raised the issue of why lesbian activism is often discussed in connection to feminism. This kind of discursive practice signals to them the assumption that without the "packaging" of feminism, lesbianism has no legitimacy in itself. Other lesbians who believe feminism is important for lesbians respond:

> Feminism fights against . . . the inequality between men and women. Queer activism aims at dismantling the stratification of sex (in which husband-wife monogamous sex is at the top, and "perverse sex" at the bottom). The two movements are fundamentally different. Nevertheless, feminists must face the question of sex. And queer activists cannot avoid the issue of gender because gender is the overall framework. Feminism and queer activism take different routes, but the two should keep in dialogue. (Taida Lambda 1995: 111)

Lambda feminist lesbians aptly summarize the connection between women's identity and sexual practice. Insofar as lesbianism defines itself as women's same-sex eroticism and union, gender is already part of the definition. Whether lesbians are enamored with femininity, or disrupting the conventional definition of femininity, or forming life and support units with other women, the dynamic is not located outside gender. Feminism's critique of the straitjackets of conventional femininity as well as its project seeking women's empowerment can be appropriated by lesbians for self-empowerment. Fundamentally, homophobia does not work the same way against women as against men in a patriarchal society. The presence of lesbianism is uncomfortable for patriarchy when it means women's potential for independence and strength.

Further, Lambda feminists confirm that it would be a great oversight for feminists to confront gender oppression as if it did not manifest itself through erotic practices, cultures, and institutions. Men's stigmatization of lesbianism intensified at the beginning of women's emancipation in the modern era, and feminists would do well to contemplate this fact. Compulsory heterosexuality may be the final tool that men have for intruding into women's bonds to exercise basic control over women, who are otherwise gaining education, professions, political rights, and limited leadership. As Hu Shuwen has reminded us, the taboo on lesbianism requires analysis from women's points of view. If, after examination, there can be found no fundamental reason why any self-respecting women should think the mutual attraction and love among women are unnatural or beyond women's capacity, Taiwanese feminists cannot hesitate any longer to embrace lesbian activism as an integral part of women's collective struggle for autonomy.

Capitalism, the Mass Media, and the Mainstreaming of Homosexuality:
Will Lesbian Activism Be Different?

If a public sphere in which lesbian rights and radicalism may be openly discussed or promoted has come into existence in Taiwan, it remains debatable to what extent this public arena has adequately represented lesbian interests and viewpoints without either domesticating lesbianism or marking lesbianism as the inferior Other of society. Although largely autonomous of the state, communications and publishing in present-day Taiwan are often dictated by commercial interests. A consideration of lesbian-feminist practice in the public sphere would thus be incomplete without, first, analyzing the representations of lesbian and gay issues in the capitalist media, and second, illuminating the relation that a radical lesbian and feminist stance may have to the commercial media.

The mass media in Taiwan in the 1990s show a schizophrenic character regarding gay and lesbian issues. On the one hand, newspapers and TV stations seem friendly to gay and lesbian activism. They carry many translated reports from the West on Gay-Lesbian Pride parades, AIDS activism, same-sex marriages, and the like in Western countries.[23] The press publishes a considerable number of articles submitted by academic writers and other private observers on queer genders, politics, literature, art, film, and so on. A number of newspaper columns and radio programs have even been devoted to the discussion and sharing of gay and lesbian experiences and problems between audience and commentator or deejay. When gay and lesbian activists organize antihomophobic events, it is also common for activists to notify the gay-friendly media so that the events will be covered and publicized.[24] Indeed, it looks as if the Taiwan mass media are interested in social change, equal human rights, or the liberation of sexual preference.

On the other hand, the Taiwan media continue to reproduce the stereotype of homosexuality as abnormality and gender inversion. Most often, it is through the media rather than treatises in medicine and psychiatry that the general population learns about outdated sexological ideas. It is through the media that medical classifications are cited, disseminated, mythologized as well as vulgarized and corrupted among the populace.

Furthermore, the media associate homosexuality with sexual excitement and the criminal underworld. Since the beginning of the 1990s, the profit-oriented media have been intent on outing, hearing, and seeing lesbian and gay persons, turning the homosexual subject into an erotic-exotic object for the popular gaze, giving queer sexualities problematic visibility.

Sensational tabloid magazines such as *Exclusive Reports (Dujia baodao)* and *Times Weekly (Shibao zhoukan)* as well as a horde of other soft-core pornographic magazines have turned out stories after stories about lesbian and gay promiscuity, sexual techniques, cruising parks and bars, crimes, murders, and suicides. Some of these reports are voyeuristic; many are plainly fantastical. They portray gays and lesbians as sneaky, alien creatures whose secrets the reporters can pry into and reveal to the general, "normal" public's satisfaction.[25] The case is especially pronounced in the case of lesbians. Unlike gay males, as a community lesbians were little heard of by the public until the late 1980s. The media's excitement at discovering lesbians was tremendous. It was predominated by a craving for seeing lesbian sex and observing spectacular transgender types. Lesbians' political struggle to make their erotic preferences visible and legitimate in the public sphere thus runs dangerously close to the pervasive hypersexualizing of women in the commercial media. The label of same-sex sexual orientation all too easily reduces women to one-dimensional beings in the popular imagination, reinscribing hierarchical power relations between men and women, as well as between heterosexuals and homosexuals.

The schizophrenic or hybrid character of the Taiwanese mass media alerts us to the possibility that theories on the relation between the mass media and social liberation that either completely denigrate or extol the capitalist media capture only part of the truth. Mark Poster points out that media theories until recently imagined media communication as "unidirectional speech" according to "a broadcast model": there are very few production centers and a large number of recipients. Moreover, most media theorists' characterization of human subjectivity reduces it to either side of the autonomous-heteronomous divide. Working with the broadcast model, pessimistic theorists such as Theodor Adorno argue that the media impose on the masses a uniform false consciousness (Poster 1995: 3–22; Horkheimer and Adorno 1986: 120–67). By contrast, optimistic theorists turn the broadcast model completely around. As Hans Enzensberger claims, "For the first time in history, the media make possible a mass participation in a productive process at once social and socialized, participation whose practical means are in the hands of the masses themselves" (cited in Baudrillard 1988: 207).

If we observe the recent disarray of media representations of gay and lesbian sexuality in Taiwan, however, it seems that what determines the rational or pernicious ideological character of the media does not have a straightforward correlation to either the concentration of capital or the monopoly of production means. The best example is the China Times media conglomerate. The same enterprise can issue a report on a Gay Pride parade in New York in its daily, carry an article on the subversiveness of queer gender performativity by Taiwanese feminist scholar Zhang Xiaohong in its evening paper, put out a fabricated erotic and scandalous story on lesbian or gay crime in its weekly, and still publish avant-garde novels of gay or lesbian themes under its book-publishing division. In other words, the monopoly of production means has not prevented the possibility of ideological diversity. The media do not give the masses one choice but multiple choices. At the same time, clearly the capitalists and the professionals running the media apparatuses evaluate and select what is to be published. The masses may make submissions, but they are far from being in possession of the production means.

The relationship between audience and the media in a capitalist society should be reconceptualized as an interactive and mutually penetrating one. The media, which have certain privileges over the masses in the structure of production and communication, cannot simply impose something on the masses. Rather, the media have to assess the market. They must guess what their audience wants, how many types of audiences there are, and how large their numbers are. The media constantly modify their communication according to the market's response. On the other hand, the media also "develop markets" (*kaifa shichang*). They provide surprises and innovations; they advertise fresh items and commodities to the public.

Given this interactive model between the capitalist media and the public, if homosexuality has become one of the most trendy and best-selling topics in the Taiwanese media and commercial publishing, is it because lesbians and gays have become such a distinctive and powerful consumer group that their emotional needs and erotic interests must be catered to, or because lesbian and gay sexualities have been domesticated and eroticized as an article of entertainment and curiosity for an audience that defines itself as normal? It seems to me that both explanations are valid, and they do not have to preclude each other. If the diverse production of homo-eroticism by the China Times conglomerate suggests anything at all, it is the fact that in a mature capitalist economy, the detection and creation of market division are essential to the media's profit making and maintenance of public credibility. The media in Taiwan are catering to a multitude of coexisting markets within the larger general market. Because of these markets' diversity in tastes and needs, the media are "schizophrenic" in their communication about sexuality. To satisfy the audience's dissimilar demands in terms of homosexuality, the media must open avenues for critical discussion, intelligent analysis, rational reportage, and the latest information on gay liberation from Western "advanced countries" while they capitalize on homoerotic sex and scandal.

Perhaps the fact that homoeroticism has been so successfully commercialized in Taiwan in recent years shows precisely that there is no easy, clear demarcation between straightness and gayness, and that although the general society may pose itself as straight, it is heavily invested in queer pleasures. This is good news on some level. On another level, however, the amazing compatibility between capitalism and gay and lesbian sexualities is troubling. In contemporary Taiwan, there have been other kinds of "minority politics" in the public sphere. For example, the dire economic and cultural situations of aboriginal Taiwanese peoples (*yuan zhu min*) have made some of aboriginal descent appeal to social justice, to rally for the restoration of aboriginal cultures, and to seek economic and political empowerment for aboriginal peoples. And yet the identity politics of aboriginal peoples never took flight in the mass media. Unlike gay and lesbian sexualities, the issues of aboriginal peoples did not prove to have general appeal and market value. Given the contrast, we may have to ask why gay and lesbian sexualities have entered the mainstream commercial media of Taiwan so easily. Are gay and lesbian sexualities limited in the challenges they pose to society? Have they become mainstream within a mere couple of years because sex and love are what capitalism has always capitalized on and consumed? If so, how can gay and lesbian identity politics be a truly progressive politics? How can it stop being assimilated by mainstream ideology? Does it want to? Is there any difference between lesbian politics and gay politics?

In 1996, a brand-new move to "mainstreamize" gay and lesbian identities took off. If the mainstream ideology in Taiwan is represented by capitalism, an analysis of this new formation can help us measure the distance between gay and lesbian identities and the mainstream. In June 1996, the first commercial gay and lesbian magazine in Taiwan, *G & L: Passion Magazine* (G & L: Re'ai zazhi) was launched. *G & L* is vastly different from previous Taiwanese magazines devoted exclusively to queer sexualities and cultures, which are represented by lesbian magazines limited in budget and distribution network. In a month, the beautifully made glossy *G & L* sold more than fifteen thousand copies at the price of NT $200 (US $8) a copy in Taiwan, and the publisher had to run a second press. The magazine envisions its customers to be "gays, lesbians, and all open-minded young gentlemen and ladies." The main editor of the magazine, An Keqiang, predicts in the "Prelude" to the inaugurating issue: "The time is ripe for creating a gay/lesbian magazine that provides tips on living, leisure, and consumption" (An 1996: 8).

The inaugurating issue of *G & L* is characterized by male-centrism and outright consumerism. The magazine speaks to gay men, heterosexual women, and heterosexual men much more than to lesbians. Erotic images of half-nude males, and other gay male interests, occupy 90 percent of the pages of the magazine. As readers' responses printed in the following issue point out, the inaugural number is disappointing in offering little to lesbians (*G & L* 2: 12). Essentially, there are only two pieces related to lesbians. The first one is a short interview with two Taiwanese lesbians who have come out with pride, Sharon and Antonia, which constitutes the strongest political statement in the entire issue. The other piece concerning lesbianism consists of a series of photos of two feminine female models and a male model, all fashionably dressed, posing in different combinations, to show that "three is better than two" (*G & L* 1: 120). It is not difficult to see that these images advocating bisexuality reinscribe male claims to lesbian bodies. The bisexual combination, two women plus a man, is remotely reminiscent of the traditional Chinese polygamous ménage à trois. By presenting such an arrangement, the magazine shows itself fully aware of the difficulty in making lesbianism acceptable to mainstream society without introducing male privilege. In their looks and dress, the female models affirm in every way society's ideal of delicate female beauty. Lesbianism means double visual pleasure for the male gaze.

The magazine unabashedly embraces consumerism. The main topic of the inaugurating issue is a story called "The Culture of Gay and Lesbian Consumption in Taiwan: The Customer Is Always Right. Long Live Queers!" (Taiwan tongzhi xiaofei wenhua: Guke zhishang, tongzhi wansui). Its authors opened it with a candid and unreserved endorsement of capitalist consumer culture:

> Our age is characterized by the motto "Business is guiltless, and consumption is right" (Shangye wu zui, xiaofei you li). . . . The number of gay and lesbian consumers is large. They form an emerging market. They are a consumer group that businesses and advertising companies are eager to develop. Gay and lesbian issues are no longer serious agendas about human rights, dignity, and resistance. They can be sold as a commodity. (*G & L* 1: 19)

This introduction amounts to arguing that being queer or pro-queer means no more than buying and using certain fashionable merchandise symbolizing good queer taste. It argues that gays and lesbians are just part of the highly capitalized society of Taiwan like everyone else. Certainly, there is more than a grain of truth in this assertion. If queer identity is based on sexual orientation, queers are probably heterogeneous from one another in matters other than sexual orientation. Also, they are probably the same as nonqueers in many respects. Indeed, gays and lesbians do not occupy any particularly disadvantaged and exploited social strata in terms of economy. Since gays and lesbians have the money to spend like everyone else, the article argues, they deserve service and respect from others. Money at once justifies and levels difference.

Nevertheless, the magazine's capitalist justification of homoeroticism provokes questions. Is changing one's status in the consumer culture—moving from the object consumed by others to the consuming subject targeted by advertisements—the sign of liberation? If money is the route to liberation, is the real distinction in society that between rich and poor rather than straight and gay? Is class the ultimate oppression? How can gays and lesbians who claim to resist oppressive social structures effortlessly embrace capitalist materialism and the economic class inequality it entails? To whom does *G & L* primarily speak? Middle-class gays interested in Guy Laroche perfume, Armani suits, and gay porn videos? If *G & L* perceives lesbians to have less purchase power than gay men or to be less interested in conspicuous consumption (as indeed the magazine's distribution of content indicates), does this mean that lesbians deserve less respect than gay men? A capitalist evaluation of people's worth and rights is problematic, to say the least.

Perhaps those who produce *G & L* magazine believe that there is no denying the fact that homosexual people are no more and no less concerned with universal social justice than nonhomosexual people. They believe that to say homosexual people are different from mainstream society in any respect other than in sexual preference would be untrue and oppressive in itself. Claiming to serve gays and lesbians, *G & L* has taken an ambiguous stance on gay and lesbian identities. It declares that to disturb the oppression based on erotic object choice, gay and lesbian identities must be demystified and shown to be absolutely ordinary. It is important because as long as there remains the discursive production of homosexuals as a social Other, whose sexual preference is thought to crystallize a multitude of insurmountable differences from the usual society in inexplicable ways, homophobia and oppression persist. At the same time, *G & L* magazine argues that gays and lesbians' difference must be affirmed. And its way to affirm erotic difference is through capitalism. It perceives gays and lesbians as in need of custom-made entertainment and merchandise different from what the straight society seeks, and the magazine promises it will entertain gays and lesbians and give them the most up-to-date information on the commodities that really suit them. G & L constructs gay and lesbian identities as the same as that of mainstream society in essence (that is, in the need to consume), and only different from mainstream society in the objects of consumption.

Radical lesbian discourse, as discussed in an earlier section of this paper, apparently departs from such a consumerist, depoliticized interpretation of lesbian practice. Radical lesbianism challenges the existent power hierarchies in social institutions: in the patriarchal, heterosexual family, the normalizing pseudoscience, the state's law on marriage and family, as well as the exploitation of lesbian gender and sex by the capitalist media. What it strives for is not just the comforts and conveniences of a particular lifestyle, but also a systemic, structural change. It aspires to develop an ethics of love distinguished from coercion, violence, and exploitation. Recognizing the reality that lesbians are doubly oppressed as women and homosexuals, lesbian activists cannot afford not to confront male domination in even a so-called free capitalist economy. The momentum of the radical lesbian movement comes from a critical, oppositional stance. What lesbian activism will do is precisely carry on serious agendas of "human rights, dignity, and resistance," which G & L dismisses. Until society takes lesbian rights seriously, lesbians and feminists will continue to build a distinctively female-imagined community on the basis of counterhegemonic publications and writings by lesbians and feminists.

Because of their ambiguous and stupefying ideological effects, the commercial media will not likely be the major means by which radical lesbian feminist discourse maintains its momentum in Taiwan's future public sphere. Lesbian feminist discourse has to find alternative ways beyond commercialization to keep its cutting edge while disseminating itself. Fortunately, with the latest developments in communication technology, noncommercial publishing and the public forum have been greatly facilitated. Central to this phenomenon is the Internet. Taiwanese lesbian and feminist publications have traditionally been printed with limited local circulation, but recently there have emerged electronic feminist lesbian journals able to reach large audiences on a global scale. One good example is G-Zine (Hong peiji, http://r703a.chem.nthu.tw/~rpgs/gzine/index.html), an electronic journal featuring incisive comments from feminist and lesbian activists in Chinese text and purposefully "offensive" graphics. The Web site is created and maintained by the Gender and Society Studies Group (Liangxing yu shehui yanjiushi) at National Tsing Hua University in

Taiwan. While arguably academic and "ivory tower" in origin, the reach of *G-Zine* easily transcends geographic locations because of the World Wide Web, and its appeal is potentially populist given its dramatic visual presentation. Its democratic potential is illustrated by the fact that e-mail responses to *G-Zine* have traveled across a variety of borders from nonacademic Chinese readers in North America, Hong Kong, and mainland China, as well as from within Taiwan itself.

Similarly, within the past three years the Chinese electronic BBS (bulletin board system) has come to play an important role in the public discussion on homosexuality in Taiwan. Many young people, especially college students, meet others of similar sexual preferences as well as argue with their opponents on the Net. According to a recent listing (June 1996), there are more than forty BBS domains set up by students in different universities in Taiwan that have bulletin boards called Members of the Same Sex. Bulletin board communication has many characteristics conducive to the formation of a critical public sphere. Communication is decentralized and interactive. It can be either one-to-one or one-to-many. Access to the Internet is wide open and mediated by little capital or social prestige. Thus it allows a greater level of democratic participation in opinion interchange than the traditional media. Finally, Internet communication is extremely private as well as public. An Internet user's speech online is not supervised from above, and the speech is sent out freely to a public, albeit in cyberspace. It is somewhat paradoxical that the postmodern Internet corresponds in many ways to Habermas's nostalgic, humanistic ideal of the public sphere of modernity, "audience-oriented privacy." If the Internet continues to maintain relative autonomy from commercialization and monopoly, radical movements in Taiwan such as lesbian activism and feminism are likely to increasingly employ it for carving out and maintaining a critical public sphere. We have reason to hope that as opinions become contested and liberalized in cyberspace, transformations in this emerging domain of the cultural imaginary will catalyze changes in the material conditions of so-called reality as well.

NOTES

Unless otherwise noted, all translations from Chinese into English are mine.

1 Mayfair Yang has argued about the emergence of a public sphere independent of the state as a capitalist market economy develops in mainland China in recent years. See Yang's introduction to this volume.

2 Baudrillard claims: "Simulation is no longer that of a territory, a referential being or a substance. It is the generation by models of a real without origin or reality: a hyperreal" (Baudrillard 1988: 166). "What characterizes the mass media is . . .

noncommunication—if one accepts the definition of communication as an exchange, as the reciprocal space of speech and response, and thus of *responsibility*. . . . Now the whole present architecture of the media is founded on this last definition: they are what finally forbids response" (207–8).

For a concise account of optimistic as well as pessimistic theories of the relationship between media and social liberation, see Poster 1995: 1–22.

3 For example, the feminist magazine *Women's Awakening* was run on a deficit from 1982 to 1995 by the Awakening Foundation, which mainly relies on donations. In June 1996, the foundation started another women's journal, *STIR* (Sisters In RevolT), a trimonthly.

4 In contrast, late imperial Chinese laws did criminalize certain circumstances of male-male anal penetration, if not male homoeroticism in itself. These codes defining the circumstances of "illicit sex" (*jian*) between males show that male-male penetration is acknowledged as sex, and that as a result it is subjected to some regulations regarding violence and social hierarchy. The regulations were class and status specific in the Qing code (Sommer 1994). On the issue of modern Chinese legal codes related to male homosexual behavior, see note 9.

5 The representative text in this regard is Li Yu's 1990 play *Pity the Fragrant Companion* (Lian xiang ban).

6 See, for example, Shan Zai 1911: 36–38. The Republican term *New Women* designated women with a so-called modern outlook and lifestyle.

7 For a controversial argument about the regulatory effect of male sexology on early feminists' same-sex bonding in Europe, see Faderman 1981: 239–53. See also Newton 1984.

8 According to Charlotte Furth, unlike in Western sexology, "no kind of sex act or object of desire was singled out in [traditional Chinese] medical literature as pathological. . . . They included no catalogue of 'perversions,' and procreative efficacy alone defined the sexually healthy" (Furth 1988).

9 Modern Chinese laws in both Taiwan and mainland China have not criminalized homosexual behavior in itself. On the mainland, the criminal code of 1980 has one law (no. 160) that pertains to man-boy rape and forced sodomy (*ji jian*). These acts are punished as a type of the behavior of "rascals" (*liu mang*) (Gao et al. 1989; Liu Fuchu 1991). In Taiwan, there are police regulations concerning obscene behavior in public that can be applied to male homosexual behavior depending on the location of the erotic act.

The Hong Kong law is a different case. Modeled after the British legal code, it criminalized homosexual behavior per se for many years. In 1991, the Hong Kong government passed a law to decriminalize homosexual behavior, partly in response to the gay rights movement in Hong Kong since the late 1980s, led by the queer activist organization Ten Percent (*Shi fen yi hui*) (Zhou and Zhao 1995: 160–77, 180–81; An 1995: 345).

10 Havelock Ellis, "Sexual Inversion in Women" (1895), cited in Newton (1984: 561). Although this particular article by Ellis may not have been translated into Chinese, his other writings that were translated similarly put forth the model of "sexual inversion" and confuse sexual preference (which concerns object choice) with the issue of gender identity (which concerns the subject).

11 Esther Newton, as well as George Chauncey Jr., has argued that, historically

speaking, male sexologists like Ellis were not entirely wrong about the masculinity of the early lesbian persona. Both critics maintain that masculine identification was a necessary strategy for early twentieth-century British and American women to make an outright statement about their physical desire for other women (Newton 1984: 561).

12 See "The School-Friendships of Girls" (Ellis 1920: 368–84), translated into Chinese as "Nü xuesheng de tongxing ai" (Same-sex love among female students) by Xie Se (pen name) in 1927. Ellis's attempt to pronounce heterosexual love as more real than girls' school friendships is loaded with male anxiety. Recently, Marjorie Garber has elegantly put forth a different interpretation of adolescent homoerotic love in boarding schools: no passion is ever false (Garber 1995: 297–334).

13 Homosexuality did not reemerge until the 1980s as a touchable topic in the public allowed by the Communist state, such as in the print media and on the radio. In addition to media discussions, many books in popular psychology and sex education have been published in the mainland in recent years, a considerable number of which include sections on homosexuality. See, for example, Liu Dalin et al. 1992. However, most of such texts claiming to offer scientific knowledge rehash outdated early sexological theories of homosexuality as gender reversal and psychological abnormality. Beginning in the 1980s, certain Republican books introducing early European sexology on homosexuality as sexual perversion have also been reprinted, such as Pan Guangdan's translation of Havelock Ellis's *The Psychology of Sex* (Xing xinlixue, 1946) and Zhang Minyun's *Xing kexue* (Sexual science, 1950). Hong Kong sociologist Zhou Huashan points out that despite the fact that homosexuality was no longer considered a psychological disorder by Western medical authorities after the mid-1970s, contemporary mainland Chinese medical sources still classify homosexuality as a psychiatric disease (Zhou 1996: 9–12). However, in 1994 the disease model of homosexuality was debunked in a joint statement made by more than fifty Chinese experts in sexual science, psychiatry, public health, law, and ethics at the end of a groundbreaking conference, "Meeting on AIDS Education and Special Sex Problems" (Aizibing jiaoyu yu teshu xingwenti yantaohui) (Zhou 1996: 20–21; An 1995: 53–57).

14 The founding of Between Us in 1990 was reported in the radical magazine *New Culture* (Xin wenhua), which also published autobiographical stories and political statements by members of the group. Later on, from a feminist stance the Awakening Foundation declared support for the lesbian group. The group gained much publicity in 1992. Taiwan TV Company (TTV) broadcast voyeuristic videos on the Taipei lesbian scene, and Between Us issued a public statement to denounce the reportage as exploitative and detrimental. Supported by a letter signed by thirty writers, artists, and critics published in *China Times* (Zhongguo shibao), Between Us succeeded in making TTV apologize. See the chronicle in the first publicly issued lesbian magazine, *Ai bao* (Love Journal, founded in 1993) 2 (1994): 8.

15 The resignifying project extends into print. The first number of the second publicly issued lesbian magazine in Taiwan, *Girlfriend* (Nü pengyou) focuses on the meanings and pleasures of the bodies of those who identify as tomboys (tangbao) in the Taiwan lesbian community. See *Nü pengyou* 1 (August 1994): 4–14.

16 The first GLAD was celebrated, with film screenings, performances, discussions,

and candlelit lakeside conversation, on the campus of National Taiwan University on June 1, 1995 (Ji et al. 1995).

17 Of course, not all female homoerotic practices have the political effect of overturning male domination or are even critical of male domination. Feminist consciousness is to some extent independent of female homoerotic practice.

18 See, for example, Ling Shuhua's "Rumor Has It That Something Like This Happened" (1926), Ding Ling's *Summer Break* (1928), Lu Yin's "Lishi's Diary" (1923), and Ye Shaojun's "The Forgotten" (1922).

19 Zhang Xiaohong, an influential heterosexual feminist in Taiwan, is representative of this position. See Zhang Xiaohong's remarks in Hu et al. 1995.

20 There are many women's organizations in Taiwan, and the Awakening Foundation is but one of them. Nevertheless, Awakening is currently the most politically active and theoretically sophisticated feminist group in Taiwan. In my discussion in this section of the paper, the words *women's movement* and *feminism* refer to what the Awakening leads and represents. See also Lee Yuan-chen's contribution to this volume.

21 Description of the situation is based on comments by Hu Shuwen, Gu Mingjun, Wang Ping, and Ding Naifei in *Funü xinzhi (Awakening)* 159–163 (1995: 8–12).

22 The relationship between feminism and lesbianism has been explored in many feminist groups (*nü yan she*) and lesbian groups on university campuses in Taiwan. However, such discussions have seldom been published to reach a wider public. Although the participants in the debate over feminism and lesbianism at the Awakening Foundation were limited to members of the foundation, since the discussion was published, it became available to a wider public in print, and readers may respond to the debate by making submissions to the journal, phone calls to the foundation, and so forth.

23 For example, in June 1994, the Taiwan mass media were among the many in the world that celebrated the twenty-fifth anniversary of the Stonewall riot, by reporting on the Gay Pride celebrations in the United States that month. The Stonewall riot symbolically marked the beginning of the American gay and lesbian liberation movement (D'Emilio 1983: 231–33). On June 27, 1969, police raided the Stonewall Inn, a gay bar in the heart of Greenwich Village in New York. The customers at the Stonewall that night, including transvestites, lesbians, and gays, responded unusually by putting up a struggle with the police. Crowds of gays and transvestites fought with the police in the streets of the Village for two nights. "Before the end of July, women and men in New York had formed the Gay Liberation Front" (D'Emilio 1983: 233).

24 For example, Taida Lambda held a press conference upon the publication of their book *We Are Lesbians*. The first GLAD at National Taiwan University was also well publicized by the media.

25 Some of the earliest voyeuristic media reports on Taipei lesbians include "Exploring a World That Shuts Men Out" (Huang Manying et al. 1991: 32–45) and "Revealing a Hundred Secrets in Female Homosexuals' Sex and Love: How Do They Do It without the 'Thing'!" (Su Yaping et al. 1991: 25–38). These reports generally focus on butch-femme role playing in the lesbian bar. They stereotype butch lesbians as "female men" (*nanren po*)—impostors posing as men, who lack penises—and femme lesbians as normal women who are somehow weak or confused enough to be sexually exploited by the so-called "crystal sex-demons" (*boli qingmo*). The reporters'

curiosity for lesbians' sex centers on the question, "How do they do it without a penis?" Their language deploys puns and mock versions of classical idioms and romantic verses to ridicule lesbianism, suggesting that lesbianism is an inauthentic substitution or imitation. The early reports conceived of "female homosexuals" as counterparts to male homosexuals, who used to be the only homosexuals the public had heard of. For a while, the sensationalist media called lesbians "female crystals" (*nü boli*), a term derived from the Taiwan slang word *boli*, which designated male homosexuals. The lesbian bar was described as a new "crystal paradise" (*boli leyuan*). The traditional term for male homosexuality, "cut sleeve" (*duan xiu*), was also used to represent lesbianism.

6

Women on the Edges of Hong Kong Modernity:

The Films of Ann Hui

The career and films of Ann Hui On-wah in the past three decades inscribe the transitional history of Hong Kong cinema from a state of being
dominated by imported English language and Mandarin films to the production of a corpus of indigenous language films of artistic quality and
merit. Hui herself is, in turn, an agent in bringing this history into being.
In significant ways, this cinematic history bears witness to a critical conjuncture in Hong Kong's recent history: a rapid urbanization that radically
redrew the physical and sociocultural contours of the territory; the emergence of an indigenous middle-class elite newly aware and confident of
itself and largely oriented to local issues and concerns; and the domination
of bourgeois aspirations toward material well-being among a majority of
those who had yet to share the territory's growing prosperity. Between
1979 and 1996, Ann Hui made thirteen films, and she is the only woman
filmmaker of her generation to have been consistently active in Hong
Kong cinema.[1]

A number of systemic features, underpinned and guaranteed by continuous economic growth, characterizes Hong Kong's recent modernity.
British colonialism nurtured, in both conscious and unconscious ways, the
identification of modernity with Western forms of bureaucratic and institutional management, and the embrace of Western technology, despite

the fact that the colonial administration, backed by local elites, was averse to the development of Anglo-American forms of democratic politics. A Westernized and increasingly technologized corporate culture began to make significant inroads into the inherited cultural traditions and practices of the majority Cantonese population in Hong Kong and began to be manifest at all cultural levels. The continuous negotiation of contact and conflict between the imported and the inherited, local and Western, became the quotidian reality of Hong Kong. The myriad forms that such negotiation took not only left indelible marks on the physical landscape but also generated the push toward a Hong Kong cultural identity in which entrepreneurial brinkmanship and flexibility, as much as a sense of in-betweenness and unbelonging, are writ large.

Ann Hui's education and training as a filmmaker show a distinctly Westernized orientation that is characteristic of the middle-class generation that came of age in the sixties. After completing her undergraduate and M.A. studies in English and comparative literature at the University of Hong Kong, she enrolled in the London Film School.[2] But right from the start of her cinematic career in 1979, her films attempted recurrently to distance, dislocate, and disrupt the corporate push toward economic success, Western lifestyles, and technology that characterizes Hong Kong's modernity. In configuring cinema as critical practice, Hui's optic frequently turns to the forms of inherited Chinese cultural life as they endure in Hong Kong, and to Chinese history framed by Hong Kong's location on the temporal and spatial edge of two empires. This "Chineseness," mediated by a Hong Kong vantage point, constitutes the counterdiscourse to modernity in Hui's films. But Hui's ethnic scenes and narratives are never merely celebratory, triumphalist, or nativist and retrogressive. In composing them, she shows the same hesitation and anxiety that characterize her doubtful reception of modernity.

Looking both toward the West and to Chinese traditions, Hui visualizes the complex transactions of modernity and countermodernity out of which Hong Kong's cultural identity develops its special features. She has a sharp eye for contest and conflict; in her narrative and visual thematics, she remembers the voices, scenes, rituals that are marginalized and suppressed, at times conjuring the phantasms of what modernity has interred. Her films make visible a critical social discourse that has to contest, often in unequal combat, with the corporate momentum toward a Westernized and technologized modernity under colonial patronage. Hui and her contemporaries of the Hong Kong New Wave cinema, Tsui Hark and Alex Cheung, whose films first appear in 1979, were not the first in Hong Kong filmmaking to think of cinema as a social medium.[3] What distinguished their films was an intense reflexiveness about forms of cultural identity that were recognizably local but subsumed by the dominant bourgeois imaginary. Hui's early films symptomatize the discontent of her generation with its nascent consciousness of a so-called Hong Kong identity hybridizing inherited Chinese and imported Western characteristics, but that also places itself against the glamorized spectacles of economic success and social advancement that dominate official and commercial media. In a public sphere heavily, if never overtly, regulated by colonial censorship laws, and in the absence of a civil society yet unformed, the New Wave cinema directors assumed the mantle of cultural workers chiseling and mining at the edges of Hong Kong's modernity, locating fissures where they existed and bringing them into public view.

Like her New Wave contemporaries, Hui began her career not in local film studios but in television. After returning to Hong Kong from London, she first worked for Television Broadcasts Limited (TVB) where she shot a few travel programs, then moved on to the government-funded Radio and Television Hong Kong (RTHK). In its conscious, if not overt, inculcation of civic values and the concept of a Hong Kong identity and community, RTHK really came into its own in the seventies. The three RTHK docudramas of the period—*Northern Star, Under the Lion Rock,* and *ICAC* (the acronym for the Independent Commission Against Corruption set up in 1974) put into circulation the images of Hong Kong's "progress" from a refugee haven to a distinctive social system in which both inherited Chinese values and modern institutional management work hand in hand under the guidance of colonial rule. Within the constraints of its institutional role, RTHK did try to present itself as critical and pluralistic and, as such, modeled itself on the BBC, against the Americanized TVB. Like the BBC, RTHK had always claimed autonomy from the government in its programming decisions and did not adopt an overtly propagandist agenda evident in other state-sponsored media in the region. In its attempts to constitute Hong Kong as what Benedict Anderson (1991) has called an "imagined" and "communicative" community, its cautious tolerance of criticism and dissent generated a quasi public sphere blurring the boundaries between government and civil society. In this respect, it departs from other state media in the region driven by unitary functions to the exclusions of difference (Dissanayake 1994: xii–xxi).

But while it offers the simulacrum of a diversified public sphere, RTHK has to operate within the government's censorship powers, which are wide-ranging in scope.[4] Ann Hui's own productions for RTHK were subject to censorship. *The Bridge*, in the series *Under the Lion Rock*, was nearly held back for its perceived criticism of the policy and bureaucracy of the Housing Authority, and two of the *ICAC* episodes she made in 1977 were actually banned because they supposedly attacked the police and civil servants. Hui had never explicitly connected her move from television to cinema with these experiences of censorship, but a cynicism about governmental and quasi-official institutions permeates her first film, *The Secret*, and works in tandem with its broader critique of colonial modernity. As a woman filmmaker, Hui quickly established herself as a pioneer in a profession monopolized by men; as a social critic, her films centralize and individualize women subjects in ways that the earlier Cantonese cinema had rarely attempted.

Drawing their inspiration from the aesthetics of Western avant-garde filmmaking, and their audience from a burgeoning young middle-class, Hui's films, like those of the New Wave cinema, broke decisively with the Cantonese-language films of the past. In the poverty and privation of the fifties and early sixties, realist Cantonese cinema was the main source of entertainment for the majority working-class population, while the more affluent preferred imported English-language or Mandarin films. There is no question that this cinema was replete with stereotypes of women, but in their representations of women's subordination they spoke to the realities of women incapacitated by a patriarchal culture of labor, and the complicity of Chinese patriarchy with colonial rule and economy.[5] During this period, studios with left-wing affiliations, while still technically conservative, also produced films that tried to critique women's victimization, and it is in these productions, rare though they may have been, that the emergence of women's countercultural agency was best visualized.[6] But in the aftermath of the 1967 riots, many of those who worked in the left-wing studios were either imprisoned or joined the commercial television stations, and the profession as a whole witnessed, as a constituent of Hong Kong's structural transformation, the defeat of an incipient socialist modernity.[7]

The tentative visualizations of socially progressive women figures in the left-wing cinema disappeared as the commercially productive but ideologically conservative media moved into public consciousness, fueling and communicating the dominant work ethic of early modern and capitalistic Hong Kong. During this period, women continued to receive less pay than men, and their dependent, subordinate, and at best supportive roles in family and workplace were taken for granted not only by men, but often by the women themselves. Veronica Pearson and Benjamin Leung (1995) have delineated the three mutually supporting reasons for women's low sociocultural status:

> Gender inequality in Hong Kong is intricately related to and sustained by several distinct features of the society: it is a predominantly Chinese society; it is a British colony; and it is a capitalist economy whose well-being has been heavily dependent on low labor costs enabling its exports to compete successfully in overseas markets. . . . These three dimensions interrelate in providing the context in which individual women in Hong Kong seek to play out the script of their lives, and in which they search for meaning to their experience. (4)

Patriarchal control underpinned and integrated inherited Chinese, colonial, and capitalistic cultures, circumscribing and defining individual woman subjects and their places in early modern Hong Kong. An emergent Hong Kong cultural identity that hybridized Chinese and Western cultural elements was unmarked by gender consciousness until the women's movement in Hong Kong took shape and gathered momentum in the eighties.[8]

The New Wave filmmakers were beneficiaries of early modern Hong Kong, which had produced a small, but growing, middle-class cinema-going public like themselves. As such, the social and critical discourse in the films of Hui and her New Wave contemporaries could not avoid inflection by the bourgeois paradigm itself. One of the strongest signs of this inflection in Hui's early films is the way in which women subjects continue to figure as subordinated to men or victims of patriarchal domination, or to define their identity exclusively by romance.[9] The complex interiority of these women subjects and their spectacular visuality coexist in uneasy conjunction with narratives that by and large rehearse their traditional discontents.

In her public statements, Hui has denied time and again that she is either political or interested in women's subjects and feminist issues.[10] Her earlier projects exemplify the gender blindness that underpins Robin Wood's claim, made two decades ago, that for the cinema director and critic "to 'live' historically need not entail commitment to a system or a cause; rather, it can involve being alive to the opposing pulls, the tensions, of one's world" (1977: 46). In these earlier films, Hui's preoccupation with the cultural contestation that underlines everyday or topical events, though often focalized by women protagonists, tends to neglect women and gender issues. This neglect can be seen as a sign of the incorporative power of capitalistic discourse in Hong Kong's early modernity: Hui's insightful mappings of the fissures of modernity fail to take into account the continued sociocultural inequalities that afflict women both at home and in the workplace, and that underpin industrial production and economic progress.

In Hui's more recent films, there is a very noticeable difference, and it can be said that these films have taken a distinct feminist turn. The focus on woman's history and agency in these recent films imbricates an urgent political self-recognition that complicates and transforms Hui's earlier critique of modernity. Through visual narratives of women's histories and subjective transformations, these films fracture the patriarchal determinations of old and also chart recognizable passages toward a horizon of the "modern" in which utopian ideals of equality, compassion, and sociality are never lost sight of.[11] In relocating women, Hui's more recent films also renew the inspiration of modernity when its achievements, at a critical historical moment in Hong Kong, seem to be particularly under threat from the resurgence of essentialistic ethnic rhetoric and ethnocultural orthodoxies. At moments of existential and ontological crisis, these women figures speak to the cultural and political instability that has afflicted Hong Kong in the passage to 1997. It is a significant aspect of these recent films that in narrating women's struggle toward becoming autonomous subjects, Hui invokes the past in order to mobilize its energies in the present; often, these energies are visualized as disruptive, and at times they develop fearful tyrannical power, but in mobilizing them the films also focus and refocus on the possible sources of cultural change and renewal within Chinese ethnic traditions and practices.

To substantiate the claims I have made, I will in the next section explore in detail four of Hui's films: the first, *The Secret* (1979); *Princess Fragrance* (1987) from the middle period; and the more recent *Song of Exile* (1990) and *Summer Snow* (1995). This detailed exploration is crucial in order not to simplify and reduce the films into transparent social records of changes in women's situation in Hong Kong during the past two decades. The films are not merely cinematic texts foregrounded by a larger contextual backdrop but are, in themselves, cultural documents that fuel the dynamics of Hong Kong culture as much as they draw on such dynamics for inspiration and energy. Mediatized and widely circulated, they have significant visibility and, in turn, make visible certain complex transactions of women in society, enabling them to enter into dialogue with other contemporaneous cultural narratives and discourses. In the nineties, the dominant tendency of studies on women and gender in Hong Kong, at least in sociological discourse, is linear and progressivist, moving from earlier moments when women's issues and the women's movement were hardly visible and received scant attention in the public sphere through the critical massing of women's groups to their current vigorous participation in both public sphere and civil society.[12] My selection and discussion of Hui's films, in the main, map onto this modernist narrative. But through detailed studies of the films, I also wish to show how Hui delineates the woman question in different locations, and how the changes in her artistic optic enact the falterings and disruptions of the modernist narrative.

The Secret, set in Hong Kong in 1970, is based on the murder of a couple whose defaced and mutilated bodies were found on a deserted hillside frequented by monkeys. In the sensationalized reports in the local press, there were hints of simian interference. Seizing on the topicality of the murder, Hui shoots the film as docudrama but focuses her narrative through the juxtaposition of two women figures, Yuan, the supposed murder victim, and Ming, her friend, who takes on the role of detective. Since the woman murdered is discovered wearing Yuan's clothes, both the police and her family assume that Yuan is killed together with her fiancé, Cheuk. Before long, Yuan's ghost starts to haunt the neighborhood; while others in the community are thoroughly unnerved by Yuan's ghost, Ming initiates an investigation that leads to the discovery that Yuan is still alive and in hiding. Ming uncovers Yuan's predicament as the third point of a triangulated relationship with Cheuk and another woman, a ballroom hostess, and her culpability in the murder that necessitates her feigned death and ghostly return. The last violent sequence in the film revisits the clearing in the wood where Ming has finally located Yuan, heavily pregnant with Cheuk's child. The film cuts from the present confrontation of the two women to flashbacks of the murder when the ballroom hostess, enraged by Cheuk's decision to abandon her for Yuan, pierces him with a long barbecue fork and is, in turn, struck repeatedly with a stone by Yuan. Yuan, by now completely unhinged by the murder and her fugitive existence, turns on Ming. Only through the timely intervention of an old woman who lives near the crime scene is Ming saved and Yuan able to give birth to her child before her own exhausted death.

Yuan is figured as the traditional Chinese woman, suffering, silenced, the victim of patriarchal sexuality, while Ming seems to embody her modern antithesis, active and self-determined. Through this superficial juxtaposition, the film excavates the subterranean dynamic of modernity and countermodernity, and the way in which the interlocking of the two frames women's subjectivities.

Yuan's spectral return, which provides the film with some of its most gothic and visually spectacular sequences, is linked with scenes of the necromantic rituals of her blind grandmother. Immobilized within a room, restrictive and claustrophobic in its gloominess, the old woman strikes a figure of maternal loss and desolation whose only recourse to action is through an atavistic spiritualism. But the film also suggests, through the reaction of the other characters in the neighborhood, that the old woman's necromancy has invoked Yuan's return, and the first hints of Yuan's haunting of her home community come through the old woman's report that she has felt her granddaughter's presence in the room. Through Yuan and her grandmother, Hui visualizes a specific bond between women that fuses the ties of blood with their inherited roles as bearers of a Chinese ethnic primitivism that is marginalized, repressed, and rendered invisible by the city's modernity, but that continues to structure the life of women, of the old, and the small backwater community in which they live. As Yuan's alter ego, Ming seems to have moved away, at least partially, from this community of women and the suburban space it occupies, and in her investigation she operates in the quotidian and apparently transparent spaces of modern institutions and discourses—hospitals and forensic and police procedures. Unlike the female detectives of earlier Cantonese cinema, who are frequently endowed with superhuman cognition and martial expertise, Ming appears in the mode of the "Western" detective, acting within the bounds of human and everyday possibilities, motivated by curiosity but remaining detached and objective even as she is drawn deeper and deeper into the mystery of her friend's death.

The recurrent site of narrative action is composed in frames of a group of prewar buildings in an older quarter where both Yuan and Ming live. "Home," as the film signifies, is the in-between cultural space on the fringes of urban modernity where primordial significations continue to circulate. Their presence is invoked in ritual, spectralized as haunting, and symptomatized in the inhabitants' fearful reaction to Yuan's ghostly revenance. As the film's visualization of Hong Kong, this home space clearly departs from the celebratory images of the colony thrust into public consciousness by the official media[13] and the predominantly glossy exteriors of the commercial cinema. In another spatial configuration in the film's narrative, this home community is intermediate between two alternative visual locations: the clearing in the wood where the bodies were found, which in the film's flashbacks figures as the primitive space of ritualistic sacrifice, and the hospital and police station, which signify modern institutional spaces. Yuan's self-consuming desire for Cheuk and her submission to his chauvinistic fantasy lead to her communal exile, and the ultimate alienation of being an outcast in the land of the dead. Ming's move away to the modern institutional spaces shown in the film to be controlled mainly by men is highly circumscribed by their disinterest, if not outright hostility. The women's dislocations imply the gradual fragmentation of the home space, and by further implication, of a traditional Hong Kong within the orbit of residual, and decadent, Chinese ethnic archaisms. But the film also eschews the bright-light images of modern urbanization, and as woman's space, and home space, the film's spatiality is tinged overall with a gloomy indeterminacy that signals woman's social disaffiliation and subliminal derangement as subjects, and a Hong Kong in its passage through an ambivalent modernity.

In the final sequence of the film, Ming is saved, not through her own actions, but by the intervention of an old woman who lives in an isolated shack nearby. The appearance of this old woman has been prepared for in earlier scenes where she hysterically protests against the arrest of her idiot son, whom the police originally mistake for the murderer. Her hysteria, which contrasts with the silent isolation of Yuan's grandmother, speaks of an alternative and quasi-anarchic maternalism that the film projects as awesome and transgressive. If Yuan and Ming are co-opted, in their different ways, into the film's ambivalent modernity, the two maternal figures present women subjects whose resistance to the "modern" has cast them into extreme marginality. Both maternal figures appear to have privileged access to primitive forces that endure at the very edges of the city, but that erupt periodically to contest their own disappearance. Together with her idiot son, the second woman lives outside of the local community, in a ramshackle dwelling near the wood without any modern conveniences. The idiot is first characterized by simian manners and gestures, and then shown dressed fantastically in the clothes of ancient village women long discarded by Ming and Yuan. In their appearance, the way they live, and the perception of them as "mad" by the local community, the mother and son embody and gather, in one direct thrust, the film's countercultural discourse. The old woman's hysteria and the idiot's simian contortions disrupt the rational logic of Ming's investigations and haunt the main narrative as another ineffable reminder of the film's own chthonic impulse. In the suspicion of the idiot as murderer, and his mother's violent outbursts, the film insinuates the alignment of this impulse with violence. Ultimately, however, this alignment is shown to be the mistaken prejudice of those who are framed by rationality and modernity as "normative": the police are wrong about the idiot, and even Ming herself, for all she manages to discover through her quotidian investigation, could not have escaped death without the intervention of the idiot's mother. Cheuk's masculine objectification of Yuan, and the patriarchal insidiousness of institutional procedures that underpin the narrative of the murder and its investigation, are counteracted, challenged, and disrupted by the film's visualizations of maternity and its discontents.

But it is precisely the film's alignment of maternity with both Chinese cultural primitivism and extreme social marginality that is dark and troubling. As a critique of the repressions of patriarchy and modernity, this alignment develops its own argumentative force and spectacular visuality, and the film contemplates the place of women amid the dissolution of ancestral structures with an aesthetic thoughtfulness previously unseen in Cantonese cinema. But as a projection of woman's resistance, poised at the beginning of Hong Kong's recent modernity, it is, even for its own time, regressive and self-consuming. *The Secret* lays down the contours of Hui's initial filmic ambivalence about women's position and subjectivity in which the exploration of agency is heavily circumscribed by a continued investment in what inherited strictures will both allow and afford, and increasingly reincorporated into an ethnocultural determinism that is, by history and definition, patriarchal in its social exemplifications. As such, her films tread the narrow path between the critique and reinvention of tradition and estrange tradition even at the same time as affirming its continued power to structure, co-opt, and exclude women's subjects. Despite the experimental and auteurish treatment of her films, and their eschewing of the melodramatic and stereotypical narratives about women in earlier Cantonese cinema, they articulate a pragmatic realism in the imagination of the possibilities and, always, the limitations of change and newness. This in itself not only typifies an ideological scrupulousness in her own films but forecasts the highly *negotiated* discourses on Hong Kong cultural identity in the eighties as 1997 begins to cast a giant shadow.

Hui's films of the middle period, which include *Love in a Fallen City*, *Romance of Book and Sword*, and its sequel *Princess Fragrance*, move away from a Hong Kong setting to the broader contours of recent Chinese history in continued attempts to locate transitional moments when the modern impacts, complicates, and dislocates the binding structures of tradition. *Love in a Fallen City* begins in Shanghai in the 1930s and moves to colonial Hong Kong—two cities that, albeit differently, stood at the vanguard of China's experience of Western modernity at the time. Based on a novel by Eileen Chang Ai-ling, *Love* retrieves, remembers, and memorializes the checkered history of modernity as it struggles to emerge on China's geographical and cultural frontiers. *Romance* and *Princess* move further back in time to narrate the moment when the Manchus, under the Qianlong emperor, conclusively overwhelmed the political resistance of the remnants of the preceding Ming dynasty and their allies, the Huei ethnic minority. In narrating the defeat of resistance, *Princess* underlines the recent politics of Chinese history as the triumphal history of empire. The fact that the Manchus were "foreigners," as opposed to the Ming loyalists who were ethnically Han Chinese, carries the resonances of contact and conflict between Chinese and other ethnocultures that are central to Hui's thematics. But more significantly, the films problematize resistance in the context of an asymmetrical relation between dynastic power, with the organization and technology it commands, and marginalized communities whose strengths and resources are minimal by comparison.

Through their complex thematics, these films develop an optic on Hong Kong's contemporary situation in the mideighties. Ever since the signing of the Sino-British Joint Declaration in 1984, which guaranteed no change in Hong Kong's way of life for fifty years after 1997, debates on Hong Kong's cultural and political identity, suppressed by corporate identification with capitalistic enterprise and restrictive colonial laws on freedom of expression since the sixties, returned with a vengeance.[14] Hui's films constitute Hong Kong cinema's thoughtful interventions in this public sphere debate, and her paradigms of cultural destabilization take on a recognizable political inflection. In *Princess*, for instance, the antiquated structures of belief first narrated in *The Secret* are mapped onto the struggle of the minority Huei community, allied with the Ming dynasty remnants, against the Qing imperial juggernaut. The antiquated and the residual: the alignment of these two discourses constitutes that fragile space of cultural and political resistance, while Qing imperial "modernity" is projected as ruthlessly masculinist and politically and militarily brutal. In the defeat of the former, the film develops allegorical inferences about Hong Kong's contemporary situation and is full of foreboding about Hong Kong's reincorporation into Chinese sovereignty after 1997.

At the same time, these films rehearse, in separate but related ways, the Chinese woman's involuntary passage between multiple subjectivities and "homes"—natal, ethnic, patriarchal—and how she plots a trajectory of her own self-fulfillment amid great adversity. These films configure a number of vantage points on women's predicament in the tortuous passages of Chinese modernity: unconscious derangement by the split in patriarchal culture between a nascent modernity and traditional authoritarianism, or their mutual reinforcement, which strains to breaking point women's psyche under patriarchal bondage; a conscious self-alienation, and its corollary, an alienated self-consciousness that produces a failure not only of corporate identification but also of community with other women. Hui's women characters, in their subjective and social estrangement, figure as outposts marking but also displaced on the edges of modernity at different times and places in China's recent history. Some of them embody what Julia Kristeva, in another but related discourse on the stranger and estrangement, calls "an agonizing struggle between what no longer is and what will never be": others try to live "neither before nor now but beyond . . . bent with a passion that, although tenacious, will remain forever unsatisfied" (1991: 10). Hui's vantage points on women's identity, past and present, exemplify the complicated transactions of this difference grounded on Hong Kong's own decade of uncertainty in the 1980s.

While both *Romance* and *Princess* are relentlessly bleak in staging the defeat of woman's perspective on history and women's history, it is in *Princess* that Hui focalizes the contests between men and women, empire and periphery, and empire and its others, through the woman subject. The titular heroine of *Princess* is Hasili, the second daughter of the chief of the Huei minority ethnic community under threat of conquest and genocide from Qing imperialism. In the original novel by Louis Cha (*Jinrong*) on which the film is based, Hasili is a semimythical figure of ethereal beauty, important but not central. Another crucial departure from the original novel is the insertion in the film of the Myth of Mamier, whose grip on the imagination of the Huei, and especially of the princess, signifies the film's historical determinism. *Princess* begins with the meeting between Hasili and Chen Jialuo, the hero of Cha's novel and the leader of the Red Flower Brotherhood, the band of Ming loyalists, predominantly male, who are rebelling against Manchu rule and whose exploits are the focus of the prequel, *Romance*.

In the opening sequences of *Princess*, Chen is on his way to the desert homeland of the Huei to inform them of an imminent Qing attack; at the edge of the oasis where Chen bends down to drink, he catches his first and fascinated glimpse of Hasili. Their romance unfolds as Hasili leads Chen to her tribal camp through the Huei homeland composed as an arcadian space where the natural and the pastoral are integrated, water is the enduring source and symbol of an ancient way of life, men and women have their own roles that foster gendered initiatives but are also compatible, and young women have autonomy in choosing their male partners. This visual geography of utopia, detailed and consummate, is unsurpassed in any of Hui's movies; the rituals of spiritualism that in *The Secret* symbolize a suppressed and atavistic cultural heritage are replaced by the verdant and life-enhancing images of the Huei homeland on the margins of the Qing empire. Utopianism, marginality, community: through the Huei, Hui maps the ground of minority resistance, and in the princess the contours of this resistance are embodied in a woman subject who, more than any other in Hui's films, articulates a political idealism justified in inherited beliefs. These beliefs are twofold, looking in one direction toward the Huei's Islamic faith and in another toward contemporary bonds of kinship. The threat of Qing conquest becomes the historical crisis when religious faith, faith in life and community survival as sacrosanct, and faith in romantic love coordinate as exigent pressures on Hasili, establishing at once her inalienable subjectivity, and its ultimate proof in self-sacrifice.

It is the paradox of selfhood and sacrifice, and selfhood *in* sacrifice, that exemplifies the dilemmas of estrangement outlined by Kristeva. In her historical situation, Hasili is poised on the cusp of "what no longer is"— that is to say, a life justified in inherited tradition unsustainable under the encroachments of empire—and "what will never be," or the realization, no matter how partial, of political and romantic utopianism, in an autonomous peripheral space. Her narrative in the film is a movement from the now to the "beyond," to borrow Kristeva's terms again, a narrative of passion unfulfilled and inimical to fulfillment within her historical circumstances. As the Qing forces mobilize on the borders of the Huei homeland, Hasili, accompanied by Chen, volunteers as emissary conveying the Huei message of defiance to the Qing commander, and before they leave she confesses her love to Chen and her readiness to lay down her life for her people. This will-to-act in both private and public spheres makes Chen's indecision in the military campaign look unheroic, and his self-control in love prudish. The asymmetry between the artless princess with her loyal band of tribesmen and the cruelty of the Manchu commander pitches primordialized innocence and community against a barbaric primitivism made even more savage because of its access to technology. The advantage of the former is revealed in an exemplary display, when the Huei manage to drive back the Qing attack and win moral and poetic justice, in the first half of the film.

In the second half, the film attempts to visualize and communicate an aura of Hasili's greatness, but it is also here that its failure is most observable. This failure was misconstrued by some early reviewers as the result of an unsuitable choice of actress, but it actually raises far more complex issues. The aura of the princess should derive fullness from the sequence right at the heart of the film when she and Chen lose their way in a desert storm, until they eventually stumble on the ruins of the lost city where

Mamier, the mythical Huei heroine, was once captive. In the ruins, the princess and Chen read the inscription on a stone tablet and reconstruct Mamier's tragedy in the present. Mamier's voice is heard narrating her capture, rape, and impregnation by a tyrant, her forced separation from her Huei lover, and how Huei resistance against the tyrant ended in defeat and her own suicide. As she narrates, the scenes of her tragedy are enacted, but the sequence is hurried, histrionic, and garishly colored, completely at odds with the aversion to melodrama habitual in Hui's films, and the significant thematic import it is supposed to carry in *Princess*. In trying to be mythical and dream-like, the sequence only manages to achieve a kind of comic-book slow-motion effect. The cuts to the princess are equally hurried, reducing her and her companion to whispering, prying, voyeurs of the ancient revelation, rather than awestruck visitants initiated into an ancient communal myth of which they are also supposedly the latest inheritors. The symbolic significations of the sequence—as the prophecy of the princess's and the Huei's tragic fate, and mythical structuration of history—are undermined by the inadequate visual texture and rhetoric, and this seriously diminishes the princess's tragic grandeur that might counterpoint the film's portrait of Qing triumphalism.[15]

In their second imperial campaign, Qing forces destroy the Huei community, and the princess is captured and brought to the imperial capital, where she at first resists the lecherous designs of the emperor Qianlong. Persuaded by Chen to put community before self, Hasili acquiesces but at the purification ceremony in the mosque before her marriage to Qianlong, she stabs herself. In this act, she reenacts Mamier's suicide as ritual in the present and fulfills an ancient myth as prophecy. Huei cultural myth and narrative point toward a determinism structuring the community's history and woman's subjectivity and disable both communal resistance and woman's agency. The princess appears as the doomed challenger of the fatal order of things, the woman in love, the shaman who crosses the ethnic spaces of Huei and Qing, and temporal boundaries between the historical present and mythical past, and is destroyed by her passage. Her suicide, an act to preserve her purity in the first instance, enacts the extinction of Huei heritage and imperial history's bloody purification of its Others. In the final scenes of slaughter, the leaders of the Red Flower Brotherhood are outmaneuvered by Qianlong and fall one after the other in a massacre. Only Chen is left unhurt; the last dramatic confrontation shows him throwing away his sword with the parting words to Qianlong that to kill him would only mean a worse emperor will follow. In this self-recognition of defeat, marginality and minority resistance confirm the irresistible triumph of the juggernaut of empire. It is a bleak diagnosis. Resistance is weak, flawed, and pointless; modernity is hateful, and the only thing to be said for it is that it might be even worse.

With *Princess*, Ann Hui seems to have exhausted the politicized cinematics of the middle period. Perhaps it would be more accurate to say that the films of this period exemplify an aestheticized politics,[16] in that they seek to construe the problematic of Hong Kong's identity under Chinese rule while obfuscating the relations between the cinematic sign and its cultural and political referents. *Princess* relocates the themes of Hong Kong identity in a distant geography and imperial history, and in repeatedly denying an interest in politics, Hui treads a canny middle path between cinema's sociopolitical significations and its aesthetics. As cinema, *Princess*, as we have seen, is very uneven work; its bleak optic on Chinese history as history of empire and the closures it imposes on resistance and woman's agency suggest a cul-de-sac vision in the long road ahead to 1997 and beyond, and strike a particularly hesitant note in the local discourse, emerging in the mideighties, on Hong Kong's identity as difference from both traditional and mainland China, and from the West.

The three more recent films, *Starry Is the Night, Song of Exile,* and *Summer Snow,* return to Hong Kong locations and focus, in a conscious contemplation, on woman in Hong Kong history of the decade before 1997. This does not mean a turning away from Chinese cultural identity in Hong Kong's modernity, or from the remapping of primordial meanings that is the burden of *The Secret* and *Princess*. But the routes of cultural memory take a more distinctive woman-centered and feminist turn in these three recent films as they cross, once again, the boundaries between Hong Kong and China, and the terrain of individual and community narratives.[17] *Starry Is the Night* concludes Hui's imagination of women in love, and romance as the determinant of woman's subjectivity is marginalized in the other two films. Gender relations continue to be important, but the space vacated by the drama of romantic love is taken up with explorations of filial and kinship bonds, and by forms of love between men and women that speak to a more inclusive sociality. The films visualize women's subjectivity through a plurality of sociocultural mediations, and in so doing they open up an engagement with recent Hong Kong and its changing identities that is more direct than in her previous films. Politics, understood as the contestation of power in the public domain, also recedes as a narrative dynamic, and woman's empowerment takes place across a number of sites and discourses, in the home and workplace, both traditional and modern.

What remains consistent with the earlier films and is further augmented is the force of memory and history: both *Song of Exile* and *Summer Snow* show women confronting the paradoxes of memory, their own and those of other characters who have the most impact on their efforts at self-determination. Through the thematics of individual memory, Hui implicitly narrates the collective memory of Hong Kong's recent modernity against the push of the rhetoric of oblivion, which seeks to cast recent constructions of Hong Kong identity as inauthentic and colonialist.[18] In the nascent nationalistic discourse of Hong Kong's return to the "Motherland," the narratives of the past three decades of Hong Kong's modernizing experience and the socio-cultural bonds they generate are exiled and replaced with narratives that stress ethnic, cultural, and political continuities between Hong Kong and the Mainland. The emergence of a nationalist discourse of "return" speaks of assimilation rather than difference, of centristic reincorporation rather than the accommodated autonomy of "one country, two systems."

Song of Exile implicitly confronts this discourse with an alternative narrative of return and homeland.[19] It also takes up the earlier themes of woman's struggle against male-centered histories framed by romance as in *Starry Is the Night* or epical conflicts of power as in *Princess*. Memory is the site of this struggle, and *Song of Exile* maps the tortuous, circuitous, and above all, ex-centric routes that this struggle takes as the woman protagonist, Hueyin, tries to negotiate her own past with those of her parents and through them, with the historical conflict between China and Japan in the twentieth century. The film begins with Hueyin's last days as a student in London when she is summoned back to Hong Kong by her sister's marriage, thus missing an interview for a job at the BBC. This is the first of the film's many returns; each is framed by the unfolding history of Hueyin's family, and her own changing self-identification within it, especially as it relates to the bond between her and her mother. Beginning with the narrative of Hueyin, the film extends its reach to the story, hitherto unarticulated within the family, of her mother's history, and the two women's narratives are folded into one another to become the complex sign of Hui's reconstruction of contemporary Chinese history from women's vantage points.

On her return to Hong Kong, the long-standing conflict between Hueyin and her mother is quickly resumed, and the film unravels the complicated history of this conflict through flashback sequences of the family's life in Macao during the Second World War. In these flashbacks, the young Hueyin appears as the unwitting accomplice in her mother's marginalization by her in-laws. The mother is figured as silent, cold, and detached in contrast to the grandparents' loving care, and the child turns away from the mother, refusing to join her and her father when they leave Macao for Hong Kong. Even when Hueyin finally rejoins her parents, the alienation continues, and as her father dies, and her younger sister marries and emigrates to Canada, mother and daughter are left to confront each other and their conjoined but also conflictual past within a "home" space emptied of natural and familial bonds. The film shows the difficult process of their reaffiliation, and it begins when Hueyin first discovers the Japanese nationality of her mother. As she accompanies her mother on her return to Japan after three decades of exile, Hueyin's disjointed memory of affliction is reconnected in a new narrative that bonds the two of them in a common history. Most of the second half of the film is shot in Japan where Hueyin, unable to speak Japanese, watches her mother reenacting the communal affiliations of her youth; marginalized and excluded, she begins to understand her mother's early silence and internal exile in the marital home and from the Chinese community. The immobilizing ties of childhood and youth inscribed in her mother's behavior toward her brother and friends in Japan impel Hueyin to assert her difference; she begins to revalue the narrative of their mutual alienation and moves to overcome the physical and emotional barriers between them. In this part of the film, the mother's narrative takes over in flashback sequences, her distraught reunion with her kinsfolk and ex-lover, and oral accounts of her meeting with Hueyin's father in China during the last days of the Japanese occupation in the forties. Hueyin perceives that change is her prerogative; her mother is too old and entrenched in her parental dignity to make the moves of reconciliation.

In the final scenes, mother and daughter return to Hong Kong where Hueyin, stabilized in a reconstituted narrative of affiliation, finds her own place in a career as a producer of news programs for a local TV station. The exile has returned to her first home—Hong Kong in the seventies— but this Hong Kong is substantially different from that visualized in *The Secret*. Through news flashes edited by Hueyin of local protests against corruption that led to the establishment of the Independent Commission Against Corruption, the sequences on Hong Kong in *Song of Exile* summarize its early modernity as a period of nascent social consciousness and activism toward reform and change.[20] This strong sense of place is augmented by Hueyin's visit to her ailing grandparents, who have moved back to China shortly after 1949. While both women's early subjectivity is scripted by their hybridized Chinese and Japanese histories and the conflict between the two, it is through Hueyin, the young Hong Kong woman, that the film bears witness to an autonomous desire toward change and self-invention, and a commitment to finding her own place in a changing

Hong Kong community. In mapping this dynamic of individual change onto Hong Kong's early modernity, *Song of Exile* inscribes both the woman and the community's liberation from history as inherited parental and nationalistic determinations. Of all Ann Hui's films, it strikes the most positive note about the will-to-change, and woman's agency in putting change in place, in a reaffirmation of the enduring bonds of family and community.

Summer Snow accentuates the historical consciousness that Hui has displayed and explored in all her films, and its domestication in the individual family (fig. 1). But unlike *Song of Exile, Summer Snow* refocalizes the contest between narratives of woman's subjectivity through a gendered relationship that pits an ordinary, lower-middle-class working woman and housewife against her father-in-law. At the same time, *Summer Snow* is located in Hong Kong and the quotidian realities of life and hardship of the contemporary Hong Kong woman in situ. What is equally significant and timely is that the film implicitly argues for the endurance in Hong Kong of inherited and quotidian Chinese cultural practices, especially as they relate to women, that have not been erased by colonial history, but also imagines their renewal in the contemporary moment.

Unlike Hueyin, the woman protagonist of *Summer Snow*, Mrs. Suen, is neither young nor Western-educated, but she lives the multiple and often conflictual lives of women under the sign of modernity. She is a housewife burdened not only by domestic chores and the task of looking after her father-in-law, husband, and teenage son, but also by her work in a small business importing toiletry items from mainland China. In the central conflict between her and her father-in-law, the patriarch of the family, *Summer Snow* interweaves gendered narratives of memory and visualizes their contest. She endures the overt dislike of her father-in-law, who at the beginning of the film appears as a detestable authoritarian demanding her total submission and goes out of his way to humiliate her. In these early moments, Suen is the abject, "colonized" by patriarchal tyranny, and her abjection intensifies when her mother-in-law, her only source of support in the family, dies suddenly.[21] Most of the film narrates in meticulous and often humorous detail Suen's slow and hesitant transformation from abjection. In this passage, she maintains her traditional places as mother, wife, daughter-in-law but also renews them in ways that signal the film's perception of cultural change as it takes place within individual families, and how it entails a more equal partnership between woman and man, wife and husband, mother and son.

After his wife's death, the patriarch is diagnosed as suffering from Alzheimer's disease, and the family, especially Suen, exhausts itself trying to

Figure 1. Director Ann Hui (right) and actress Josephine Siao (who plays Mrs. Suen) on the set for the Hong Kong film Summer Snow.

protect him from his own life-threatening behavior. The patriarch's mental confusion is symptomatized by short-term memory loss so that he fails to recognize his children and grandchild, and his obsessive reenactments of his earlier career as a fighter pilot in the nationalist airforce battling the Japanese in the Second World War. His sense of self, and the patriarchal narrative of history he embodies, contracts into a truncated narrative of epical heroism. Such diminishment is at first difficult for Suen to resist, for only in becoming part of his narrative—and playing along with his memory fantasies—can Suen access his interiority and contain the disruptiveness of his behavior. This entails the displacement of the ongoing narratives of her own subjectivity as wife, mother, and worker and leads to sudden disruptions within family life. She finds herself in conflict with husband and son and marginalized by a younger, female competitor in the office, a glamorous new immigrant from mainland China. One by one, her support systems fail: husband and son become frustrated and unhelpful, and the day-care center that initially accommodates the patriarch rejects him because of his vagrant tendencies.

The film visualizes Suen's predicament and exhaustion but focuses above all on her strength under duress, amplifying an ordinary woman's fortitude with vignettes of other women who strive, despite their straitened circumstances and privation, to care for men who are old and sick in their own families and the community. In its consistent attention to women's patience and endurance, the film interweaves and makes visible a narrative of their heroism that counteracts, displaces, but also works in tandem with the patriarch's epical memory. In this respect, *Summer Snow* is Ann Hui's most detailed and accomplished project to date in retrieving and liberating Chinese women's history from its patriarchal determinations and her own previous defeatist optic. At the same time, it reconciles, through the growing imaginative and emotional empathy between daughter and father-in-law, the conflict of gendered histories and posits this reconciliation as the source of the family's rapprochement and renewal. The apparently limited scope of the domestic narrative belies the complex ambition of *Summer Snow*: it relocates history as women's history and visualizes cultural regeneration predicated on the intimate revolutions in women's place within individual families.

In the office subplot, the young immigrant contests Suen's indispensable assistance to the male boss. Again the contest is focalized by memory; Suen is used to keeping an inventory of the company's stock, clients' orders, and dates of delivery in the private storehouse of her memory. Against this, the younger woman pushes for computerization and for a time wins the boss's confidence with her glamorous appearance and technological expertise. Through the two women, the film reverses the oppositions between Hong Kong and mainland subjects and aligns the former with the contemporary renewal of traditional practices while embodying in the latter the frenzied rush toward a technologized modernity. When the computer breaks down, the business operation has to rely once more on Suen's prodigious memory. In this narrative, the film's skepticism about technology's necessary displacement of inherited forms of memory pushes into the contemporary moment Hui's earlier critiques of Hong Kong's bourgeois modernity. *Summer Snow* revisits most of the preoccupations that I have examined in the earlier films. Now, a modernity that is entrepreneurial and technology-led is seen as subject to amnesia, as disabling in its way as the pathology of a traditionalism that is ghostly—like the patriarch, a captive of the dead past. *Summer Snow* enacts a critique of both; in it and in the person of a family woman and clerk in a toiletries company, Hong Kong's modernity finds its latest and not unworthy embodiment.

In *The Secret* and *Princess Fragrance*, Hui maps the intersecting contours of patriarchy and modernity as the grid within which women are both confined and struggle to stake claims on their own subjectivity. These women are figured as bearers of veridical details or ethical ideals, but defeated as social agents, and as such, situated in uneasy and anxious relationship with the material world, and in extreme instances, perpetual and irreversible exile from it. It is a paradox of these early films that the centrality of the women figures as spectacle points insistently to a vantage point that sees their past and present decentering from society and culture.

In her more recent films, Hui seems to have turned away from the broad canvases of politics and society to the milieu of family and home, and with this there is a perceptible shift in her stance on women as agents of change. In their traditional places as daughters or daughters-in-law, these women seek self-transformation and enable the reparation of disrupted kinship and social bonds. But despite its ostensible focus on individual and familial renewal, this feminist turn has broader social implications, for it posits the dislodging of women from traditional positions of dependency within the family as the basis for their social empowerment and agency. Hueyin's liberation from her mother's memory is coterminous with their reaffiliation, and the narrative sequencing of the film proposes that this reinvigorated bond between the two generations of women becomes the ground of Hueyin's engagement with a reformist agenda through her work as a journalist. From a different generational perspective, *Summer Snow* reconfigures Mrs. Suen as the cohesive force of family renewal, and her return to a position of centrality in the workplace. While the films of other nineties' directors like Wong Kar-wai celebrate postmodernist dislocations and symptomatize urban decadence and transitional hysteria, Hui's recent films, like *Song of Exile* and *Summer Snow*, have become increasingly realist in their optic on women's continuous struggle to unsettle and disrupt the orthodoxies that prescribe relations within the Chinese family as an inherited social institution, and to imagine and enact its restructuration. Through the narratives of the two women, young and middle-aged, from the middle and lower-middle classes, the films point toward the emergent formation of Hong Kong civil society from the bedrock of individual and familial changes wrought by women in different locations, and the collective strength of their aggregation. For all her narrative peregrinations, Ann Hui's films have in the main been configured as social critiques and utopian projects. Her future cinematic passage, post-1997, into the ambivalent intersections of postmodernity and ethnic and nationalistic corporatism, will certainly be worth waiting for.

NOTES
I am grateful to the following for their help in enabling the writing of this essay: Terry Boyce, Chris Hutton, Douglas Kerr, Li Cheuk-to, Shirley Lim, Jimmy Ngai, Nicola Nightingale, Shu Kei, Elizabeth Sinn, and Helen Siu. Special thanks to

Elaine Yee Lin Ho

Estella Tong for sourcing some of the films, and to Ann Hui for answering my questions.

1 I have periodized Hui's films in the following order: the early period includes *The Secret* (1979), *The Spooky Bunch* (1980), *The Story of Woo Viet* (1981), and *Boat People* (1982). *Love in a Fallen City* (1984), *Romance of Book and Sword*, and its sequel, *Princess Fragrance* (1987) are considered as films of the middle period, while the more recent films include *Starry Is the Night* (1988), *Song of Exile* (1990), *My American Grandson* (1991), *The Zodiac Killers* (1991), *Summer Snow* (1995), and *Ah Kam* (1996). This essay will focus on films in which women play significant roles and leave out those in which they are insignificant or simply act out cinematic, gender, and cultural stereotypes. The latter include the women characters in *The Story of Woo Viet* and *Boat People*, two films that are otherwise of considerable interest in their handling of the topical issue of the exodus of refugees from Vietnam in the early eighties and questions of diasporal Chinese identities. Hui's penchant for the topical can degenerate into purely market concerns as in *Zodiac Killers* and *My American Grandson*, two recent films with insignificant women characters. In her response to my comment that these two are her most "commercialized" films, Hui agrees: "Yes. [They] were made not really with the market in mind, but I listened more to my boss." *Ah Kam*, her latest film, once again displays this tendency. It is ironical that while a number of her more "artistic" films did not earn enough money at the box office to please their investors, the films shot to appease the financiers or the market fared no better.

2 It is interesting to note that Hui's master's thesis (1972) was on the novels and films of Alain Robbe-Grillet. She explored Robbe-Grillet's "main concern—a denial of all 'significance' or pre-established 'values,'" and showed special interest in the anti-traditional devices he employed in different "phases" of his work (Hui 1972: i). The conscious search for alternative spaces and identities, and experiments with montage and temporal dislocations in her cinematic narratives, especially in the early films, resonate with Hui's graduate academic work.

3 For preliminary studies of the Hong Kong New Wave and its cinematic context, see Kung and Zhang 1984, Ma 1988, and Lui 1988. At the moment, there is no extended work in English on the subject.

4 Through the Television and Films Authority, and latterly, the Television and Entertainment Licensing Authority (TELA), the government vets all mediatized productions. Television programs are regulated by powers enshrined in the *Television (Standards of Programmes) Regulations* (Hong Kong Government 1964). Paragraph 4 of the subsidiary legislation, for example, states that "Programmes broadcast by a licensee shall exclude material which is likely (a) to offend against good taste or decency; (b) to mislead or alarm; (c) to encourage or to incite to crime, civil disorder or civil disobedience; (d) to discredit or bring into disrespect the law or social institutions including any religion; and (e) to serve the interest of any foreign political party." On a number of occasions, the government has invoked these laws to prevent the shooting or showing of films that are perceived to be potentially destabilizing locally or that might lead to trouble with China.

5 As Janet Salaff observes, while women's labor had been central to "an export-dependent economy, beginning with the labor-intensive textiles and garment machining in the 1950s," their participation in the workforce continued to be seen as transient and superfluous, subject to the fluctuations of external demand for locally

made goods, and unprotected by any governmental legislation against their employers' exploitation through enforced redundancy when there was a downturn in trade (1981: 20). Their wages were also kept low, "and young women are assumed by management and the Department of Labor to be indifferent to long-term job security" (20). That is to say, despite their crucial presence in the industrial and manufacturing sectors, women were still largely identified by their places within Chinese family, which was and continued to be patriarchal in its structure. The Hong Kong Council of Women, set up in 1947, was largely an expatriate, upper-middle- and middle-class group whose charity work was confined to members of their own class. They would not have been part of the audience of the indigenous Cantonese cinema.

6 See, for example, *Love and Passion* (1964) produced by the left-wing studio Chi Luen, which targets the destructive impact of capitalistic modernity on familial bonds and woman's intellectual and social advancement. The woman protagonist is a Western-educated architect who contests patriarchal and colonial authority and attains a measure of self-sovereignty through suffering and subterfuge. In another popular genre—that of martial arts films—the gothic mood and charismatic counter-traditionalism of the heroine in *Green-Eyed Demoness* (1967) is particularly interesting. The eponymous demoness has prodigious martial arts skills and is positioned as the cultural outsider, battling against three villains figured as the standard-bearers of Chinese cultural orthodoxies and patriarchal authority: a Confucian scholar, a Buddhist monk, and a Taoist priest. In separate modern and traditional settings, the two films narrate woman's fulfillment through social and cultural transgression, and insofar as the women protagonists emerge triumphant, they provide unusual counterblasts to the conformist visual thematics of most of the Cantonese films of the time, which place a premium on male social agency and masculine satisfaction in gender relationships. Informative studies on the Cantonese films of the earlier period include Lai 1982; Lin 1982; Law 1984; Du 1986; Ma 1988; and Chan and Law 1996.

7 In 1967, riots inspired by anticolonial sentiment and the ideology and rhetoric of the Cultural Revolution exploded into violence on the streets of Hong Kong. After the riots, in its heightened anxiety about civil disorder and social discontent, the government took the initiative in fashioning an environment where some form of local and communal identity could be nurtured without, however, the need to open legal channels for public debate on or popular participation in the political process (Turner 1995). In this executive-led project, Hong Kong belatedly exemplifies, despite its colonial situation, what Jürgen Habermas observes of Western modernity: "The modern state, that is the tandem of bureaucracy and capitalism, has turned out to be the most effective vehicle for accelerating social modernization" (1996: 282). The sixties' riots mark a watershed in many aspects of Hong Kong's passage to modernity, not least for the cinema. For a study of Chi Luen and the work of other studios with left-wing sympathies, see Yu 1982, Fonoroff 1988, and Lai 1982.

8 See *The Other Half of the Sky* (1992), and other annual reports from 1985 of the Association for the Advancement of Feminism in Hong Kong; Choi 1993; Wu 1995; and the essays in Pearson and Leung 1995.

9 Besides Hui's *The Secret*, the two other classics of the New Wave in 1979, Tsui Hark's

The Butterfly Murders and Alex Cheung's *Cops and Robbers*, are equally uninnovative in their imagination of women subjects.

10 In an interview in 1982, Ann Hui said, "I really do not understand politics. I don't know if it's too simple so I don't care to understand it, or it's too complicated, so I don't understand it" (Li 1982: 20, my translation). More recently, Hui has distanced herself and her films from the issue of 1997 when she was asked what she thought about using the medium of film to raise questions about the handover and Hong Kong's future: "The biggest problem is that this involves the whole of society, and you don't know where to begin. . . . My personal view is that without sufficient time, there is no way one can filter the issues, and so it's impossible to shoot a film. There has to be enough time for research; it takes patience. There is no need to rush into films about the question of 97" (Wei and Lao 1990: 17, my translation). Earlier, in 1988, on the subject of herself as a woman director, Hui said, "If you don't ask for social advantages as a woman, you don't get the disadvantages. . . . Women directors are not even an issue now [in Hong Kong]. You don't hear people saying 'Ah, there's an interesting woman director. Look what a woman can do'" (Lam 1991: 6). In answer to my questions as to whether she is especially interested in making films on women subjects, she has said, "No, I'm not," and adds, "I seldom reflect on my identity as a woman."

11 These films exemplify John Orr's contention, in speaking of the aesthetics of Western cinema, that "the reflexive nature of the modern film, in its capacity for irony, pastiche, for constant self-reflection, and for putting everything in quotation marks, are not 'postmodern' at all, but on the contrary, have been an essential feature of cinema's continuing encounter with modernity" (1993: 2). My own discussion has a more specific reference point in Hong Kong's recent history but also distances itself from recent discussions of Hong Kong culture within "postmodernist" frames (Abbas 1994).

12 Choi Po-king's 1995 study of the period between the mideighties and midnineties, which begins "with the building up of the local women's movement in the process of decolonization, and ends with its diversification in its confrontation with problems associated with political transition" (102), is an outstanding example of this tendency. See also Hong Kong Association for the Advancement of Feminism 1992, 1993; Choi 1993; Wu 1995; and the essays in Pearson and Leung (1995).

13 The Government Information Service performs a crucial function, as an ideological apparatus, in composing and disseminating images of Hong Kong as economically vibrant and politically consensual (see Man Joseph Chan 1987, chap. 6). The involvement of the government in the design and manufacture of the bourgeois imaginary is discussed by Turner 1995.

14 The past five years have seen an increasing, and urgent, self-reflexiveness in Hong Kong on questions of a local identity. In the domain of literature, the arts, and culture, see especially Ho 1995; Leung 1995; Sinn 1995; Turner and Ngan 1995; and Clarke 1996.

15 For debates on the film among reviewers, see Shu 1987.

16 I have borrowed and adapted Walter Benjamin's phrase "aestheticization of politics" (1970). In 1987, three years after the signing of the Joint Declaration in which Britain and China agreed on the transfer of sovereignty and launched the long transition to 1997, the problematic of Hong Kong's political future was just beginning

to take shape. Without a tradition of public sphere debate, serious discussions over the future were confined to small elite groups that were involved, directly or indirectly, in working out the complicated mechanics of the transition. In the months to come, these groups came under increasing public pressure to define and formulate their positions vis-à-vis political and constitutional development up to and beyond 1997. *Princess* represents not only an individual artistic vantage point but is also evocative of an anxiety about *engagement* in the mideighties, when filmmakers had to reassess their own cinematics and, like other cultural workers, explore relocations with the rapidly shifting contours of sociopolitical change. Hui and her New Wave contemporaries took different routes: the cinematic career of Alex Cheung, for instance, stuttered while Hui, like Tsui Hark, continued to work within the parameters of commercial cinema while trying to expand its capacity for self- and social reflexiveness.

17 Recent works mapping ethnic and feminist contestations in different locations include Spivak 1987; and Mohanty, Russo, and Torres 1991. For specific discussion of such mappings in contemporary Chinese cinema, see Chow 1991.

18 In his discussion of films like Louis Malle's *Lacombe Lucien* and *The Night Porter,* Michel Foucault (1989) discusses cinema as the site at which popular memory contests its erasure by official "histories" and re-members the dispersed imaginations of resistance.

19 See Choi 1995 for a discussion of the politics of the women's groups in Hong Kong as they diversify between those with pro-China and nationalistic orientations and others with a strong sense of Hong Kong identity.

20 Lui 1995 offers a detailed account of women's participation in politics.

21 In Mrs. Suen's relation to her father-in-law early in the film, certain traces of Kristeva's complex constitution of the subject as abject can be seen: "It is not the white expanse or slack boredom or repression, not the translations and transformations of desire that wrench bodies, nights, and discourse; rather it is a brutish suffering that 'I' puts up with, sublime and devastated, for 'I' deposits it to the father's account . . . : I endure it, for I imagine that such is the desire of the other" (1982: 4). "Abjection," Kristeva further observes, "is always brought about by that which attempts to get along with trampled-down law" (19). As the film goes on to show, the patriarch, as the embodiment of immutable cultural power and hegemonic historical narrative, has become deranged and incoherent, although this fact is unknown to Mrs. Suen and the family in the film's opening sequences.

FILMOGRAPHY

(Titles of Cantonese language films have established English translations.)

Chan Lit-bun

    1967 *Green-Eyed Demoness.* Hong Kong Film Co.

Wong Yiu

    1964 *Love and Passion.* Chi Luen Film Co.

Hui On-wah, Ann

    1979 *The Secret.* Unique Film Co. Ltd.

    1980 *The Spooky Bunch.* Hi-Pitch Co. Ltd.

    1981 *The Story of Woo Viet.* Pearl City Films

    1982 *Boat People.* Pearl City Films

1984 *Love in a Fallen City.* Shaw Brothers (HK) Ltd.
1987 *Romance of Book and Sword.* Yangzijiang Film Co. Ltd., Tianjin Film Studio, Yindu Corp. Ltd.
1987 *Princess Fragrance.* Yangzijiang Film Co. Ltd., Tianjin Film Studio,Yindo Corp. Ltd.
1988 *Starry Is the Night.* Shaw Brothers (HK) Ltd., Thomson (HK) Ltd.
1990 *Song of Exile.* Gaoxi Film Co., Zongyiang Film Co.
1991 *My American Grandson.* Taiwan Golden Film Co., Shanghai Film Studio
1991 *Zodiac Killers.* Taiwan Golden Film Co.
1995 *Summer Snow.* Golden Harvest Entertainment Co. Ltd.
1996 *Ah Kam.* Golden Harvest Entertainment Co. Ltd.

PART III

Masculine

Nationalism

and the Male

Public Sphere

7

Dai Jinhua

(Translated by Yu Ning,
with the assistance of
Mayfair Mei-hui Yang)

Rewriting Chinese Women: Gender Production

and Cultural Space in the Eighties and Nineties

Writing the History of the Other: Cultural Production of the Chinese Male Elite

In retrospect, the main body of Chinese cultural production in the 1980s
was written history prompted by a strong impulsive longing for utopia. It
was a special kind of suffering with a mixture of ecstasy and despair bright-
ened by a hopeful star of liberation. That is why the circle of cultural producers in mainland China was fascinated by allegories of the ruins and
wastelands of our traditional culture, and by the dances of death and quiet
extinction in the self-perpetuating cycles of Chinese history. With the
root-searching novel, the movement of historical-cultural retrospection,
and Fifth Generation films as its forms of expression, a hidden and clearly
contrasting set of binary oppositions involving time and space depicts for
us a tragic view of Chinese history. On the one hand, there is the circular,
close-minded, conservative, violent, benighted, and traditional culture; on
the other hand, there is the linear, open-minded, progressive, democratic,
civilized, and global (or Western) culture. In the discursive milieu of China
in the eighties, this binary construction of history is certainly asymmetrical, identifying the modern West as the norm, and depending on notions
of progress and modernity as the comforting objects of faith. Indeed, in
the China of the 1980s, progress and modernity became the collective

ideal and faith that elite intellectuals held on to in their tragic, desperate, and stubborn way.

The cultural ethos of the eighties is an extension of the profound process of "internal exile," which started during the May Fourth Movement earlier in the twentieth century, as Chinese intellectuals came to adopt a Western view of history and alienated themselves from Chinese culture. In the 1980s, China's national history once again was alienated as the history of the (Western) Other, so that an outsider's gaze turned this history into a space of failure, a space in which the possibility for progress is absent, and a time that is forever recurrent yet forever lost in the cyclical movement of history. While these 1980s interpreters of Chinese history saw themselves as cultural and political rebels, they also positioned themselves as discursive subjects suspended awkwardly in between the discourse of the Other, which they embraced, and the traditional native discourse from which they could not quite separate. That is to say, in adopting a Western view of Chinese backwardness, Chinese intellectuals put themselves in a difficult position, since they themselves are deeply attached to and rooted in the cultural tradition they came to objectify and reject. This longing for roots is revealed in Fifth Generation film director Chen Kaige's maiden work, *Yellow Earth*, in which Gu Qing, the People's Liberation Army soldier and outsider to the village, could never penetrate or become part of the ancient culture of the village rain worshippers on the yellow earth. Han-han, the village mute boy, turns against the crowd of local worshippers and runs toward Gu Qing, the promise of outside salvation, and attempts to throw himself into a new life. However, when he arrives on the horizon, Gu Qing has disappeared, and Han-han encounters nothing but a broad and empty expanse of land. This failure of salvation suggests a verdict on and a rejection of the possibilities of an outside Western discourse to save the ancient culture; it reveals a deep identification with a process of spiritual wandering across the yellow earth.

All this goes to show that cultural production in the 1980s became a discursive space for a marginal culture of male elite intellectuals. It became their indictment of the Father and their struggle to replace him and his culture. Simply put, it was an attempt to counter traditional Chinese culture with Western civilization. One may even say that the awkwardly suspended narrator and the outside gaze came with the apparition of the individual imported from the West. If there was a common master narrative in mainland Chinese culture in the second half of the decade, it was the father-son relationship. In such an accusatory and subversive narrative, Chinese history became a space filled with gory scenes of father figures killing sons, in which a culture of son killers, or a cannibalistic banqueting culture, is depicted as the fundamental feature of traditional Chinese culture. Father-son conflict became the most important and repeated paragraph in history's open plot, with the castration complex as a metaphor for political persecution. The central symbol in such a historical scene is the parched and bleak land and the starving men without women.[2] The parched land suggests the end of the ancient Chinese agricultural civilization, and men without women symbolizes the discontinuity of the bloodline of the patriarchal clan or "Chinese community." If we read these as an allegory of the end of Chinese and Eastern civilization, then we must accept their internal interpretation of the allegory: the evil man with a beautiful wife stands for the socially powerful but sexually impotent man (appearing in the story as "the elder" or "the Father") who takes away and possesses the woman who should rightfully belong to the healthy younger man.

Within this particular cultural space and mode of writing, women are exiled in a dual sense. First, women in such a father-son conflict are presented as objects of men's desire. Within this narrative context, as the forbidden fruit or the object of lack for men, women serve to reveal the fate of men to be rejected and exiled from history and the father-son hierarchy. Second, in this allegory of Chinese history with a father-son relation as its central metaphor, women must accept the terms of the male-identified culture. That is, she must dress up as a man or become a version of man, or she will lose any space or opportunity to speak as a full historical or discursive subject. Meanwhile, the male author of the historical allegory occupies the position of a dreaming person, a subject with a split identity. On the one hand, he is the all-knowing author of the gaze, the transcendent narrator adopting the role of the individual imported from the West, and the spirit of the cultural hero who will save China. On the other hand, he also identifies with the timid, murdered, or castrated son, who is weak but rebellious. Thus we may call the cultural narrative of Chinese male elite intellectuals in the eighties "the story of the son's generation."[3] When the father-son hierarchy and the son-destroying culture are represented as the power structure of traditional Chinese society, Chinese history becomes a paradoxical progress of death and extinction, and the narrator of such stories becomes both the sacrificial victim of the narrated death ceremony, as well as the righteous judge in social discourse.

Yet there is an even more profound self-contradiction than the tension between the condescending outsider's gaze and the deprived and about-to-be murdered son within the male elite narrating subject. Although the history of the Other is written as the history of the clan based on blood ties, and thus as the history of the Chinese self, the outsider's gaze that is adopted by the narrator still poses a problem. It reveals the decline and death of a traditional culture that nevertheless continues to be intricately connected with the elite Chinese male narrator through blood ties. Although in political television shows such as *River Elegy*, the decline of the yellow earth culture indicates that finally China will be accepted and embraced by the vast and wealthy "blue ocean civilization" of the West, traditional culture is not to be eliminated. In the vision of elite intellectuals of the eighties, traditional culture is not so much a ghost from the past that they must exorcise today as merely a tax that must be paid for a modernized tomorrow. It was in the 1980s, when a sense of crisis was created by buzz words such as *China's global citizenship* and *storming the pass*, that modernization (that is, Westernization) took off again, as if entering some sort of competition or life-and-death gamble for the fate of the nation and national rebirth. Even though traditional culture is put at stake in this game, and although the risk of losing it exists, in this discursive system the development of the nation becomes the battle of the century, with Victory, or Death as its battle cry. Yet this embracing of the myth of modernism and impulsive longing for utopia have still not resolved the dangerous tension between Westernization and nationalism. Therefore, the writing stance of the male intellectual cannot be as simple or decisive as his rational choice for modernization. That is why participants of the historical-cultural retrospection movement never resolved their dilemma between critical retrospection and roots searching, patricide and father seeking, and denouncement and admiration of traditional culture.

Among these works, Mo Yan's novel *The Red Sorghum* reveals a typical symptom of roots-seeking literature. It was Mo Yan and his *Red Sorghum* (1992) that established the pattern of "muscular and heroic grandfather and timid and pallid father." Such a pattern is not so much a "destructive retelling" of the Father's history as a helpless pacing back and forth in the giant shadow of patriarchal power; not so much a rejection of patriarchal history as a resignation to the ending of the bloodline of the hero, or the shame of a mixed-breed sorghum. In this pattern, symbolic patricide becomes at the same time a pursuit of the idealized Father. This subject position of being both inside and outside traditional culture and historical allegory constantly renders impossible the completion of the rebellious presentation of history. Theirs is the history of the Other, but at the same time the history of the self; it is the denouncement of history's power structure and castration drive, yet at the same time a yearning for blood ties or traditional culture in a journey of roots seeking. Thus, this wavering gaze is necessarily invested with the painful tug of complex ambivalent emotions. Under this gaze, even as the Chinese nation is portrayed as a paralyzed space of eternal failure, what also develops at the same time is a desire to rescue this history from the state of flux, in a desperate effort to crystallize it in lasting images of our national culture.

The Emergence of Popular Culture

Beginning in the early eighties, popular culture became a follower and replicator of male elite culture, finding commercial support to situate itself among elite discourse, mainstream ideology, and the daily life of the masses. In the mid- and late eighties, what emerged from this awkwardly positioned popular culture was a rather noticeable phenomenon, the exemplary success of best-selling novels and serial television historical dramas set in the late Qing dynasty.[4] Interestingly, the elite mode of writing the Other's history of China was applied in popular culture to the Qing dynasty, especially the late Qing, this most appropriate of symbolic signifiers.[5] First of all, the history of the Manchus, a national minority that had conquered and ruled the Han nationality, became a historical narrative that could most readily win the masses' identification of them as the Other. Even in the historical-cultural retrospection movement, the unstated yet clearly accepted premise is that the Han people are the subjects of Chinese history and the cultural mainstream. Second, as the last dynasty in Chinese history, the Qing is taken without question as the symbol of corruption and cultural decline. And it was the late Qing dynasty, when China reluctantly opened its doors to the Western powers' gunboats, that in the wounded national memory marked the beginning of China's "Western" or "modern" complex. The Qing dynasty is beyond a doubt the guilty villain that started the hundred years of blood and tears in early modern Chinese history. Third, another unstated consensus is that the last years of the Qing dynasty were written in the history of one woman—the Empress Dowager Ci Xi (Yehenala)—who seized the reins of male state power. Such a narrative pattern was transformed in the process of mass interpretation into an attack by innuendo of the Cultural Revolution as the handiwork of "that woman," Jiang Qing, Mao's radical leftist wife. More openly than elite culture, the popular narrative repeated the ancient saying that "woman is the source of evil and calamity."

In the 1980s, in a discursive space organized by a powerful grand narrative and a complex and entangled national identity formation that exiled the position and subjectivity of women, China began a new period of rewriting its women.

In the early and mideighties, in the cultural inscription of elite male intellectuals, the exile of women from history was explained away as the dispossession of men. That is, men's refusal or inability to possess a woman was due to their self-exile or their being exiled by the patriarchal order from history. In the history writing of the late eighties, however, women began to appear quietly on the historical scene. In most roots-seeking novels of the mideighties, women were presented in the image of the "large-breasted and wide-bottomed" Mother Earth.[6] In the New Wave novels of the late eighties,[7] however, women were depicted as sinister and perplexing; they climb and maneuver like destructive vines in the history of the Other. Rather than help continue the bloodline from father to son, they confuse and contaminate the ethical system, the social order, and the holy bloodline by constantly changing their masters. Women are no longer the abyss of desire or the gate to manhood, but a gap and a barrier, keeping the young male protagonist, or the son, out of history.[8] However, although the New Wave novelists are purer and more decisive than the roots-seeking novelists in their critical-political cultural stance, this cannot help them successfully resolve or save them from their uncertain suspension in history, and the anxiety that comes with their self-alienation from a cultural tradition to which they are still deeply connected.

It was as if by chance that a woman officially entered the scene, or reemerged, in Zhang Yimou's maiden work *Red Sorghum* (1987). This time the woman appears right in the male protagonist's lustful field of vision: the film opens with seven close-ups of Gong Li, all under the male characters' desiring gaze. The appearance of this woman successfully resolves the male anxiety over being suspended outside the scene of history, or the father-son narrative. Furthermore, she imaginatively releases and alleviates the great tension between China and the world, and between traditional culture and modernization. The allegory of national extinction is here replaced by a national myth of the explosion of primitive vital energy; the humiliating memories of our race are erased by an indomitable hero who successfully resists foreign aggression. Yet the woman becomes a mere sacrifice, first on the altar of male desire and initiation to manhood, and again in the ceremonial scene of the national myth. In the final scene, it is at the side of a prostrated woman that the man can stand tall as a hero.

Zhang Yimou's choice of foregrounding a woman might have been an exceptional case, but in the last year of the decade, 1989, the expressions of extreme trauma by male intellectuals unintentionally helped the reemergence of women. In the final year of the eighties, China's historical calamity deeply frustrated elite intellectuals' optimistic illusion of ending the tragic cyclical history of Chinese culture and thereby entering the linear historical development of "human progress." It also effectively thwarted their utopian impulse to embrace the myth of modernity and its inevitable triumph over the "feudal" past. When a medieval ending was imposed on a postmodern text, what followed was necessarily a confusion of time and space that cast doubts on their previous convictions of linear discourse. It started to dawn on them that the show of military force may be more a symptom of modernity than feudalism. As a result, the mainland circle of cultural producers in the early nineties suffered from severe aphasia. Reality, as the coordinate or parameter of history writing, lost its clarity and certainty. Male elite intellectuals could not decide whether they had missed a historical opportunity to join the world and enter a Golden Age through the Gate of Eden or had lost a utopia constructed merely in discourse. At this juncture, *woman*, as a familiar and predetermined symbolic signifier, became an effective word to dispel this aphasia and a safety valve to release the pressure to explain a confusing political reality and its nameless anxiety. [Since women have been thought of by male intellectual discourse as the realm of timeless space outside history, woman was the perfect signifier to release them from their quandary and confusion of grand narratives, to escape from their painful helplessness in concrete history, and to enter into a third grand narrative of human history, the timeless relationship between men and women.]

In 1990, *Yearning*, the Mainland's first television soap opera serial, was broadcast and immediately started a shock wave that swept across the countryside and cities alike in China. It contained a most familiar image—a self-sacrificing and submissive woman who devotes herself to her husband and educates his son—which successfully diverted the profound frustration of the whole society with the previous year's events, the Tiananman Square trauma. The effect was indeed shocking. So much so that the Women's Federation publicly complained, "This television serial has pushed back the liberation of Chinese women by fifteen years." Suddenly, images of women penetrated the dusk of historical memory of New Wave novelists and became the main character in historical narratives. Thus gender came to replace the father-son binary and was positioned at the center of Chinese history. An important and interesting development is the shift of the Chinese historical setting from an open yet failing space—the ancient and huge expanse of the yellow earth, the vast and lavish sorghum field, and the boundless poppy field (as in Su Tong's *My Hometown of Maples and Poplars*)—to a sealed-off and obscure internal space—the ancient dye house built after a model from a classic reference book (as in Zhang Yimou's *Ju Dou*), the haunted mansion of the Chen family (as in Su Tong's *Wives and Concubines;* and Zhang Yimou's *Raise the Red Lantern*), the ancient yet female yin-dominated mansion of the Cai family (as in He Ping's film *Red Firecracker, Green Firecracker*), and the delicate yet ruined brothel and nunnery in southeast China (as in Su Tong's *Rouge Powder* and Li Shaohong's film *Rouge Powder*).[9] The spatial enclosure compares Chinese history to a prison and sets up an exotic Oriental wonder for the Western gaze. This is the same iron house that Lu Xun used to symbolize the core of Chinese culture, but now it imprisons only women. Thus women, in their roles of timeless characters, become the scapegoats of history.

Among these works, Su Tong's narratives are the most typical. In his work, women are depicted as both inmates and guards. At once separated yet connected by hatred and conspiracy, they jostle against and abuse each other. In Su Tong's allegories, just as men are held together by history's perpetual power struggle, the interdependence between the master and the slave, and the exchanging and sharing of their women, women are also held together by their struggle against each other for men, and by their indescribable, irrational hatred for each other. They need men not out of desire but because of greed and spite; they are entangled in struggle not to possess men but to acquire crumbs of power from men so that they can hurt other women. Such unutterable hatred does not end with death. The most hideous image can be found near the end of Su Tong's novel *Another Kind of Woman's Life* (1993b). Left unfinished on the embroidery frame of the old maid Jian Shaozhen is a portrait of another woman, Gu Yaxian, with a pair of scissors stuck in between her pink lips. In this historical portrait where women are the main characters, they are made to bear both the load of historical unconscious and the historical task of castration. It is woman who is both the officiant at the sacrificial ceremonies of a dark history as well as the victim who is offered as ritual sacrifice. She is history's co-conspirator, but at the same time she is also sacrificed by history.

In this manner, the history writing practiced by male elite intellectuals in the eighties was successfully transformed. In the classic patriarchal discourse, women represent a spatial rather than temporal existence. As a result, women's image and women's world order coincided precisely with the spatialized and cyclical narrative of Chinese history. At the same time, as the eternal Other in a patriarchal society, women are made to act out a Chinese historical drama that replaces the Father's history with a new history of the Other, which is the self-Orientalizing male elite narrative.

Thus historical narrative in the nineties re-presents women in such a way that male authors can absorb and resolve the problem of Otherness in their adopted Western narrative of the 1980s. That is, the figure of woman allows the male narrator, as the dominant historical subject, to write a story of the Other (or a narrative of China from a Western perspective) as if he were writing the history of the self. In this way, male authors can denounce history without placing themselves in an awkward, suspended position. But Su Tong and those like him did not know that their gory, cruel, and charming stories about women were not only going to resolve the strangeness and opaqueness of the complex Chinese male historical narrative but also win them a ticket "to the world," or the attention of the West.

The Game of Gender Switching

After a few long and depressed years, 1993 witnessed the sudden arrival of a commercial tidal wave and the radical progress of modernization. However, this time reality shed the rosy idealism of the eighties and was no longer represented as the Gate of Eden to a Golden Age. What is clearly presented now is a future that will be rescued by material wealth, a future showing the brazen and greedy face of utilitarianism. Shocked by reality a second time, mainland China's intellectual circle is faced with a cruel pressure to accept the status quo and at the same time must respond to the allure, embarrassment, and threat presented by the new reality. Western culture and Western material civilization now appear without the pleasant blue-colored comforting embrace and paradigm of spiritual salvation, which had figured in the idealistic imaginings of intellectuals in the 1980s. Instead, the West now brazenly poses itself as competition and threat. Encroaching on the Chinese cultural market, multinational capital breaks in through China's window like Zeus in a storm of gold. This invasion more clearly defines the position of a Third World country and the status of its national culture. Chinese male elite intellectuals must now struggle under the pressure and the embarrassment of real life. In addition, they have to face another severe reality—the subtle, complex, and lowly cultural situation and status of a local scholar in the shadow of a more powerful global post–Cold War discursive realm.

Chinese male intellectuals are familiar with the textual rules surrounding gender, politics, and power. But in the cultural-linguistic milieu of this new world order, the interchangeability and synecdochic equivalence of gender, *race*, and power come into operation on a larger scale according to similar rules that are now working against the male elite. Interestingly, just as Chinese male intellectuals were anxiously looking for possible ways to avoid or remove the rules, toward the end of the eighties Chinese women authors started to see through the secret of the global power game as the result of their own painful gender experience. Zhang Jie's novel *There Is Only One Sun* (1989) depicts an ugly and bizarre picture of East-West conflict under the sun that shines over the whole world. She directly addresses the anxiety and fear that the Chinese male intellectual experiences in the face of the Western world. In the novel, an Asian witch takes advantage of the opportunities afforded by her gender and race and plays these roles out successfully, thus "happily" marrying a white man. Meanwhile, the most beloved Chinese male protagonist drowns himself in despair near a sunny nude beach in a Western country. These episodes bitterly and satirically reveal that the rules governing the gender-power binary can also be applied to the race-power relation so that women are dominated by male power just as other races are dominated by Western power. Similarly, another woman author, Wang Anyi, presents the humiliating adventure of a famous male Chinese writer in "My Uncle's Story" (1991). With tongue-in-cheek humor, Wang describes an absurdist and tantalizing scene of how her uncle was frustrated in his attempt to exercise male power over a Western woman. Instead, he had to be submissive to the Western woman's racial and linguistic power. This obvious cultural fact reveals a bitter yet well-hidden secret of the Chinese male intellectual situation today.

In the nineties, the important reality facing Chinese culture is the need to acknowledge and submit to the rules of race, gender, and power established by the West. Indeed, rather than conquering the West, the Chinese films nominated for an Academy Award in the early 1990s fall in this very pattern of the gender-race binary, where even the superior force of the Chinese male gender must submit to the more powerful principle of Western race privilege. Both of the films that did so well in the West, *Raise the Red Lantern* (1991) and *Farewell, My Concubine* (1993), fully display the cruel fate of Chinese culture in a Western-dominated world. In *Raise the Red Lantern*, with its old cyclical structure of the passage of time from one summer to another, director Zhang Yimou dramatically removes from view the patriarch of the Chen mansion. The only master now is the classical Chinese prison-like square, enclosed courtyard. In this spatial structure, wives and concubines no longer engage in internal strife and mutual abuse for the entertainment of any male character in the film, but are framed by a presumably objective camera in an aesthetic, tragically beautiful, and balanced picture (fig. 1). In this manner, women become the absolute protagonists of the historical narrative and the only objects of visu-

Figure 1. *Women enclosed within walls: a scene from Zhang Yimou's film* Raise the Red Lantern.

al observation. The audiovisual structure of the film successfully replaces the male master-slave logic with a female abusing/abused logic as the core of the historical ordeal. More important, the structure described above also reserves the male gaze position vacated by the old patriarch Chen for the gaze of the Western male film viewer. In *Raise the Red Lantern*, Zhang Yimou constructs an image of China through and for the lens of Western culture. He manufactures an Orientalized female image and paints a Chinese screen of beautiful maidens. Faced with the discursive context of the West and its cultural market, Zhang Yimou chooses to assume the position of a female in the global order of gender, race, and power.

Chen Kaige's film *Farewell, My Concubine* is a more complex narrative. What is most revealing to me is one of Chen's most important revisions of Li Bihua's original novel. Chen has completely changed the gay orientation of the character Cheng Dieyi, having him appear in the film as a charming woman only on the stage, but not a homosexual off-stage. The person whom the character Cheng Dieyi loves is only the Heroic General on the stage, not his coactor and childhood buddy Duan Xiaolou, as in the original novel. Thus Cheng Dieyi's freedom from homosexuality allows director Chen Kaige to identify himself with this character. I would argue, however, that director Chen's identification with a feminized character such as Cheng Dieyi is not due to any sympathy of minds between two crazed and idealistic artists but represents an unconscious acknowledgment on the part of Chen Kaige of the need to accede to the self-feminization of Chinese male intellectuals, so as to facilitate their "march" into the Western cultural market. This is a fact that he does not want to face but has to face.

On another level, the switching of gender roles occurs in a different manner. The nineties is a decade of desire rather than a decade of action. In this decade, mainland Chinese intellectuals fall prey to a desperate anxiety as they openly accept the dollar as the criterion for cultural achievement and regard acknowledgment and awards from Western culture as the highest standard of success. In this process, they project the male subject's castration anxiety onto someone else, using the game rules of gender politics as an imaginative means to resolve their awkward predicament. That someone else is an unpleasant new image of the hysterical, greedy woman who becomes an anchor for the floating ship of the post-1989 mainland culture. In the popular novels of the nineties, works such as Su Tong's *A Guide for Divorce* (1993a), *Yang Bo, the Married Man* (1993c), and Wang Shuo's *Die but after the Throw*,[10] the women are greedy, cruel, irrational, and nearly mad; their aim in life is nothing but to constantly create disaster in the lives of men. Because of these women, men suffer, die, or gasp desperately for breath in a hell on earth. They become weak, timid, humiliated, and spineless. In such a chilling picture of mundane life, women are taken as the obvious cause for the sordid reality and for men's anxiety and are held responsible for the tragic fate of men. In this manner, the shock, frustration, and pressure of dealing with the larger threatening world in the period between the 1980s and '90s, are all transferred onto women. Thus, the project to subvert and change the social status quo becomes an effort to perpetuate the gender order, and reflections on the political and historical fate of the nation become the presentation of the male subject's individual suffering. In this way, the male narrator brings about the pardoning of men at the expense of women's exile.

Women's Writing and Women's Cultural Space

Although Chinese culture in the New Era (post-1979 period) can be seen as patriarchal culture's counterattack against the gender equality of the previous era, the emergence of women's writing is nevertheless one of the most important new developments on the cultural scene. However, the problem is that while men's writing openly presents its male perspective as the mainstream paradigm to be followed, women writers are always vague in the expression of their gender. This is a dilemma of discourse: Chinese women's liberation was granted and has been supported by the existing regime, and up to now most women's welfare has been actually protected by the existing system. Because of this, the subversive position of some elite women intellectuals is difficult: if they pose as political dissidents, they necessarily become the ally of the male elite intellectuals and thus actually acquiesce, or at least tolerate, men's "rewriting" of women. Meanwhile, as a voice of gender and political resistance against the official discourse of "women's liberation," women's writing stresses gender differences. Yet that stress, on the one hand, leads them into the old rut of classic gender essentialism and, on the other hand, makes it easy for the patriarchal discourse to appropriate. In the nineties, the Third World native intellectual's cultural predicament suppresses women's cultural expression under a different excuse, demanding an identification of Chinese women with Chinese men. Chinese intellectual discussion of postcolonial culture has also provided another forceful argument to male elite intellectuals' attack on feminism and international sisterhood. Because of this, when women consciously resist the retaliation of patriarchal culture and insist that women speak in their own voices, they are often accused of adopting the sickly tone of official discourse and are easily dismissed as a kind of female identification with the state apparatus. That is why since 1979, despite their admirable effort, women intellectuals have failed to establish a women's cultural space. However, entering and sharing men's cultural space have allowed them to break the monolithic maleness of that space with multiple voices.

In the mid- and late 1980s, important trends in women's writing of history and present reality were to discover the tragicomic aspects of women's existence; to depict how this strange creature that is female self-identity is the product of a patriarchal society; and to show how men, as masters, often become the toys and fools of the gender order that they themselves created. Even though most women writers deny that they are feminists, their writing often engages in unexpected ironic attacks and subversions of the patriarchal gender order. In their writing about women in history, women writers in the 1980s have at least accomplished the writing of disconnected episodes of women's history as full historical subjects.[11] In the nineties, however, Chinese women's writing begins to wear a new face, and their consciousness of and demand for women's cultural and physical space emerges despite various difficulties. First of all, women's writing breaks out of the male elites' pattern of grand narrative and national allegory to describe the everyday life of women in an undecorated style and a detached voice.[12] Second, women's writing begins deliberately to continue a female tradition that can be traced back to the forties and even earlier to what was called boudoir literature.[13]

The most noteworthy works thus produced are the autobiographies and semiautobiographies by a group of young women born in the sixties. They bravely write "my body" and "my self," narrate their gender and sexual experiences, and record their fear of and longing for sisterhood and lesbian relationships.[14] Not since 1949 has women's writing entered the cultural scene in a more shocking manner than it does now. However, patriarchal culture, especially patriarchal commercial culture, has at the same time started an operation in order to use and then sacrifice this rich resource of women's culture. Brave and frank confessions of women are constantly dug up and invested with commercial valence. Male publishers and male critics time and again repackage women writers' candid expositions of the female body, female desire, and their self-inquiry into a marketing formula: "My body, my self, and my monster." By means of repackaging, male publishers and critics transform women's self-narrative and self-questioning into the lustful gaze of the male voyeur. But women's writing continues to appear in a clearer and more forceful voice, resisting the new cultural exploitation. The resistance is unprecedentedly clearer and more forceful, and also fully conscious of the present state of women's gender existence. It is deeply introspective, once again transcending and subverting the old gender order to a new cultural level.[15] Sisterhood is no longer defined in the narrower lesbian sense, or in the sense of women's escapist utopia, but has become a clear depiction of a female space and an expression of an ideal feminist society.[16]

Among the cacophony of the market and the loud patriarchal voices, women's resisting voice is indeed still weak and marginal, and it often immediately encounters the condemnation and hostility of the dominant patriarchal culture. But clearly, their voice is breaking out from a common space shared by men, women, the state, and the market. Women are striving to establish a cultural and physical space for themselves, but they have a long way to go before they can break out of the encirclement of patriarchal culture and oppressive society.

NOTES

1 The root-searching novel was one of the most important trends in Chinese literature of the mid-1980s. It was so dubbed mainly because of Han Shaogong's essay "The Roots of Literature" (1985). Representative works include Han Shaogong's *Father, Father, Father* (1992), Ah Cheng's *The Chess Master* (1992), Mo Yan's *Red Sorghum*

(1986), and Wang Anyi's *Xiao Bao Village* (1986). See Liu 1992. The movement of historical-cultural introspection was an intellectual reexamination of Chinese history and culture from a critical political perspective, as exemplified by the television series *River Elegy* (1988). Fifth Generation films refers to those directed by a group of young directors after 1983. Representative works include Chen Kaige's *Yellow Earth* (1984) and *King of the Children* (1987), Tian Zhuangzhuang's *Sketches from the Hunting Ground* (1983), and Zhang Yimou's *Red Sorghum* (1987).

2 Similar works include Zheng Yi's root-searching story *Old Well* and the film of the same title (1987) directed by Wu Tianming, Teng Wenji's film *Ballad of the Yellow River* (1989), and Hou Yong's film *Bleeding Sky* (1990).

3 See *Qiu Ji* (Anonymous 1988).

4 Representative works include the film *Magic Whip* (directed by Zhang Zi-en, 1988) and *The Soccer Knight of Beijing* (1989).

5 Representative works include the television serials *The Last Emperor, The Romantic Prince,* and the films *The Last Empress* (starring Liu Xiaoqing) and *Tan Si-tong.*

6 The image of the mother with large breasts and a wide bottom is the most important female image in roots-seeking novels. In 1995, that image even became the title of Mo Yan's latest novel, *Feng ru fei tun* (Large breasts and wide bottoms) (1996).

7 The New Wave novel was one of the most important literary trends in mainland China around 1987, and these works reveal bold avant-garde experimental styles. Representative authors include Su Tong, Yu Hua, Ge Fei, and Ye Zhaoyan.

8 Also see Su Tong's "The Poppy Family" and "Rouge Powder" (1992c, 1992a); Ge Fei's "Green and Yellow" (in Chen Juntao 1992a); and Ye Zhaoyan's "The Story of the Date Tree" (in Chen Juntao 1992c).

9 See Su Tong 1992b, 1992a.

10 An interesting fact is that in 1992 when the novella by Wang Shuo was rendered into a television series, the scriptwriter attached two other stories by Wang Shuo to the end of the novella, thus making it into a story of a hysterical heroine, who through the help of a man and his love finally returns to her family and his arms. This rendition became extremely popular at the time.

11 Works of this kind include Wang Anyi's *Thirty Chapters of the Flowing Stream* (1990); Tie Ning's *The Rose Gate* (1989); and Chi Li's "Gazing" (1993).

12 Of these works, the more conspicuous ones are Chi Zijian's "A Journey into the White Night" (1995), and Jiang Zidan's "For Whom Does the Mulberry Smoke Rise?" (1995).

13 The more important works of this group are Wang Anyi's novel *The Long Ode of Lost Love* (1996); works by the young woman author Xu Lan (1995); and works by Meng Hui (1994).

14 Representative works include "A Toast to the Past" and "No Place to Say Goodbye" by Chen Ran (1992b, 1992a); Lin Bai's novel *One Person's War* (1992); and Lin Bai's "The Chair in the Winding Corridor" and "Water in the Bottle" (1995a, 1995b); and Xu Xiaobin's "The Double Fish Constellation" (1995).

15 The woman author Xu Kun has published "Brighter and Brighter from Now On" (1995), and that work lies between fiction, nonfiction, and criticism.

16 See Chen Ran's article, "Gender Transcendent Consciousness and My Creative Writing" (1994), and her novel *Breaking Up* (1995).

FILMOGRAPHY

Ballad of the Yellow River. (Huanghe Yao). Directed by Teng Wenji. 1989.

Bleeding Sky. (Tian Chuxue). Directed by Hou Yong. 1990.

Farewell, My Concubine. (Bawang Bieji). Directed by Chen Kaige. 1993.

Judou. Directed by Zhang Yimou. 1990.

King of the Children. (Haizi Wang). Directed by Chen Kaige. 1987.

Magic Whip. (Shen Bian). Directed by Zhang Zi-en. 1988.

Old Well. (Lao Jing). Directed by Wu Tianming. 1986.

Raise the Red Lantern. (Da Hong Denglong Gaogaogua). Directed by Zhang Yimou. 1992.

Red Firecracker, Green Firecracker. (Pao Da Shuangdeng). Directed by He Ping. 1993.

Red Sorghum. (Hong Gaoliang). Directed by Zhang Yimou. 1987.

River Elegy. (He Shang). Directed by Wang Luxiang. 1988.

Rouge Powder. (Hong Fen). Directed by Li Shaohong. 1995.

Sketches from the Hunting Ground. (Liechang zhasa). Directed by Tian Zhuangzhuang. 1983.

Yellow Earth. (Huang tudi). Directed by Chen Kaige. 1984.

Susan Brownell

8

Strong Women and Impotent Men: Sports, Gender, and Nationalism in Chinese Public Culture

The People's Republic of China (PRC) has been a relative newcomer to the transnational world of sports due to its withdrawal from the International Olympic Committee and international sports federations from 1956–1979 in protest over their recognition of the Republic of China on Taiwan. Through "Ping-Pong diplomacy," sports were strategically used by the Communist Party in the developments leading to the PRC's admission to the United Nations in 1979, and since that time China's international sports involvement and the sports media that cover it (particularly television) have grown by leaps and bounds. The story of international sports in China, however, has an unusual twist. In the rest of the world, sports are a notoriously male-dominated realm: the scale of professionalized male sports dwarfs that of female sports, the most ardent fans are typically male, and the sports media are dominated by men (and the list goes on). In China, by contrast, female athletes have had greater successes than male, hence they have been the heroes in the resurgence of this globally repositioned Chinese nationalism since 1979. In particular, the victory of the Chinese women's volleyball team in the 1981 World Cup is identified by many Chinese as the pivotal point in their rediscovery of national pride after the devastation of the Cultural Revolution (1966–76). What do sports as a transnational cultural form contribute to a Chinese public sphere or public culture? Have Chinese sportswomen, who have been so vociferously heralded by the state feminist project as shining examples of its success, played any role in the emergence of a feminist public sphere autonomous from the state?

Public Sphere and Public Culture

Previously, I have argued for the use of the phrase *public culture* rather than *public sphere* (Brownell 1995: 67–70). My argument was based on many of the same critiques of the public sphere concept that Mayfair Yang covers in detail in her introduction and chapter in this volume. However, like Yang, I wish to retain Jürgen Habermas's emphasis on communicative structures and a public space for discursive formation. In this chapter I describe a realm in which public opinion is formed, national symbols are debated, and a national image is set apart from international and subordinate regional images. I pay particular attention to the communicative structures of television, print media, film, and public ceremonies. This is the realm I call public culture. It is the main arena in which social groups (including agents of the state itself) contest and attempt to manipulate the various phenomena of nationalism. Because this realm is not clearly autonomous from the state in China, it does not seem to qualify as a "public sphere"; yet, at the same time, it is possible to detect emergent public spheres within the broader realm of cultural debate. Some are quickly squelched by the government, some fizzle out on their own, and a few begin to approach the Habermasian ideal of the public sphere. I prefer to retain public culture as my overarching analytic category, and to view these emergent public spheres as utopian projects that take shape, but never fully achieve their ideals, within this category—which does have a definite shape and structure and is not itself a utopian project. As Yang notes, "To look for a particular historical public sphere is a performative act that contributes to bringing it into existence" (introduction to this volume). In this chapter, I will show that a feminist voice was almost entirely absent from the public culture of sports. By outlining some of the spaces that this voice could have occupied, and communicating it to female sports scholars in China, I hope to contribute to bringing it into existence and adding it to the emerging feminist public sphere in China. I also hope to contribute to a better understanding of this emerging feminism by analyzing why feminist voices were absent in discussions of Chinese sportswomen. The most important conclusion of this analysis is that the structure and nature of Chinese nationalism in sports tended to mask or even exclude a feminist voice. This analysis leads to an altered understanding of Habermas's concept of the public sphere because it shows how the cultural logic of gender and nationalism in the overarching realm of public culture can shape—and even restrict—the public spheres that emerge out of it.

To a great extent, the public opinion that is formed in the realm of public culture consists of a national consciousness, or a consciousness of nationhood (*Public Culture* 1988; Appadurai and Breckenridge 1988; Kelly 1990). Many debates are entangled with this consciousness of nationhood, and certainly the position of women is one of them. However, as Yang discusses in her chapter and as I will discuss below, these debates about gender-in-the-nation often manage to accomplish an erasure of the feminist project at the same time that they foreground gender as a national issue.

In China, the debates that occur in the realm of public culture are often strongly shaped by the official discourses of the party-state, either because it seeks to control them, or because counterdiscourses emerge in almost direct opposition to it, so that it has essentially set the terms of the debate. Thus, these debates tend to privilege the category of nation over all other kinds of identities, whether transnational, subnational, sexual, ethnic, and so on. Yet public culture is caught up in all of these relationships and may be viewed as a node or crossing point in them, so that even when debates appear to be about nationhood, closer analysis will reveal the involvement of other identities as well.

Another reason I choose to use the phrase *public culture* results from my commitment to the concept of culture—so long as it is used in a way that is informed by the current multiculturalism. I want to argue for an understanding of public sphere or public culture that directs our attention to debates about culture, including rituals and symbols and other forms of nonverbal performance. One problem with Habermas's public sphere concept is that it neglects the importance of rituals and symbols, which are very important in the Chinese political process. Habermas has been criticized for overemphasizing rational-critical discourse and neglecting the link between citizenship and theatricality, such as public festivals (Garnham 1992: 360). In our times, major international sports events are an important kind of public festival (MacAloon 1984). By paying attention to their symbolic and mythic dimensions as well as the debates that surround them, we can begin to understand the cultural logic that shapes understandings of public life; this logic constitutes the framework that gives a definite shape to public culture as an analytical category. By paying more attention to culture, this kind of focus should help us understand the distinctiveness of a Chinese public sphere and avoid the criticism that we are imposing a Western model on a Chinese context.

Women's Volleyball and Television—A Transnational Public Sphere?

Mayfair Yang has argued that during the Maoist period the mass media helped to create a homogeneous national culture, partly by constructing an us-versus-them image of a Chinese nation threatened from the outside (1997: 293). This was one means by which the state was able to fully appropriate nationalism, so that nation and state came to be integrated into a single entity (292). However, she finds that in recent years the increasingly transnational mass media (her essay concentrates on television) have contributed to the detaching of Chinese subjectivity from the state and the deterritorialization of Chinese nationalism, which is now increasingly linked with Taiwan, Hong Kong, and the Chinese diaspora. This opens up the possibility of the emergence of a transnational public sphere that is no longer grounded in any one nation-state. Indeed, Benjamin Lee has argued that such a transnational sphere of Chinese public criticism had already emerged in the aftermath of 1989. He states that "in some cases, the leading edge of change lies in the intersections and interstices of processes beyond the nation-state that have their own global infrastructure" (1993: 174).

At first glance, television would appear to be the mass medium that most transcends national boundaries, and telecasts of international sporting events would appear to be the most remarkable example. The cumulative number of worldwide television viewers of the Olympic Games is exceeded only by the Football (Soccer) World Cup; the Olympic Opening Ceremonies probably attract the single largest global audience, with more than one billion people around the world watching the same event (Larson and Park 1993: 6). However, it is not clear that sports telecasting is at the leading edge of the emergence of a transnational public sphere, because its technological infrastructure as well as its content tend to reinforce distinctions between nations at the same time that they create new interconnections between them.

The live telecast of the 1981 World Cup in women's volleyball illustrates the transnational and nationalist aspects of sports television. When the Chinese women won the final match, it was China's first victory in a major Olympic sport (table tennis was not then an Olympic sport). It marked China's reentry onto the world scene after the isolation of the Cultural Revolution. The tournament was played in Japan, and in the final match the Chinese played the Japanese, who had won the previous World Cup in 1977 and had dominated the sport for many years. The victory thus represented an evening of scores with China's Asian rival and former oppressor. Defeat of China's other main global rivals, the Soviet Union (third) and the United States (fourth), made the victory even more meaningful. Despite the November cold, fans had converged around televisions set outside in public spaces like courtyards and alleys, while others crowded around televisions in auditoriums and homes. Many, if not most, of these viewers did not normally follow sports. When the live broadcast came to an end, there was a spontaneous outpouring of patriotic emotions. People flooded the streets, weeping openly, embracing, and setting off firecrackers. College students gathered on campuses, banging drums, chanting, and lighting bonfires.

The victory would probably not have had nearly the same impact if it had not been viewed as a live television broadcast by millions. Yet the technology that made it possible was a relatively recent development out of the regional growth of television in Asia. Only three years before, Hong-Kong based Television Broadcasts Limited (TVB) began to provide coverage of major sporting events for members of the Asia-Pacific Broadcasting Union, the largest regional broadcasting union in the world, serving more than two billion persons (Read 1993: 508). The central government in China had regarded television so lightly as a propaganda tool that there was not even a national broadcasting station until 1980, when China Central Television (CCTV) was created out of the Beijing Television Station that had been serving as the national broadcaster. In 1981, CCTV did not plan to broadcast the volleyball World Cup games live, but viewers called in to demand it for the China-U.S. semifinal match. Frenzied inquiries finally produced a link with Pacific Satellite only moments before the China-U.S. semifinal game appeared on the screen (*Xin Tiyu* 1981: 22).

In linking up with transnational flows of culture, therefore, sports television led China's other realms of television. Many kinds of new technology were first used for major sporting events, such as instantaneous satellite transmissions and international sharing arrangements. This technology provided the infrastructure that enabled the public debates surrounding the volleyball championship. It also thrust the members of the Sports Bureau at CCTV into relationships with members of the international community for which they were ill-prepared, due to their poor English and lack of international experience (this was one reason for their reliance on Hong-Kong based TVB, with Hong Kong serving as a mediator between the PRC and the rest of the world in this as in so many other realms). Thus, the technology and the people required to run it were increasingly sucked into global networks. At the same time, however, the content of the broadcasts certainly reinforced national boundaries rather than transcending them. In part, this was because the mainland Chinese controlling this technology were not the cosmopolitan elites with little allegiance to the nation-state envisioned by theorists of transnational culture (*Public Culture* 1988: 3) but, rather, were people with relatively little international experience whose allegiances lay squarely with the Chinese nation. Moreover, nationalism is built into the very structure of international sports and sports ritual. The Olympic Games and other major events actually require athletes to represent particular nations, marking their representation in rituals such as the awards ceremonies and parade of athletes, and in symbols such as uniforms, flags, and anthems. This pageantry exploits the fact that national allegiance is a large contributor to spectator interest.

These regional and global structures already had a certain male bias built into them long before China joined the game. Men's professional soccer was already well established as the most popular sport worldwide, with heated rivalries between nations; the Olympic Games and international sports generally showered more money, opportunities, and attention on men; the sports media moguls were men; the majority of sports journalists were men.

Similarly, in China the people who shaped the image of the women's volleyball team were mainly men. The 1981 victory was the event that made sports commentator Song Shixiong's name a household word. It was also Song Shixiong who made vivid the television image of the team that was broadcast across China. In an interview, he told me that he had carefully prepared the image that he would propagate beforehand.[1] In order to more fully understand the players, he watched them practice. He described their training as "very bitter." He saw them cry, yell at the coach, sweat, fall to the floor. He saw them when they were so tired that they could not climb up stairs. He also "learned from women's volleyball," and it inspired him to work harder at his own job. He wanted to communicate this to his television audience—not just to report on the game, but to let the audience know what it took to get to that point. I asked him how he felt when the team won the championship. He said that when they played the national anthem and raised the flag, he was very moved. I asked him if tears came to his eyes. He acknowledged that they did, "But I still had to exercise restraint." Song's portrayal of the team was clearly shaped by his own nationalism, which reflected the popular Chinese nationalism of the time. He was a man, and, as I will argue below, the popular nationalism was essentially masculine.

And so, although the global sports television infrastructure opened up the possibility of the emergence of a transnational public sphere that was somewhat autonomous from the party-state in mainland China, this process did not necessarily open up new spaces for feminist voices. Further, it is not clear that international sports will begin to make the nation-state obsolete in the coming "postnational" global order predicted by Arjun Appadurai (1993: 419–20). To the extent that transnational television strengthens Chinese nationalism, and to the extent that this nationalism is gendered male, the linkages with transnational television will only strengthen the male subject-position. On the other hand, the 1996 Atlanta Olympic Games, "the women's games," were seen by many as a turning point in international sports, so there may be hope that international sports telecasting will be more friendly to feminist positions in the future.

Women's Volleyball and the Print Media—A Public Sphere?

Television was only one of the myriad channels by which public opinion about the 1981 victory was expressed and shaped. Newspapers carried front-page headlines in red; magazines devoted entire sections to day-by-day accounts of the victory and diaries of the athletes. Artists dedicated musicals, poems, and paintings to them; a book was written about them. The vast majority of these artists and authors were men. One notable exception is the feature film *Seagull* (*Sha ou*), which was directed by Zhang Nuanxin, a female filmmaker. The possibilities for a feminist understanding of this film will be discussed further below.

Everyday people as well as elites felt compelled to reach out to the team. In the time immediately following the championship, more than a hundred groups and individuals sent them gifts, including Young Pioneer scarves, Youth League pins, school badges, commemorative badges, valuable food items, embroidery, metalwork, and fresh flowers. Famous artists sent them a seal, calligraphy, artwork, and statues created in their honor. More than thirty thousand letters were mailed to the team members; star spiker Lang Ping alone received more than three thousand. Thousands of letters were written to editors of newspapers and magazines and sports departments of television and radio stations.

This practice of making public private written forms like letters and diaries was extremely important as public opinion about the victory took shape. The role of letters is similar to that described by Habermas for the "literary public sphere" of eighteenth-century Europe. Through them, Habermas argues, the subjectivity developed in the intimacy of the family was extended into a public realm between private individuals and the state; later, the literary public sphere was used to defend the interests of the privatized market economy from the incursions of the state (1989: 49, 51). The publication of private sentiments is an important means of creating a third space between private and public subjectivity in Chinese public culture as well. Letters to the editors of newspapers and magazines, television talk-show hosts and commentators, and public leaders and institutions have been an important means of popular expression for many decades, even in the Maoist era. It is also common for the recipients of these letters to reply to them publicly. The coach of the women's volleyball team, Yuan Weimin, wrote a best-selling book titled *My Way of Teaching* (Wode zhijiao zhi dao) (Yuan 1988), describing it as his reply to the mail he had received over the years. These ritualized exchanges of letters and gifts between individuals and public figures seem to play a more important role in Chinese public culture than in contemporary America. They are thus one example of what is uniquely Chinese about Chinese public culture.

Of course, the letters that were published were selected for their harmony with official discourse. Only a few of the letters mailed to the team were ever made available to the public. In 1996, when I tried to track down the letters sent to the team, I was told that the bags had been thrown away sometime earlier in the 1990s; several people told me that it was probably because no one considered that they might have historical significance. However, it is also the case that when a Chinese sports scholar requested to look through the letters in the early 1980s she found that she was only able to gain access by pulling connections and promising to return all of the letters when she was finished. The reason, she was told, was that many of the letters were written in blood (a customary way of expressing deep emotion). The implication was that making public examples of such extreme emotion could be potentially dangerous.

It is possible to get a general idea of the emotions that compelled ordinary people to write the team from the multitude of letters, poems, and songs that were published in newspapers and magazines. The letter writers often linked their own pain to national humiliation in a way that blurred the boundaries between individuals and the collective nation. A recurring narrative goes as follows: the women's volleyball team endured extreme physical and psychological pain, persevered against overwhelming obstacles, and finally succeeded in their long quest, in the end redeeming their own suffering and China's national humiliation. The traumas of the

Cultural Revolution had only officially ended in 1976. Average people were inspired to persevere in leaving behind the past in order to redeem their own suffering and China's humiliation. Thus, the overriding emotion provoked by the 1981 victory was grief and its redemption. "Scar literature" had already begun to give public expression to this grief in the form of novels and short stories; the women's volleyball victories provided not just a catharsis, but also a vindication of sorts. A letter written by a middle-school teacher in Hunan to *Sports News* (Tiyu bao) echoes my analysis:

> Women's volleyball's tears of victory and the inspired tears of the hundreds of millions in the TV audience—what do they mean? They mean that victory doesn't come easily, they mean that the Chinese people need victory, they need the sweet dew of victory to moisten the spirit that was wounded in the past. (Wang 1981)

In sum, these letters contributed to a popular nationalism that was not entirely state-orchestrated. They contained the seeds of antiparty sentiment because there was a feeling of national unity based on the shared grief of the Cultural Revolution period and a desire to leave all that behind. What role did gender play in this rediscovered nationalism?

The Erasure of Gender by the Party-State

These moments of spontaneous, popular nationalism were never completely autonomous from the party-state, and the party quickly tried to harness the outpouring of nationalism to its own service. The official discourses about the volleyball victory were, for the most part, characterized by the "erasure of gender and sexuality in the discursive and representational space" that characterized Maoist China (see Yang, chap. 1 in this volume). This erasure was a result of the larger project of national redemption. As Yang puts it, the liberation of women was only a means to the end of the liberation of the nation, and thus it was ultimately subordinate to the larger nationalist project.

How did these *young women* come to stand for national unity and honor? In the current of patriotic fervor, their gender was usually subsumed by their Chineseness. Indeed, the thing that was remarkable about the official discourse of that time was that the team's gender and issues such as women's liberation or the state feminist project were not emphasized to the degree one might expect. By far the more prominent theme was that the team had realized the long-held revolutionary dream of erasing the label of "the sick *man* of East Asia" (*dongya bingfu*—the male bias is present in the original Chinese *fu*). When specific people are named as the dreamers of this dream, they are all men. The victory was said to fulfill the dreams of former Premier Zhou Enlai, who had first invited a Japanese volleyball coach to China to help the women train; Marshal He Long, the popular first director of the State Sports Commission; and Ma Qiwei, one of the key figures in the introduction of Western sports to China and the first women's volleyball coach after the founding of the PRC national team in 1950. Were there any historically significant women whose dreams were fulfilled on that day? Their voices are absent from the newspaper and magazine accounts and the official histories.

The welcoming speech made by an elderly high official at the airport was typical in its absence of gender and teleological history:

> That your victory stirred the heartstrings of one billion people has deep historical roots. . . . When we were young, people from the outside world cursed us as "the sick men of East Asia." . . . This time, when we saw the five-star flag of our ancestral land rising up to the solemn accompaniment of the national anthem, we old folks could not stop the hot tears from rolling down. Only under the leadership of the Chinese Communist Party was this day made possible. (in Rong et al. 1984: 429)

Of course, the women who made up the team had their own dreams, and some of them were fulfilled after their victory. It is a common practice to appoint star athletes to political positions; this is said to demonstrate that "the state has not forgotten." The first-string team members were appointed as delegates to the National People's Congress and other political positions; three of the women were given high positions in the Sports Commission system, and one in the People's Liberation Army (PLA) system. However, the person whose political star rose most rapidly was Yuan Weimin, the male coach who led the team to its first three victories. He subsequently became vice director of the State Sports Commission and a member of the Party Central Committee.

One reason that gender did not figure prominently in the official nationalism was that these athletes were the product of a sports system that deliberately erased gender differences. Removed from their families and put into sports boarding schools, they had been subject to military-style discipline from a young age. Sports team rules are especially draconian with respect to gender and sexuality. The provincial, municipal, and national teams administered by the State Sports Commission forbade athletes to have romantic relationships with members of the opposite sex, and sex segregation was strictly enforced in the dormitories. Violation of these rules could result in expulsion from the team. Until the late 1980s, athletes were allowed to be engaged only after the ages of around twenty-four (for women) and twenty-six (for men) and were not permitted to marry while still competing. This contrasted with the minimum legal ages for marriage of twenty (for women) and twenty-two (for men) for the general populace. Since the late 1980s, it has become possible only for star athletes in their late twenties or older to negotiate with their teams to allow them to marry. In an influential article that critictized the sports system, "Superpower Dream," Zhao Yu commented that "not a few leaders and coaches of professional sports teams stand guard against love as if they were standing guard against a flood" (1988: 182). Zhao states that this is because they believe love has no place in the military discipline of the sports team. Also, providing the facilities for families and children would divert resources away from the main goal of sports success.

In addition, the dress code on sports teams forbade women to wear long hair hanging loose over their shoulders. Until very recently, sportswomen were required to wear their hair short or tied back in public, including in competitions. If tied back, the ponytail or pigtails should be low on the head because a high ponytail was considered too provocative. Several famous male coaches also forbade their athletes to wear face cream, makeup, or high heels. Even today, it is not regarded as proper for an athlete to draw attention to her femininity, because it is considered to show a lack of a properly serious attitude. Although in the 1990s market forces began to unleash sexuality from the enforced masculinization of the Cultural Revolution period, change was much slower to come to sports teams than to society at large. Athletes who have grown up in this sort of atmosphere often experience a kind of awakening when they retire and begin to look for a husband. For example, a former basketball player decided to take a modeling class after she graduated from the Beijing University of Sports in the early 1990s. She told me:

> On the sports team when I was younger, we were forbidden to dress up. Long hair over the shoulders was forbidden. We always wore our hair in a ponytail or pigtails. All the Chinese athletes did. . . . I didn't even have the idea of makeup in my brain until I took the modeling class. . . . I had short hair like yours and an athlete's demeanor . . . the way I moved and carried myself, and my hunched back. . . . I learned to have confidence in my appearance, to improve my posture, and to carry myself like I'm somebody. . . . I did find another boyfriend [after her first one, a male teammate, broke up with her]. . . . I got into fashion modeling because I thought it

should be a kind of aesthetic appreciation (*yishu xinshang*), it should be elegant (*wenya*).

Ironically, in the 1990s many of China's runway models were former athletes who had been chosen for their height. The repressive sports background was often cited as a reason for the low level of grace and aesthetic awareness among Chinese fashion models.

In 1981, the women's volleyball team had neither the opportunity nor the social context for this awakening. They were the products of a militarized disciplinary regime in which a masculine appearance symbolized the proper fighting spirit. This was the kind of woman that represented the Chinese nation.

Gender in Popular Nationalism

And why should we be surprised? For they were, after all, carrying out the dream of restoring a national honor that was, in many ways, a masculine honor. Although these women are highly regarded in China, most people still comment that if the Chinese men's soccer team could win the World Cup, then you would *really* see a celebration.

While the official discourse and the state sports system erased gender as an issue by creating women athletes in the image of men, in the popular nationalist discourse something more subtle was going on. People were aware of the gender of the team, but their gender was often secondary to their nationality. When they retired several years later, their marriages were reported in the media and followed with interest by the public. People also commented on their appearances. It was widely commented that Yang Xilan was young and pretty, while Lang Ping was not very attractive.

Still, they were Chinese first and women second. An example of this view is found in one letter, sent to the team by Chinese students studying abroad in West Germany, which mentions the team's gender only to quickly subordinate it to their Chineseness:

> You have simultaneously demonstrated before the eyes of the world the modesty and goodwill of the Chinese people, the traditional virtue of Chinese women, the fighting spirit of today's young people, and superlative ball skills. You've told the world, "These are the Chinese!" (in Cao 1985: 139)

While I would not want to take anything away from the inspiration that millions of women received from their victory, I have also observed that the most active and visible fans seemed to be male, most of whom were probably college students. Young men seemed to dominate the welcoming ceremonies at the airports during the team's string of world championships over the next seven years. Among the letters the team received were thousands of love letters and proposals of marriage.

Of course, the athletes became an oft-cited example of the liberation of Chinese women under the Communist Party, but at the popular level they also became a source of pride for Chinese women. An example is a young Beijing university student who told me that she and her friends found glee in challenging sexist statements from male students by asking, "So what's wrong with the *men's* volleyball team?"

Ironically, the string of volleyball victories in the 1980s occurred at a time when, despite the repression of femininity on sports teams, the bodies of sportswomen had become the first site for the reassertion of the masculine gaze in the popular media. This was probably due to the fact that the clothes worn by women in many sports reveal the body more than typical street clothes do. This baring of the body was permitted by the state because of its promotion of top-level sports. Hence, calendars, magazine covers, playing cards, and postcards at that time often featured gymnasts in leotards, swimmers in bathing suits, tennis players in short skirts, and so on, while Western-style swimsuit calendars were still banned as pornography. When, after a heated debate, the State Council allowed the State Sports Commission to approve the wearing of bikinis by women bodybuilders in 1986, women bodybuilders quickly became a favorite image in these media, and their photos could be seen on the fronts and backs of magazines having nothing to do with sports. In other words, in this period when China was just emerging from the Cultural Revolution and the power of the market had just barely started to assert itself, the masculine libido of the state was still minimizing gender differences by exerting a masculinizing effect on sportswomen, but the masculine libido of the market was already beginning to mark gender differences by selling the sportive female body. Of course, this body did offer a hard and strong alternative to the soft and passive-looking models inspired by Hong Kong and Taiwanese fashions.

Zhang Nuanxin's Seagull *(Sha Ou)*

While most of the popular images of the volleyball team were created by men, one influential exception was the popular feature film *Seagull*, filmed in 1981 before the World Cup victory. Cowritten (with Li Tuo) and directed by Zhang Nuanxin, a prominent Fourth Generation director, this film is typical of the films made by women about women, which Dai Jinhua criticizes because they were still made from a male point of view (see Dai's contribution to this volume). *Seagull* is, for the most part, an example of this trend. However, it does open a small window for a feminist reading.[2]

Seagull portrays the bitter life of Sha Ou, a member of the national volleyball team, who is played by an actual second-string team member. The film opens with her and her teammates tripping across a grassy field toward the camera in their red China uniforms. Sha Ou's voice explains, "Every person has her dream. My dream was to defeat the Japanese volleyball team and to be the champion." The year is 1977, the Asian Games are three months away, and she is twenty-eight years old and nearing the end of her career. She recalls, "If only we could win, I was willing to pay any price and make any sacrifice. But I didn't know that the sacrifice was that great, the price that high."

The story then begins as she is pulled out of practice to go to the team clinic, where she is told that she has a serious back injury and that to continue playing will risk permanent paralysis. We are thus introduced to the tragic mood that pervades the film from beginning to end. Through most of the film, Sha Ou is sullen, stubborn, sobbing, and suffering. When she wins only the silver medal in the 1977 Asian Games, she is so bitterly disappointed that she tosses the medal into the ocean on the boat back from Hong Kong while seagulls soar in the distance. However, her sadness is briefly allayed when she reads in the newspaper that her boyfriend, Shen Dawei, a member of the mountain-climbing team, has successfully conquered Mt. Everest. Everything seems beautiful for a moment: she tells her mother that she is happier than if she had succeeded herself, and that she will now retire, go through with her oft-postponed wedding, and devote herself to being the "head of the support team" (*houqin buzhang*) for her husband. Her brief happiness is shattered when an avalanche kills Dawei on the way back down. Her will collapses like the crashing snow of the avalanche. In her lowest moment, she recalls a time when they visited the Yuan Ming ruins together. Dawei, who is older, wiser, and something of a mentor, explains to her that the palace was burned by the imperialist powers: "Whatever could be burned was burned. Only these stones remain." These words echo through her mind, drawing a parallel between her own personal loss and China's most poignant symbol of national loss. The allegory motivates her to return to the national team as an assistant coach. In the airport before Dawei left, Sha Ou had recounted that her most ruthless coach had been a woman in her thirties, whom Sha Ou had once called Tiger Yu in a fit of temper. Coach Yu had vowed not to marry until she had won a world championship. When she was finally unable to make the international traveling squad, she had no choice but to marry, but she put her hopes on the younger women. Like her, Sha Ou now mercilessly pushes the next generation of women to greater performances.

The wedding party of her friend and former teammate, Lili, highlights the film's recurring conflict between marriage and the vindication of national honor. Lili, who had never been as tough and single-minded as Sha Ou, was always a bit of a flirt, but she has now achieved happiness. Dr. Han, the team doctor who had always harbored strong feelings for Sha Ou, attends the wedding and is now a widower with a young daughter. The daughter follows Sha Ou into Lili's bedroom, picks up one of Lili's trophies, and says, "Look at me—I'm a world champion. Auntie, are you a world champion?" Sha Ou answers sadly, "No. Auntie isn't a world champion. Auntie is nothing." The little girl tells her not to be afraid, that one day she will be a world champion. Dr. Han enters the room, and it soon becomes clear that he is about to propose marriage, and it looks like Sha Ou has decided that marrying him will make her into something, and she will accept. Her dead boyfriend Dawei had asked Dr. Han to look after her just before he left to climb Everest, noting that "girls will inevitably have their weak moments," and so one man had essentially handed her over to another. Unfortunately, just at this moment she tries to pick up the daughter, collapses, and knows that she will never walk again.

The movie ends with her in a wheelchair in the hospital. She has just heard that the women's volleyball team has won the world championship. Although she had refused to watch, she agrees to go to the TV room to watch the end of the broadcast. (The ritual importance of television is marked by shots of her friends and colleagues around a TV set at the national team center and her mother and family at home, uniting everyone in spirit if not in space.) She arrives in time to hear the voice of Song Shixiong, the television announcer, saying, "The people thank you. The nation (*zuguo*) thanks you." As she wipes tears from her cheeks, we hear Sha Ou's voice conclude, "Friends say being an athlete is too bitter. . . . Not me. If people could really change things, if I could live it all over again, I'd still want to be an athlete, I'd still want to play ball, I'd still want to be a world champion." The final scene shows a new generation of young volleyball players bouncing across a field toward the screen in their red China uniforms.

This film could have been made by a man in that it echoes the elements of Chinese nationalism that I argue are constituted from a male subject-position. The women clearly have to choose between marriage and volleyball, so that their main sacrifice is their womanhood (with the implicit understanding that wifehood and motherhood is what makes a woman a woman). And after all, the one who ends up happy and healthy is the married Lili, not Sha Ou. Sha Ou achieves her success under the tutelage of a male coach, doctor, boyfriend, and even at one point a male cook. They are all concerned and supportive, while the most ruthless person is the female Coach Yu whose place Sha Ou later takes. Coach Yu and her own mother are also the only people whose authority Sha Ou openly defies.

However, there is a small space for a feminist interpretation if we compare this film to the official discourses discussed above. In those discourses, the women's volleyball team realized the hopes held by several generations of men. This film, by contrast, is very much about a female lineage, which I believe reflects the female subject-position of the director, however tentative. The lineage extends from the bitter thirty-year-old coach to Sha Ou to Sha Ou's students to Dr. Han's daughter. The people most strongly committed to national honor are women. Only the woman coach has the nerve to tell Sha Ou that her problem is not physical, but the lack of will power. It is often the men who try to dissuade them from putting themselves through such suffering. Sha Ou has "traded the second half of her life for a game," as Dr. Han had pleaded with her not to do, and the film leaves no hint that her future holds anything other than a wheelchair in a small room. The extremely tragic tone of the movie offers the possibility of understanding this film as a criticism of the cruel self-sacrifices made by women who were ultimately tougher than the men who guided them. The female lineage within a male structure is reminiscent of the "women's community" described by Margery Wolf (1972).

"The Yin Waxes and the Yang Wanes": Debates on Gender and Nation

The women's volleyball victory was only one of the first in a series of breakthroughs on the world scene by Chinese sportswomen. Since the 1980s, women have, on the whole, had more success in international sports than men. This has been true in basketball, soccer, track and field, swimming, judo, weightlifting, softball/baseball, and so on. Only in gymnastics, diving, table tennis, and badminton have Chinese men achieved successes comparable to the women. The superiority of Chinese sportswomen has been a constant topic of debate—both conversational and published—for more than a decade now. It has been expressed in the aphorism, "The yin waxes and the yang wanes" (*yin sheng yang shuai*). In classical iconography, the phoenix represents the female and the dragon the male: the big question is why the "phoenix has taken off first." The answers that have generally been given are that women's sports worldwide got a later start than men's and that they tend to get less government and economic support than men's sports; hence, the level of competition is lower, and therefore women's gold medals are easier to attain than men's. The Chinese government has given relatively equal support to men's and women's sports since its inception, and this gives Chinese women a relative advantage over women from other countries. It also proves the superiority of women's position under socialism. Finally, Chinese women are more obedient than Chinese men, and sportswomen train harder than sportsmen (fig. 1). For example, a 1988 newspaper article argued that

> the majority of China's female athletes possess Chinese women's character-istic ability to "eat bitterness and endure hard labor" (chiku nailao). They train hard, they have a tenacious way of doing things, they are disciplined, listen to instructions, have a strong commitment to their work and a strong sense of responsibility. Not a few coaches reflect that this is why female athletes are easy to coach. (Yan 1988)

Elsewhere, I have analyzed the sources of women's obedience at length (Brownell 1995: 213–37; Brownell 1996). I argue that women, especially peasant women, are obedient and able to "eat bitterness" because they are born into a low status in life and sports are a way out for them. While sportswomen's ability to endure pain has been much valorized in the press, no one has looked below the surface of their "spirit of sacrifice" to see the underlying logic of the social inferior who sacrifices herself for higher-ups in the social hierarchy.

The fact that the subject-position in these debates is essentially male is evident in a debate that took place in 1987, when the sports media gave much coverage to a new phenomenon: two married female athletes, one of them with a child, had won gold medals at the 1987 Chinese National Games. This development was heralded because it was said to destroy outdated stereotypes about life stages. In analyses of why it was that foreign women continued to win medals after marriage and childbirth while Chinese women usually did not, the conclusion was that traditional Chinese stereotypes were the problem. For example, one newspaper article noted that "internationally, not a few female athletes enter their second 'golden age' after marriage, but we've had difficulty in accepting this and for a long time have emphasized the so-called weaknesses of the Eastern female" (Miao 1987). If one substitutes men for we in the last sentence, the essentially male subject-position in this view is exposed.

In conversations, sportspeople usually explained that a woman's attention

Figure 1. A runner and her male coach at the 1986 Haidian District Middle School Athletics Meet in Beijing. Photograph by Susan Brownell.

becomes "scattered" (*fensan*) after childbirth and she can no longer concentrate on her training. In fact, it seemed to me that the real problem was the double burden, which affected the performance of athletes even more so than women in other professions, given the physical demands of their trade. Yet no one I talked to explained the problem in this way. Ye Peisu had retired to marry and have a child over the vehement opposition of her male coach. In 1987, she came out of retirement to win the high jump at the National Games. She told me that she didn't know what to expect but thought she would just "try and see." She said she was only able to manage it because her mother helped her with child care. Even so, she often brought her young daughter with her to the track, where she played in the sand in the long-jump pit or was rotated among Ye's training partners when they were resting between workout assignments. Ye only managed a one-year-long comeback.

The absence of any discussion of the double burden is the reason that I feel the subject-position in these debates was male. Both male and female athletes who had married and continued competing were few, because of the general team policies against it. However, it seems significant that the one married male athlete whom I interviewed did not name child care or household duties as his major obstacle to continued improvement. Instead, he said his main problem was to manage the relationship between his mother and his wife. So long as the relationship between the mother-in-law and daughter-in-law was a good one, he told me, it was entirely possible to train after marriage.

Finally, another issue that was totally absent from these discussions of female athletes was that the superiority of sportswomen existed only in the realm of active athletes. After retirement, and in the Sports Commission hierarchy, women's positions were generally inferior to men's. There was only one woman in the top levels of the State Sports Commission and the Chinese Olympic Committee—Zhang Caizhen, a vice director of the State Sports Commission. In 1990, only 19.4 percent of China's 18,173 professional coaches were women (Riordan and Dong 1996: 147). This figure suggests that as much as 80 percent of China's female athletes were being coached by men. Occasionally, one hears rumors of physical and sexual abuse. Ma Junren, coach of the world-record-breaking long-distance runners, publicly stated that he had sometimes hit his athletes (*Liberation Daily* quoted in *China News Digest* 1995a). Yet, needless to say, there has not been a whisper of this in the Chinese press.

Gender: Nation as Female, State as Male

Events that surrounded the victory of the women's volleyball team in the 1985 World Championships illustrate the predominance of the male voice in both the official and popular aspects of the Chinese nationalism that was expressed at a moment when a potential public sphere seemed to be taking shape. The events were set into motion on September 18, 1985, when several thousand Beijing University students gathered at the school's south gate and pasted up big-character posters to protest the party's handling of the anniversary of Japan's invasion of the Northeast in 1931. Some posters took the occasion to denounce Japan's "economic aggression" against China and the lack of democracy in China. One night in November, dissident students pushed pamphlets under dormitory doors calling on students to demonstrate in Tiananmen Square on November 20, the date on which the women's volleyball team would play Japan for their fourth straight world title, and when the final game in the first-ever Sino-Japanese Go championship would take place. The letter ended by claiming, "This is a day in the history of contemporary China-Japan contacts on which to feel proud and elated, and the patriotic enthusiasm of the entire Chinese people will show an unprecedented upsurge."

The Chinese won both events. A few hundred students showed up in Tiananmen Square and were greeted by a horde of Western journalists who had obtained copies of the dissident letter. The students sang the national anthem and shouted slogans for two hours until they were dispersed by security officials with bullhorns (*Time* 1985: 50).

In the next week, the go and volleyball teams were brought together with university students on at least six different occasions for "welcoming meetings" (*huanying yishi*). These state-choreographed occasions are common when victorious teams return to the homeland, and are characterized by elaborate national symbolism in the absence of any real exchange of opinions. At Beijing University on a blustery day in November, the team members, coaches, and university president—clad in down coats—were seated on the rostrum in the concrete grandstand at the May Fourth sportsfield. For four hours they took turns giving speeches and receiving gifts. While this might seem dull by American standards, the fervor of the several thousand students who attended made the situation potentially dangerous. The margins of the crowd expanded and contracted in waves as the students on the outside pressed forward eagerly to see and were repelled by the students in the core fighting back for space. Some students were injured. Several of the women spoke briefly, with the longest speech by Lang Ping. However, her voice and those of the other women were clearly in the service of the state: they repeatedly emphasized the hospitality and friendship shown to them by the Japanese, in contrast to the accusations of Japanese aggression that had been declared in the students' big-character posters two months earlier. When they were finished, Yuan

Weimin speechified for more than an hour. Students read congratulatory letters. There was a ritual exchange of gifts: the Beijing University women's volleyball team gave the women fresh flowers, and Young Pioneers tied red scarves around their necks. In return, the women were asked to sign a volleyball to be mailed to the front-line soldiers on the southwest border in order to "express their common fighting spirit, their desire to win glory for the nation" (see the account in *Beida xuetongshe* 1985).

In this ceremony and in the discourses described above, whether official or popular, and in the dissident letter, a distinct woman's voice was never expressed. Most of the key actors were male: the high officials were all male, the people who spoke the longest were male, most of the people who offered the letters of congratulations and gifts were male, and the dissident letter writers were reportedly male. The crowd at the welcoming ceremony seemed to be predominantly male (in Brownell 1995: 86). Yuan Weimin was presented as the spokesman for the team. The only interaction involving just women was the exchange of gifts with the university women's volley-ball team. Overall, these choreographed exchanges gave the impression that these women were able to reach their full potential under the guidance and tutelage of men. If they represented women's place within the Chinese nation, then it was apparent that this women's space was thoroughly circumscribed by men. These women who symbolized national unity and progress were clearly subordinated to a (masculine) party-state.

This symbolic structure can be expressed in the formula woman : man :: nation : state. Woman obeys the guidance of man just as the nation or the people obey the guidance of the party-state. Clearly, the vaunted obedience of female athletes has greater political resonances. From the official point of view, there is a certain logic that young women were successful signifiers of the Chinese nation. From the popular point of view, there was also a certain logic. For one of the main emotions that the team was officially supposed to—and sometimes actually did—inspire was love of country. An example is from a letter written to the team by a disillusioned university student:

> You have aroused again the love of country in the bottom of my heart. . . .
> [You] have lit the flame of my love which had already died out. . . . In ten
> years this was the first time I felt my heart beating—along with the strong
> rhythm of the pulse of the nation; in ten years this was the first time I felt
> the honor of being human—China's pride. (in Cao 1985: 137)

If, as I have argued, the subject-position in this popular nationalism is that of a heterosexual man, then who better to signify the nation, the object of his love, than young women? Once these events were set into motion, these young women resonated with the symbolic structure of Chinese nationalism and the public culture that shaped it. I do not think it is a coincidence that the 1989 student demonstrators in Tiananmen Square were predominantly male as well. Since Beijing University was one of the hotbeds of unrest in 1989, it is likely that many of the fans of the women's volleyball team in 1985 may have been sitting in the square in 1989 (I know that at least one was). Hence, my description of their nationalism has broader implications. Craig Calhoun observed that in 1989 the national essence was presented as primarily male (1994: 192). As I have suggested, I believe that women tended to relate to the team in a different way, which was potentially subversive of the interpretations of the masculine state and nationalism. However, this subaltern perspective never fully took shape in public culture.

And so it would not be accurate to say that the popular fans viewed the volleyball team as masculinized women whose gender was insignificant or forgotten; the picture is more complicated than that. Instead, I would argue that these discussions and representations of sportswomen continued some of the themes of Chinese nationalism over the past century that have been discussed by feminist scholars in China and abroad. Essentially, these scholars have shown that modern nationalism in China has been characterized by the trope of female bodily suffering and self-sacrifice as a signifier of a male nationalism, which saw itself as wounded by and impotent against Western and Japanese imperialism (Barlow 1994a; Duara 1995a; Liu 1994; Meng 1993). The subject-position in this nationalism is male; women must suffer because men are impotent to right the injustices done to *men* through their women. Thus, female suffering is above all a sign that men need to pull themselves together and do something about it, which is a source of much self-flagellation among Chinese men. It seems to me that this theme has also been an undertone in discussions of Chinese sportswomen, including in the film *Seagull*, and that it explains why debates that are very much about gender can avoid addressing feminist concerns.

Feminists writing on the emergence of the public sphere in Western Europe have shown that it emerged in opposition to another sphere defined as private—the domestic realm, which was women's realm (Eley 1992: 307–19). As Joan Landes has argued, "It is as if man's subjecthood could only be attained at the cost of woman's subjection" (1984: 29). In China in the 1980s, women were not relegated to a private sphere; instead, sportswomen as public symbols of the nation were very prominent. Nevertheless, Landes's statement holds true for China as well, because ultimately this entire construction of gender-in-the-nation was from a male point of view that did not allow a voice for women's real problems and concerns. And so it would appear that whether we are talking about proto-public spheres in Western Europe or in China, the obstacle for women is that the overarching public culture is still constructed from a male point of view.

Postscript

In the 1990s, the state control of the sports system loosened and market forces began to influence female athletes. While this change liberated some female star athletes from the disciplinary rigor of the state, it subjected them to the even more inevitable forces of the market. The relative equality in financial resources devoted to men's and women's sports was shattered in 1995 with the commercialization of men's soccer and basketball and the formation of corporate-funded professional leagues. Men's basketball and soccer were judged to have the potential to earn money; women's basketball and soccer were not. This was true even though the women's teams were among the top five in the world, while the men's teams were not. One of the key arguments in support of this capitalist-style professionalization was that it would improve the level of competition and propel Chinese *men* toward Olympic gold medals.

However, the market also brings its own kinds of freedom. In 1993 and 1994, the superstar sportswomen were the world-record-setting long-distance runners who were trained by the draconian coach Ma Junren. By 1995, his star runner Wang Junxia had led a rebellion of the "Ma Family Soldiers." They had left his tutelage and started their own team, complaining that he had kept large portions of their prize money and claimed the three Mercedes cars they had won at the 1993 World Championships. Wang told Reuters, "We simply couldn't take it any longer. We had absolutely no freedom. We were all on the brink of going crazy. The pressure was too intense; we couldn't take it" (*Track and Field News* 1995: 59). Wang found herself another coach and went on to two outstanding performances at the 1996 Olympic Games, where she won one gold and one silver medal.

As sports become more commercialized and athletes more cosmopolitan, the tightly structured relations between state and nation described above will change, and athletes will no longer be so closely allied with the party-state. However, female athletes will probably find that while they are less subject to the masculinizing pressures of the state-controlled system, they are more subject to the masculine gaze of the market, which dictates that sportswomen who are attractive to men get more commercial sponsorships. Because the development of Chinese sports is now so thoroughly intertwined with television, and because Chinese television is rapidly becoming more dependent on the advertising revenues offered by joint-venture and multinational corporations, transnational market forces will probably increasingly shape the production of the images of sportswomen. This may liberate these women somewhat from the roles required of them by Chinese nationalism, but I am not optimistic that it will liberate them from the boundaries imposed by the masculine libido.

Perhaps the latest turn in Lang Ping's life will serve as a possible sample of what the future has to offer. After many years in the United States, she returned in 1995 to take over as the national coach of the women's volleyball team. The team quickly turned around its eighth-place finish in the 1994 World Championships and became a medal contender. When the Chinese team toured the United States shortly before the 1996 Atlanta Olympic Games, Lang Ping received raucous standing ovations from the Chinese members of the audience, much to the surprise of many American spectators, who had no idea what a national icon she was. The team won the silver medal in Atlanta. Members of the Olympic delegation told me that this rapid turnaround was not due to her skills as a coach but, rather, to her presence as an inspiring symbol.

Quite a lot of discussion was stimulated by another transformation: Lang Ping had, since she was last in the limelight, become quite attractive, to the point of being nearly unrecognizable. Despite the tremendous admiration and even love that was felt for her as an athlete in the 1980s, it was generally agreed that she was not very pretty. At the 1996 Olympic Games, she sported stylish glasses and a shoulder-length, bobbed haircut. Her formerly heavy-lidded eyes now seemed larger, and indeed her entire face seemed different. The rumor among the Chinese Olympic delegation in Atlanta was that she must have had cosmetic surgery to have changed so much. Since cosmetic surgery is quite popular now among Chinese celebrities, especially the double-eyelid operation to make the eyes larger, this was not improbable. However, after comparing her photos from the 1980s with the official team photo in 1996, I concluded that she had not necessarily undergone surgery. The difference could have been that between a woman in her twenties with short, boyish hair whose life revolved around a volleyball court and a cosmopolitan thirty-plus woman who had learned to use makeup and hairstyles. Lang Ping's metamorphosis is truly a sign of the changes in Chinese women's self-presentation. This is where the economic reforms are leading Chinese women: if even Lang Ping's appearance is subjected to such harsh scrutiny, and her team's success attributed to her value as a symbol rather than her skills, then surely no one is free from the tyranny of stereotypical feminine beauty.

It is to be hoped that, at least, a feminist voice will begin to emerge in the debates going on in the public culture of sports. Change has been very slow in sports scholarship. As of yet, the handful of female sports scholars have been unable to develop a feminist viewpoint. The obstacle is that the successes of Chinese sportswomen have provided a superficial appearance of women's equality or even superiority that has proved difficult to penetrate because even women view it from the primarily male subject-position that I have elucidated in this chapter. It will probably not be until after the superficial appearance of equality is lost under the market reforms that this voice will emerge.

NOTES

The fieldwork on which much of this paper was based was carried out in 1985–86 at Beijing University and in 1987–88 at the Beijing University of Physical Education. The latter period was supported by a dissertation-year fellowship from the Committee on Scholarly Communication with the PRC, with funds from the U.S. Information Agency. Part of the textual research was supported by a Richard Carley Hunt Grant from the Wenner-Gren Foundation for Anthropological Research (1993). Later materials were collected during a project funded by a University of Missouri, St. Louis, Research Award and a University of Missouri Research Board Award (1995–96).

I would like to express my intellectual debt to Mayfair Yang, whose challenging comments and stimulating work greatly shaped this essay.

1 All interviews and Chinese sources cited in this chapter were translated by the author.

2 *Sha Ou* (Seagull) was produced in 1981 by Beijing dianying xueyuan, qingnian dianying zhipianchang.

9

White Women, Male Desires: A Televisual Fantasy

of the Transnational Chinese Family

From the Field to the Set: Acting as an Anthropologist in Shanghai, 1995

A stint as lead actress in a Chinese television drama was not part of my anthropological fieldwork as I originally envisioned it. But one of fieldwork's
many unexpected turns was the opportunity to participate in the production of an award-winning Chinese television movie, *Sunset at Long Chao Li*.[1]
My official role in the drama was to play the American wife of a returned
Chinese scholar; unofficially, I was also the cultural and linguistic intermediary, who not only translated for other Americans on the set but who was
also variously called on to "authenticate" images of Americans in both the
drama and in real life. Not surprisingly, perhaps, my commentaries and
interlocutions were often dismissed or reinterpreted by my Chinese colleagues, producing unexpected outcomes. Thus, this essay is partially an
effort to come to terms with the ways in which the Chinese male creators
of the drama constructed me as a "foreign" and "modern" woman during
the production and, more generally, the ways in which Caucasians—the
quintessential foreigners—are deployed in constructions of Chinese identity. Specifically, this essay links a textual interpretation of *Sunset* to larger
questions regarding the construction of a modern Chinese transnational
identity originating on the Mainland but encompassing a new global order
of economic and gender domination.

The drama, whose critical acclaim in China derived partly from its purportedly innovative script, addresses the rapid transformation of Shanghai in the 1990s, its differential impact on older and younger generations, changing conceptions of marriage and family within a transnational context, and conflicting views about what constitutes a modern Shanghai and Shanghainese identity, as the city and its people refashion themselves into China's international and cultural center. Most striking, perhaps, is the presence of two foreigners in a drama depicting the lives of a three-generation "Shanghainese" family. An elderly father, his son, the son's Caucasian wife, and her Caucasian son comprised the Zhou family; there were no Chinese women. Although this family configuration might, at first blush, suggest American incursions into the sacrosanct realm of the Chinese family, I argue that the gendered and racial implications of this representation actually reveal the aspirations of elite Chinese men to dominate and define the terms of a transnational Chinese modernity in the late twentieth century.

Analyzing the gendered and hierarchical nature of the Chinese and foreign roles in *Sunset* provides insights into the cultural salience of at least three contemporary social phenomena: China's growing economic and political role in the global arena; the perceived threat to China's "masculinity" through the trafficking, or loss, of women to overseas Chinese and foreign men (which dovetails with concerns about China's dominance in the transnational capitalist sphere); and the challenges faced by Chinese women (and men) as they negotiate the opportunities and limitations accompanying these changes. My concern is twofold: first, to interrogate the ways in which images of foreigners, and especially white women, are utilized to create a transnational ideal of modern urban Chinese identity—an identity that simultaneously depends on and promotes ideals of global capitalism like freedom, openness, wealth, individual expression, and personal fulfillment; and second, to examine how the absence of Chinese women from this drama serves to restructure racial and gender categories in such a way that essentialized characteristics of Chinese womanhood are transformed into a masculinist vision of modern, desirable femininity that even white women can fulfill.

Televisual Culture and the Formation of
National Publics and Transnational Subjectivities

The notion of a transnational Chinese identity is both predicated on and constitutive of the global flows of capital, people, and culture around and across the Pacific Ocean—flows that have intensified and accelerated commensurately with the economic reforms in mainland China over almost two decades (Ong 1993; Ong and Nonini 1997). In the final decade of the twentieth century, the open door facilitating these flows is increasingly a technological door in which television and other forms of electronic mass media provide the vehicle of transport. By the mid-1990s, China's TV audience had grown to 900 million people, or 75 percent of the mainland Chinese population, and more than 90 percent of urban households own at least one set (*China News Digest* 1995b; Wang Shaoguang 1995).

As a medium of both cultural creation and mass dissemination, television can simultaneously generate and reflect alternative visions of possible worlds and selves and play a crucial role in the formation of national debates and "publics" in the home country and across national boundaries (cf. Abu-Lughod 1993; Grewal and Kaplan 1994). Visual media, and especially television, are particularly effective in this regard because they rely on "spectatorship" and the generalizability of certain desires in a viewing public (Lee 1993). Thus, despite charges of cultural homogenization or imperialism associated with television viewing, the transnational aspects of TV can also play a role in linking Chinese-speaking populations around the world (cf. Yang 1997; Zha 1995; Liu 1995b), allowing the transfer and transformation of images and desires for modernity.

A starting point for this analysis, then, is the recognition that China's urban coastal centers like Shanghai are sites that not only consume, incorporate, or transform Western cultural productions but also *produce*, both independently from and interactively with Western sources, their own images and values of what it means to be Chinese, Shanghainese, and a woman or man, in the transnational sphere in which China variously and selectively constructs itself as both distinct from, and just like, the "rest of the world." The meteoric growth in Chinese programming in recent years (Lull 1991; Yang 1997) highlights the importance of examining the ways in which Chinese themselves utilize expanded technological opportunities to "imagine" new possibilities for identity, agency, and modernity (cf. Anderson 1991). One way is suggested by the rapidly increasing televisual portrayal of foreigners, constructed through *Chinese* imaginaries, projected into the homes of common mainland citizens. During my fieldwork, many people commented on the number of foreign roles in Chinese dramas and in response to my queries suggested that foreigners increased the show's popularity or interest (*qu*) for the viewing public.[2] Moreover, the inclusion of foreigners in TV dramas provides a real and symbolic opportunity for

Chinese to "connect to the world" (*guoji jiegui*)—to realize China's aspirations for greater economic, political, and cultural leadership in the international arena.[3]

Turning the analytic gaze on locally produced mass media can counter "orientalist" discourses (cf. Said 1978) by decentering the West as the global site for the production of images of modernity and freedom, and by viewing the flow of culture, knowledge, and power around the globe as multidirectional, crisscrossing national boundaries in the constitution of new forms of identity and power (Appadurai 1993; Grewal and Kaplan 1994). But interpreting local television productions as sites of public expression and cultural contestation does not necessarily reveal a subaltern vision of the world otherwise obscured by American televisual imperialism. Lila Abu-Lughod (1993a, 1993b) points out that in most countries television is at least partially state controlled, and television productions often reflect the concerns of the cultural or political elite. These politics of production mean that television shows that appear on the air conform broadly to national discourses and cannot be seen as independent, counter-hegemonic challenges to the political order. Indeed, although they decenter the West as the producer of global modernizing discourses, these programs may reproduce locational and political inequalities within a given nation, and their analyses must take these complex dynamics into account. In a similarly cautionary stance toward their democratic potential, Nancy Fraser (1992; also Yang, introduction to this volume) has highlighted the ways in which "public spheres," by their very definition, have historically reflected male concerns and reinscribed gender divisions, marginalizing women's voices and concerns into the "private" domain.

These caveats are particularly relevant to the interpretive analysis of Chinese television serials, even in the contemporary period of flourishing growth in the mass media industry. Despite expanding freedoms in the arena of cultural production, state censorship continues. Moreover, for the most part, the access and opportunity to take advantage of the more open environment remain in the control of men. Thus, most of the images and debates that circulate in the Chinese public via television reflect male perspectives and conform, at least in broad terms, to state dictates. As a drama written, produced, and directed by Shanghai's male and self-proclaimed progressive cultural elite, *Sunset* presents a particular strain of masculine narrative that hinges on the reimagination of Chinese identity in the transnational sphere. As such, the drama suggests China's transcendence over Western domination but does so on masculine terms that reinscribe gender inequalities in the modern Chinese family and nation.

Figure 1. *The Zhou family enjoys a pleasant outing in a scene from* Sunset at Long Chao Li.

Family, Gender, and Race in an Innovative Television Drama

Described to me by the director as a "Chinese *On Golden Pond*," *Sunset* dramatizes the conflict between the young and old generations in one family, the Zhous (fig. 1).[4] Zhou He, an elderly Chinese architect world renowned for his work even in the present, lives in a *shikumen* rowhouse complex called Long Chao Li that he himself designed in his youth.[5] Now widowed and living alone, he awaits the homecoming of his son and only child Zhou Tong, who studied architecture in America and is returning to China for the first time after a protracted absence. Zhou Tong writes his father, telling him to anticipate a "pleasant surprise." The surprises Zhou Tong bring are neither anticipated by nor pleasant for Zhou He: a Caucasian American wife, Margie, and her Caucasian American son from a previous marriage, Billy, *and* a plan to demolish Long Chao Li and replace it with a commercial plaza. What ensues is Zhou He's gradual revelation that his generation and its accomplishments are a thing of the past; that they must make way for the younger generation to create a modern city on their own terms, and the realization that perhaps that vision is not all bad; that the "joining" of East and West—both literally and metaphorically through Zhou Tong's marriage and architectural designs—is the hope for Shanghai's future. Zhou Tong, for his part, must negotiate the treacherous path between remaining a filial son (by preserving his father's heritage and lineage) and becoming accomplished and dispassionate in ways that the West (embodied by his wife's father, who heads the construction company backing Tong's project) will recognize and acknowledge.

Produced by Shanghai TV's new production company, Quest (Qiusuo)—which had already received acclaim for its high standards—Sunset was promoted as innovative and noteworthy from the outset.[6] Unlike many television dramas with exaggerated melodramatic or comedic themes, Sunset addressed a serious social topic: the demolition of "traditional" Shanghainese homes (the shikumen) to be replaced with shopping malls, modern skyscrapers, and Kentucky Fried Chicken outlets. Of the physical landscape of the city, the screenplay posed the question, "How much and what kind of change are we Shanghainese willing to accept to assume our place on the modern world stage, and what must we do to retain our Shanghainese identity?" The importance—not only symbolically but also politically (Zha 1995)—of projecting the image of a modern and forward-looking city through the plot is demonstrated by the censors' one criticism in their otherwise laudatory evaluation: that the title, Yesterday's Sunset (Zuori de Xiyang), conveyed too bleak and obsolete a feeling rather than a sense of contemporary relevance.[7] The censors suggested instead Sunset at Long Chao Li (Xizhao Long Chao Li). This name change was intended, the director told me, to shift the focus away from the passing of the elderly man and his generation and toward the demolition of a physical construction and its obsolete way of life.

Sunset—the abbreviation I use to encompass both the old and new titles—also examined the changing demographics of Shanghainese families: children sent overseas for study who are irrevocably transformed by that experience, the threat and promise of the growing number of marriages with foreigners, and, ultimately, what constitutes a modern Chinese family in turn-of-the-century (indeed, turn-of-the-millennium) urban China. Turning on its head the more common practice and representation of Chinese women married to, or at least sleeping with, foreign men,[8] Sunset offered a new twist: the lead female character Margie is a white woman; her professionally and romantically successful husband Zhou Tong, a mainland Chinese man. Indeed, of only five total roles in the entire script, two were white Americans; none was a Chinese woman.

The absence of Chinese women in this drama constitutes an effort by elite male TV producers to contest dominant images of China and "Chineseness" in the international sphere, and to present an alternate (self-) representation of Chinese modernity. This alternate vision highlights China's pursuit of global dominance in the twenty-first century—a dominance that depends in part on reimagining the nation as masculine and (sexually) desirable (Ong 1993), especially in relation to the West. By representing white—*not* Chinese—women as the object of Chinese male desire, this configuration of Chinese-Caucasian sexual relations eclipses Chinese women in three significant realms: as symbols of the Chinese family/nation, as agents in the pursuit and construction of a transnational Chinese modernity, and as legitimate subjects in the constitution of their own sexuality and desire. In this story, then, Chinese women are written out of the very dimensions of Chinese life that represent, and are represented as undergoing, the greatest transformation in the late twentieth century.

This erasure of Chinese women should be distinguished from the "gender erasure" of the Cultural Revolution period described by Yang (this volume; also Dai 1995a). Although the majority of television serials in the contemporary period still include Chinese women in leading roles, my discussion emphasizes the ways in which a particular representation of the *transnational* Chinese family displaces the Chinese woman as crucible of family and culture. In her place, an idealized image of desirable femininity, incorporated by a foreigner, is contrasted to dominant Chinese masculinity. In a sense, essential feminine characteristics are universalized (across at least Caucasian and East Asian female bodies), offering Chinese men opportunities for dominance both at home and abroad. Thus, it is not *gender difference* that is erased in this depiction of the white-Chinese heterosexual relations but, rather, *Chinese women* as the necessary embodiment of desirable womanhood.

The notion of the transnational Chinese family is crucial in this context. The depiction of the Chinese family as one peopled by foreigners seems the very fulfillment of *guoji jiegui*—connecting to the world—in a television production. And notably, this "connection" occurs through the drawing of foreigners *to* China rather than by exporting Chinese overseas. That is, *Sunset* is neither the story of Chinese victims and victors in America (see Liu 1995b; Yang 1997) nor of successful capitalist "astronauts" from other East Asian cosmopolises (see Ong 1993). Rather, by locating the story in China (and specifically in Shanghai), spinning the plot around the negotiations and impact of transnational circuits of power and capital, and having the domestic (and subordinate) sphere occupied by Caucasians, mainland Chinese men are depicted as central agents in the modernization and internationalization of both the family and the nation, and Shanghai is reinscribed as an international city both connected to and on par with other global cosmopolises.

Shanghai Cityscape as Setting and Metaphor for Chinese Modernity

The setting of this drama in Shanghai is significant on several levels. First, Shanghainese see themselves, and are seen, as inhabiting China's most international city and the one that combines the "authentic Chineseness" of the Mainland with the international (meaning primarily European) influence remaining in architecture and lifestyle from Shanghai's 1930s heyday as the "Paris of the East." As a leading industrial center, and one on which Deng Xiaoping bestowed his blessing by advocating development of the Pu Dong New Area Special Economic Zone in 1992, Shanghai is poised to reclaim what most residents feel is its rightful place as the commercial and cultural heart of China (*wenhua zhongxin*).[9]

Inhabiting this perceived pinnacle of Chinese culture and living standards, Shanghainese feel that they can do better only by leaving China (see Liu Xin 1997). The "West," or flight to the West (Ong 1995), symbolizes a kind of freedom that most Chinese feel remains elusive in China. Shanghainese women, considered among the more beautiful and well educated in all of China, are frequently courted by overseas Chinese men seeking mainland brides, and many young women have also become wives and mistresses to the growing population of foreign businessmen in Shanghai. The city thus acts not only as a site for the trafficking or "export" of Chinese women, but also as a dynamic site for the re-creation of Chinese families in China. Although the Zhou family in *Sunset* inverts the typical gendered configuration of this transnational Chinese family, it nevertheless retains a consonance with the growing Shanghainese reality of marriage overseas and does so by reinscribing Shanghai as the key site for this intertwining of sexuality, money, and modernity in China (see Hershatter 1992).

Indeed, Shanghai has a claim to Chinese modernity in a way that no other mainland city does. Its history of semicolonialism to Western and Japanese powers can be read two ways: on the one hand, it points to a historical relationship of "inferiority" that China wants to overcome; on the other hand, this history has given its citizens an openness to the West unmatched by other Chinese cities. Shanghainese often told me that they, as compared to other Chinese, could more easily "accept" (*jieshou*) the now seemingly pervasive Western influences. Thus, the West, and the perceived middle-class lifestyle of white Americans in particular, provides the model of modernity to which many Chinese aspire, and that Shanghainese see themselves uniquely positioned to achieve.[10]

This dual reading of Shanghai's history in relation to the West—as simultaneously one to overcome and one to make use of—contains a paradox that can also be read in the script of *Sunset* through the metaphor of Shanghai's unique architecture. Ostensibly, the plot centers on the father-son conflict over the demolition of a *shikumen* housing complex that, in the words of Zhou He, is the site of Shanghai's "unique way of life"—a middle-class life of the now-nostalgic 1930s Shanghai.[11] Rather than being built around a courtyard as is typical of traditional *hutong* homes elsewhere in China (which are viewed as the architectural basis for the extended three-generational families that have been the norm in China for centuries), *shikumen* are two- to three-story rowhouses built along long alleys, or lanes (*lilong*), dotted with vendors, bike and shoe repair stalls, and fruit and meat stands, comprising large complexes that often constitute an entire city block (see Lu 1995; Pellow 1993: 404–9).

The paradox in this view of Shanghainese lifestyle originating in this architecture is, of course, that the design and construction of these homes were influenced by the European presence in Shanghai in the early twentieth century. The *shikumen* resemble urban European rowhouses in design and were built in the late nineteenth and early twentieth centuries to accommodate Shanghai's growing population resulting from the combination of industrial growth due to foreign investment, and war and poverty in the countryside. While the poorest of Shanghai's new residents lived in shacks on the outskirts of the city (see Honig 1992), and the wealthiest few capitalists in mansions, an emerging middle class of that period—the educated, modern citizens of Shanghai's republican era (Wakeman and Yeh 1992)—lived in the *shikumen* homes.

Despite their historically modern status, in the plot of *Sunset* the *shikumen* occupy the symbolic location of traditional Shanghainese homes counterposed to what *now* constitutes modernity: a cityscape of towering high-rises and commercial plazas that meet international standards of late twentieth-century urban architecture. This transformation of the *shikumen*, from embodying 1930s' "modernity" (derived from international influences) to 1990s' "tradition" (opposed to contemporary international influences), parallels the passing of the old generation of modern Shanghai citizens to make way for the new. This passing is embodied in the father-son relationship in which similarities between the two are explicitly drawn, showing the continuity of Chinese culture, but clear distinctions also point to the direction that China must follow to earn its rightful place in the twenty-first-century global arena.

Kathleen Erwin

Constructing Chinese Manhood: Father and Son as the Chinese Family/Nation

The estrangement and reconciliation between Zhou He and his son provide the dramatic core of *Sunset;* father and son together represent China's past, present, and future. Their roles represent what Lisa Rofel (1994a: 713) has called the seizure of the "torch of nationhood" by male intellectuals in the 1990s, allowing for a rediscovery, or reformulation, of Chinese masculinity.

The symbolic location of Chinese culture and identity in the male leads can be discerned in several ways. "Old Shanghai," embodied in the aging and failing Zhou He, achieved a certain prominence in the first half of the twentieth century, when the man swallowed his anger ("Wo chile yikou qi," says Zhou He of his youthful encounter with foreign developers who scoffed at his plans to build Long Chao Li) and forged ahead despite European and Japanese semicolonialism. His early success starts Zhou He on a distinguished career, which contributes to China's international status. Early in the plot, we learn that his design for a Jiangnan-style garden in San Francisco has earned him recent acclaim in the U.S. press. But in the sunset of his life, Zhou He is once again charged with protecting Chinese culture and lifestyle against foreign incursions. The dual threat of renewed foreign intrusion comes from the investors from America who want to replace the *shikumen* with a commercial plaza, and from the addition of Margie and her son to his respected Chinese family. Zhou He's initial rejection of both represents China's commitment to preserving the fundamental Chineseness of the family and nation, even in the contemporary period of reform and opening to the West.

For his part, Zhou Tong represents modern China on the brink of the twenty-first century. The entire characterization of Zhou Tong is consistent with the growing popular image in Asia and worldwide of the transnational Chinese businessman (Ong 1993): he has one foot in China and one overseas; his interests and successes benefit China and contribute to familial gain, while also meeting "international" standards. This image has growing salience on the Mainland, especially in the city that views itself as the Hong Kong of the twenty-first century. And, I would argue, this portrayal is consistent with the male playwright's and directors' *own* self-image and worldview, which they project through Zhou Tong.

By marrying the daughter from a "wealthy and influential" American family, Zhou Tong is shown to be professionally successful and sexually desirable by international standards. His marriage visually counters the perceived assault on Chinese nationhood posed by its loss of women via marriage to overseas Chinese, and especially Western, men. The fact that foreign men are considered more desirable husbands clearly reinforces notions of Chinese male inferiority. Margie's choice of Zhou Tong not only inverts this relationship by making Chinese *men* the object of desire, but given that Margie's first husband was Caucasian, it also points to Tong's equality with (or even superiority to) white men. Moreover, that Zhou Tong would marry a widow suggests his own modern open-mindedness, and willingness to eschew traditional expectations for a young and virginal wife.

Importantly, despite his American wife and education, Zhou Tong's own fundamental Chineseness remains intact. His architectural designs contain elements of the highest classical forms in Chinese architecture, and the burdens of filial piety torment him as he pursues his plan to demolish Long Chao Li to win success in the eyes of his American father-in-law. Indeed, Zhou Tong remarks that his design will show that "Chinese too can build world-class architecture that reflects the international mood at the turn of the century." A pregnant Margie holds the promise of the quintessential heir to the cosmopolitan and transnational Shanghai: a half-Chinese progeny who embodies the best of East and West. This heir—originally conceptualized as male, but later changed to an unknown sex (again suggesting the director's own open-mindedness)—fulfills Zhou Tong's filial obligation to produce descendants of the Zhou family line.

Ultimately, Zhou Tong's return to America at the end of the movie, leaving behind his dying father, represents the flight of the nation from *its* dying past in pursuit of freedom, and new possibilities for China to incorporate, on its own terms and under the leadership of Chinese men, elements of the West that can contribute to the advancement of the motherland. In a word, Zhou Tong embodies a modern China struggling to discard the shackles of tradition and still retain male supremacy in the family and in the nation.

The engaging premise that these two generations (Zhou He and Zhou Tong) represent China's national integrity in the face of pre-Liberation and post-Tiananmen foreign imperialism, however, hinges on the implausible scenario that a man whose son is now only thirty years old was a designer of housing built primarily in the first three decades of this century. Leapfrogging over the entire generation that came of age under Mao allows both the rejection of an antiquated lifestyle and the inspiration for modernity in masculine terms to be cast against the backdrop of Shanghai's more distant pre-Liberation past and the specter of Western (male) domination, rather than against a still-present, and emasculating, socialist state (see Rofel 1994b; Zhong 1994).[12] Moreover, by highlighting Shanghai's continuing connection to the West, this formulation allows mainland men to envision a modern *transnational* masculinity in which they can dominate a new global order in both economic and sexual spheres. But to do so, they must expunge the feminized nation/self.

China's Global Dominance: Expunging the Feminized Nation

Throughout this century, and in a variety of contexts, Chinese women have symbolized the nation's achievements and deficiencies in its pursuit of modernity (Barlow 1994a; Chow 1991; Hershatter 1992; Li 1992; Liu 1995a; Zhang 1994; Chatterjee 1993). Analyzing the popular 1990 television drama *Yearnings*, Rofel (1994b) has suggested that the female lead in that drama, Huifang, represents a feminized China based on a post-Tiananmen reformulation of national identity that foregrounds the personal familial sphere (embodied by women) and female self-sacrifice. But Rofel and Zhong Xueping (1994) have also pointed to an emerging trend among predominantly male writers and directors to represent modern Chinese identity as masculine, and Chinese masculinity itself as desirable. Moreover, by the mid-1990s, urban Chinese, and especially Shanghainese, have increasingly imagined themselves as part of a modern *transnational* space; to occupy this station equal or superior to the West, the Chinese nation must be perceived as masculine in relation to the West.

The hierarchy of gender and racial relations represented by the Zhou family both produces and reflects this growing perception that a strong and desirable China is moving to the world center. By dramatizing the conflicts among the Zhous brought about by China's rapid transformation, *Sunset* retains the formulation of national identity in the personal familial sphere but clearly emphasizes male agency in the transformation of Chinese family/nation. As the only woman in the story, Margie's singular presence renders invisible any female-female social relations in the representation of Chinese modernity (see Dai 1995a). Moreover, the conspicuous absence of Chinese women—even (or especially?) in their more powerful roles as mothers-in-law and family matriarchs (see Wolf 1972)—renders invisible their contributions and "self-sacrifice" on behalf of the family/nation and acts as a means of eliding their real or imagined connections (sexual and otherwise) to the West, and the transnational sphere. In short, the Zhou family graphically illustrates the expunging of the feminized nation from a vision of Chinese transnationalism emerging from the Mainland.

This representation, moreover, is not an isolated aberration. A particularly popular serial, broadcast in Shanghai in the summer of 1995, was *Foreign Women in Beijing* (Yangniu Zai Beijing). Ostensibly a copycat inversion of *A Beijinger in New York* (Beijing Ren Zai Niuyue; see Liu 1995b; Yang 1997), this comedy-drama cast two white women as Americans in Beijing. One, like Margie, is the virtuous modern wife of a Chinese male lead; the second is a sexually promiscuous woman who is also the object of male Chinese desire. The details of plot are beyond the scope of this essay, but the similar configuration of Chinese male–white female sexual relations and the absence of Chinese women in leading roles suggests that the serial shares more in common with *Sunset* than with its supposed prototype.

The prominent role of foreign women in these television dramas is crucial to the formulation of this shift in self-representation as China looks toward the new millennium. Casting white women in leading roles, especially explicitly sexualized roles in relation to Chinese men, suggests that mainland men, at least those of a particular social location, can possess and even dominate their objects of desire—the modernity and freedom attributed to the West—through the acquisition of American women.[13] For China to achieve its sought-after position as a world leader equal or superior to Western nations, the feminized China must literally and completely disappear and be replaced by a male lead whose success is validated by and in the West. Moreover, when Chineseness is located in the male lead and head of household, the Chinese family (as locus of Chinese culture and identity) can propagate, even with a foreign wife.

Destabilizing the Trope of the Foreign Woman

Notably, Zhou Tong did not go to America and marry a Chinese American, or an African American, woman. As a modern woman of good background, Margie *had* to be white (see Schein 1994).[14] Her racial and gender traits together make her the ideal wife for a transnational Chinese businessman in the Zhou Tong image. A devoted wife and mother, Margie also provides Zhou Tong with an essential link to the West, both culturally and through her father's business. Her actions and dialogue are peripheral to the plot, making her role much more symbolic than substantive. Margie continually admonishes her husband to speak frankly with his father regarding his plans and to make "realistic" choices—not "emotional" ones derived from feelings of filial piety. Her appreciation for Chinese culture and ability to speak Chinese, despite her sometimes culturally inappropriate gestures (like kissing her father-in-law's cheek upon his presentation of a family heirloom), make Margie a likable character who simultaneously challenges and reinforces the stereotype of the foreign woman.

Although the Chinese term *foreigner* (*waiguo ren*) literally refers to any non-ethnically Chinese person, in common usage its application is more specific. Foreigners are modern, wealthy, and unable to speak comprehensible Chinese. They have blue eyes, prominent noses, and blonde hair. The term conflates all people of European descent, regardless of nationality.[15] *Waiyu* (literally "foreign language") is used almost exclusively to refer to English, implying that *all* foreigners are English speakers. Foreign women are at best "romantic" (*langman*) and "open" (*kaifang*), referring to their sexuality, and more likely, licentious. The fact that all whites are seen as embodying this universal image can be demonstrated by an exchange I had with a cab driver: "You speak Chinese so well," he said. "If you didn't have blonde hair (*huang toufa*) and blue eyes (*lan yanjing*), I would have thought you were Chinese"—this despite my almost-black hair and brown eyes. When I pointed these characteristics out to him, he proclaimed with some confusion, "Well, you still have a big nose (*gao bizi*)!" At other times I was asked which of my parents was Chinese, since my dark coloring and Chinese language skills indicated that I could not be completely foreign.

Through much of the production, I clung naively to the belief that I could change this unitary view of foreigners, and especially white women, shared by the directors and crew.[16] Although in preproduction I managed what I considered a small victory—convincing the director that my dark and prematurely graying hair need not be dyed blonde—I soon realized that my interventions did more to transform their view of *me* as a foreign woman than it did to transform their stereotype of foreign women more generally. For example, to their insistence that "all foreigners wear fur coats," I argued in vain that many Americans oppose the wearing of furs, and most Americans cannot afford them anyway. I finally had to concede that Margie, described as coming from a wealthy family, might indeed wear fur. Living proof that my arguments were ill-conceived efforts to throw them off track, Billy's real-life mother, the blonde, blue-eyed wife of an American corporate executive stationed in Shanghai, arrived on the set daily wearing one of *two* genuine fur coats she had brought with her to China.

During the course of the production, other differences emerged between Billy's mother and me that served to simultaneously reinforce the foreigner stereotype and affirm an intermediate position that I (and Margie) could fill. For instance, I joined the rest of the cast and crew in eating "box lunch"—a usually less-than-gourmet, mass-produced assemblage of rice, meat, and vegetables sold in Styrofoam boxes with disposable chopsticks—whereas Billy and his mother brought their own sandwiches and American snacks to the set. But the essential foreignness of Billy and his mother was confirmed when the filming went well over schedule, stretching from the initial seven-to-ten day commitment to more than three weeks. Exhausted and frustrated, Billy, with his mother's consent, refused to return to the set. For the director and crew, it was inconceivable that an actor would abandon a production after establishing a relationship and signing the contract. The threatened withdrawal reinforced for the Chinese that foreigners (especially Americans) do not care about relationships (*guanxi*) or feeling (*ganqing*). My ability to successfully mediate the disputes, and convince Billy and his mother to return, further reinforced the perception that I understood Chinese ways of thinking and doing things and therefore was not really like other foreigners.

Thus, although Billy's mother and I were both American women, the contrasting presence of what the Chinese saw as the "authentic" foreign woman—one who had blonde hair, wore fur coats, smoked cigarettes, ate sandwiches, and could not speak Chinese—placed me in an explicitly intermediate position. As the dark-haired, Chinese-speaking interlocutor and cultural intermediary, I presented an alternate image of desirable modern womanhood that coincided with the one the directors wanted to present in Zhou Tong's ideal wife: a foreign woman who validates essential aspects of Chinese culture while providing a link to the West. What I believe they saw in me that was consonant with their Margie ideal was an ability to act *zhongguotong*.

Zhongguotong: *Sinicizing the Foreign Woman*

The reconciliation of the dissonance between the image of the foreigner and an individual foreigner who is liked or admired is expressed in Chinese through the complimentary phrase *zhongguotong* (literally, "thoroughly Chinese," referring to a foreigner perceived to have mastered Chinese customs and language; a China expert).[17] The concept of *zhongguotong* provided the directors with a construction of modern womanhood that encompassed characteristics of an ideal foreign wife to a successful cosmopolitan Chinese man representing Shanghai's future. That I behaved in ways acceptable, and even desirable, to Chinese—that is, my own status as *zhongguotong*—indicated to the director that I could convey that through Margie. Indeed, he and other crew members told me repeatedly that I did not need to "act" (*biaoyan*) for the role; I could merely be myself. The me they saw was an idealized *zhongguotong* wife who could symbolize Chinese men's success in moving to the global center in the twenty-first century. The bestowal of *zhongguotong* status itself acts as a self-affirmation to the Chinese. That is, the indication by foreigners of respect and appreciation for what are "essential" Chinese characteristics—a self-orientalizing process (see Ong 1993)—validates China's ascendance in the eyes of the West.

Speaking intelligible Chinese is the primary prerequisite of *zhongguotong*. Most Chinese I met, and certainly the educated Shanghainese who were the focus of my research, recognized that language conveyed not only words but the ideas and practices of Chinese culture. Margie's ability to speak Chinese and adapt to Chinese culture was an essential criterion in establishing her as an acceptable replacement to a Chinese wife for Zhou Tong. Margie's first words in the movie are to address Zhou He as *Baba* (father) and to instruct her son Billy to call him *Yehyeh* (paternal grandfather). These forms of address also show that Margie recognizes Zhou He (and not her own or her first husband's father) as the rightful patriarch of their family.[18]

Providing further assurances of Margie's credentials as an acceptable daughter-in-law, even by the "old" Chinese standards embodied by Zhou He, Zhou Tong's first exchange with his father establishes Margie as college educated and a student of Chinese culture. Her appreciation for Chinese culture and earnest efforts to behave appropriately (by visiting the Zhou family village and bowing to the ancestors) are rewarded when Zhou He presents Margie with an heirloom his departed wife left for her future (and presumably Chinese) daughter-in-law. And it is ultimately Margie who proposes a solution to her husband's quandary that allows him to remain a filial son: that they utilize Zhou He's renovation plan for Long Chao Li to save the homes from demolition. Margie's *zhongguotong* status is sealed when, in one of the final scenes, Zhou He bestows on her a Chinese name, Yufeng (Jade Phoenix), representing the "most auspicious symbols" of Chinese culture.

Desire and Virtue: The Dual Framing of Margie's Sexuality

Sexuality was a key framing of Margie, and the characteristic that remained most ambiguous in her construction as an ideal *zhongguotong* wife. To fulfill such an ideal, Margie had to be virtuous; but as a foreigner, she also had to be open and unconstrained by China's repressive past. The notion that foreigners, and especially foreign women, are more sexually open than Chinese was one that was held by virtually all of the Shanghainese men and women I encountered during my fieldwork.[19] They dismissed as preposterous my suggestion that America was actually a very sexually conservative country; it might not be as "chaotic" (*luan*) as represented on TV and in the movies, some conceded, but America certainly was not conservative (*baoshou*) like China.

Nevertheless, openness was something that, in breaking with the repressive Maoist past, urban Chinese felt increasingly able to pursue. I was often told, "Chinese are just like foreigners now. Everyone is having an affair; unmarried couples are living together; marry one day, divorce the next. It's still conservative in the countryside, but Shanghai is very open." These widely shared beliefs are also notable because of the dual positioning of the speaker: on the one hand, (all) Chinese are contrasted to (all) foreigners, affirming their essential difference; on the other hand, Shanghainese have a unique position, as modern and urbane vis-à-vis "the rest of China," described as the countryside. Other urban centers disappear, and Shanghai is made *the* sexually modern counterpoint to China's rural conservatism.

Thus, representing Margie's sexuality was an opportunity for the Shanghainese filmmakers to affirm themselves as modern, innovative, and open (see Barlow 1991; Hershatter 1996); it also exposed and coincided with their own investment in constructing elite Chinese masculinity and femininity in relation to the Western Other. The director was adamant that *all* films and television movies in China now have a sex scene, and that there would be a crucial gap in the story if the "natural" relationship between husband and wife was not visibly consummated on screen. When I declined to do a sex scene in bed, remarking that the dialogue was unrealistic, even humorous, the scene was moved from the bedroom to the living room, but the dialogue remained unchanged. The director's accommodation (or misaccommodation) emphasizes the importance of Margie's sexuality in confirming both foreign women's essential sexual openness and Zhou Tong's desirable masculinity.

To the director (who conferred in his decision making with others on the crew), the *crucial* aspect of that scene entailed Margie's sexual pursuit of her husband. That is, before calling her father in America to discuss progress on the construction project, Margie *had* to say, as she chased her husband into the bedroom, "I want you first" (*Wo xian yao ni*). In this male fantasy, Margie's role as pursuer does more than reinscribe her as a modern, open woman; it also suggests that modern *and* foreign women not only find Chinese men sexually attractive, but actually sexually pursue *them*. Thus, this scene, or more particularly the line "I want you first," was so crucial because of its dual contribution to the construction of Chinese masculinity and modernity (and in the process, modern womanhood) as open, nonrepressed, and one in which wealthy Chinese businessmen constitute the objects of attraction.

The Model Modern Wife: A Transcendent Feminine Ideal

Despite his desire to highlight Margie's sexual openness, the director still wanted Margie to fulfill the idealized role as a virtuous wife and good mother, worthy of the Zhou name. Debunking his father's assumption that Margie is a licentious American woman whose chaotic sexual relations resulted in her motherhood ("Meiguo de nannü guanxi jiushi luanqibazao de"), Zhou Tong remarks, "Billy is Margie's son from a previous marriage. Her first husband died in a plane crash. Margie comes from a wealthy and influential family." Her status as a widow (not a whore), and as the cultured daughter of a wealthy, influential American businessman, confirms in Margie the sexual propriety required of an ideal wife.

Margie's character is clearly delineated as a wife and mother. Margie's own mother is never even mentioned, though, further establishing her as a woman whose entire social and familial networks are configured through men. Moreover, in the process of filming, Margie's professional role was strikingly diminished, from a virtually equal partner in her husband's venture in the original script to merely a mediator between him and her own father in the final production. That is, scenes depicting her fulfilling wifely duties remained, while scenes depicting her as a business partner or as a representative of her father (namely, the West imposing its will on China) were considered unnecessary—even compromising—to the image the director wanted to portray.

The essential criterion for a desirable wife, then, is one that fulfills an idealized image of a modern "virtuous wife and good mother" (*xianqi liangmu*; see Honig and Hershatter 1988; Yang, this volume). The modern virtuous wife and good mother, like her idealized Confucian predecessor, produces the next generation of male heirs for the family lineage. But in contrast to the Confucian ideal of an uneducated woman, subservient to her husband and his lineage, and virtuous even to the point of committing suicide upon her husband's death (or remaining chaste if her betrothed died [see Elvin 1984, Carlitz 1994]), this modern reincarnation is (1) educated and cultured (*you wenhua*); (2) sexually open enough to affirm Chinese manhood (but importantly, only within the institution of marriage); and (3) connected to the West, with its commensurate associations of freedom, wealth, and international recognition. Thus, the domestic, female sphere in the modern Chinese family/nation need not necessarily be Chinese. In fact, to achieve dominance in the transnational arena, the model wife is best embodied by a foreign woman with *zhongguotong* qualities.

As the representation of that model, Margie is neither completely foreign nor truly Chinese. Her big nose, fur coat, and sexual assertiveness mark Margie with the visible trappings of essential foreignness, but her education, cultured status, and desire for a Chinese husband allow Margie to be sinicized as a modern *xianqi liangmu*. The resulting composite of modern womanhood occupies an intermediate and shifting position between, or perhaps transcending, the poles of Chinese and foreign. This transcendent ideal foregrounds Margie's gender difference (vis-à-vis Chinese men) and mitigates her racial difference (vis-à-vis Chinese women)—a relational stance that is visually facilitated by the absence of Chinese women in the story. That is, with respect to her status *within* the modern Chinese family, Margie's role as wife and mother reinscribes "traditional" gender relations by defining "modern womanhood" in domestic terms that transcend racial dichotomies. Gender difference is thus presented as a universal given conferring male dominance and relegating women to the home. In contrast, "Chineseness" (through sinicization) becomes an achievable, expansive characteristic that allows Chinese male dominance to extend beyond the domestic realm into the transnational sphere.[20]

Domination through Sinicization: Absorbing the West

The reconstitution of mainland Chinese masculinity in the transnational sphere depends in part on its capacity to dominate, or absorb, the West through sinicization. In *Sunset* it is not only American women, but also America's sons (its future), who are subject to the tutelage of Chinese men. Through the course of the drama, eight-year-old Billy is radically transformed from Margie's Michael-Jackson-loving, air-guitar-strumming American son into Zhou He's Chinese-calligraphy-painting, Kun-Opera-singing *zhongguotong* grandson. The shift in Billy's identity and loyalty is quite marked. When Margie and Zhou Tong decide that the struggle over the fate of Long Chao Li has made staying in the Zhou household untenable, Billy sides with Zhou He: "*Yehyeh* says that living together is what makes a family. . . . You can leave, but I'm not going! I'm staying with *Yehyeh!*" Not only is Billy expressing his desire to remain physically at the side of the Chinese patriarch, he is also expressing allegiance to the traditional Chinese value on family. Later, when Margie's father rejects her proposal to use Zhou He's renovation plans to save Long Chao Li, Billy again takes a stand against any attempt by the (masculine) West to dominate China/Zhou He: "*Waigong* [maternal grandfather] is bad! I won't let him tear down the houses *Yehyeh* built!" Like his mother, Billy's complete sinicization is ultimately symbolized by his embrace of the Chinese name Zhou He bestows, Tian Long (Heavenly Dragon); "I'm a dragon from America!" Billy exclaims delightedly. The choice of this auspicious name, which symbolizes the Chinese nation itself, is also an almost literal fulfillment of the Chinese wish that one's sons become dragons ("wang zi cheng long").[21]

A more subtle manifestation of this absorption of the West by Chinese transnationalism can be found in the fifth character in *Sunset.* Uncle Xu is Zhou He's lifelong friend and coresident of Long Chao Li. Our first visual image of Xu portrays him using *qigong* healing techniques on Zhou He.[22] When Margie is later introduced to him, she remarks that Xu's demeanor is "just like an English gentleman." To this Zhou Tong replies that Xu went to England as a young man to study Western medicine. After returning to China, he took up the study of Chinese medicine and later became a master of *qigong* and *zhou yi ba gua* divination. "Everyone calls him Xu Banxian," concludes Zhou Tong, that is, "half-mystic."

These mystical Chinese powers—and not Xu's study of Western medicine—we later learn, are the secret to Zhou He's longevity. When Zhou He is hospitalized for treatment of an unspecified cancer that has metastasized throughout his body, Margie, expressing her own belief in the superiority of Chinese medicine, begs Xu to cure Zhou He. Xu replies, "If I had not been treating him with *qigong* for the past two years, Old Zhou would not be here today." Thus, Xu, a Chinese man, not only embodies the refined manner of English gentry, but through his mastery of Chinese medical secrets, he also achieves a level of wisdom and healing power superior to Western medical training. That is, he demonstrates that a Chinese man can absorb, and then improve on, the esteemed achievements (in both civility and science) of the West.

The Gender and Locational Politics of Televisual Production and Transnational Chinese Public(s)

As a short series of only two segments (ninety minutes total), and one lacking the exaggerated melodramatic elements of many popular serials (recovered long-lost relatives, illicit affairs, and so forth), *Sunset* did not gain the avid following earned by many longer-running TV serials in China (Lull 1991; Rofel 1994b; Zha 1995). But the drama nevertheless did achieve notable critical acclaim and garner significant coverage in newspapers, TV guides, and magazines. Nominated by Shanghainese critics for best short-run serial in three international television festivals in 1995 (in Sichuan, Guangzhou, and Beijing), it ultimately won an award as an "outstanding" (*youxiu*) production in the Tenth Annual Asian Television Festival in Beijing. The award recognized *Sunset*'s excellent cinematography and innovative portrayal of socially relevant content.

Despite these accolades, *Sunset* could hardly lay claim to a radical reformulation of Chinese modernity outside dominant discourses. In fact, coming as it did from sanctioned circles, the critical acclaim might most strongly point to *Sunset*'s conformity to a set of images and ideals that appeal to China's primarily male political and mass-media elites. The portrayal of a successful, returned Chinese scholar/businessman undertaking a foreign investment project that contributes to China's modernization dovetails with the economic and political goals of the Chinese state to promote "socialism with Chinese characteristics." In terms of gender representations, *Sunset* also conforms to established elements of symbolism and plot found in more mainstream productions. Like many 1980s' tales, it focuses on father-son conflict in the working out of national predicaments (Rofel 1994b; Dai, this volume). And like *Yearnings*, it valorizes a "virtuous wife, good mother" ideal—albeit a modernized version—for the female heroine.

To the extent that Chinese women viewers might aspire to emulate Margie in their own imaginings of modern womanhood, they would hardly find in her characterization a radical image. Indeed, one female interviewer found it incomprehensible that Margie, whom she described as a "virtuous wife, good mother" (*xianqi liangmu*), could be portrayed by a self-described American feminist scholar.[23] Her surprise is well warranted. In *Sunset* the sole female character is peripheral to the action of the plot, which emphasizes male agency in the modernization of Shanghai's architecture, material life, and family structures.

More importantly, Chinese women are completely absent from this vision of urban Chinese modernity and transnationalism. Their once-sacrosanct role as the vessel of the Chinese family, and therefore Chinese culture, is doubly displaced. As Chinese, their cultural/racial responsibilities are taken up by a new vision of Chinese manhood that embodies and transmits essential Chineseness both within the reconstituted modern family and beyond, to the sinicization of the West. As women, their gendered/sexual claim on Chinese men is dismissed in favor of an idealized modern Western woman, who nevertheless fulfills traditional female obligations as producer of heirs and object of male desire. This bifurcation of the domain constituted by Chinese womanhood in the construction of a new (masculine) narrative of Chinese transnationalism eliminates any visual representation of female homosocial networks, of women's desires (sexual and otherwise), and of women's participation in the reconstitution of Chinese families and modernity as transnational.

These aspects of *Sunset* suggest that the representation of women and articulation of independent women's voices on Chinese television remain largely circumscribed by masculinist and state ideologies. But the fantasy scripts of Chinese television dramas constitute only one venue for the imagining and enacting of transnational Chinese subjectivities and publics. In practice, it is far more common for Chinese *women* to marry overseas Chinese and foreign men, thereby reconstituting the modern Chinese family in transnational terms. As China's most educated female population, Shanghainese women also have growing opportunities to be employed in foreign joint ventures or to travel abroad for work or study. These trends suggest that far, from being marginalized by the structures and practices of transnationalism, Chinese women play a crucial role in establishing links across borders that foster greater connections between Shanghainese and the world.

And though women's contributions to the formation of transnational linkages are masked in *Sunset*, the production should not be dismissed as categorically sexist or merely unrealistic. It is *Sunset's* vision of the transnational Chinese family in Shanghai, and of Chinese transnationalism emanating from the Mainland, that marks it as innovative within the context of television serial production in contemporary China. The story highlights Shanghai as a magnetic, global center—attracting foreigners and overseas Chinese to the Mainland—rather than as a locus for the export of Chinese to the West, and to other sites in the Asia Pacific. This portrayal places China, rather than the Chinese diaspora, at the vortex of Chinese transnationalism and allows urban mainland men, in particular, to envision themselves as central participants in the "triumphalist narratives" of Chinese transnationalism that Aihwa Ong (1997) has described.[24] They symbolically grasp the "torch of Chinese transnationalism," at least in their home country.[25] This representation of China's claim to global dominance taps into national pride and aspirations for the twenty-first century that mainland men and women both can embrace.

Thus, the televisual images generated in *Sunset* reflect not only the gendering of a transnational Chinese imaginary emanating from the Mainland; they also reflect national and other locational politics in their site of production (see Abu-Lughod 1993). By attending to the hierarchies of place that make some sites of Chinese transnationalism more desirable, and more influential, than others, *Sunset* calls attention to the multiplicity of positions from which articulations of Chinese transnationalism are generated—from Shanghai to Hong Kong to southern California to Henan (see chapters in this volume from Shih, Rofel, Li, and Ho; Yang 1997; Ong and Nonini 1997). In each locale, the desires of men and women may overlap as much as they diverge,[26] and the politics of televisual production may foster greater national or local cohesion than transnational alliances based on gender or ethnicity. Television may be especially effective in generating shared images and narratives of gender and transnationalism. But to comprehend its implications for, and effects on, transnational Chinese public(s), we must remain attuned to the *multiplicity* of means and positions from which the variously located, mobile, empowered, and constrained subjects of Chinese transnationalism act, speak, and dream.

NOTES

My fieldwork in China, which presented me the opportunity to become a television actor as well as ethnographer, was made possible by the generous support of a National Science Foundation Graduate Research Fellowship, and by the University of California at Berkeley Vice Chancellor's Fund for Research. I am extremely grateful for this financial support, without which my extended stay in China would have been impossible. I am deeply indebted to the makers of *Sunset*, and especially Feng Danian and Liu Zhixin, for giving me the unique opportunity to participate in their production. I hope my analysis has done no injustice to their creativity, skill, enthusiasm, and sense of fun. Many people have generously contributed their time to read and comment on drafts of this essay. This version benefited immensely from the thoughtful and incisive critiques of Aihwa Ong, Gail Hershatter, Lydia Liu, Mayfair Yang, Liu Xin, Wang Zheng, and Karen Franklin. I am also grateful to Aihwa Ong for suggesting the title. The findings and opinions expressed here are my own. I have tried to incorporate my readers' suggestions but remain responsible for any errors, omissions, or failure to adequately address their thoughtful criticisms.

1 I became involved in the production after being introduced to the director by a mutual Chinese acquaintance. Unless otherwise noted, the information, descriptions, and other materials discussed in relation to this production are derived directly from my own experience acting in the drama and talking with the directors, actors, and crew during and after the production. I kept detailed notes on my conversations and experiences and have in my possession a copy of the script and the final film on video.

2 In the dramas I saw and heard about in 1995, rarely were the foreigners depicted as family members (with the exception of *Foreign Women in Beijing*, which I discuss later

in this essay). My analysis here is limited to the representation of foreigners, especially white women, in mainland Chinese families.

3 The expression *guoji jiegui* literally means "connecting the international tracks" (like train rails) to link China to "the world" in a two-way mutual interchange. This expression has been a popular slogan in urban China in the 1990s, and its implication of a mutual interchange between China and the West highlights the global restructuring that I argue is central to the reimagining of a transnational Chinese masculinity.

4 This comparison to an Academy Award–winning American film itself points to ways in which Chinese define themselves and view their own modern representations through and against Western (or specifically American) media.

5 *Shikumen* literally means "stone arch gate" and refers to the entryway to the complex. The *shikumen* design is most like what we call rowhouses or perhaps brownstones. See Lu (1995) and Pellow (1993) for descriptions.

6 Following Deng Xiaoping's 1992 southern tour (*nanxun*), Shanghai established a second radio and TV entity called *Dongfang* (Orient, or Eastern), making it the only mainland city with more than one official broadcasting corporation (Yang 1997). The competition created by *Dongfang*, generally perceived as more independent and innovative, led Shanghai TV (STV) to create a new company, *Qiusuo*, to produce its own innovative dramas. Following closely on the heels of *Qiusuo's* first production, the popular *Debt* (*Niezhai*), *Sunset* was expected to fulfill this mandate and thus received substantial coverage in local newspapers. Indeed, one article in *Liberation Daily* began: "After 'Debt' what new quest is 'Quest' undertaking? The recent completion in filming of 'Yesterday's Sunset,' a story which chronicles the life of an elderly Shanghainese man. . . ." (*Jiefang Ribao*, Friday April 7, 1995).

7 All productions must be approved by censors at the municipal or provincial level before they can be broadcast. The censorship process includes a written evaluation of the film, the direction, plot, cinematography, and so on and rates productions in relation to each other. Lull (1991) and Chang (1989, esp. 212–28) describe the administrative and political organization of Chinese broadcast corporations.

8 See, for example, *A Beijinger in New York*; also see Liu 1995b; Yang 1997: 305–8; Shih 1997.

9 In comparison, many Chinese, even outside Shanghai, see Hong Kong as less authentically Chinese not only because of its former status as a British colony but also because (like Guangzhou) its lifestyle is dominated by Cantonese language and culture. Beijing is China's "political center" (*zhengzhi zhongxin*). Interior cities are seen as inferior to coastal ones in terms of culture as well as economic development.

10 Although mainland Chinese modernity can clearly be seen as modeling itself on the consumer economy and lifestyles of East Asian centers like Taipei, Hong Kong, Singapore, and even Tokyo, Shanghainese people tend to downplay this influence and emphasize the particularly Western flavor of Shanghainese lifestyle.

11 Indeed, many people throughout my fieldwork tenure recalled for me the significance of these houses in creating this unique Shanghainese lifestyle. The relationship of architecture to lifestyle is of course not unique to China. Paul Rabinow (1989) has elaborated this relationship in *French Modern: Norms and Forms of the Social Environment*.

12 Notably, *Sunset* makes no reference to the Cultural Revolution (1966–1976), and

even allusions in the original script to Communist Liberation (1949) and the Maoist era were eliminated during filming, thereby ignoring the impact of thirty years of socialism on an entire generation of Chinese citizens. In particular, those born between 1948 and 1953, called the *laosanjie*, are considered China's "lost generation." Born into war and poverty and buffeted by political campaigns of the 1950s and 1960s, they came of age during the Cultural Revolution and lost educational opportunities; they were the first generation on whom the one-child policy took effect, and in the economic restructuring of the 1980s and 1990s they are among the most likely to be laid off (*xiagang*). See Erwin (1998) for discussion.

13 Lydia Liu (1995b) makes a similar point in her description of Wang Qiming's humiliation of the white prostitute in New York in *A Beijinger in New York*.

14 Louisa Schein (1994) analyzes the symbolic content of white women as fetish in China, and particularly among the Miao people. She suggests that the overarching trope of the white woman eclipses any variations in their representation. Although I agree with much of Schein's analysis, I believe the distinction between the trope of the foreign/white woman and the sinicized Margie is of particular significance in the imagining of a Shanghai-centered masculine Chinese transnationalism, as depicted in *Sunset*.

15 That *foreigner* is marked as white (except in the most general pronouncements of non-Chineseness) is illustrated by the common use of *heiren* (or *feizhou ren*) to describe blacks and Africans (of any nationality) and *riben ren* to describe Japanese (never to be confused with Chinese); other ethnicities are also specified as necessary.

16 This stereotype of the foreign/white woman itself comes from filmic images in Hollywood that shape, in part, how Chinese (re)construct these images.

17 Lu Xun borrowed the term *Zhina tong* from the Japanese *Shinatō* to refer to "China experts," who expounded on the essential characteristics of the Chinese race (cf. Liu 1995a: 52–53, 463). I thank Lydia Liu for pointing this out to me. In current popular usage, *zhongguotong* has complimentary connotations toward a person who has seemingly mastered essential characteristics of appropriate Chinese behavior.

18 An additional interpretation of these terms is that the appellation *Baba* highlights the modernity of the Zhou family, since the traditional term a woman would use to address her father-in-law is *Gong-Gong*. *Yehyeh*, also used to address any elderly man two generations senior to the speaker, may not have particular significance in terms of implying loyalty to the family lineage. I thank Lydia Liu for pointing out these alternative interpretations.

19 This perception of American women, of course, is not unique to Chinese people. It is widely held throughout most of the world outside Europe, Australia, and the Americas (Stoler 1991; Schein 1994). See also note 16 above.

20 Frank Dikötter (1990) discusses shifting conceptions of "race" in Chinese cosmologies, including nonbiological, cultural achievement of "Chineseness." I thank Emily Chao for suggesting the relevance of Dikötter's work here.

21 The second line of this saying, "wang nü cheng feng" (wishing that one's daughters become phoenixes), can similarly be seen as Margie's transformation into a "Chinese" daughter through the bestowal of her name Yufeng (Jade Phoenix), as discussed earlier in this essay.

22 See Nancy Chen (1995) for discussion of the revival of *qigong* healing in urban China.

23 The interview appeared in *Shanghai TV Weekly* (Shanghai Dianshi Zhoukan) September 1995, A15.

24 See also Donald Nonini (1997) for discussion of the ways in which relatively localized men in the sphere of Chinese transnationalism create "fantasy scripts" to escape their embodied localizations within the nation-state.

25 I have amended this phrase from one turned by Rofel (1994b), who has described how Chinese male intellectuals "grasp the torch of nationhood" (as discussed earlier in this essay).

26 In her contribution to this volume, Shu-mei Shih makes a similar point with regard to the politics of national origin shaping response to a murder case in southern California.

PART IV

Transnational

Crossings of

Gender Images

and Feminist

Discourse

10

Li Xiaojiang

(Translated by Zhang Yajie, with editorial assistance by Mayfair Mei-hui Yang)

With What Discourse Do We Reflect on Chinese Women? Thoughts on Transnational Feminism in China

In this essay, Li Xiaojiang, a prominent feminist on the Mainland, reviews the modern history of discourses and ideologies, their Chinese and Western genealogies and usages, and examines how they have constructed, appropriated, and changed Chinese women. She pays special attention to the specificity of language and terminology and shows how, in the post-Mao reform period, new imports of Western feminist discourse enter into a very different linguistic and historical context, in China, where they will engender different interpretations. Given Chinese women's special historical experiences with the Communist Revolution, not only will some aspects of Western feminist discourse be irrelevant, but they can also cause confusion and damage to the new feminist movement in China.

An explication of key terms and concepts imported into China from the West can be found at the end of this article. It shows how the specific interpretive context of these terms make them highly problematical in the context of Chinese women's historical experiences.

The various terms given to woman (*nüren*) have brought confusion to our thinking. The terms *furen, nüzi, nüxing*, and *funü* all carry with them a special connotation and ideological background. In everyday speech and conversation, women are always fixed in a particular position defined by their specific historical era. This essay will consider the language and discourse of a Chinese women's movement, and the problems encountered in the process of using Western discourse to address Chinese situations.

I chose the word *nüren* (women) for the Chinese title of this paper with the aim of using its etymology to reveal its ontological sense. Here, the word *human* (*ren*) is ontological and refers to a being of human subjectivity. Thus, it differs from the notion of sex (*xing*) and the notion of gender (*xingbie*). The other part of the term, *nü*, is not the same as *female* (*ci*), which refers to the sex of other animals in nature, because in the Chinese language *nü* can only refer to the sex of a human being. The terms *woman* (*nüren*) and *man* (*nanren*) already reveal their social character, since they refer to "human beings who have a socialized sexual character." At the same time, both the terms *nü* (female) and *nan* (male) are attached to the term *human being* (*ren*), whereas the English word *woman* is attached to the word *man*. Therefore, in China, no matter how far women's liberation is carried out, there is no need to launch another revolution in our conceptual scheme, because in our language the term *woman* (*nüren*) is not predicated on *man*. Furthermore, if it were not for the sake of facilitating communication between China and the West, it would be redundant to introduce the notion of gender (*shehui xingbie*) to the Chinese language, since *nü* and *nan* are already understood as social, and not natural, beings.

Chinese women today have reached an impasse. We have expended great efforts to improve our position; however, we are now unable to clearly perceive the significance and effects of these actions. Consequently, thinking about how we are to conceptualize our situation becomes an important action in our practical everyday life. For a long time now, by passively accepting a given, ready-made discourse, we have allowed ourselves to be controlled. When we start to construct discourse ourselves, we may unwittingly overturn a certain power structure. In addition to the spiritual liberation we may gain from unifying speech and action, what is perhaps more important is the changing of our subject-position. In changing our task from that of reflecting on women to the task of encouraging *women* to engage in active reflection, the first problem we encounter is, with which discourse do we reflect on women?

In the past half-century, the lives of Chinese women have undergone a tremendous transformation. Different generations of women, each with their distinctive historical traits, are concentrated within a single historical period. Due to the power of historical discourses, the difficulties of communication between different generations of women are not decreased but increased. At the same time, because of reform and opening up to the world, new information and ideas from the so-called developed countries, carrying with them, no doubt, "advanced" foreign discourses, have entered our country. Due to the very different historical conditions in each place, these ideas not only pose as obstacles to dialogue between China and the West, but they also further confuse the already ambiguous and disoriented discursive world of Chinese women. As a result, Chinese women mistake today with yesterday and unnecessarily add to their burdens of psychology and life.

It was Tani Barlow, a woman scholar in the United States, who first deconstructed the discursive world of Chinese women. In recent years, she has published several articles on this subject (1989; 1994a; 1994b). By focusing on terminology and conceptual systems, she has analyzed the historical changes in views on women in Chinese society and uncovered their particular political and cultural meanings. Her work is very stimulating. She shows how discourse answered the needs of a historical era and its political demands and suggests how we can trace the changes in history by following the changes in discourse. However, her schema still leaves unanswered several questions: how does discourse change people's minds and change the course of history? From what sources does the power of a discourse derive? How does discourse affect women and how does it get accepted by them? The answers to these questions cannot be provided by a text, that is to say, they cannot easily emerge through the mere deconstruction of a text.

The present essay does not propose to deconstruct discourse from a text. On the contrary, I shall try to return discourse to its context, in order to see how different ideologies provide different discourses with which we can reflect on women, and to see how different discourses can motivate women to create their own gender roles, social practices, and founding myths of women's liberation. Human beings are created by society, as matter is created by nature. Discourse has an important role in this creation. Especially in China, where the notion that the superstructure can react back on the economic base was particularly emphasized due to political demands, discourse becomes subordinate to ideology and becomes a monotonous gauge of political consciousness. Thus, the original cultural connotation and semantics in discourse are denuded; discourse becomes a standard by which people's actions are molded, and it ceases to be a language reflecting people's inner experiences.

The "we" in this essay stands for living Chinese women today and their collectiveness. A basic characteristic of the history of contemporary Chinese women is that they have been molded collectively. In this process of being molded as a tool of ideology, discourse plays a primary role in both overturning and constructing history.

Discourse, Context, and Ideology

Once discourse is isolated from the text, the analysis of context must go beyond the structure of the text and enter into history—the life circumstances of the people who employ the language—to deconstruct the historical relations between discourse and human beings. So far, three distinct discursive worlds dealing with Chinese women can be clearly discerned, precisely corresponding to three different historical phases. The first discursive world can be called traditional discourse, that is, native discourse. In the terms *little woman* (*xiao nüzi*) and *old woman* (*lao furen*) are reflected the lives of women that continued for thousands of years. Confucian and Daoist teachings, their moral rules and ritual regulations, are all constructed as part of this discourse. Although this discourse was created totally by men and directly serves a male-centered society and subordinates women to men, it has not lost its power to influence women, nor has it reduced the degree to which women self-consciously accept it. The production and spread of texts such as *Commands for Women, Canons for Women,* and *Women's Analects* have enabled male discourse to be reborn in the fertile soil of women, thus greatly enhancing the vitality of this discourse.[1] With Confucianism as its orthodoxy, Chinese culture built an effective tradition of obedience in which behavior is normalized through the manipulation of discourse. As far as women are concerned, there is an additional layer of restriction: women's behavior was also normalized by male discourse.

Ironically, although this discursive system has a venerable history and is deeply embedded in our national culture, it has become very alien and remote to contemporary Chinese women's sensibilities.—so much so that were it to be totally cut out as a segment from our history, Chinese women would not feel any pain of separation. We do not need to argue here the advantages for women's liberation of being separated, if possible, from tradition—we have perhaps already dwelled on this too much elsewhere. As long as it is still this nation that lives, breathes, and works on this stretch of land, it is impossible to be cut off from our history completely. However, it is possible to have breaks in discourse, and it is precisely these breaks that result in historical disjunctions. This is all the more evident in the fact that we can only understand history through historical texts; therefore, discourse not only modifies history but also makes up history. Subsequently, in the radical transformation of our discourse, we have come to lose a great part of our history, and in this process, we have lost ourselves. At the same time that we lose our capacity to take hold of history, the possibility for our autonomous thinking is also foreclosed. It seems to me that, in order to live sensibly today and restore our capacity for autonomous thinking as human beings, we must reconsider and answer certain questions that we thought we had already clarified and put to rest: What forces severed our discourse in history and are thereby responsible for the break that occurred in our language, for the loss of autonomy in the production of our national culture, and for the cutting off of Chinese people's everyday life from its origins? Can language and practical life really be alienated and cut off from history? If not, what has been abandoned, and what has been preserved? What was the historical force that propelled this revolution in national discourse?

Anyone with any historical common sense will realize that there is a distance of a whole century between our today and our yesterday, which is just the second historic stage this paper is going to discuss. In relation to the past of China, there is indeed no history for the twentieth century that took place on this soil, and perhaps no future as well. This has been an alien century, and it has alienated us from our past. However, through its own special twentieth-century discourse, it has constructed a solid edifice for our contemporary life. This means that we must first overcome and climb over its railings before we can stride into and assume our own century tomorrow.

More than a century ago, along with the entrance of Western weapons and vessels of war, and its missionaries and opium into China, also came Western ideology. Put another way, while the West invaded and attempted to swallow China, it also offered China weapons to save and strengthen itself, that is, thought, and the weapon of a new way of thinking, a new discourse. What gives us much food for thought is that our people's behavior at that time was to rally together against the external threat, returning blood for blood extracted, returning cannon fire for cannon fired, and learning how to fight back against the foreigners using their own firearms. However, in the area of thought, the backlash was turned inward, to criticize and revolutionize our own culture. The reaction here was to borrow from the foreigners' weapons of thought to rally together against the *internal* threat. From the Hundred Days Constitutional Reform of 1898 to the May Fourth Movement of the 1920s, the revolution in ideology surpassed any developments in the political, economic, and social realms of China at that time. Spurred on by the East Wind of the national wars against external enemies at that time, this revolution in ideology took root in people's hearts.

This East Wind of national war was conducted in a pure and authentic Chinese style, to resist external enemies such as the Russians, the Japanese, and Western imperialists. The West Wind was the new ideology of Western learning, consciously introduced by Chinese intellectuals. This new Western discourse came in two sets, from two different backgrounds.

The first set came from the Enlightenment, the product of capitalist industrial civilization and the French Revolution. Its central idea was that of "natural rights." The notion of "human being," that is, the abstract individual, became the central focus in its humanism. Its key words were *freedom, democracy,* and *equality*. At the beginning of this century, Chinese intellectuals did much to translate, introduce, and import this set of discourses into China. It was used to fight against the autocratic emperor system, to criticize the myriad social maladies of the time, and to appeal for national self-strengthening and social reform. From this was derived a new discourse for women, simply encapsulated in the notion of "the new woman" (*xin nuxing*). A series of literary figures involved in this notion's formation brought about a whole set of discourses concerned with the role of the new woman in casting off the feudal family, breaking away from feudal morality and ritual practice, and pursuing freedom and liberating individuality.

The second set of discourses was socialist, a product of Marxism and the victory of the Russian October Revolution. Its central content was class struggle (*jieji douzheng*). Class was the epitomy of key terms and decided the character of the masses in this ideology, which not only obliterated human individuality but also weakened human gender attributes. Instances of such a discourse include the slogans "Workers of the world unite,"[2] "For the liberation of humankind," and such characteristic Chinese phrases as "Times have changed, so men and women are the same" (shidai butongle, nan nu dou yiyang), "Women can support half the sky" (funu neng ding banbian tian)—there are too many to mention all of them. As far as objectively existing "individuals" and "human beings with gender" are concerned, and as long as they are subsumed under such banners, it is impossible to avoid being made into self-conscious agents of revolution as well as targets of the revolution. It follows that the key words derived from this discourse can be nothing but *revolution, liberation,* and *equality*. Discourse here is not only the tool of ideology and class struggle but has also become a political weapon for integrating the disparate social forces together into a whole. Like the first discourse, the political function of this discourse is evident; it works to overturn any previous authority it encounters.

Despite the contrast between a concern for the individual and a concern for the collective, these two ideologies were both progressive for Chinese society at that time. When Western discourse was imported into China at the beginning of this century, Chinese intellectuals did not draw a clear line between them. Hence, they were usually intertwined with one another. For instance, the former does not talk about class struggle but of "equality"; the latter rejects "freedom" but also upholds the same conception of "equality." In a healthy and normal society, people using different discourses should be able to live together harmoniously, and this is also the basis on which the "Hundred Schools of philosophy can contend." The difficulty arises when the different ideologies to which the discourses belong follow different and mutually exclusive political lines, forming two completely different and opposed militant camps. The so-called Cold War was actually a war between ideologies, and the main weapon in its direct confrontations was nothing but discourse. Against such a background, the word *revolution* created a whole linguistic context of its own. As soon as this linguistic signifier appeared, it summoned up an entire set of normative behavioral expectations and rules that formed its own self-sufficient system dictating everything from the motivation of thought to behavioral goals. It was this Cold War political environment that castrated this term, deprived it of its rich cultural connotations, and transformed it into a standardized norm for controlling human behavior. Thus, it was no longer a tool for social self-reflection, and with the loss of tools for thought, the process of thinking was put to an end. When a discourse becomes a weapon for making war, the hearts and minds of the people also become the battlefield for the Cold War. For example, the so-called self-reform (*ziwo gaizao*) movement, where subjects were made to criticize and remold themselves according to political dictates, was a special product of this linguistic environment.

Before the end of the Cold War not long ago, it was the discourse of revolution that enjoyed the greatest frequency and widest spread in China. This discursive dominance spanned the changing of eras marked by the year 1949, from the resistance against imperialism and feudalism to the Great Cultural Revolution. Chinese women remolded themselves in this revolutionary environment,[3] and perhaps they were also objects of revolutionary remolding. They were both the targets of the revolution (since they were tied in with the feudal institution of family and kinship) as well as the weapons of the revolution (since their liberation was a goal of the nation-state). Against the background of revolution, Chinese women completed two leaps at the same time: the first out of the feudal family and into society, and the second out of feudal society and into the modern sense of the nation-state. It is at this new historical junction that Chinese women came to be called women comrades (*funü tongzhi*).

Tani Barlow has noted the relationship between the appellation *funu* and revolution (1994b), but she neglected the original special context out of which this term emerged. Among the revolutionary soldiers, when the issue of gender emerged in language, only the term *funü* could be combined with the word *comrade*. (Can you imagine calling a woman *"nüzi* comrade," a *"nüxing* comrade," or a *"nüren* comrade"?) That is why when subsequently this term was spoken by itself, it still retained the connotation of *revolution*. In consulting the early documents of the revolution, we can easily find that this term was associated with this special linguistic context because there were really women in the ranks of the revolutionary forces, and therefore, men were in search of new terminology with which to address the "new women" (*xin nüxing*) in their company. Here it is worth reminding ourselves that among the "new women" in the early years of the twentieth century (including those who became revolutionaries later on), few called themselves or called women as a group *funü*. It is only after the founding of the Communist Party that this term prevailed among the ranks of the revolution. The writings of Mao Zedong provide a typical example in this regard. In his early reports made as an observer of peasant women's living conditions, Mao called women *nüzi* (Mao 1986), but when he became leader of the party, he called women in his own camp *funü*, or more politely, *funü* comrades. In this way, discourse was not only a weapon of revolutionary war, but later could also be a tool serving the revolutionaries according to the requirements of changing situations.

Under these historical conditions, feminism suffered a worse fortune than the other Western "-isms." It fell into the hands of men when entering China and was immediately dismembered by the two main Western ideologies that had taken root in China. In the early stages, male Chinese thinkers unanimously employed feminism as a tool against feudalism, and before women themselves had fully encountered feminism, they submerged and stifled feminism in the heavy currents of nationalism and social revolution. In the first set of discourses, feminism's spiritual quest for freedom was preserved. However, these sentiments were only expressed in works of literature, so they became literally discourses in "the text." The second set of discourses preserved the original core of feminism, that is, equality, but at the same time, it also stressed that equality between men and women must only proceed alongside of and at the same pace as "the liberation of the proletarian classes." After the year 1949, in the postliberation period, women were liberated, and so the problem of women disappeared. The category of women and sentiments of feminism then vanished in the great ocean of "equality." As a consequence, one can see that it is not that contemporary Chinese women refuse Western feminism, but that the discourse of feminism was rejected historically during the course of the liberation of Chinese women. Due to this period of history that saw the disappearance of feminism, even if it were possible for contemporary Chinese women to hold a dialogue on an equal footing with Western women, Chinese women do not or cannot think about women in terms of feminist discourse. Today, although the confrontation between the two main ideologies has subsided, what has not disappeared are the different contexts and connotations behind seemingly substitutable or translatable concepts (like equality), which inhabit both discourses. These connotations continue to burden that period of ultimately untranslatable history, a history not experienced by Western women. Herein lies the difficulty of exchange between the worlds of Western and Chinese scholarship on women.

The Uniqueness of Chinese Women's History

Reflecting back over the history of our generation of Chinese women—in other words, over the historical process of the construction of modern Chinese women—we have had a very unique experience compared with either traditional Chinese women or Western women. These experiences are like fruit produced in a utopian garden, with distinctive marks of ideology. They are fruit worth a thorough chewing by ourselves, our people, and even our future generations.

First, as "human beings with gender" (*you xing de ren*), that is, as women (*nüren*), we almost never received any kind of sex education, having experienced neither family education in the form of such texts of traditional female education as the *Daughter's Sutra*, nor the influence of modern feminist ideas. All special educational programs for and about women were suspended for more than thirty years from 1949 to the mid-1980s.[4] Our generation went through childhood, puberty, and adolescence in an era of "genderless ideology" (*yishi xingtai wuxing zhen*) and "asexual" (*feixinghua*) consciousness.

A very interesting phenomenon is that although the traditional way of calling women "little women" (*xiao nüzi*) has given way to *funü*, and there is the saying that "women can hold up half the sky," still, virtually no women like to be called or identify with the term *funü*. This term conjures up particular historical and cultural connotations that its bearer is married, adult, senile, and old-fashioned. We have noticed that on college campuses and in school life, few people use this term. Instead, people prefer to use the terms nü (female) *students*, nü *classmates*, and nü *youth*. In social life, all women who have work units and professions identify with the terms nü *worker*, nü

teacher, and nü *cadre* or nü official, rather than *funü. Funü* is a general designation in official documents or is used by officials to address women at formal meetings. It has become difficult to use it in reference to a particular
person because the word is now held in contempt by women and has been
abandoned by society. It is now only suitable for women who are jobless
and hanging around in urban neighborhoods or in the village—women
who have not been able to find a female professional title. This group of
women will eventually be assigned to the only women's organization in
China since Liberation, the Women's Federation. The rejection of the term
funü by "liberated" professional women suggests at least two kinds of inner
psychological stances: one tries to sever any connection with a historical
category of women through an identification with one's profession; the
other seeks to relate to the title of their social position while trying to
break away from their female gender position. Talk about revolution of
the self: are there any people who are more filled with revolutionary consciousness and more thorough in erasing a part of themselves as Chinese
women?

Second, in the political education we received after Liberation, there
was actually nothing that particularly aimed to establish equality between
men and women. Equality between men and women was postulated a priori as the antecedent condition for the birth of a new society. By means of
the New Marriage Law of 1950, the Constitution (1954), and a whole series of political movements, equality moved from being an ideology to the
realm of political power. No longer was it a discourse for the people to
think out problems and issues: it became a standard and norm for regulating behavior. Under such conditions, what kind of discourse can we still
use to think about women? Frankly speaking, for a long time we never
really reflected on the question of women. This is not because "the times
have changed, so men and women are alike," but because the discourse for
reflecting on women was reduced to the slogan "Equality between men
and women." We could only be women within the narrow confines of its
definition of women. It was a straitjacket wherein right and wrong, good
and bad were all determined in advance, so that it was not necessary or
even possible to think, but only to act. Thus we learned to be just like men.

Third, let us turn to the question of women's liberation. Our generation
was born in a social atmosphere that held that women had *already* been liberated. Through the use of such idioms and slogans as "New China" and
"After Liberation," it was taken for granted that Chinese women were new
and liberated. To our mind, liberation was not only in a "completed tense"
(Luo 1986), which we did not need to seek anymore; it was also a promise

made to us by society rather than a responsibility for every person to work on. The general attitude was that since we are socialist we must already possess equality between men and women. Thus the relationship between women and society was established as one of women's dependency. Just as in the period before Liberation, women were dependent on the family and on men and therefore could be constructed and shaped by them, today, women are dependent on society, on the party, and on the state. Although they have gained liberation, women are doomed by their passive role in this liberation. It is no wonder that in the process of struggling for liberation, we have gradually lost parts of ourselves, so that not only is it difficult to become masters of our fate, we are also no longer capable of being women. Under the banner of equality, in order to prove that "men and women are the same," women took the plunge into revolutionary consciousness and action, without regard to fame, gain, or consequences, and without distinguishing between right and wrong. So we had various Iron Girl Teams and March Eight Teams. Both in the Great Leap Forward state-orchestrated movement and in the violent behavior during the early stages of the Cultural Revolution, women did their best to participate just as the men. Although these efforts did reveal the degree to which we had achieved equality between men and women, at the same time they revealed our ailment. Liberation that departs from the humanistic spirit can become destructive and lead to inhuman behavior, to destroying others, and to destroying ourselves.

Before the 1970s in China, first we had a Cold War with the West and then a "debate" with the Soviet Union. As a result, both sets of discourses imported from the West have been cut off from their origins due to the periods of hostilities with the outside world. An important consequence of the ensuing stress on "self-reliance" was the ascendancy of the slogan "Long Live Mao Zedong Thought!" Thus we were drowned in a vast ocean of Maoist discourse, into which we plunged our entire youth. We devoted our hearts and souls to pushing equality between men and women to its ultimate extreme. We did not stop employing Maoist discourse until a long time after the Cultural Revolution. It was only after this that we began to think about women.

In the tightly sealed environment of those times, there were no new discourses and no new ideological worlds. So what force was it that helped us to break through the ideological confinement that had molded and constructed us, to walk out of yesterday and head for today? It was life, none other than women's lived experiences. Our generation of women can take our own life experiences to prove that the feelings and emotions of real life are the most effective weapons with which to overturn a dominant discourse of power. While losing our control over language and even our ability to think reflectively, life experiences become a potential form of discourse that can smash through the barrier encasing us in discourse. They can cast doubt on consciousness that has become rigidified and institutionalized. Real-life experiences enable us to say "No!" to discourses that try to construct and regulate our lives.

Our third historical phase started amid the discursive world that had molded and constructed us. In the 1980s, women writers' first gesture—"searching for the self" (xunzhao ziwo)—promptly and accurately expressed the embryonic spiritual quest of our generation of women. For a long time in China, to speak of the self was to be a social rebel. Many people find it difficult to recognize that a pioneering quest such as going "in search of the self" was started by precisely the people who have been most looked down on, that is, women. From the search for the self in literary texts, the quest was broadened to the popular movement of "the self-recognition of women" (nüxing ziwo renshi), and thus began Chinese women's new journey from "self-reliance" (zili) to "the self as master" (zizhu).

The search for the self was the real starting point from which Chinese women began to reflect on themselves from an active subject-position. Women's self-recognition was Chinese women's manifesto of rational awakening. To disentangle women's "self" from the midst of "men and women are alike"; to retrieve women's experiences from the world of discourse constructed by men—these steps are unprecedented in the history of China. Based on these efforts, a new field of "women's studies" (funü yanjiu), which takes women as the "subjects" of history, emerged for the first time and started to construct a women's discourse. Furthermore, the awakening of "women's collective consciousness" (funü qunti yishi) is fundamentally transforming women's traditional dependence on family, men, society, and the state, so that they can start a life where the self is in charge.

Interpretations and Misinterpretations of Some Key Terms

Due to the peculiarities of our history described above, when we reflect on the situation of women, there may be significant differences between ourselves and Western women in our understanding and employment of some key terms and phrases. These differences will unavoidably create obstacles in our mutual exchanges. Due to the limitations of space, I can list no more than a few key terms in this article in order to show some important semantic differences, and to provide a basis from which future research can mount deeper deconstructions and make more clarifications.

Liberation (jiefang). This is one of the most popular words used by Chinese women. In its particular ideological context in China, there are two important elements of this notion that are defined a priori; both are indispensable in Chinese women's understanding of women's liberation. The first element is revolution and the second element is class. The complete semantics of this term can be seen in this phrase: "Strive for 'liberation' through 'revolution' in solidarity with the oppressed classes." This notion of liberation must include two basic qualities: one is a collective spirit (for the whole of humankind); the other is a genderless character (men are also liberated along with women). In English, the words *liberation (jiefang)* and liberty *(ziyou)* are synonymous and etymologically linked, so they are naturally intertwined in conception and usage. However, for Chinese, and even for Chinese women, the word *liberation* does not necessarily carry the connotation of *liberty.* So it is hard for Chinese men and women to associate liberation with freedom, and even harder for them to reflect on the liberation they have already gained from the viewpoint of personal liberty. Lack of freedom is precisely one of the important characteristics of Chinese women's liberation.

Furthermore, because *liberation* is politicized in ideology, the word is used in different senses even among Chinese women. For instance, *liberation* seems to be a taboo word in Taiwan. For a very long time, women who strove for liberation in Taiwan dared not talk about women's liberation for fear of being accused of "connecting with Communists."

Consciousness (yishi). This is a new word that Chinese women have started to use to reflect on women. It emerged in the process of "searching for the self" in the 1980s. The words *women's consciousness* and *self-consciousness* are central to the discourse of women's studies and women's education in the post-Mao New Era. This concept is marked by distinctive features, such as the emphasis on individuality, the agency of the active subject, and gender. The English word *consciousness* can be understood as both *consciousness (yishi)* in the sense just noted, and also as political consciousness *(juewu)* (Wang Zheng 1995: 110). If we were to translate this term into the Chinese *juewu* and put it into a Chinese text, it would have a totally different sense from today's notion of consciousness *(yishi).* The concept of political consciousness in contemporary Chinese usage has a particular political linguistic context: it is often associated with class and revolution, from which it derives its meaning and its positive connotation. What is set up in opposition to political consciousness is precisely consciousness (*yishi*), which is often associated with the concepts individual and bourgeois. With its powerful connotations of individuality, spontaneity, gender, and sexuality, it would seem that *yishi* stands in rebellion against political consciousness (*juewu*).

Equality (pingdeng). This word is probably the word with the biggest difference in meaning and connotation between the discourses of Chinese and Western women. The main reason for this difference lies in the practical relationship between equality and women's lives in China and the West. For Western women, equality is a goal and banner; it is the core of feminism, and also an important marker of women's liberation. Its frame of reference is men. However, for Chinese women, equality was the very principle that constructed our history and environment, and it is also an important component of our practical everyday lives.

I once wrote a paper expressly on the topic of the gain and loss that we have experienced in implementing the principle of "equality between men and women" (*nannü pingdeng*), and its impact on Chinese women (Li Xiaojiang 1995). When China was in a miserable state, our equality was to have an equality of misery, so that the sharing of misery was both the price we had to pay for equality as well as an intrinsic part of equality. Under the banner of "equality between men and women," it is not surprising that Chinese women never had any energy to enjoy and make use of their equality. On the one hand, Chinese women have had an abundance of life experiences in that they have tasted their fill of equality's bitterness and sweetness and endured a stabbing pain that is difficult to express in words. On the other hand, this period of history has enabled them to thoroughly understand the world of men; in this world still laden with hardships and war, it is indeed difficult to maintain one's attraction to the goal of becoming like men.

Women's studies (funü yanjiu). This is also a new concept that emerged in the post-Mao New Era and coincided with the West's own developing dynamism of gender studies. The West's gender studies were developed on the foundation of women's studies. However, in China women's studies and gender studies cannot be made interchangeable or allowed to collapse into each other. Even if they emerge together, this does not mean that the latter is the product of the development of the former, nor that the former should develop into the latter or serve as a transition into the latter. There are three reasons for this. First, the former (women's studies) has a political nature, while the latter (gender studies) is purely academic. Second, the former is all about agency and subjectivity, and the latter is about methodology. Third, the former is a specialized study with a clear object of study, while the latter is a broadening of scholarly topics. Due to the fact that not long ago in Chinese history women disappeared in Chinese social life, consequently, not only is it necessary for women's studies to raise high its own banner, it must be especially on its guard against getting buried again in a gender studies that resembles the myth of "men and women are the same."

The new concepts explicated above represent the most stellar thinking in the new Western feminism. However, among Chinese women they may elicit very different reactions and may even be counterproductive. Besides the above key terms, there are still some important concepts that should be mentioned.

The personal is political (gerende ji zhenzhide). This is a slogan of the radical faction in the new Western feminist movement. It is directed against the indifference and even contempt that politics and the political system in the West harbor for women's family lives and individual and private lives. While this slogan has gained wide influence in Western society, it is nothing new in Chinese society. Indeed, with regards to Chinese women, it may even bring harm. In the past half-century in China, the personal has without exception been political. In everything from relations between men and women to marriage and family relations, the hand of politics was felt everywhere. It penetrated and eventually completely appropriated personal space. Since the family and private life were women's areas of influence, not only were women objects of appropriation, but under the influence and goading of ideology they easily became the appropriators, too. All these horrible scenarios are recorded in countless literary works, and they remain indelibly etched in people's memories. Thus, we would hesitate to politicize the space of the personal again, which is also often women's space. With this example, it is not difficult for us to understand that the same concept in different societies might have entirely different implications and consequences. A simple transplantation of a concept into a very different context may cause confusion, and even tremendous harm.

Women's rights are human rights (nüquan shi renquan). This is the slogan that has been shouted the most loudly in the West in recent years. It is directed against the fact that traditional Western concepts of human rights left out women's rights and did not express women's interests. Here "equality between men and women" still lies at its core, and there still remains a demand of male-centered society to grant women the same rights as men. China, on the other hand, is different. In the past half-century, Chinese women have actually obtained too *many* rights and benefits that they originally had not expected. Today, these gains stand in striking contrast to

Chinese women's general indifference to the spread of human rights in society, and their lack of sensitivity to women's own rights. Therefore, perhaps what Chinese women need today is precisely a converse slogan: "Human rights are women's rights." Only this reversed slogan can help Chinese women change their traditional view that the issue of rights and power is either decided on by the will of others, or that society can be relied on to guarantee their rights. It is only by alerting Chinese women in this way that they will self-consciously push further the process of the democratization of Chinese society, that they will really grow to become concerned citizens, and that they will embark on the path to political maturity.

Sisterhood is power (jiemei tuanjie jiushi liliang). This slogan was brought into China at the Fourth UN Women's Conference in 1995 by Western women, but it has little drawing power for Chinese women. The reason is very simple: as compared with the slogan "Unity is strength," which has been trumpeted for several decades in China, this unity only of "sisters" seems a bit weak both in spirit and scope. Another slogan we have been promoting in recent years that is very close to this is "Women's collective consciousness." While "Sisterhood is power" exhorts individuals to march toward the collective, this other slogan seeks to detach a women's collectivity from the total collectivity of "men and women are the same." The former is directed at ordinary women who are powerless and weak; the latter is directed at intellectual and professional women who have ability, social status, and influence. The former urges women in solidarity to oppose a male-centered society; the latter calls on women elites to come to consciousness and throw themselves behind the women's movement. As to the objective of a new Chinese women's movement today, if it is simply advocated as a movement of women, it cannot mobilize even ordinary women. This is not only because women's progress in developing countries depends eventually on social progress in the society at large but, even more important, because the whole of Chinese society, including men, has actively participated in and promoted the liberation and progress of Chinese women. Against such historical experiences where the whole society was mobilized, to call only on sisterhood would not only be ineffective, it would also sound as though we were forming a "small faction" out of a "great unity" and would thus leave the impression that one is forsaking something better that we had, and embracing something more narrow.

I have examined certain key terms and phrases above to stress the differences between their Chinese and Western textual expressions and contexts. However, this is not to rule out their similarities. Such similarities form the basis on which different societies of the world coexist and the objective point of departure for recognizing differences. However, if these similarities and common points of departure are exaggerated and treated as the means and ends of human existence, then the result could be dangerous, making each society or individual lose themselves in an imposed uniformity. We in China already have learned painful lessons in this regard. Under the banner of communism, in replacing individuality with notions of commonly shared human nature, the society lost sight of humanity and the humane. Similarly, under the slogan "Men and women are alike," we relinquished the category of women. These are all lessons learned in our lived experiences, and today they serve as the basis of our wisdom. Therefore, my position is to be skeptical of any elevation of the experiences of only a segment of humanity to the status of global truth (or to the rank of universally applicable solution). In extending one's wisdom globally, one also runs the danger of losing oneself. Therefore, in the end we must return to the ancient and profound philosophical adage "Know yourself!"

NOTES

1 *The Commands for Women* was authored by Ban Chao in the Han dynasty; *The Canons for Women* (thirty volumes) was by Queen Zhang Sun of the Tang dynasty; *Women's Analects* (twelve volumes) was by Song Ruohua of the imperial palace in the Tang dynasty.
2 I discovered that the English word on Marx's gravestone is *workers (gongren)* rather than proletarians (*wuchan jieji*).
3 See the preface (in Li 1994c).
4 In May 1985, I organized a class on women and domestic policy and lectured on the topic of women's self-recognition at the Women Cadres School in Henan Province. The reestablishing of women's education programs soon spread throughout the country.

11

Gender and a Geopolitics of Desire:

The Seduction of Mainland Women

in Taiwan and Hong Kong Media

The prime function incumbent on the socius has always been to codify the
flows of desire, to inscribe them, to record them, to see to it that no flow
exists that is not properly dammed up, channeled, regulated. When the
primitive *territorial machine* proved inadequate to the task, the *despotic machine*
set up a kind of overcoding system. But the *capitalist machine* . . . finds itself
in a totally new situation: it is faced with the task of decoding and deterritorializing the flows.
—Gilles Deleuze and Félix Guattari, *Anti-Oedipus: Capitalism and Schizophrenia*

The increasing economic integration of Taiwan, Hong Kong, and China
has in recent years spurred, in both popular and academic arenas, their
imaginary fusion into a single entity called "Greater China."[1] Scholars
have recently begun to explore the cultural manifestations and consequences of this integration, especially in light of the developments in mass
media such as popular music (Gold 1995) and film,[2] where coproductions
and cultural "joint ventures" (*hezi*) are becoming common.[3] On the one
hand, given the need for strategic marketing and market penetration beyond national boundaries, such coproductions tend to render ambiguous
which "state" they are speaking for or against. On the other hand, the
availability of electronic mediation has greatly facilitated the traffic of

popular cultural productions among these sites. The combination of these two factors—political ambiguity and easy access to mass-mediated cultural productions—has further sparked the consideration of the potential emergence of a public sphere in this region outside the direct intervention of the "states" involved. Is culture, then, like economy, becoming more and more integrated in these sites, so that a "transnational Chinese culture" (alternatively, "pan-Chinese culture" or "global Chinese culture") is now being created, particularly since they already share a putatively similar cultural heritage, languages, and customs, as some would claim?[4]

Little has been said about how gender inflects such a perceived economic and cultural integration, however, and, conversely, how such an integration effects a specific kind of gender economy.[5] My inquiry here concerns the relationship between gender, mass media, and the question of a pan-Chinese public sphere. As I see it, late twentieth-century ethnic Chinese capitalism in mass-mediated cultural productions in the China–Hong Kong–Taiwan (hereafter *zhong gang tai*) region operate through two contradictory gestures on the plane of gender: mass media targeted for consumption throughout this region strategically suppress native patriarchal and nationalist sentiments in order to maximize market expansion, while media aimed at local audiences tend to resuscitate and reconsolidate native patriarchies and nationalist/nativist sentiments.[6] Inscriptions of gender in the latter case, which is the focus of this paper, particularly mainland gendered subjects in Taiwan and Hong Kong media, are never divorced from political tensions that have been periodically mounting in the region. In fact, it is the site of gender representation that has attracted the heaviest concentration of political anxieties; their cultural correlates can be found in the increasing calls for a cultural nativism in Taiwan, as well as in the earnest attempt of Hong Kong cultural workers before 1997 to carve out a unique identity vis-à-vis China. The increased migration of mainland women to Taiwan and Hong Kong in recent years has played a significant part in a complex trajectory of anxieties intimately enmeshed with the volatile political and economic relations in the region, and the representations of mainland women in mass media (newspaper, television, and film) are thereby full of patriarchal injunctions against these women's threat and contamination (in the case of Taiwan's "mainland sister") and fantasies of their containment and assimilation (in the case of Hong Kong's "mainland cousin").

From analyzing these anxieties in the representation of mainland women in mass media in Taiwan and Hong Kong, I suggest that the perceived economic integration is by no means a fait accompli, nor does it translate into or should it be equated to cultural and political integration. The disjunctions and contestations in the cultural and political arenas challenge the facile narrative of a coherent pan-Chinese capitalism, which operates entirely according to the economy of capital, and thwart easy assertions of the emergence of a pan-Chinese culture in this region. More specifically, I suggest that the interweaving of political, economic, and cultural anxieties in the figure of the mainland woman consistently precludes the emergence of a gendered public sphere in these sites and systematically undercuts the "transnationalizing" tendencies in current discussions of issues pertaining to these women. This is a much more complex question and, indeed, an entirely new question, going beyond the prevailing paradigm of the contradictory relationship between gender and nationalism, where the women involved were often revealed to be further oppressed by their Third World nationalist patriarchies under colonial or neocolonial control.[7] As I mention elsewhere, in these earlier discussions on gender and nationalism, the boundary of each discourse has been generally delimited to the geopolitical nation-state and its violation at the hands of unwelcome invaders, hence *woman* becomes the third term in the binary, Manichean struggle between the colonizer and the colonized (Shih 1996a). The *zhong gang tai* mediation of gender, however, is in reality a transnational and multiangular social phenomenon created through the migration of media and people, but its discursive constructions are characteristically "national" in sentiment. Yet this "national" interpretation is itself highly ambiguous: Hong Kong is fated to become more and more closely integrated into China (despite the current policy of One Country, Two Systems), and Taiwan is under direct threat of forceful reunification with China, which makes the designation "national" more of an approximation than an accurate rendering of intense nativist feelings felt by the majority of Taiwan's populace and now a decreasing number of people in Hong Kong. If one posits that the ambiguous interplay between the transnational and the national indicates the new social formation in the late capitalist world in general, where the transnational flow of goods, commodities, and peoples has achieved a degree of denationalization and deterritorialization, the specific gender representations in the *zhong gang tai* context exemplify an opposite effort to nationalize or territorialize politics and culture due to the perceived political, cultural, and economic threats posed by transnational migration. In the end, the notion of "Greater China" itself is revealed to be heavily Chinacentric, since the perspectives from other diasporic Chinese communities, especially Taiwan, are clearly opposed to integration, whether economic, cultural, or political.[8]

It will become apparent in the following analysis that native feminists in Taiwan and Hong Kong simply tolerate and sometimes strategically evoke the "national" when dealing with issues regarding mainland women. This is because the migration of mainland women into their midst, as well as rampant adultery of Taiwan and Hong Kong businessmen working in China, have seriously compromised and threatened the interests of native women. In such a context, Taiwan and Hong Kong feminists appear allied with the larger cultural and economic nativist movements in their societies. If they were silent in the face of patriarchal disparagement of mainland women in popular media, however, these feminists did not condone the same patriarchy's further oppression of native women through its members' extramarital relationships with mainland women. If nationalism was strategically tolerated so as to sharpen the focus on native women as the real victims, the erstwhile twin of nationalism, patriarchy, was nevertheless denounced as the agent of abuse. Feminisms in contemporary Taiwan and Hong Kong have moved away from the dichotomous model of "women versus the nation" in which the nation is equated with patriarchy, and therefore antipatriarchal voices were always either dismissed or brandished as antinational and traitorous. It was this paradigm of women versus the nation that had earlier told women they would have to wait for national liberation before women's liberation could be accomplished (Jayawardena 1986; Gilmartin 1995). By disembedding patriarchy from the nation, we can more clearly delineate, deconstruct, and resist the assumptions of patriarchy. The multiangulation of gender relations within the *zhong gang tai* region by a complex of historically specific issues then offers a new paradigm for studying gender in a changing Third World, parts of which are fast approaching the First World in terms of economic status, and projects a new geopolitics of desire in an age of blurred national boundaries.

Beleaguered Communities

Chinese New Year, 1996. The second trial in the murder of a mainland Chinese woman dragged on in Orange County Supreme Court, and southern California's Chinese community continued to be reminded of the tragedy of transgressive relationships between the mainland Chinese and the Taiwanese. As with the first trial that had ended in a hung jury, local Chinese newspapers related the daily events in court on the front page of the local news section. A crime of passion: the murdered woman is the mainland Chinese mistress of a Taiwanese businessman, and the accused murderer is his wife. The story began when the businessman, Peng Zengji, left his wife and children in Taiwan to open a factory in China to expand his business and there found himself a mistress, Ji Ranbing. He eventually moved Ji Ranbing and their newborn baby to an apartment in southern California, not far from where his two children by his lawful wife lived and went to school as "little overseas students" (*xiao liuxuesheng*). Lin Liyun, the wife, allegedly encountered Ji Ranbing during one of her visits to southern California. She had been aware of Ji's existence for several years and was alleged to have gruesomely murdered both Ji and her baby son.

If one does not take into account the complicated political, cultural, and economic transactions within Greater China, the story reads like another instance of the moral failings of a patriarch ruining the lives of two women and their children, and a classic case of the wife's internalization of patriarchal values and displacement of her anger over her husband's adultery onto the mistress and the symbol of the mistress's power, the male child. The Chinese community in southern California, split between mainlanders and Taiwanese, was, however, uniformly reticent regarding Peng's wrongdoing. Peng's public declaration of love for his murdered mistress in the local newspapers provided Mainlanders in the community with moral ammunition to defend Ji's adultery as an act of genuine love, allowing them to sympathize with her publicly, and to offer assistance to her tear-stricken father and sister who came to southern California to attend her funeral. Peng therefore could not be accused by the mainlanders: to accuse him for his moral lapses would degrade the murdered victim and her family with whom the mainlanders needed to sympathize in solidarity. On the other hand, Peng could not be accused by the Taiwanese immigrants either, who feared that it would deepen discord in an already split community of mainlanders and Taiwanese. The Taiwanese showed their solidarity instead by rallying around Lin, the wife, and later, when she was pronounced guilty, by establishing the Friends of Lin Liyun Association on Mother's Day in 1996, visiting Lin periodically, seeking the governor's pardon, and providing legal and psychological counseling to her and her family.[9] If in old China male polygamy had been sanctioned by the seamless operation of patriarchal power, in the Chinese diaspora in southern California, adultery was beyond reproach because of the fissures among the various ethnic Chinese immigrants who embodied the political, cultural, and economic tensions in their native places. These tensions complicate the roles and functions of gender and disallow the emergence of a translocal voice of antipatriarchy.

If, however, the Chinese diaspora in southern California can be tentatively called a community, albeit a split one, in contradistinction to other racial and ethnic groups, the same could not be said of Taiwan, China, and Hong Kong. The crisis situation in their interrelationships in the mid- and late-1990s renders the epithet "Greater China" merely an indication of putative ethnic similarity and economic codependency that disguises intense animosities. China continues to renew its threats to conquer Taiwan in the name of "reunification," whose most crude manifestation was the March 1996 missile crisis, and threatens to invalidate democratic forms of culture and politics in Hong Kong through the curtailing of freedom in the media and the disbandment of the democratically elected legislature. The grand rhetoric of "reunification" that prohibits "territorial division" threatens both Hong Kong and Taiwan, whose fates are linked not only in their shared subjection to Chinese hegemony, but also because Hong Kong's "return" to mainland rule has been seen by all parties involved as a model and testing ground for the planned takeover of Taiwan. The rhetoric of "antiterritorial division" looms as the grand narrative for the containment of Taiwan, while Hong Kong's return has functioned as the authentication of China's ultimate power over Taiwan: "It is only a matter of time."

How does gender become configured in these times of crisis and potential violence? Under a thin facade of reportage realism, newspaper, magazine, and film representations of mainland women in Taiwan and Hong Kong are fraught with multiple overdeterminations to such an extent that "mainland women" as a category becomes overlaid with meanings beyond the biological and economic determinations ordinarily apparent. Although these are the bodies that serve as prostitutes and wives in Taiwan and Hong Kong, as mistresses and surrogate mothers for Taiwan and Hong Kong businessmen in coastal cities in China (that prosperous margin that is more than "China"),[10] and accordingly their representation is heavily "bodied," they carry potent political and cultural meanings in their signification. It is the uneasy tension and mutually constituting relationship between the bodied (as index to women's oppression as commodified and exploited bodies) and the socialized (as index to political and cultural complexes) that I see as central to the examination of gender issues here. Indeed, the bodied becomes so embroiled in the socialized that the latter threatens to make the question of women's bodily exploitation inconsequential.

Reading media representations of mainland Chinese women therefore requires a double attention to the categories of mainland China and women, although they inevitably intersect. In other words, using *mainland China* as a primary signifier requires a thorough contextualization in the specific configuration of relationships within the *zhong gang tai* region, but foregrounding gender will also require a reference to the transnational paradigm of traffic *in* women[11] and the traffic *of* women across boundaries. This "transnational" dimension of the traffic in women (smuggling and abduction) and traffic of women (willing migration) within the confused network of *zhong gang tai* helps to foreground the commodification, exchange, and extortion of mainland women as bodies, but the conflictual trajectories of their "national" histories immediately undermine that "transnational" reading and replace the bodied reading with a socialized reading of cultural and political antinomies. But more than mutually contradictory, the "transnational" and the "national" are also ambiguously constituted vis-à-vis each other because of the memory of their former unity and a putatively shared cultural heritage. This memory has been deployed by all three sides: by the mainland Chinese government as a rhetoric of containment; by the Taiwanese government to validate its "Chinese" culture as more authentic than that of communist China;[12] and by erstwhile Hong Kong nationalists (pro-communist or not) resisting British colonial domination and by many Hong Kongers in their recent conciliatory reception of Chinese rule. With the military threat from China, this memory and sharedness are now increasingly refuted by Taiwan, yet they linger on in various forms such as in the strategic assertions of Taiwan's cultural superiority over China. For Hong Kong, "becoming Chinese" on July 1, 1997, has required a recuperation of this sharedness with all the hoopla of ritualistic and carnivalesque celebration, even while liberal democrats have conducted frequent protests. Strategizing Hong Kong's emergent yet threatened-to-be-lost cultural identity and Taiwan's struggle for international recognition as an independent nation-state requires a subtle delineation of the "national" and the "transnational" in this region that capitalizes on both its constituents' sameness and difference in multiple, contradictory ways.

So the boundaries that mainland women traverse are not the linguistic ones that often trace national boundaries: those who go to Taiwan often speak the Taiwanese dialect because the same dialect is spoken in Fujian province, albeit with a slightly different accent, and those who go to Hong Kong often speak the language of its populace, Cantonese, also the language of Guangdong province. For the independence-oriented intellectuals in Taiwan, to hear Taiwanese-inflected Mandarin spoken by mainland prostitutes rounded up by the police and interviewed on television is more than unnerving: the difference necessary to maintain and police the boundaries of national identity is absent in this case. The threat to Taiwan's independence is in this sense the threat of similarity: if a large number of illegal immigrants from China succeed in crossing the Taiwan Strait, China need not resort to military means to conquer Taiwan. Without the convenient marker of language or ethnic difference, and without a ready-made discourse of independent national memory and culture, Hong Kong and Taiwan cultural imaginaries must turn elsewhere for the recognition, production, and consolidation of difference. It is within this specific context that I endeavor to decode the representations of mainland women in Taiwan and Hong Kong media and locate a new geopolitics of desire.

Sexualizing the "Mainland Sister"

In the imagined community of the new nation, women are admitted only with reservation and only as sex.

—Rey Chow, "The Politics of Admittance"

The conjunctural elements that comprised the historical moment of the mid-1990s in which the specific semantic field of the "mainland sister" (*dalumei*) in Taiwan was generated may include the following: the early 1990s had witnessed increased official and unofficial contacts between Taiwan and China and an unprecedented rise in bilateral trade, yet the storm of rage expressed by the Chinese government over Taiwan president Lee Teng-hui's unofficial visit to the United States in June 1995 threatened a total breakdown of the painstakingly fostered relationship. Even before Lee's visit, however, anxiety over Taiwan's relationship with China ran deep in popular and official discourses alike. This can be illustrated by the extent to which the sensationalist book *August, 1995* (Zheng 1994), which predicted China's invasion of Taiwan in August 1995, gripped a paranoid Taiwan readership. And when August 1995 actually rolled around, political analysts and newspaper columnists conjectured about the possibility of actual invasion based on the book's scenario.[13] By 1996, however, with China's military exercises opposite the Taiwan coast conspicuously asserting China's will to conquer Taiwan, the scenario of invasion, no longer confined to the realm of imagination and the market, triggered a massive exodus of Taiwan's foreign currency, an immigration frenzy, and necessitated the Taiwan government's intervention in the stock market for fear that a drastic fall would irrevocably damage business confidence.

Although the late 1980s and early 1990s had seen a mushrooming of independence-oriented cultural production in Taiwan, the political crystallization of which was the establishment of the Democratic Progressive Party (*minjindang*), the rhetoric of independence had been losing popular support because of the overwhelming threat by the Chinese government that an assertion of independence would be tantamount to an invitation to invasion.[14] Late 1980s and early 1990s confidence that Taiwan was economically more advanced than China, that Taiwan could teach modernization techniques to China, that Taiwan could make money by conquering the virgin market and exploiting inexpensive labor in China, and that Taiwan was culturally more modern and sophisticated than "backward" China (Shih 1995) was instead replaced by a deep sense of ambivalence toward all transactions with China: Is Taiwan's economy becoming too dependent on China? Will Taiwan businesses lose their investments in China if tensions mount? On a smaller scale, can Taiwan businessmen in China still act the rich compatriots asserting their economic superiority when China itself is increasingly becoming richer? To put it differently, as China's market economy modernizes, what markers of culture can be deployed to show Taiwan's superiority? Or, are there any realms left with which Taiwan can comfort itself vis-à-vis China's political hegemony or resist that hegemony, when economic gaps are gradually being bridged, ironically in part because of the efforts of Taiwanese businesses?

Increased legal and illegal immigration of mainland Chinese to Taiwan has not decreased hostility but instead heightened Taiwan's anxiety of contamination and fear of takeover by the Chinese. The migration is necessitated by Taiwan's lack of labor resources and the difficult marriage market for native males, and it is fueled by the "gold digging" (taojin) aspirations of some mainland Chinese men and women. In the mid-1990s, they came legally and illegally in droves: laborers were recruited to work on ships and construction sites, mainland women were smuggled over by Taiwanese "snake heads" (shetou—human smugglers) for prostitution, and marriage services organized trips to China and helped with the eventual immigration of Chinese brides. Related to the migration of Mainlanders to Taiwan was also the prevalent phenomenon of Taiwanese businessmen in China taking mainland mistresses (the southern California murder trial is an example of this), and the practice of husbands involved in an infertile marriage finding surrogate mothers in the Mainland. These surrogate mothers, as expected, often caused marriage crises for the married couples, as they sometimes remained mistresses to the men.

It was roughly within the intersection of these social junctures that the "mainland sister," the dalumei, came into being as a media construction in the mid-1990s. Who is this dalumei in Taiwan? Popularized by sensational stories in newspapers of sexual exploitation, the dalumei is a woman who in most cases serves as a prostitute, willingly or otherwise, and who in some cases successfully disguises as native and gets to make money as a singer, waitress, bar hostess, or beautician. The word *mainland* (*dalu*) suggests economic backwardness and hence the quest for monetary gain; and the term *little sister* (*mei*) suggests the means by which the quest is conducted—by way of sexuality and youth. *Mei* in classical parlance has often been used to designate the female lover, and when applied to a young woman in a certain context, unambiguously refers to the woman's low social status and exploitability. The *dalumei's* two prime signifiers are money and sex: her desire for money makes her a readily available sex object, which provides moral justification for her exploiters ("she herself wants it"). As such, she is different from mainland women (*dalu nuzi*) whom Taiwanese businessmen take as mistresses or who marry Taiwanese and become "mainland wives" (*dalu taitai*). But there is no epistemological clarity between the terms *dalumei*, *dalu nuzi*, and *dalu taitai*, as the latter two can easily be reduced to *dalumei* if the enunciator at any moment wishes to denigrate the mainland woman he or she encounters. So when a *dalu nuzi* is found to be residing in Taiwan illegally, she is immediately called *dalumei*; when a *dalu nuzi* is seen as undeserving of an arranged marriage with a native husband, she is reduced to a *dalumei*. But if *dalumei* prostitutes were found and rescued by the native police from their indentured sexual labor, they are bestowed the honorary title of *dalu nuzi* so that the moral authority of the police can be subtly asserted.[15]

The *dalumei* in newspaper and magazine representations is most often a flat character, whose singular obsession of "searching for gold" seems to lead her to any activity that will fulfill that goal. Newspapers sometimes carry sensational stories of her sexual abuse, which curiously make her even more seductive. The paradox is due to a kind of performative contradiction: newspaper coverage that is meant to arouse people's concern over the problem ends up turning the reports of *dalumei* into tantalizing tales of sex and money. The stories are consistently about their involuntary and voluntary engagement in the sex business, and their labor is given explicit numerical monetary values. It is customary, for instance, to report how much the smuggling fee was, how the *dalumei* paid for it or was forced to pay for it, and what is happening to the *dalumei* at present in terms of her financial status. A small headline for a news item on *dalumei* in September 1994 reads, "Receiving 350 Customers—the Price for Coming to Taiwan." The article details that the fee for smuggling two *dalumei* into Taiwan via Thailand with false passports was serving 350 customers each, which, at NT $1,000 per customer, translates into NT $350,000 (US $14,000). The two prostitutes paid off their smuggling fees in less than five months and had been keeping 40 percent of each transaction for themselves until they were caught.[16]

While earlier accounts of *dalumei* exploited for sexual labor expressed a certain concern for their well-being,[17] in representations since the 1995 fallout with China, even forced sexual labor is depicted with a tinge of ironic humor. A February 3, 1996, news item depicts how three *dalumei* were saved by the police just when they were being forced into prostitution and notes that one of them had had the "adventure" of having breast implants. The obvious jab here is at the *dalumei* who pretended that they did not realize their impending fate. Why else would a *dalumei* get breast implants? The absence of moral concern in the article is striking, as the *dalumei* has become not the object of sympathy (which would have confirmed Taiwan's moral superiority) but the object of derision. This is because while earlier stories concentrated on how inhuman the smugglers had been in deceiving the *dalumei* into indentured prostitution, more recent stories tell of how these *dalumei* willingly came to become prostitutes under a contract with their smugglers to pay off their smuggling fee through their sex work. The support of the society is therefore unnecessary. Rather, the fact that they can now come to Taiwan without paying the smuggling fee in advance shows how vulnerable Taiwan's border is to their infiltration. Hence, concern for the welfare of the *dalumei* is replaced by alarm at the ever clever and "corrupt" *dalumei* who are contaminating Taiwan.

The popular Taiwanese news magazine *China Times Weekly* has published at least two special reports on the *dalumei* question. The first of these appeared in January 1993 and dealt not with the *dalumei* at home but with the *dalumei* in China, conflating mainland prostitutes and mainland mistresses of Taiwanese businessmen. As the semantic field of *dalumei* in Taiwan is saturated with illicit sex and money, the *dalumei* in China is characterized by an insatiable greed for money, luxury, and material goods. The article, tellingly titled "Dalumei Love to Kill Taiwanese Men," describes three stages in the relationship between *dalumei* and Taiwanese businessmen in a pseudo-analytic and pseudohistorical manner. The reporter defines the first stage as occurring between 1988 and 1990 when Taiwan businesses started to expand into China. This was when Taiwanese businessmen were lured by the ready availability of beauties in China, and the mainland women were equally impressed by the tenderness of Taiwanese men. The sight of these women walking down the street with Taiwanese men did not trigger much attention or prejudice from the local population, as opposed to their having Caucasian and black lovers. Unlike Hong Kong lovers who tended to speak little Mandarin, and Japanese lovers whose male chauvinism was unacceptable, Taiwanese men spoke Mandarin and were tender. Racially and linguistically compatible, the two sides found perfect romantic matches in each other. This was the period of easy conquest for Taiwanese men: they showed their tenderness, bestowed some money and small gifts of jewelry, and the women were easily seduced.

In the second phase, 1990–1991, it became harder for Taiwanese men because those previously willing mistresses were no longer satisfied with a few hundred yuan of foreign exchange currency[18] or a few dozen pairs of stockings but demanded substantial amounts of gold and money. In the third phase, *dalumei* became even more expensive to maintain. By 1992, monthly expenses for keeping a *dalumei* had risen from US $1,000 to US $2,000. She also typically demanded a purchased apartment (around US $200,000). But the Taiwanese businessmen still preferred having a *dalumei* over a mistress in Taiwan because the latter was still more expensive (about US $3,200 a month) and entailed a greater risk of discovery by the wife. The article ends with the following remarks addressed to Taiwan businessmen: "Let me ask you: Do you like to be showy and exaggerate your wealth? Do you slap your face to make it appear plump? Do you dye your hair to seduce women? I advise you to conduct a self-examination, because today's mainland beauties are no longer so easily taken."[19] The reporter also gives another warning: court the *dalumei* with your money and you are the one who will suffer, because she will demand more and more from you. There is a reason why the Chinese call you "simpleton com-patriot" (*daibao*) instead of "Taiwan compatriot" (*taibao*), he notes, and he warns that "increasingly smarter dalumei are happy to eat up the simpleton compatriots." While the pseudohistory of the relationship between Tai-wanese businessmen and mainland women, replete with financial statistics, reads like a man-to-man mistress guide or sexual adventure guide, the warnings uttered by the report present a reverse scenario of exploitation that paradoxically subalternizes the Taiwanese businessmen. It calls for a controlled exercise of financial power to better manipulate the women and avoid being manipulated in turn.

A second special report appeared in the December 1995 issue of *China Times Weekly*. It included some new information regarding the *dalumei* and their activities in general and had an interview with three of the fifty-seven *dalumei* then held at the women's detention center in Hsinchu. It reveals a wide spectrum of social backgrounds of the *dalumei* but emphasizes their shared desire for money as the prime motivator for their migration to Taiwan, as exemplified by the newly coined saying "The old Gold Moun-tain is in the United States, but the new Gold Mountain is in Taiwan!"[20]

The three *dalumei* interviewed are presented as having not the least bit of shyness or shame: they brag about their success making money and vow to try to return to Taiwan after deportation. The threat of *dalumei* is therefore that of massive migration: the article says that no one "dares" figure out how many *dalumei* are actually in Taiwan besides the fifty-seven detainees. The article ends with the story of a *dalumei* connected with high government officials in China, noting that the Chinese government has been known to employ *dalumei* as spies to work in bars and restaurants in Chinese coastal cities frequented by Taiwanese businessmen, and concluding that some *dalumei* in Taiwan may be communist agents sent by the Chinese government.[21] *Dalumei* as money chaser is now replaced by the projection of national security concerns as China has begun to conduct its ostentatious military exercises.

Dalumei represented as a sexualized body hungry for economic gain, hence exploitable and prone to the sexual conquest of Taiwanese men, reflected a fantasy of Taiwan's economic power, here translated into sexual power. When this power was threatened by *dalumei*'s clever maneuvers, the Taiwanese businessmen were reminded of their status as "simpleton compatriots," and the *dalumei* has increasingly come to embody a threat. She is not merely a threat to Taiwanese businessmen's pocketbooks, but a generalized threat to Taiwan capital and industrial advantage as Taiwan becomes more and more dependent on Chinese labor and the mainland market. She is even a threat to Taiwan's national security. If the Taiwanese government earlier considered the entry of Taiwan businesses in southern China as a strategy of "connecting with the South and approaching the North" (Hsu, Li, and Shiao 1991: 152–60)—Taiwan capital as capturing southern China and loosening control from Beijing—now Taiwan investment in China is increasingly perceived to be vulnerable to the whims of the communist government and has become a liability. The rumor that Taiwanese business tycoon Wang Yung-ching planned to build a large-scale chemical factory in China instead of Taiwan sent nervous government officials scurrying to Wang's door, and when Wang publicly announced in early 1997 that he had already begun construction in China, Taiwanese officials were extremely embarrassed and had to announce that if it were found to be illegal, Wang would be punished. The desire and fear in Taiwan's economic and political relationships with China uncannily parallel the media representations of the *dalumei*. The *dalumei*, a gendered embodiment of *dalu* (mainland), incarnates for the readership the economic threat of usurping and exhausting Taiwan capital through her seductiveness and the political threat of migration, infiltration, and invasion. The call to Taiwanese businessmen to exercise self-control is now underscored by a heightened sense of urgency because of the national implications: Stop being seduced! Stop being duped! Stop making yourself more vulnerable!

Elided in all these heavily troped representations of *dalumei*, however, is not only the actual physical maltreatment of mainland women, but also the fate of native women in Taiwan. The situation of native women is of great concern for local feminists because the availability of the *dalumei* undoubtedly threatens their desire for monogamy and equality, not to mention economic security. More precisely, native patriarchy can take full advantage of the availability of the *dalumei* to further consolidate its arbitrary domination over native women. The story of a Taiwanese woman who killed her children and committed suicide after her husband's affair with a mainland mistress led to complete neglect of his family is not just a story of the increasing peril felt across the Taiwan Strait, but also a story of a modern-day Medea. So when native feminists marched on the streets in 1995 against teenage prostitution in Taiwan, they did not include *dalumei* prostitutes in their agenda: the real subalterns might well have seemed to them not the willingly exploited *dalumei* but the native women who have had to endure their husbands' infidelity. This explains why Taiwanese feminists have been reluctant to take up the issue of *dalumei* at all, prompting Lee Yuan-chen, a local feminist leader, to say, "The *dalumei* issue is a blind spot in our feminism."[22] Hence, the unabashedly patriarchal tone of the media representations of mainland women—as desirable and easily exploitable bodies and then as embodiments of threat—goes unchallenged by local feminists. The responses to the Chinese murder trial in southern California are thus conditioned: Lin Liyun, the Taiwanese wife, is seen as the victim by Taiwanese women. Her alleged murder of the mainland mistress may well symbolize for them the collective revenge of the Taiwanese wives.

The most eloquent testimony to this local-oriented feminist endeavor to help the wives of adulterous Taiwanese husbands is a book-length study of the phenomenon coauthored by a famous feminist lawyer named Qiu Zhang and Lin Cuifen. The book is titled *One Country, Two Wives* (1994), a parodic reference to the Chinese Communist Party's slogan of "One Country, Two Systems." In this book of legal analyses of many representative cases and their consequences for local wives, Qiu and Lin not only offer biting criticism of the adulterous husband Peng Zengji in the California murder case but also suggest to the wives that instead of killing the mistress the smarter solution would have been to castrate the husband. They reason that killing the mistress resulted in a very difficult legal situation for

Lin the wife (who was later sentenced to life imprisonment), whereas castration, according to Taiwan laws, would merely have been considered an "injury," for which the greatest punishment is only two years in prison. Likewise, they offer legal counsel throughout on such issues as property possession, divorce, and child custody, condemning patriarchal Taiwan laws and the corrupt husbands they protect. In this book, those mainland women who willingly comply with Taiwanese men's demands are depicted as usurpers, gold diggers, and opportunists, thereby provoking some measure of nationalist sentiment, but the main target of criticism is consistently Taiwanese patriarchy. Theirs is an adamantly local feminist voice that, while drawing subtly on nationalist sentiments to fight against the infiltration of the Other women, vociferously condemns patriarchy from the perspective of the local wives' "double loss" of husband and money (Qiu and Lin 1994).

Despite the local focus of this feminism, however, it clearly does not at all cohere to single nation-state–based discussions of the relationships between gender and nationalism as mutually contradictory. Instead, there is a strategic appropriation of nationalist sentiments in order to raise the feminist consciousness of women. The battle here instead is that between forces of deterritorialization and reterritorialization from a gendered perspective; this battle eventually plays itself out in local-specific feminist politics that resist transcontext theorizations of gender. This does not imply that this adamantly local feminism is therefore unable to dialogue with other feminisms across the world. Rather, it suggests how no single feminist position can account for the ideological simultaneity of various feminist positions arising from different contexts, that feminist struggles should not and could not be articulated in universalistic terms of transparent translatability across different locations in the world.

Feminizing the "Mainland Cousin"

It's vital to have possession of this memory, to control it, administer it, tell it what it must contain.
—Michel Foucault, "Film and Popular Memory"

The typology of mainland women in Hong Kong in the mid-1990s was more variegated due mainly to a long history of immigration from the Mainland to Hong Kong, their easier access to Hong Kong, and their presence in varying strata of Hong Kong society. Although Hong Kong society mainly consists of Chinese immigrants who came in earlier periods, there was considerable prejudice against those "new immigrants" (*xinyimin*) who were considered Chinese rather than Hong Kongers.[23] It was to this group of mostly lower-strata individuals that mainland women belonged, although occasionally there were successful entrepreneurial and professional new immigrant women who became visible in society. In Hong Kong, there were *dalumei* prostitutes as well, whose appellations were often based on their places of origin: *Tianjinmei* for those from Tianjin, *Hunanmei* for those from Hunan Province, *beimei* for those from Northern China in general, and so. In 1995 alone, an unprecedented number of more than one thousand illegal mainland prostitutes were caught by the police.[24]

But the more urgent issue, as in the case of Taiwan, was the prevalence of mainland mistresses for Hong Kong businessmen. The large-scale adultery captured media attention in late 1994 and early 1995, when statistics of Hong Kong businessmen having mistresses in China—the so-called keeping a concubine/mistress (*bao ernai*) phenomenon—were revealed. It was reported that Hong Kong men had collectively sired about three hundred thousand illegitimate babies with their *ernai* in China, about 5 percent of the entire Hong Kong population of six million (Ifumi 1995), with the entire bordering city of Shenzhen in the Chinese Special Economic Zone becoming a "village of *ernai*," and with China ironically dubbed the "*ernai*-providing sphere" (Liu Xin 1995; Ifumi 1995).[25] These mainland *ernai* have been easy prey for adulterous Hong Kong businessmen, one feminist journalist in Hong Kong taunts, because they are "inexpensive and of beautiful quality" as well as compliant to the demands of Hong Kong businessmen in exchange for financial gain, unlike native Hong Kong women, who need pampering and demand equality (Liang 1995). A betrayed Hong Kong mother of three was rescued from an attempted suicide, another woman killed her adulterous husband, yet another castrated her husband, and several other incidents of tragedy were publicized (Liu Xin 1995).[26] In late 1994, a group of angry Hong Kong wives protested to the Hong Kong government to demand the curtailing of rampant adultery between their husbands and mainland women,[27] and there began debates and proposals to criminalize the *bao ernai* phenomenon through new legislation. The opposing parties to this call for criminalization came up with the shocking proposal to legalize the *ernai* with the argument that Hong Kong businessmen needed to have their sexual desire satisfied while sojourning for long periods for business purposes (Liang 1995).

The situation for local feminists in Hong Kong is perhaps even more urgent than that for Taiwan feminists due to the sheer quantity of such incidents and the overwhelming number of illegitimate children who will very likely have the right of legal migration to Hong Kong. For native women in general, their struggle for equality is severely undermined by the overwhelming surplus of women available to Hong Kong men, who no longer need to succumb to native women's demands since earlier gains in gender equality were due in part to the shortage of women and the necessity for native men to compete for them (Ifumi 1995). Native wives also face the fate of losing both the money and the husband, as with Taiwanese wives, and their shared fate with Taiwanese wives has not gone unnoticed (Liang 1995). The first book on women's services and women's groups in Hong Kong notes how the main agenda of one of the community centers for women is to offer support for the wives whose husbands work in China. The Hong Kong feminist perspective, like that of the Taiwan feminist, is to see the *bao ernai* phenomenon as a social problem that has victimized native women (New Women's Promotion Association 1995: 135–36, 63–64). Feminism in both contexts is vigilantly local, an impassioned attempt to defy the compromise of feminist ideals resulting from the transnational migration of ethnic Chinese men and women across borders.

Beyond the obvious similarity between the conditions of native women in Taiwan and Hong Kong, however, I am also interested in delineating a peculiar category of mainland women in Hong Kong's popular imaginary, the *biaojie*. This highly ideological category does not exist in Taiwan, but its explication offers crucial vantage points in understanding how ideological issues became gendered in the mid-1990s and, more critically, how this category becomes the playing field of a certain nativist urgency to define a Hong Kong cultural identity destined to gradually become extinct with the retrocession. Taiwan has in recent years been flaunting its democratization as a way to repudiate the communist system both symbolically and pragmatically, with its erstwhile Marxist-leaning intellectuals and politicians having long lost any calling in the society. But for Hong Kong, ideology is of imminent importance, since it is situated between a globalized capitalism and a communist system that has promised to institute an ideological stranglehold. The ideological category of the *biaojie* is a communist cadre whose name literally means older female cousin. While her male counterpart, the *biaoge* (older male cousin), may be positively innocent, old-fashioned, or engaged in immoral behavior such as robbery and bribery, the *biaojie* tends to denote a set of mostly negative characteristics: backwardness, unfashionableness, lack of proper etiquette and culture, and an inclination to use bribery and connections.[28] Both terms probably originate in the term *biaoshu* (maternal uncle), used in the Cultural Revolution model play *Red Lantern* as a code name for underground communists during the anti-Japanese War in China (Weng and Ah 1965). When circulated in Hong Kong, *biaoshu* fittingly served as a metonym for the generational difference in the relationship between the "motherland" and its putative "child," Hong Kong. In the pre-1997 climate of Hong Kong, during which the "return" to the motherland was construed by some as a transition from British colonialism to "ancestorland colonialism" (*zuguo zhimindi*) or a process of "recolonization" (*zai zhimin*), the implications for the relationship with "maternal" relatives became increasingly problematic.

To contextualize my analysis of the representation of *biaojie*, I will present a necessarily broad description of the historical junctures of Hong Kong in the mid-1990s in terms of politics, economy, and demographics, followed by a more sustained inquiry into the cultural scene. It is no exaggeration to say that the primary obsession of the Hong Kong populace in the mid-1990s was the approach of the 1997 retrocession to China. The June 4, 1989, massacre in Tiananmen Square had mobilized Hong Kong's democratic forces against the communist regime and injected a sense of urgency into their efforts to democratize before the arrival of communist rule. The legislative election of September 1995 registered an overwhelming success for the pro-democratic forces. Economically, there was a curious boom contributed to by rising real estate prices and a prosperous stock market (partially fueled by the infusion of so-called Red Capital from China), which Ackbar Abbas characterizes as an ironic phenomenon of "doom and boom" (1993: 3). The demographic changes were apparent as Mandarin was more frequently heard on the streets of Hong Kong. Mainland immigrants were also becoming more and more visible, since they could acquire the round-trip certificates (*shuangchengzheng*) or smuggle themselves into Hong Kong relatively easily.

Conversely, due to the imminence of return, the previously thoroughly commercialized cultural arena, especially the mass media, became increasingly obsessed with delineating Hong Kong's unique cultural identity vis-à-vis China in the years leading to 1997.[29] The mass media's desire to construct a Hong Kong identity reflected and paralleled the desire of the populace, as seen in the results of a public poll taken in February 1995. Thirty-six percent of the respondents claimed that they were "Hong Kongers," 32 percent "Hong Kong Chinese," only 20 percent "Chinese," and 12 percent "British Chinese."[30] The percentage of Hong Kong residents who more or less claimed a Hong Kong identity amounted to almost 70 percent, if we consider "Chinese" in "Hong Kong Chinese" as merely an ethnic designation. Concomitantly, there was an upsurge in a kind of identity discourse that strategically evoked British colonial history as a constitutive element of Hong Kong identity in order to distinguish it from China. Rey Chow, a prominent Hong Kong diasporic intellectual in the United States, for instance, saw Hong Kong's coloniality as the better of two evils and defined British colonialism as "a form of opportunity, in which the daily experience of oppression is synchronized with a self-conscious search for freedom in alternative forms." So even though British colonialism had been a form of violence, it was one that was "lived as an alternative to greater violence elsewhere," *elsewhere* undoubtedly referring to China (1993: 199). In a different article, Chow defined Hong Kong's emergent cultural production as "impure" and presented a vision of an "alternative" culture or community in a "third space" between British and Chinese cultural systems (1992). She carefully avoided the term *hybridity*, as popularized by Homi K. Bhabha (1994) and as that which celebrated the obliteration of the violence of colonial history and instead insisted on the notion of impurity with which she emphasized both the oppression and agency of the colonized in a situation of successive colonialisms.

A different formulation of Hong Kong identity, as posited by Quentin Lee, saw hybridity as the means to deconstruct "the illusion of cultural purity" envisioned by both Chinese nationalism and Hong Kong Occidentalism (that is, worship of the Occident), thereby disenabling domination from both directions (1994: 19). Lee here treated hybridity and impurity as one and the same. However, this impurity/hybridity discourse was also criticized by others who saw it as intertwined with the English gaze, since it was British colonialism that also selectively legitimated Hong Kong's hybridized cultural production (Chu and Wai 1995). The other potential danger in the impurity/hybridity discourse is this: if the essential difference between China and Hong Kong is the former's purity and the latter's impurity, what prevents China's contemporary cultural elements from becoming part of the impurity of Hong Kong after 1997? Could not contemporary Chinese cultural elements be incorporated in such a way that Hong Kong's impurity becomes another justification for an innocuous multiculturalism? In the absence of "nativist" paradigms of culture, any assertions of the unique constitution of a Hong Kong identity are bound to be at best tenuous, if not problematic. This is because the option of imagining a "national" identity (as in Taiwan) is not available for Hong Kong.

As the return to the "motherland" was described as domination by yet another colonizer, the return promised a kind of "postcoloniality" that only mocks the implications of the prefix *post* (Abbas 1994) because decolonization does not mean liberation or independence. The more futile the search for a unique cultural identity, however, the greater the urgency and desire. Nick Browne's description of the temporal mode of 1990s Hong Kong cinema as "future anterior" to suggest the "complexity of an impending return that threatens to be a future undoing of its past achievement" underscores the paradoxes in the search for a cultural identity (1994: 7). This paradoxical search for a cultural identity that is premised on its very impossibility or futility can be understood in terms of Susan Stewart's discussion of nostalgia:

> Nostalgia is a sadness without an object, a sadness which creates a longing that of necessity is inauthentic because it does not take part in lived experience. Rather, it remains behind and before that experience. Nostalgia, like any form of narrative, is always ideological. The past it seeks has never existed except as a narrative, and hence, always absent, that past continually threatens to reproduce itself as a felt lack. Hostile to history and its invisible origins, and yet longing for an impossibly pure context of lived experience at a place of origin, nostalgia wears a distinctly utopian face, a face that turns toward a future-past, a past which has only ideological reality. This point of desire which the nostalgic seeks is in fact the absence that is the very generating mechanism of desire. (1993: 23)

The search for a narrative of Hong Kong identity is, like nostalgia, paradoxically premised on its absence and its lack of lived experience; ultimately, it is a utopian dream that generates longing precisely because of its impossibility. Hence the temporal mode of this desire is the "future-past" or "future-anterior": the prospect of the future engenders an anxiety over the loss of the past because that loss is guaranteed. Hence the desire to find an object, a souvenir, as the memory marker of a culture. Hong Kong films are in this sense fantastic souvenirs of a culture that could not exist as an autonomous entity and an attempt to appease the anxieties of the nostalgic.

The production of about half a dozen films about the *biaojie* in Hong Kong cinema may be understood as the souvenirs of a past; thus the "essences" of Hong Kong culture become a prime focus of representation through their contrast with those of China, represented by the *biaojie*. But the films do more than nostalgically evoke unique Hong Kong cultural elements, for they also project possible future narratives beyond 1997. These films range from farce, comedy, and romantic drama to pornography, but a particular series of four movies made by the director Alfred Cheung titled *Her Fatal Ways* (*biaojie ni bao ye*, literally, "Mainland cousin, bravo!"), produced between 1990 and 1994, provide ideal sites for examining the political and cultural negotiations these films project onto Hong Kong's relationship with China precisely because they are hyperbolic, farcical, and bombastic.[31] In the films, *biaojie* is the narrative figure whose changing relationship with Hong Kong symbolizes those possible scenarios of Hong Kong's past and future, albeit in somewhat crudely mimetic fashion as the genre of farce dictates. To borrow a Freudian trope here, these film enactments can be likened to the child's "fort-da" games, enacting the disappearance and appearance of Hong Kong in an attempt to use symbols (films) to control its absence and further make sense of its impending future.[32] This sense of control is further communicated by the genre of the films, farce, which displaces anxiety with laughter. The pleasure thus gained is an exercise of power and control, even though it may only last for the duration of each film.

The *biaojie* herself is an amalgam of comic effects in the four-part movie. Played by Hong Kong actress Cheng Yu Ling, she is a masculine, gun-wielding kung fu master, party cadre, policewoman who crosses the border to Hong Kong to track down mainland criminal elements. A typical, de-gendered "iron lady" (*tie niangzi*, who stands at the ideological forefront), Shuonan (literally "great man") lives and breathes communist ideology. She walks a wide, masculine gait, speaks in the loud voice of authority, and spews official rhetoric, and, as to be expected of a party cadre, all signs of femininity and sexuality are erased. The comical effects are achieved by what may be called the ideological malapropisms of her behavior and language in the different context of Hong Kong. Here, her ideologically correct behavior and language are eminently misplaced, and they become comedic material for the audience to laugh at. But there is a further twist: Shuonan becomes more and more self-conscious about her behavior and language, which have been exclusively dictated by communist ideology, and she gradually awakens to her own deeply repressed desires. At times, Shuonan herself consciously applies dry, clichéd ideological rhetoric to deal with awkward situations that might otherwise force her to betray her own innermost desires and wishes.

The split between the ideological self and the private self is thereby constructed along clear lines. The suppressed, private self is discovered soon after she enters seductive, urban capitalist Hong Kong, and it is gradually released. It is through her transformation that we see an explicit confirmation of the culture of Hong Kong. This process of transformation is most explicitly depicted in part 1 of the series, since this is when the *biaojie* first comes to Hong Kong. For a party cadre who is not supposed to harbor any bourgeois desires, she quickly, and of course secretly, desires to become feminine—she applies lipstick, wears dresses, and falls in love. In an unguarded moment when she is with a Hong Kong Chinese policeman played by the supremely handsome and likable Tony Leung, she exclaims at the beauty of the colorful neon lights seen from the upper deck of a double-decker bus. Her exclamation confirms the superiority of Hong Kong culture because it is spoken by a staunch Communist Party cadre who has heretofore been very careful to hide her fascination. The confirmation also comes from its contrast with an earlier scene in which she lectured on the art of spitting and spit right out the bus window and into the mouth of a passing motorcyclist. Her transformation from an uncouth cadre with no taste or sensibility to a woman longing for beauty and love (and from a primitive bus to a double-decker bus, the crowning symbol of urban Hong Kong) is as dramatic as the confirmation of Hong Kong's cultural superiority. The film consistently posits the universal validity of beauty and pleasure in the bourgeois capitalist mode and identifies those elements that constitute Hong Kong's superior culture. Abstract qualities of humaneness, civility, subtlety, and emotional concern for others are wedded to material manifestations of capitalism: state-of-the-art technology, bustling urban scenes, products that speak to individual desire (lipstick, cable television, and fashionable clothes), and above all the "rule-by-law" legal system represented by the Hong Kong police. These qualities then add up to an inventory of Hong Kong, set in opposition to China and Chineseness as represented by the *biaojie*.

As the films progress, the *biaojie* becomes increasingly comfortable displaying her feminine self. In each of the four movies, Shuonan falls in love with a Hong Kong man, even though her falling in love is in some ways devastating since it subverts what she is supposed to represent for China. By the end of the last of the four movies, there is a definite prospect of Shuonan marrying a man in Hong Kong, since now she has decided to remain in Hong Kong as a permanent resident. So the evolution of the four movies is also a progression toward the completion of Shuonan's journey: from crossing the border back and forth, Shuonan settles down in Hong Kong and vows to be "more Hong Kong than Hong Kongers." The policewoman who lectured on the art of spitting on the bus to Hong Kong, who sang with such a high-pitched voice that glasses shattered in a karaoke bar, who ate with her left hand so as to be ideologically correct, whose gaudy makeup made her look like the "red woman soldier" (*hongse niangzi jun*) from Cultural Revolution model operas, now readily absorbs and displays bourgeois values and becomes another Hong Kong woman among many. Her appearance changes accordingly: her thick, dark-rimmed glasses and long straight hair become continuously modified in the four films into thin-rimmed glasses and slightly wavy hair; her baggy shirts and pants are replaced by attractive, form-fitting shirts and skirts; her loud, masculine voice softens into a gentle, feminine one; and her wide, dramatic gait gives way to sensual steps. With the prospect of marrying a local man, her Hong Kong-ization can be said to be complete. What Hong Kong does to her is to arouse in her the "universal" longings of a woman and regender her into the feminine role.

Beyond "modernizing" the *biaojie* into a feminine, bourgeois capitalist, and thereby confirming the universalizing capacities of Hong Kong capitalism, the films also explicitly engage in discussions of 1997. In the first film, made in 1990, 1997 is rarely evoked, and when it is, its threat is not yet directly felt. So in the last scene of the movie when Shuonan says good-bye to her first Hong Kong lover at the border, she hands him a note on which she has written, "After 1997 maybe we can cooperate again." By part 3 (1992), we see the entire staff of the Hong Kong political bureau confessing to a high mainland official, Qian Li, who is visiting Hong Kong.[33] They tell him the sins they committed against China and seek forgiveness, for fear of retaliation after 1997. In the fourth installment (1994), 1997 becomes a powerful obsession and fear for the Hong Kong characters involved. Another mainland woman, Xiao Ru, is strategically seduced by a half-British, half-Chinese policeman, Oliver, because Xiao Ru is the daughter of the general who will be in command of the People's Liberation Army to be stationed in Hong Kong. Seducing her would translate into having influence over the general's decisions regarding Hong Kong, and this will directly affect Hong Kong stock prices and other financial conditions. In fact, her seduction is a conspiracy of the entire police department to ensure Hong Kong's financial future and the policemen's own financial security. The last scene of the movie at the border is painfully explicit. In that scene, we see Oliver "using connections" (*kao guanxi*) to ensure his future in the manner of a mainlander. He says to Xiao Ru's father, "Mr. General, this is my identification card, please remember me. I will remain in Hong Kong after 1997." Again, the scene is farcical, yet an ominous sense of reality looms.

Together, the films project a set of negotiations with the Mainland, even as the latter is consistently made the object of laughter. Shuonan's romantic encounters in Hong Kong actually involve men of different races: she falls in love with two ethnic Chinese in the first two films, but by the third film, it is a biracial man (half-British, half-Chinese), and in the fourth film, a Scot. And it is only with the Scot that her love is fully reciprocated and a union is expected. To venture an allegorical reading here, the union of the Scot (who represents the colonial government) and the Chinese mimics the political cooperation between the British and the Chinese governments who have decided Hong Kong's fate without the participation of the Hong Kong people themselves. In a similar manner, the man who seduces Xiao Ru is half-British, suggesting the occlusion of the ethnic Chinese Hong Kongers whose fate is beyond their control. In contrast, the fact that the *biaojie* is infinitely seduceable by Hong Kong men and readily replaces her mainland culture with Hong Kong culture also presents a narrative of assimilation. "Modern," "cultured," and capitalist Hong Kong, it is suggested, can "civilize" the backward Chinese and thereby neutralize the effects of the 1997 takeover. At the very least, the capitalist seductions of the city can soften the hard mainlanders to such a degree that perhaps 1997 will not be as traumatic as expected.

This optimism regarding Hong Kong culture's power of assimilation is validated by the immense influence Hong Kong mass media have exerted in southern China. As director Alfred Cheung pointed out in an interview, Hong Kong television has been transforming the ideology of sixty million people in southern China, and the influence of this "Hong Kong cultural zone" is reaching farther and farther north (Shih 1996b). In the language of the Hong Kong Cultural Studies Collective, this formidable force of Hong Kong mass culture is the "Northward Imaginary" (*beijin xiangxiang*) whose advance cannot be blocked.[34] The feminization of the *biaojie* in *Her Fatal Ways* then, embodies this optimism, and in this narrative, curiously, time is on the side of Hong Kong. The apprehension about 1997 can then be disregarded by projecting a vision into a more distant future, when China will become more and more capitalistic in the Hong Kong mold and may eventually eschew monolithic communist rule.

What goes unsaid in this optimism, of course, is the potential vulnerability of such assertions of cultural power (derived from the universalizing power of Hong Kong capitalism) in the face of blatant exercises of political power. Taiwan's recent clashes with China may foreshadow this. The projection of Hong Kong's cultural power therefore may well be another fantasy equally fracturable in the face of China's political authority, and its assimilating potential quite exaggerated. What came to be dubbed as "Hong Kong Cultural Imperialism" is criticized not only by ultraconservative, state-sponsored, nationalist leftists, but also by the so-called Chinese postcolonial critics whose compulsory critique of all nonnative forms of culture makes them equally weary, though differently from the ultraleftists, of Hong Kong mass culture's incursion on the Mainland. The immense creative energy emanating from a population of 1.4 billion threatens to assimilate Hong Kong mass culture into its fold rather than the other way around. Seen in this light, the projection of the feminizing supremacy of Hong Kong mass culture can be construed as a fantastic imagining of power and agency for Hong Kong beyond 1997. While Taiwan media resorted to nationalist sentiments to reject the lures of mainland women and thereby asserted Taiwan's moral supremacy and economic leverage, Hong Kong media's recourse to a feminizing capitalism as the means to carve out a cultural identity may be quite futile when China itself has been vigorously advancing on the route of a flexible, market-oriented, "socialism with Chinese characteristics" in the post-Mao, and now post-Deng, years.

Gender and Public Sphere

If Taiwan media representations of the *dalumei* can be largely decoded as manifestations of the fear of contamination, the Hong Kong films analyzed above imagine a narrative of assimilation and domestication in order to neutralize China's political power. The divergent encodings of mainland women are suggestive of the different degrees of autonomy available for Taiwan and Hong Kong. Whether or not the availability of autonomy is ultimately an illusion for Taiwan, given the looming threat of military invasion from China, Hong Kong's lack of autonomy is ineluctable due to the gapless succession of colonial controls. In light of such antithetical underpinnings in the representation of mainland women in Taiwan and Hong Kong mass media, the mass media's potential for the construction of a pan-Chinese public sphere in the *zhong gang tai* region remains a rather unlikely prospect.

Classic discussions of the public sphere in the tradition of Jürgen Habermas saw its relationship with mass media to be an oppositional one (Habermas 1989), whereas reconsideration of this relationship generally fell into two modes: the celebration of the deterritorializing potential of mass media and its capability to form a transnational public sphere, and the similarly celebratory perception of mass media as the site of peripheral cultures manufacturing alternative identities against domination. Arjun Appadurai's notion of mediascape and Miriam Hansen's discussion of the deterritorialization of public sphere based on the transnational flow of electronic media are examples of the former mode; Bruce Robbins's discussion of mass media as the potential site for disenfranchised minorities or marginalized collectivities to articulate their cultural identities is an example of the latter (Appadurai 1993; Hansen 1993b; Robbins 1993). China scholars have also debated the question of the public sphere, asking whether there was a public sphere in imperial China (*Modern China* 1993) and whether certain locations can be found in today's transnational landscape for a Chinese public sphere. Tu Wei-ming's conception of "cultural China" as the realm of common awareness of all Chinese beyond geopolitical boundaries has been identified as the possible site of a Chinese public sphere (in Madsen 1993: 197). In relation to mass media, Mayfair Yang recently charted the transnationalizing tendencies in Chinese identity formation in China in the age of diaspora and free-flowing mass media (Yang 1997). In the conceptions of both cultural China and transnational China, the authority of hegemonic statism is undermined by virtue of the scope and dynamics of these conceptions. While Yang locates the agency of antistatism in the urban Chinese populace in China, Tu would locate sites external to geopolitical China as the vital areas of cultural China.

The specific constitution of *zhong gang tai* as a possible public sphere remains problematic, however, because of the absence of the basic premises of "communication" and "rational-critical discourse" as in the Habermasian paradigm, even if one allows for historical differences between Habermas's Germany and today's *zhong gang tai* region as the departing point of theorization. Assertions of China's political power over Taiwan and Hong Kong in the mid-1990s, fueled by the reorganization of power due at the time to the impending death of Deng Xiaoping and its unpredictable consequences, were made vigorously and conspicuously. Taiwan and Hong Kong therefore resorted to asserting economic and cultural power as a means to resist China's political power, but such forms of resistance, as manifested by their media's representation of mainland women, are fraught with a sense of impossibility and apprehension. Inasmuch as mass media in Taiwan and Hong Kong have afforded moments of fantastic narrativization of power, one can perhaps ascertain the potential of mass media as a form of resistance. However, in the overlapping of "state" powers of China, Taiwan, and the colonial government in Hong Kong, as well as in China's ever tightening policy over Taiwan's claims to independence and its post-1997 policies of containment of Hong Kong, the room for generating truly alternative identities that will be recognized as such in the international arena is very limited. If "Greater China" as an entity is largely an economic trope, the prevalence of oppositional dynamics in mass media's gender representation exposes the impossibility of imagining it as a culturally harmonious entity. Hence, representations of mainland women in mass media emphasize their cultural difference from the women of Taiwan and Hong Kong and are filled with patriarchal injunctions and eroticizations.

In the end, they are ironically made to become linking agents for the patriarchal kinship system in the region—Taiwan and Hong Kong men do have unions with Chinese women either legally or illegally—but their "linking" function triggers the fear of contamination in the case of *dalumei* and the fantasy of assimilation in the case of the *biaojie*.

Such a situation also portends the untenability of a gendered public sphere in the region. Although Taiwanese feminist groups have incorporated aspects of mainland culture to empower themselves and imagine solidarities,[35] the towering imperative of Taiwan's national well-being disallows the engagement to become any kind of universal feminist critique of women's oppression.[36] Understandably concerned with local women's status, Taiwan and Hong Kong feminist groups alike have chosen to focus their efforts on local wives as victims of the patriarchal domination of their lustful and adulterous husbands. The imagined construction of a feminist public sphere among certain select feminists in the *zhong gang tai* region would then have to be an obviously limited, classed affair, with the majority of underclass women excluded. As we have seen, in the discussions of mainland woman as represented in mass media the transnationalizing readings of "Greater China" are systematically undermined and local contingencies are repeatedly foregrounded. Ultimately, it is the critical imbalance of political power that disallows the emergence of a public sphere, gendered or not.

NOTES

The first version of this paper was presented at the Gender, Mass Media, and a Chinese Public Conference at the University of California, Santa Barbara in 1995, and later versions were presented at Tufts University, the Chinese University of Hong Kong, and Harvard University. My gratitude goes out to all members of the audiences who graciously provided their comments. Mayfair Yang read the paper in its various stages and gave insightful critiques; Ming-yan Lai alerted me to issues pertaining to Hong Kong capitalism; Leo Ou-fan Lee and Carol Breckenridge were encouraging voices. I also thank the editors and readers of *Signs*, where this article was first published, for challenging me to articulate my arguments in more precise terms.

1 For a useful genealogy of the term *Greater China* and its related issues, see Harding 1995. Although Macao and other Chinese communities abroad have been technically included in the more inclusive conception of "Greater China," discussions have revolved mainly around Taiwan, Hong Kong, and China, the three key economic players.

2 It has become customary in recent years to talk about popular culture in the region using the abbreviated term *zhong gang tai* (China–Hong Kong–Taiwan) culture. Particularly in discussion of Chinese films, the term *zhong gang tai* has been prevalent. See, for instance, the Taipei Golden Horse Film Festival's 1994 official publica-

tion, "Division" and "Reunion": A Perspective of Chinese Cinemas of the 90s. The title of this collection of articles on Chinese cinemas reveals the sense of optimism then circulating regarding the formation of a pan-Chinese cultural sphere that was not premised on the constitution of a pan-Chinese nation-state before the March 1996 missile crisis in the Taiwan Straits. See also Chiao 1993.

3 A note about romanization: the fact that Taiwanese, Hong Kongers, and mainland Chinese use different romanization systems but share pretty much the same written script poses problems for an essay that deals with all three areas. I generally follow the mainland Chinese pinyin system, the most commonly used romanization system in the United States, but I am aware of its hegemonic implications for Taiwanese and Hong Kong readers. The choice here is a pragmatic one. Exceptions to this pragmatic choice apply to widely circulated names of famous personalities and cities that may use a different romanization system.

4 Harry Harding cites the circulation of these terms, showing their prevalence in recent years. Harding himself, however, has reservations regarding the possibility of such cultural integration (1995).

5 In the context of this paper, I use the term *gender* to foreground the fact of women's genderedness as the Other of men, whose gender is made normative, universal, and is therefore functionally invisible or taken for granted.

6 I use the word *patriarchy* to connote the social, political, economic, and symbolic structure of power maintained by men for the interest of men and largely at the expense of women.

7 See Mohanty, Russo, Torres 1991; Parker, Russo, Sommer, Yaeger 1992; Chatterjee 1993; Kandiyoti 1994.

8 Although one of the aims of this paper is to deconstruct the "Greater China" ideology as espousing a problematic integrationist logic, the juxtaposition of Taiwan and Hong Kong vis-à-vis China can be construed by some, as *Signs* reviewer suggests, as a methodological enactment of this ideology. To this comment, my reply is that it is only through a direct engagement of their interrelationships that the fissures and contradictions of the "Greater China" ideology can be most thoroughly exposed, and "Chineseness" can be rethought as an ethnic rather than cultural or political designation.

9 *Chinese Daily News*, May 1, 1996. The *Chinese Daily News* is a diasporic Chinese-language newspaper published in Los Angeles with extensive coverage of news from all ethnic Chinese nations and communities including China, Taiwan, Hong Kong, Chinese America, and other South and Southeast Asian countries.

10 Coastal cities such as Shenzhen were named the Special Economic Zone where foreign investment and global trade are encouraged with tax breaks and other benefits not found in the rest of China. The Special Economic Zone has been playing the leading role in integrating China's economy with the global system.

11 See Gayle Rubin's classic essay "The Traffic in Women: Notes on the 'Political Economy' of Sex" (1984), where she argues, among other things, that the traffic in women, through marriage and other ways, has been the means by which patriarchal kinship systems are maintained.

12 See my essay "The Trope of 'Mainland China' in Taiwan's Media" (1995) for a discussion of the competing claims on Chinese cultural heritage. By the late 1990s, this claim to authentic Chineseness lost ground in Taiwan as the ruling Nationalist

Party gradually shifted from a mainland-based cultural ideology to a localist cultural ideology.

13 An ironic anecdote related to this paranoia is the sale of a computer-game derivative of the book called "Final Battle across the Taiwan Strait in August, 1995," for NT $600 (US $24) each since 1994. The computer software is published by Softworld International Corporation located in Kaohsiung, Taiwan.

14 This can be seen in the following developments: the strategic Japanism of the Lee Teng-hui government—the invocation of Japanese colonial history in Taiwan as that which makes Taiwan distinct from China—was not as valuable as political capital as it had been previously. The climactic and geological theories of Taiwan's difference—Taiwan as an island with oceanic cultural formations as opposed to China's continental formations—also seemed to be waning. Even the Democratic Progressive Party noted the necessity of toning down its independence agenda in its party proclamations when the legislative election of 1995 approached and the 1996 presidential election was in sight. In this particular climate, the New Party (xindang), the bastion of pro-unification ideology formed in 1994, won a surprisingly large number of seats in the legislative election. Although a new, more aggressively independence-oriented party, the Nation-Building Party (jianguodang), was formed in 1996, it has not been able to garner popular support.

15 My typology of the mainland women is derived from the following news reports: Chinese Daily News: August 24, 1994, A8; September 5, 1994, A1; November 2, 1994, A9; February 16, 1995, A7; February 3, 1996, A8. Also see China Times Weekly 64 (March 1993): 80–81; 62 (March 1993): 80–81.

16 Chinese Daily News, September 9, 1994.

17 For instance, an early 1900s sympathetic reception of the dalumei can be seen in a fictionalized account by Wang Benhu in his popular novel Amoi Bride (1991).

18 The foreign exchange currencies were only available to foreigners and were worth more than regular mainland currency, renminbi (people's currency), because certain upscale goods could only be bought with them.

19 China Times Weekly 53 (January 1993): 80–82, overseas edition.

20 The term Gold Mountain was coined by nineteenth-century laborers from China who came searching for gold in California. Today, one of the two Chinese names for San Francisco is still Old Gold Mountain (jiujinshan).

21 China Times Weekly 93 (December 1995): 41–51, Taiwan edition.

22 Author's personal communication with Lee Yuan-chen, April 1995, Santa Barbara, California.

23 Cheng Ying, writing for the popular Hong Kong news magazine The Nineties, noted that the term new immigrants refers to post-1980 immigrants who came not for political reasons as did the earlier waves but for economic reasons, and that this group tends to be politically pro-China (1995).

24 Chinese Daily News, November 30, 1995.

25 Similarly, the anxiety over Taiwanese marrying mainland women has triggered statistical projections that if fifty extra mainlanders were added to those mainlanders admitted to Taiwan each year, in twenty years there will be more than one hundred thousand of them residing in Taiwan (China Times Daily, July 26, 1993).

26 See also Chinese Daily News, October 7, 1994 and June 13, 1996.

27 Chinese Daily News, October 7, 1994.

28 Information provided by a mainlander-turned–Hong Kong resident, March 1995.

29 See the articles by Leo Lee, Li Cheuk-to, and Esther Yao in *New Chinese Cinemas* (Browne, Pickowicz, Sobchack, and Yau 1994) for the allegorical rendering of Hong Kong's identity formation vis-à-vis China in Hong Kong films. Ackbar Abbas calls this phenomenon "a culture of disappearance" because the interest in cultural specificity appeared just when Hong Kong as a reality was about to disappear (1994).

30 *Press Freedom Guardian,* July 21, 1995.

31 Alfred Cheung, *Her Fatal Ways* (Biaojie nihaoye) parts 1–4, is a series of films produced in Hong Kong by Golden Harvest and released in 1990, 1991, 1992, and 1994. The fact that the films were farcical and bombastic allowed expression of the most direct and unmediated desires (supposedly speaking on behalf of the Hong Kong populace) toward China because the director could always deny that the films were meant to be true representations. The success and popularity of the films in the market also attest to the degree to which the audience seemed to have related to the films.

32 John Fiske gives a succinct summary of the "fort-da" game theory in Freud: "Freud draws our attention to the infant's 'fort-da' game in which the child continuously throws away a loved object only to demand its return. His explanation is that the game is enacting the disappearance and appearance of the mother, and that in playing it the child is not only symbolizing his or her anxieties about the mother's return, but is also beginning to use symbols to control the meanings of his or her environment" (1987: 231).

33 The name of Qian Li (meaning One Thousand *Lis*) is a parody of Wan Li (literally, Ten Thousand *Lis*), member of the Standing Committee of the National People's Congress of China. *Li* is an ancient Chinese unit of distance. One *li* equals two kilometers. In another mainlander movie titled *Mainland Dundee* (Biaoge wo lai ye), a female character is named Jiang Chun (after Jiang Qing). These are examples of direct satires on mainland political figures.

34 See the special issue of *Hong Kong Cultural Studies Bulletin* titled "Northward Imaginary: Repositioning Hong Kong's Post-colonial Discourse," published by the Hong Kong Cultural Studies Program at the Chinese University of Hong Kong. For my more extensive critique of this "northward imaginary" discourse, see Shih 1997.

35 The best example of this is the publication of a women's writing script in China called *nushu,* in large part by Fembooks (*nushudian*), a subsidiary of the Awakening Foundation (*funu xinzhi*) in Taiwan.

36 A good example is Taiwanese feminists' refusal to attend the United Nations Women's Conference held in Beijing in September 1995, due to military threats by the Chinese government and its insistence that they attend as "Chinese" and not Taiwanese representatives.

12

The World Map of Haunting Dreams: Reading

Post-1989 Chinese Women's Diaspora Writings

Having nightmares is a hobby of yours; don't know since when, night-mares have been growing, and aging along with you. When they don't show up in your dreams over several days, you will be missing them, ana-lyzing why they haven't come for their rendezvous with you.

—You You, "The Screaming Wood"

Introduction: Rewriting "Diaspora Literature" (Haiwai wenxue)

Several years ago, Hélène Cixous, the versatile French feminist critic, de-livered a lecture at a conference on freedom and writing at Oxford. The title of her lecture was "We Who Are Free, Are We Free?" She remarked: "Ours is, for me, the era of a double temporality: it is the broken-backed century that [Osip] Mandelstam lamented, the twilight of freedom; and in our grating and jarring present, it is the bitter dawn of liberty." In such a "season of turmoil and anguish," nations as well as individuals are infected with "a phobia of nonidentity"—"this neurosis, this pain, this fear of non-recognition" (Cixous 1993: 202–3). In such an era suffused with the expe-rience of various border crossings, language is a floating country while writing is "nomadic," constantly pointing to the Other spaces. Mandelstam, the Russian poet who dared to challenge Stalin and was persecuted to death, titled his prose texts *The Noise of Time*, joining the distinctive chorus of writers who "have often come forward as witnesses of the noises of history" (Cixous 1993: 205). As a feminist critic and poet writing at the end of this century, Cixous is, however, also acutely aware of the gender dimension that has been so often erased in discussions about freedom, exile, and the individual voice. She places herself, and thus the figure of the writing woman, right in front of her audience: "Me, myself, who? Today myself, a woman who writes, a woman part of whose identity is therefore caught up in the drama of Writing and the drama of woman" (Cixous 1993: 202).

The recent historical reconfiguration of the Chinese diaspora constitutes a set of "postnational locations" (Appadurai 1996) in which contemporary Chinese women's diasporic writing is situated. "Diaspora literature" (*haiwai wenxue*) as a geopolitically specific category in Chinese official discourse generally refers to literature written in Chinese and published primarily in Hong Kong, Taiwan, and Singapore, but also wherever there are large Chinese communities such as in the United States. Viewed from the mainland, the diaspora—*haiwai* (literally, beyond the ocean) or *qiaoju taixiang* (residing in others' countries) in Chinese—is seen as a peripheral landscape, inhabited by those uprooted ones who have lost the vital contact with the "homeland." In the official literary discourse in the Mainland, the term *haiwai wenxue* carries a mixture of connotations compounding the familiar and the strange. On the one hand, it is perceived as exotic and even titillating as it offers descriptions of sensual tropical landscapes and sentiments (for example, San Mao's autobiographical fiction). In the late 1970s and early 1980s *haiwai wenxue* was immensely popular in China, as it functioned as an imaginary outlet for repressed sexuality and a model of modernity (as the *haiwai* as a whole was perceived as materially more advanced). On the other hand, the category also suggests exclusion and discrimination because the diasporic "wandering sons" (*youzi*) are seen as having lost their Chinese authenticity, and their use of the (standard) Chinese language as heavily adulterated by local dialects or even foreign tongues. Because much of the diaspora literature of the past was rather out of touch with the contemporary developments on the Mainland, it was also regarded as a literature doubly removed in time and space.

The horizon of Chinese diaspora writing has been significantly broadened and reconfigured since China opened its doors in the early eighties, and more dramatically so after 1989, when many mainland Chinese writers suddenly found themselves in compulsory or voluntary exile, thus physically as well as discursively relocating themselves in the diaspora. Many temporary sojourners such as students, visiting scholars, and artists decided to stay in their host countries. The fall of the Berlin Wall in the same year also ushered in a global drama of greater capital and labor flow. Within a few years, a large number of mainlanders, many of them well educated, found themselves becoming overseas Chinese, eagerly craving "authentic" Chinese food and soap operas shown on emerging Chinese-language TV channels run by this new generation of permanent or transient immigrants. This latest wave of emigration has seen a sharp rise in interracial relationships or marriages, as compared to previous generations of overseas Chinese who clustered around Chinatown. In this age of global transmigration and "adoption," traditional markers of cultural identity such as language, citizenship, passport, blood lineage, and ancestral home are becoming unstable or even contradictory reference points. Only a decade or so ago, very few mainland Chinese had ever laid eyes on a passport, not to mention having been in possession of one. Today, many Chinese writers and artists, holding variously colored travel documents, traverse different continents and communities.[1]

The new, expanded diasporic public sphere, from which an emergent feminist diaspora literature evolves, should be regarded both as a contextual and global space and a relational and transnational temporality. This broadened horizon also includes the recent technological and media expansion and globalization, and their impact on the diaspora communities. The popularization of fax machines and the coming of age of Chinese software for personal computers (and increasingly the Internet), for instance, have vastly reorganized the time and space of the articulation and transmission of the Chinese language. In March 1996, a symposium on Chinese writing across diaspora took place in conjunction with the International Writing Festival held at Brown University. The Chinese delegates were surprised to see Salman Rushdie "attending," by way of a huge TV screen, a panel on freedom and writing that was televised live. The larger-than-life Rushdie on the screen even answered a called-in question from a TV viewer. In the next few days, the palpability of this displaced and mediatized simultaneity continued to make ripples in the conversations among the Chinese writers and critics. There arose the awareness that not only Chinese literature or the Chinese diaspora but also the very definition of literature were facing new realities and in need of paradigmatic transfigurations. Clearly, the conception of the modern nations as "imagined communities" by Benedict Anderson (1991) in his widely influential book is no longer sufficient for thinking about the novel formations of cultural production and reception, beyond not only the limits of home-bound nationalism but also those of a market bound by the print media. Nor is that model sensitive enough to women's participation in the public sphere and the global experience that encompasses a horizon of heterogeneous temporalities including personal trajectories of migration, family histories, interracial encounters, and the "transformation of intimacy" as a whole (Giddens 1990: 142–43). The relationship between women and the globalization of media technology largely remains a subtext in the women's writings I discuss in this essay. There are, however, some recurrent references to the use of the computer as a different writing machine and film—especially the montage technique—as an inspiration for alternative narrative structure.

The subjects who inhabit this essay—Chinese women writers of mainland origins who have lived and written in diaspora since the late eighties—have in a concrete sense been experiencing the double "drama" that Cixous talks about. The dilemmas faced today by these world-wise women writers in particular, and the Chinese diaspora in general, are, to be sure, very different from the past. Although the quantity and influence of their writings remain limited, they have produced some indelible "noises of time" that depart radically from the *wanyue* (gracefully restrained) feminine style that has characterized the bulk of traditional female writing, and that as a received gendered aesthetic is still very much prevalent in contemporary China. Descriptors such as *graceful, exquisite, sentimental* are no longer applicable to these women's writings. Some of them are also multimedia artists, operating across a wide geocultural scene.

Among the writers to be discussed, Liu Sola, while trained as a composer, was already a prominent writer in China during the eighties. She lived in London for several years and is now based in New York producing experimental and popular music. Zha Jianying is perhaps better known for her prose writing in English in the United States.[2] She also wrote a column on contemporary Chinese popular culture in *The Nineties*, a widely read Hong Kong Chinese monthly magazine, which has recently ended publication following the Hong Kong handover. Hong Ying and You You have come to the foreground in the literary scene only recently; their prolific writings in Chinese are often more daring and experimental, exploring uncharted territories of the diaspora experience. Hong Ying lived in California before she moved to London with her husband (a prominent Chinese scholar) a few years ago. You You has spent many years in New Zealand and Australia (and short sojourns in America and Germany) and is for the moment temporarily living in England with her poet husband Yang Lian. Unlike Zha and Liu who have more or less found a place in the culture market of America, You You and Hong Ying continue to write primarily in Chinese. Xie Ye, who was killed by her estranged poet husband Gu Cheng before he committed suicide in New Zealand in 1993, was never seriously regarded as a writer in her own right but as Gu Cheng's secretary and helpmate. In a sense, the intensity and the inseparability of her tragic life drama and the drama of her writing set up a relentless mirror in which the anxieties of cultural and gender identity shared by Chinese women writers in diaspora are reflected. But what is being positively refracted from this mirror are the efforts they made to explore the space for survival and imagination, and the beginnings of an intimate public sphere informed by feminist consciousness. This essay is meant as an introduction to an emergent body of writings by these diaspora women, addressing (1) how this body of writings, hitherto overlooked by critics, participates in a growing transnational Chinese-speaking public sphere; (2) to what extent their writings, experimental and provocative in both form and content, signify a female consciousness that is specific to the recent Chinese diaspora experience; and (3) how, to a certain degree, this women's literature helps to redefine the meaning and contours of Chinese diaspora literature and acknowledges the possibilities and challenges brought by global media. Since this group of women's writings have not been translated (except for Liu Sola's *Chaos and All That*) and seldom studied previously, I will devote a considerable amount of space to presenting an overview of this particular literary landscape.

The German scholar of Chinese literature Wolfgang Kubin, in an article written several years ago, characterized the famous woman poet Shu Ting's writing as a kind of bodily writing and wounded literature (Kubin 1988). The historical background of his argument is no doubt the Cultural Revolution and the large-scale internal exile (the massive transfer of youth to the countryside) it entailed, but the body and wound metaphors are to some extent still relevant to the present discussion situated in a context of external cultural dislocation: the diaspora. Shu Ting's lyrical poetry written during the Cultural Revolution revealed the pain and poetic ethos of the internal exile and transmitted through the underground the spiritual tenacity of love and humanist faith even when confined in the prison house. The women writers of the nineties who live outside China find themselves bound for external wanderings that have less definable boundaries. Because they are travelers, writers, and women (or the ambivalent wives of more famous men) who have to constantly weave new beginnings in the tedious and fragmented web of daily life and desire, the body specificity and wounded sensitivity manifested in their writings surfaced through new expressions. The state as an authoritarian image, which once, at home, stood in direct antagonistic relation to privacy, love, and humanism, no longer serves as a monolithically abstract force that paradoxically stimulated rebellious consciousness and its kin, lyrical impulse. Nor is romantic love, which was deployed as a standard metonymy for individual expression in underground literature during the Cultural Revolution and its immediate aftermath, merely platonic or utopian anymore. For Shu Ting, gender awareness was largely limited to the sentimental search for an idealized lover (who usually has a broad shoulder and a heroic aura), and the romanticization of the mother-child relationship. Moreover, the body in her writing is highly iconic, redolent of sacrificial meanings against a politically oppressive state.

As a whole, the diasporic women's writing in the nineties is not obsessed with deploying the body as a political metaphor but, rather, with treating it as a heterogeneous and eroticized site of gender signification within a global space. Shu Ting (and her generation of women writers at large) was writing in concealment, inside the oppressive political history, and was thus inhibited from freely expressing a frontal and thorough critique of the state and sexual repression. The writings of the women writers situated in the diaspora are conditioned by the historical and spatial distance between their present dispersed lives and the immediate past and present political life back home. To a large extent, that has enabled them to be more daring in exploring the oppressive nature of that political system and also linking it with a deeply rooted patriarchal structure.

Their writings extend into many forbidden areas of Shu Ting's era. They demonstrate a far more acute sensitivity to the arbitrary nature and polyvalent potential of language. Encountering languages other than Chinese has broadened their cultural horizon and complicated their perception of literature. Their attempts to rewrite various histories (personal, cultural, and literary) and their bold probing of the continued war between the sexes in new geocultural settings often push their writings into precarious territories. Though each has her own distinctive voice and style, their writings as a whole demonstrate an obsession with dreams, a propensity for deliberate narrative fragmentation, and a frankness about female (or even feminist) perspectives. It is impossible here to account for *all* of their writings, not to mention other writers whom I do not include in this essay (such as Min Anqi, Ai Bei, Yan Geling, and Zhang Ci).[3] I have chosen to focus primarily on their fictional or autobiographically inflected works published in the literary journal *Today* (*Jintian*), a major forum for diaspora writing by Chinese writers and intellectuals who have found themselves living abroad after 1989.[4] The project is based on a preliminary "jump-reading" of the past issues of the journal since it resumed publication in Norway in 1990 (now it is based in New York), with the aim of exploring an emerging women's diaspora writing. Some of the interpretations come from "zero-degree" textual readings (à la Roland Barthes), but I also try to examine how some thematic and stylistic features are subtly or sympto-matically (with regard to the prevalent "dream logic" found in their texts) connected while posing challenges to the larger diaspora context as both a textual and experiential realm.

In linking the women's writings with an emergent diaspora public sphere in which journals like *Today* play a pivotal role, I also want to con-sider how women in specific ways simultaneously contribute to and com-plicate this still predominantly male sphere. Although their scattered writ-ing practices do not yet in themselves constitute a pronounced feminist public sphere and their readership remains limited, it is, I believe, partly the task of the critic to "bring it forth" by outlining its emerging contours, or, perhaps, in Nancy Fraser's words, "thematizing the gender subtext"— a lacuna in Jürgen Habermas's theory of the public sphere (Fraser 1989: 122–29). What I have found most remarkable are the features in their writ-ings that address shared concerns and ambivalence about the relationship between the personal and the public, China and the world, experience and representation. After some discussions on how it is that they engage with an existence of writing in a diaspora context, linguistically and (multi) culturally, I will point out how Julia Kristeva's conception of "women's time" (1986) pertains to their rhetorical strategies (which include the use of dreams, psychoanalysis, and poetic structure) in representing the double drama of being a woman and the writing woman at the same time.

Rather than confining the "women's time" expressed in their works to a foreclosed female interiority, I will anchor this *heterogeneous* temporality and subjectivity on a post-1989 "horizon of global experiences." This horizon includes a wider range of life content and subject-positions than what was allowed by the Habermasian "structural" category centered on the print media (or "public opinion") and a predominantly male institution of "free associations." Within the expanded horizon, those whose experiences have been largely excluded from the dominant discursive space find arenas for the articulation and actualization of their concrete needs and interests. The social experience that gives the horizon its contingent, concrete, and heterogeneous form is, in the words of Miriam Hansen, a protean category "which mediates individual perception with social meaning, conscious with unconscious processes, loss of self with self-reflexivity; experience as the capacity to see connections and relations (*Zusammenhang*), experience as the matrix of conflicting temporalities, of memory and hope, including the historical loss of these dimensions." This discursive inclusiveness, beyond the "perspective of class struggle," is germane to the feminist project for the reclamation of the public space, without suppressing rich and complex female experiences (Hansen 1991: 12–13).[5]

Today, *Permutations of a Public Sphere, and Women*

Before I embark on a detailed analysis of the women's writings, a short sketch of the history of the journal *Today* is in order. It heralded the emergence of an alternative literary public sphere within China in the late seventies and early eighties and more recently in diaspora. Its later stage also provided an accessible forum for the women's writings in question here.

In its underground mimeographed form, the journal was first "published" in 1978, in association with a number of mostly male poets (Bei Dao, Mang Ke, Yang Lian, Gu Cheng, Duo Duo, and others), whose modernist-inflected poetry later came to be labeled as the "Misty poetry" (*Menglongshi*). These poets, many of whom had been sent to the countryside or to factories for reeducation during the Cultural Revolution, began to experiment with a new poetic language to express emotions and experiences that were not permissible in the official literary discourse. Their poems were circulated and hand-copied by a zealous underground readership. Following the arrest of the Gang of Four in 1976 and the Third Plenary Session of the Central Committee of the Chinese Communist Party in 1978 (which is often quoted as the milestone meeting that began to open China's doors to the world), the poets and their friends in Beijing set up *Today*. In its own way, the magazine became involved in the Democracy Movement that demanded freedom of speech and publication as an essential prerequisite of the official program of "modernization." The first issue of *Today* was posted on the walls of the Ministry of Culture, on the gate of the most important official poetry magazine, *Poetry* (*Shikan*), and on the Democracy Wall in Xidan in downtown Beijing (Goodman 1981; Pan and Pan 1985). The subsequent nine issues, as well as the last three issues under the title *Today Literary Research Materials* (a strategy adopted to avoid confiscation), drew a wide readership nationwide. Hundreds of underground publications mushroomed, some of which directly imitated the style of *Today*. The magazine was, however, forced to cease publication in December 1980 following a political purge. Throughout the eighties, the Misty poets were caught in a complex relationship with the official literary apparatus, which oscillated between strategies of co-opting and denouncing the alternative literature represented by *Today.*

After June 4, 1989, many of the former *Today* members found themselves living abroad, including Bei Dao, Wan Zhi, Yang Lian, Duo Duo, and Gu Cheng. In 1990, again under the initiation of Bei Dao and Wan Zhi (Mang Ke, another founder of the magazine, still lives in Beijing), *Today* was revived in Norway, where the two were living at the time. This time around the magazine (especially since the third issue), financed or supported by various American or European foundations and academic institutions and published by Oxford University Press and printed in Hong Kong,[6] no longer has an amateur underground look. Its high-quality paper and thick volume also give it a professional and "official" appearance, though it is still officially forbidden in China. Another significant development is authors' remuneration paid in U.S. dollars, a lucrative yet respectable new source of income for Chinese writers anywhere.

The single biggest fact that distinguishes the present *Today* from its former life is perhaps the spatial dispersal of the people who run and read it. Its worldwide, albeit not always effective, distribution network, besides its current head office in the United States, includes liaisons in Sweden, Germany, France, Japan, and Hong Kong. Although the journal has reached the bookshelves of major East Asian libraries in the West, is being sold in Chinese bookstores in Hong Kong, Taiwan, and the diaspora, and has even recently (in excerpts) appeared on the Internet, the mainland market has remained limited due to censorship. Through various smuggling channels the journal still reaches a considerable number of contributors and readers there, being circulated in a fashion not too different from ten years ago. If *Today* ten years ago evolved into an expanded literary salon in Beijing and an "imagined community" nationwide, today it is a transnational entity that, besides the journal itself, also publishes a biannual collection in English translation of selected works in *Today* and frequently hosts symposiums on literary and cultural issues across the Chinese-speaking world. The journal has presented a special issue on contemporary Chinese cinema from the Mainland, Hong Kong, and Taiwan, and another on Hong Kong's culture and politics on the eve of 1997. After its resumption, the journal also actively sought a younger generation of editors and contributors. For these reasons, it cannot be simply regarded as a nostalgic, partisan (re)publication.

The amplified presence of women's voices constitutes another aspect of its recent transformation. Ten years ago, Shu Ting was probably the only prominent female contributor to the journal, although as one early member,

Zheng Xian, recalls, there were a few young women volunteers who did tedious office work that included making noodles for the male editors and visitors (Zheng 1994: 8). Now there is a sizable group of women who regularly contribute to the journal, and a few as members of the editorial board are directly involved in the decision-making process. In the section on criticism, more gender-related articles have been published. Yet on the whole, the diasporic *Today* does not have a pronounced commitment to gender issues nor does it consciously promote women's writing other than for the purpose of having an appealing diversity. The editors for both the fiction and poetry sections are all male. As the journal suffers from a chronic shortage of fiction contributors from the Mainland due to political or communication obstacles, it has offered a relatively open ground for women writers in diaspora.

It is within this emergent, and often troubled, diasporic public sphere, which is financially backed by (a tiny fraction of) the global capital, that the women writers have begun to write for survival and creative fulfillment and gradually extend into other forums and form new allegiances. Many of them know each other and are mutually attentive readers or commentators. Compared to the ordeals of a much larger number of mainland Chinese women including illegal workers in sweatshops and mail-order brides/maids as mentioned in Shih Shu-mei's article in this volume, these women writers' lives may be very privileged, as many of them are married to well-established men and can travel relatively freely across borders. Once in a while their writings do expose some unreflective self-absorption. This should not, however, prevent us from giving a due appraisal of their contributions to the formation and representation of a feminist consciousness in diaspora, however incipient and peripheral it may appear at this moment. They have boldly confronted some deeply entrenched narratives of nationalism and modernity, and the thorny issue of sexuality vis-à-vis writing in an enlarged public sphere.

The (Off) Limits of Language and Nationhood

Any consideration of writing demands a critical attention to the various predicaments and possibilities that language brings. The complex relationships between narration and nation in the wake of modernity and under the impact of colonialism have been an especially popular subject of critical discourse in the past few years (Jameson 1986; Bhabha 1990). Because language is an essential ingredient in subject constitution, early on the project of instituting a modern vernacular literature was placed at the center of the Chinese cultural drama (and dilemma). At various points in modern Chinese history the language issue has continuously surfaced in the vexed relationship between the shifting frontiers of literary writing and the contours of a modern nation-state. After 1949, and especially during the Cultural Revolution, when China's national borders were literally off limits to the outside world, the boundaries of language and the state as well as those between the private and the public largely overlapped. By now the "linguistic despotism" (*yuyan baozheng*) of the Cultural Revolution and the impoverishment of literary representation that resulted have been rewritten into recent literary history. The cultural renaissance in the mideighties has come to be regarded as a new revolution in language, which attempted to reestablish the symbolic "distance" between the signifier and the signified and carved out a space for a literature that could encompass broader experiences beyond the limits set by state ideology and censorship.

Women's writing in the eighties proved instrumental to the literary renaissance. The booming literary scene was for a moment filled with the voices of a number of middle-aged or young women writers and poets such as Zhang Jie, Zong Pu, Dai Houying, Zhang Xinxin, Shu Ting, Wang Anyi, Liu Sola, and many others. Their engagement with many previously tabooed subjects, especially the intensely personal sphere and the experience of being a woman, regendered literary discourse and brought to the foreground questions concerning the efficacy of female voice vis-à-vis old and new patriarchal formations, and the difficulty, or even the impossibility, of reinstating a feminist consciousness, which had been appropriated by state feminism in the past few decades.

To a large extent, women's writing in the eighties was preoccupied with reconstructing a gender interiority that did not necessarily enable a powerful critique of the state patriarchy and its nationalist ideology. Many women writers devoted their writing to representing the trauma of the collective repression of the immediate past and reconstructing an individual identity largely predicated on liberal humanism. Their desperate search for a new selfhood for women was often secondary to a search for a "real man" (who had been absent due to the sexual repression during the Cultural Revolution) to give the woman protection and romantic love (Zhong 1989). Can Xue, probably the most provocative woman writer of that period, shocked the literary world with her idiosyncratic experimental fiction, which made some male critics label her a "paranoid woman" while reluctantly including her in the predominantly male avant-garde writing (Lu 1993). Can Xue's radical aesthetic of "negation," however, did not open further possibilities

Zhang Zhen

≈ 318 ≈

for a self-conscious feminist imaginary, especially when her writing was uneasily lumped together with male experimental fiction. In general, women's writing in the eighties was more obsessed with carving out an "individual" space for a subject in search of a safe haven of interiority, and there was also a nostalgia for family bonding. Their critique of the state was often limited to an emotional indictment of the Cultural Revolution, and their critical edge was at times unwittingly canceled by inculcated patriotic sentiments and an unreflected faith in the renewed project of "modernity." Except perhaps for Can Xue and Zong Pu (and some women poets), the language they used to write remained mired in a received May Fourth realist tradition, and no serious challenge was launched to question its representational transparency and legitimacy.

Diasporic women's writing is more explicitly risk taking in experimenting with language. This has enabled them to reclaim experimental writing for women. Their geocultural dislocation outside the national boundary inadvertently offered them previously unimaginable vistas for reexamining the relationships between nation and representation, state and female experience. Once they step outside the doors of China, the Chinese language ceases to be a taken-for-granted reference point, nor is it simply instrumental, as it proves quite useless in most daily situations. As many of them live in major cosmopolitan cities and travel (or migrate) a great deal, the exposure to the multiplicity of cultures forces them to relativize and constantly relocate Chinese culture and language within an emergent Chinese "traveling culture" (Clifford 1992; Yang 1997). Encountering a wider range of female and male subjectivities also compels them to reflect harder on the question of gender and how it bears on their past and present experiences. Finally, writing in the exile scenario after the Tiananmen Square massacre of 1989, the women writers were caught by a deeper anger and disillusionment with the state, the reforms of which in the early eighties seemed momentarily to suggest hope and renewal.

Reading the writings of Liu Sola, You You, Hong Ying, and the others, written abroad in the nineties, one is quickly led into a series of life and textual situations where languages and identities collide. The orbiting of the body and language on trajectories outside the country of one's origin or the attempt to survive and thrive in the compounded space of multi-cultures become a continuous tension-ridden effort to break out of various encirclements. As a musician, Liu Sola has an acute ear to the sounds and dissonance in language. In *Chaos and All That* (1994), a novella written in London about a Chinese woman writer's turbulent life as a new immigrant, she takes on a seemingly playful postmodern stance to reexamine such heavy-duty themes as freedom, history, and language.[7] The novella is structured by Huang Haha's tragicomic narration under the melancholy sky of London about past and present fragments in her life; her erratic voice also momentarily delivers a self-indulgence, if not cynicism, as a "world citizen." Beneath the surface of this frivolous, or "chaotic," narration, however, lies a rather conscious effort to critically re-view some major tropes in Chinese history and tradition. Although the name of the female protagonist is Haha, an onomatopoeic reference to hearty or ironic laughter, her family name Huang alludes to the Yellow Emperor, the legendary forefather of the Chinese race. A male friend whom she constantly pokes fun at is called Lao Gu, the "old ancient." In other words, Haha is an irreverent offspring who mocks the mythic patriarch-ancestor. The narration zigzags between absurd events in London and violent episodes of the Cultural Revolution. The omnipresent "dirty words" (zanghua) are interwoven with lyrics from traditional operas and contemporary pop music, the two of which are also interpenetrated, producing a hilariously "cathartic" effect. Chaos and All That is a text reverberating with "noises" that strike the eardrum of the reader with an acoustically—and culturally—malleable language. Huang Haha is having a relationship with a certain Caucasian named Michael, yet she would always suddenly stop talking or making love to him to write letters home to Beijing. Her life is literally caught in a strange circle: "London—Beijing—classical sculpture—operas—kinship— Zhoukoudian [where the "Peking Man" was found]—ape-man—Anna Karenina—Wang Baochuan [heroine in a traditional opera]—Huang Haha." Huang Haha blurts out a big laugh while jotting down on the paper the phrase dui cuo (right or wrong), whose logic keeps evading her and the reader. The novella, in privileging the chaotic mode of narration and confronting the hybrid nature of the diasporic existence, breaks up and undercuts state patriarchy. At the same time, Liu Sola's relentless depiction of the painful immigration experience, and her reservation about interracial communication (or love), persistently put the Western notion of freedom on trial.

The murder of Xie Ye by her husband, the famous poet Gu Cheng, near their home in self-imposed exile on a small island in New Zealand in 1993 before he committed suicide himself, shocked the diaspora community and the post-1989 Chinese cultural scene at large. The tragedy not only attests to the often shrill and inchoate diasporic existence, but more crucially it reveals the spiritual and physical mutilation frequently inflicted on women by self-styled male exile heroes who are frustrated by their own cultural impotence in adjusting to the reality of diaspora. In the case of Gu

Cheng, he simply refused to learn English and other necessary day-to-day skills to survive. As a copyist, typist, secretary, and personal manager of her husband's literary enterprise, Xie Ye seems to have submerged her authorship into Gu Cheng's corpus. But she did write something with her own signature attached to it. In her autobiographical piece "Your Name Is Samuel" (*Nide minzi jiao Mu'er*) (1993b). She wrote about a heartrending mother-son relationship under the shadow of a willful Gu Cheng, who had their son adopted by a Maori family. The text is full of the boy's innocent yet precocious speech mixing English and Chinese. Once when the mother and son met during one of those rare occasions, she tried to teach him to say "Mama, I am little Mu'er [Samuel's Chinese nickname]" in Chinese, and he unexpectedly responded in English: "Mammy got funny talking." In a letter to her girlfriend who is also a mother, Xie Ye mentioned another incident. She had taught him to say "How are you?" (*nihao*) in Chinese; Samuel reproduced it as "You are fire" (*nihuo*). If Gu Cheng, the child's father, made himself a madman in the prison house of the national language even in his effort to deconstruct it, Samuel, born and raised in a new cultural milieu, has become a product of a different language (or, rather, a mixture of languages) and a hybrid Other to the homogeneous national identity, which Gu Cheng challenged with deep ambivalence and at a terrible cost.

Also the wife of an influential poet who was among the early members of *Today*, You You started writing fiction seriously in the past few years while leading a wandering life with Yang Lian. Her early short pieces published in 1993 in *Today*, such as "The Screaming Wood," "Nothing to Say," and "?" are often surreal sketches of nightmares and daydreams, symptomatic not so much of the nervousness of an emergent writer as of a writing subject who is constantly journeying between disparaging climates, exhausted by the frequency of having to move from room to room, packing and unpacking. They are also muffled cries and suppressed screams from a woman who has to make sense of her present status: an exile? an exile's wife? a writer in her own right? These short pieces are permeated with a fear of aphasia for which wood, rock, ice become condensed rhetorical vehicles as well as symbols of bodily pain experienced by the diasporic subject.

"In a Trance" (*Huangxi buxi*, 1993a), written during a trip to the United States, is a short story about a woman losing (and trying to make) sense of direction while living abroad. It delves deeper into the theme of aphasia and culture shock. The writer opens her story at the double edge of dream and language:

In the morning I was still in bed dazed with sleep when I heard someone talking in Chinese. It was as though you understood everything, but when it came down to every single word, it did not sound quite right anymore. Only when stringed together, then was it unmistakably Chinese. (35)

The female narrator could not tell whether or not she was in her apartment in the gray concrete building in the Jingsong district in east Beijing. But the loud voice of the veteran Leon speaking in English from downstairs made her realize that she was in a different country, not the street in Beijing "where every minute is full of Chinese." Although she took pains to decorate her new home in the same way as the apartment in Beijing, she has come up with a new definition about "home": "What is home? Home is in your hands; it's like two suitcases that you can pack up in five minutes and set off with. You carry your 'home' and go everywhere" (37). Home has simply become portable.

What is also interesting is that the sounds of Chinese in her "trance" do not necessarily have to come from standard Mandarin, which represents the central authority; instead, she vividly recalls the local colors of dialects of Xi'an or Gansu, where she had been a while back in China. In a sense, the multiplicity within the Chinese language and the marginality of provincial localities, when surfaced in her dream memory abroad, complicate any abstract longing for a monolithic China. Beijing, the official center of the state, becomes localized in this process of remembering.

"History's Time" and "Women's Time"

As a way to break the discursive limitations of national literature further, I will now consider the delicate relationship between what Kristeva calls "women's time" and historical consciousness manifested in this group of women's writing. To a large extent, intense female consciousness is the shared keynote and perspective of this group of women's writings. They often weave into their texts (repressed) family history, female bonding, and seemingly inconsequential daily life as a way to convey subtle critiques of the more grandiose masculine narratives of national and political history and to question their cohesiveness and legitimacy. Alternative temporalities such as those found in dreams and psychoanalysis are frequently used as rhetorical devices to foreground not only the jarringness of various geolinguistic "tenses" but also the collage effect of diaspora existence. This is not to say that their writings simply bypass significant historical events; rather, it is through the effort to write against the grain of the clichéd narratives (such as the Cultural Revolution) that they give voice and shape to some inchoate experiences. This partly explains why the prominent female consciousness in their writings is also expressive of a vigilance about the danger of slipping into any foreclosed "female essence" or a polarized female-male antagonism.[8] Living outside of China and being exposed to various other masculinities and femininities have dramatically complicated their gender consciousness, which we have already glimpsed in several works discussed earlier.

The Bulgaria-born-and-raised French feminist theorist Julia Kristeva, who was trained in the philosophy of language, has consistently rejected the temptation to demarcate the *feminine* (in French it does not carry the same connotation as *feminine* in English) as a separate semiotic category of signification, as it carries the risk of "a too rapid valorization of difference" (Moi 1986: 11). In her *Revolution in Poetic Language* (1984) she also includes several male writers to illustrate a revolutionary strain in literary modernism. In her later essay "Women's Time," however, Kristeva (who now has had the experience of pregnancy and motherhood) tries to locate a possible, if still shifting, oasis for female subjectivity against the paralyzing logic and politics of deconstructive negativity. She delineates a more salient feminist project in terms of temporality instead of the space of the "semiotic jouissance" central to her earlier theoretical preoccupation. Pointing out that the persistent tendency to define and confine women to the "space" of reproduction rather than to "time" or history is characteristic of various patriarchal traditions (including modern formulations by Sigmund Freud and James Joyce), Kristeva ascribes to women other modalities of time that have been repressed by the linear, male-dominant historical time, especially with the onset of modernity. Female subjectivity, according to her, is linked to "cyclical" time (repetition) and to "monumental time" (eternity). These inclusive and life-generating temporalities are fundamentally at odds with "time as project, teleology, linear and progressive unfolding: time as departure, progression and arrival—in other words, the time of history" (Kristeva 1986: 192–93). Within these temporal realms, many experiences such as pregnancy, agony, and ambivalence in love that are unaccountable by linear time—"which passes"—are given extraverbal expressions. With this temporal reorientation, Kristeva is able to periodize (not necessarily chronologically) three generations of feminists: the first wave of liberal feminists, who struggled for an equal footing with men in linear history; the second generation, which emerged after 1968, eager to assert difference rather than sameness between the sexes; and the third generation, which Kristeva clearly identifies as aspiring

(marginal handwritten notes: "complicate gender consciousness from strand"; "Kristeva"; "women's cyclical time and monumental time"; "women's experience as temporal")

to bridge different temporalities so as to allow for a broader conception of history and gender.

The ascendancy of linear temporality, or a specific "time conscious-ness," as Habermas underscores, was key to the project of modernity and the emergence of modern subjectivity (Habermas 1987a). The global "flow" of the modern time also effected a profound restructuring of his-torical consciousness among Chinese intellectuals. As the Chinese femi-nist critic Meng Yue (who serves as an editor for *Today*'s criticism section) forcefully argues, "in the discourse of the pioneers of the New Culture movement, the 'modern' is chiefly a temporal value"; because the Chinese reality was perceived by (male) intellectuals as "incompatible" with or "dis-located" in modernity, the "'present' simply became a synonym with 'dark-ness' and 'chronic disease'" (Meng 1992: 177–78).[9] Such a diagnosis put an invisible straitjacket on the nascent female writing heralded by, among others, Ding Ling, who for all her life was caught in a sense of guilt and frustration as a feminist writer. Joining the grand narrative time of revolu-tion ultimately did not prove to be the solution for the perpetual procras-tination of women's liberation. On the other hand, Zhang Ailing (who re-cently died in solitude in California), consciously placing her writing in a "dialogue" with the May Fourth discourse, was committed to sketching the "incomplete" modernity in China and the multiple or uneven (*cengci*) temporal-spatial dimensions in everyday life, not least in terms of gender relations. She devised "romance" (*chuanqi*) rather than the "realism" (*xieshi*) widely practiced by the May Fourth writers as a narrative mode that did not subscribe to a telos, or the drive to "complete history" (Meng 1992: 191–92). If "women's time" is poised between the nonverbal and the enun-ciative (or semantically ordered) realms, Zhang Ailing's strategy, which questions linear time but refuses to give up language altogether, is in tune with Kristeva's ultimate conviction of female writing as a vital practice to turn the female "creatures" to "creatresses," and thus to create new knowl-edge about gender and culture, and to rewrite the social or sexual contract (Kristeva 1986: 205–7).

The writings of the women writers discussed in this essay manifest a discernible tendency of wandering off the "proper" historical time of China as a modern state. However, that per se should not obscure our view of the alternative temporalities operating in their fictional or autobiographical writings. First of all, travel and wandering (without an ultimate destina-tion) embody intensely personal and visceral time experiences. The infi-nite superimposition of dreamscape, landscape, and historical backdrop receives complex patterning in the "time of working through," which includes the time of writing. The writers seem to zigzag between various regions of history and their often contending representations. For instance, Liu Sola's ambivalence between the present tense and the past perfect tense in *Chaos and All That* coincides not only with her present life in diaspora and the immediate past of the Cultural Revolution, but also with the ambivalent relationship—the entanglement and conflict—between family history and the political history in modern China.

Zha Jianying was known for her story "Go to America" (*Dao Meiguo qu*) written after she had come to the States to study literature. She served as fiction editor for *Today* for a while after its resumption in 1990. The first resumed issue has a short story by her, "Program" (*Jiemu*, 1990). It tells the story of Lingzi, a Chinese student of psychoanalysis in an American city abbreviated as Z, and her gradually routinized, or "programmed," life with her husband Pan. The crisis of their marriage, under the surface of a plain, harmonious daily life, is uncannily interwoven with the routinized practice of psychotherapy by Lingzi, who is serving as a student intern. Pan seems imperviously unaware of the disintegration of the marriage. This does not have explicit connections to any politicohistorical events; on the contrary, the repetition of daily life and the case histories of the nameless subjects of psychoanalysis, which Lingzi routinely retells to Pan in bed upon his insistence, constitute another kind of historical landscape. The names of the patients are called arbitrarily according to the order of appearance: "B, C, D, E," and so forth, either due to some professional ethical code or in order to show a typology of (non)identity in psychoanalysis. Viewed through Jacques Lacan's psychoanalytic theory, these patients' self-narratives filtered through the "discourse of the Other," or through the "intersubjective" dialogue between Lingzi and her patients, become more and more submerged in her own unconscious, especially when they are subsequently renarrativized (or "transferred") between her and Pan. The process of psychoanalysis is, according to Lacan's skeptical theory, not so much a chronologically ordered treatment predicated on a stable object-subject relationship as it is a time travel in language and the unconscious to which both the analyzer and the analyzed are subjects (in the making). The analytical procedure is thus necessarily a "time of working through." In such a time, history cannot be ipso facto reconstructed through hypnosis or other means but is always the "future anterior of what I shall have been for what I am in the process of becoming," a process unfolding in superimposed time zones of the past and the future (Lacan 1977).[10]

Lingzi's husband hardly gives heed to the fact that the "program," which has added some stimuli to their rather bland life, has in fact turned into a psychoanalytical procedure between the couple themselves. Those nameless patients who have "abnormal" gender identifications or sexual behaviors have invisibly metamorphosed Lingzi's self-perception. They range from the masochistic Mrs. B who willingly succumbs to her husband's predatory sexual acts, the lesbian Miss D who takes attractive women from men, to a certain Ms. F who pathologically lies to men, and to Mrs. G who hates and loathes her husband but lacks the courage to leave him. On an (extra)ordinary morning, Lingzi wakes up from a disturbing dream and tries anxiously to tell Pan the story of Mrs. G. The impatient husband, who only likes to listen to a case history as a lullaby, does not realize that Lingzi, after working through those multiple personalities (A, B, C, D . . .), is no longer that "sedately tender and delicately seductive" (*duanzhuang weiwan, chuchu dongren*) good wife (or Mrs. G!) who gives him soul-lifting massages in bed while telling the stories. Their marital history has come to an end and assumes the status of yet another case history. While Lingzi has changed rapidly through her "intersubjective" encounters with the Other when studying abroad, Pan stands still in his imaginary cocoon of a traditional marriage in which he thinks all along that things are under his control. In foregrounding the time lag between Pan's insensitivity and inertia and Lingzi's dramatic self-transformation, the story also epitomizes a symptomatic phenomenon in Chinese mainland diaspora: that women tend to be better at adapting and being flexible with foreign cultures. The risk of stereotyping notwithstanding, many Chinese mainland women are more inclined to explore new possibilities that are not as accessible to them at home. They are often quick learners of daily tactics and new languages, while many men (especially intellectuals) are burdened by their self-imposed mission to represent China in more formal discourses and capacities and tend to suppress the often humbling immigrant experience. They also tend to be more self-righteous about their anti-Westernization stance, which is often fueled by an uncritical nationalist fervor in spite of their critique of the status quo at home.

Now I want to turn to Hong Ying's prolific writings. The female voices in her fictional works, as in her poetry, are multiple and layered; they cross back and forth between disparate time zones. Dream or dream-like ambiance typically overdetermines her narration; even the more soberly structured "Recent Studies on Yu Hong" (1994b) manifests a sustained fascination with the "incomprehensible" dream logic that challenges public representation. What Hong Ying strives for is a representation that consciously treads the tightrope between fiction and nonfiction. Liu Sola, in her typical tomboy fashion, attempts to fill the gender gap through extensive use of conventionally masculine dirty words or even scatological references. Hong Ying, on the other hand, born in the early sixties and thus spared most of the staple programs such as being turned into a peasant or destroying temples as a Red Guard, left China in her twenties and is not as burdened by the trauma of the Cultural Revolution or China's heavy political national history in general. While both writers experiment with different aspects of "women's time" in their writing, Liu Sola seems to be more concerned with the representation of the historically monumental, whereas Hong Ying's preoccupation with the exploration of the unconscious, the body, and sexuality aligns her with the second and possibly the third generation of feminists described by Kristeva.

Several short pieces, or groups of fragments, by Hong Ying, written before "Recent Studies on Yu Hong," reveal a keen sensitivity to the *situation* of the female body as the writing body. They also reveal moments of empowerment or hopelessness in the visible or invisible war between the sexes that take place, among other venues, in the most intimate private sphere, the bedroom. For instance, in "Fingernail" (*Zhijia*, 1993), the "tender and docile" (*wenshun*) wife's "jade-carving-like" fingers, similar to the "golden lotus" bound feet for the traditional Chinese literati, are worshipped as a fetish by her husband. He wants her to grow her beautiful nails and put gloves on before washing the dishes. When making love to her, he calls her his little kitten, puppy, or little treasure as if she were his pet or a collected antique. But the wife is not insensitive to such objectification. Once when they made love, as the man was lost in his self-indulgent climax, she suddenly realized that he was "so far away." She did not say anything but thought to herself: "What is this? Can this be called lovemaking?" On a later occasion before they were to make love again, the husband, yawning, told her that she did not have to do any household chores because that might damage her delicate hands. Unable to sleep, she realized that her hands felt "hot and clumsy, and her imagination impoverished." She walked to the desk, took out a pair of scissors from the drawer, and wanted to cut off those "hateful fingers." Her culminating frustration and anger at being treated as a plaything were about to take the violent form of self-mutilation. But the "cold touch of the iron instrument" woke her up from this wild fantasy. Uttering a curse, she put down the scissors and went back to bed. The hand is simply too important for a writing woman. She discovers that her fingers ultimately belong to herself.

These and other fragments (such as "Dirty Fingers, Bottle Caps") are symptomatic of a wounded and scarred textual body and also of a young woman poet searching for an alternative form and time frame to articulate her border-crossing and taboo-breaking experiences. When Hong Ying wrote "Recent Studies on Yu Hong" (*Jinnian Yu Hong yanjiu*, 1994b), she seemed to have come to terms with her agitated night wanderings and was much more at ease with fragmentation both as (life)style and the true face of history or, for that matter, the history of female writing. This time, in order to approach her subject through many possible temporalities, the writer uses the film montage technique to establish a number of interlaced points of view. Although at the outset this text is more saliently a narrative story, it is still shrouded in a dreamy mood that accentuates the evasiveness and arbitrariness of historical representation. The story is centered on the biographical myth of Yu Hong, the pen name of a woman writer who was active in occupied Shanghai in the early forties but was subsequently purged out of literary history because she was, like some other writers such as Su Qing and Zhang Ailing, suspected of nonresistance to Japanese colonialism and too immersed in "decadent" Shanghai metropolitan life. The multiple angles of narration present to us the image of the writing woman from the early forties to the present and fuse together "cyclical" and "monumental" time in an enigmatic representational space. Yu Hong's purported granddaughter Fu Hao (her name is the homophone of *sign*), a young poet and a student at Fudan University in Shanghai, tries to befriend the reclusive woman editor who seems to hold the key to the mystery since she was responsible for publishing Yu Hong's work in the past. Through archival work the narrator exposes the negative attitude of some prominent May Fourth writers like Zheng Zhenduo toward Yu Hong and the tragic fate of the people who were involved with the elusive woman writer. Hong Ying's text thus critically confronts the master narrative of modern Chinese literary history.

The story, woven together by various discourses (diaries, photo albums, archives, newspapers, academic writings by both Chinese and American scholars, and feminist criticism), is in fact an intricate *context* that foregrounds the thorny issue of historical representability and the difficult position of women's writing within or vis-à-vis the mainstream narrative. Hong Ying also employs footnotes as a device both to parody academic writing and to experiment with a writing style that tackles both fiction and history head on. The form of the notes, in incorporating scattered pieces of history (or, rather, the histories of history) into the main text, disrupts any attempt to present a causally coherent narrative. Fu Hao's project is to revise modern Chinese literary history by reinserting Yu Hong's name in it; by so doing she herself also benefits from the restored legend, as a natural heir in the literary (matri)lineage. The information retrieved by her, mainly by poring through Yu Hong's diaries and photo albums, and through conversations with the ailing editor—which are in turn processed through her computer (a striking marker of her being a writer of the 1990s)—presents conflicting pictures or, rather, fragments that do not cohere into a solved puzzle image. The leads and traces do not necessarily point to one truth, nor can public discourse such as academic scholarship or news reports substantiate the myth hinged on multiple temporalities. The story seems to suggest that writing a history of female writing is no less an arduous adventure as writing a fictional *histoire*. Ultimately, the question of the biographical authenticity of Yu Hong does not matter anymore, as no linear time could adequately account for her *body* of writing.

Despite Fu Hao's desire to rewrite history with the aid of modern technology (computer, overhead projector, and so on), she is unprepared to confront the full breadth and complexity of an alternative history imbricated in a "women's time." It is therefore a historical irony that, as Yu Hong's sensational presentation at the university is reported in Shanghai's major newspaper *Wenhuibao* (under the title "The Historical Enigma Is Finally Resolved: The Story of the Talented Grandmother and the Granddaughter Makes a Legendary Tale"), the old editor passes away with her sealed secret and fate. The rhythm of an undying time of repetition and cyclicity, like that of the spring rain, however, will continually bring back the echoes of the name of Yu Hong:

> The secret paths crisscross, always lead her astray. History is relentless; you fool history, it will in turn fool you. The thing that has made her suffer all her life is but a tiny name, but the protest harbored in her heart has also long before decided the outcome. The riddle originates in her; whenever and however she wants to handle it, she remains its only owner.
>
> She wobbled toward the bed and carefully lay down. Pitch-black water swept away the fragments that exploded in her heart, along with everything in her memory. . . . Life reincarnates and repeats cyclically as always, though occasionally there will be exceptions. If she could ever chance upon such a rare occasion, she would take hold of it and start all over again, no camouflage, no putting up with degradation, and live like a real woman. Yes, she would try, really, she said to herself. She was determined and she did it. (82–83)

The crisscrossing paths are a pertinent metaphor for "women's time," as it does not grant any easy entry to or exit from the labyrinth of history. The old woman's death or, rather, self-imposed disappearance (and invisible reincarnation) comes as an anticlimax to Fu Hao's success in a computerized age, and a counterpoint to the public discourse in the official newspaper. The story of Yu Hong (which literally means the "remaining rainbow") is finally only a residual shadow of an elusive past. To some extent, Hong Ying (which means the shadow of a rainbow) has also "edited" her own name and her act of (auto)writing into this unofficial literary history written in the diaspora, redolent of "women's time."

The Horizon of Global Experiences

The writings of the women writers in diaspora are simultaneously embedded in and actively helping to shape the new Chinese diasporic literature at a time when both the official map and popular imagination of the geocultural contours of China are facing radical transformations. As the quantity and influence of their writings remain limited, and the privileges they enjoy in transnational travel and movement create certain social distance between them and other home-based Chinese writers and readers, it will be an overstatement to say that their creative activities constitute a distinct female public sphere per se. Instead, their dispersed lives and writings partially converge in an expanding diasporic forum represented by journals like *Today* and, more recently, *Tendency (Qingxiang)*. The two publications are now based in Iowa City and Boston, respectively, although the members of their editorial board may live beyond the Pacific or the Atlantic Oceans. Moreover, their contributors are not limited to those living outside the Mainland but include many who still have not left China even once. The distribution network is volatile, yet reaching a considerable audience through underground shipping and subscriptions (only outside the Mainland, as both journals are still prohibited there). Some of the women writers also travel frequently to China, and their works (especially Hong Ying's and You You's) appear in literary journals in China as well. Hong Ying has also been involved in editing collections of women's diaspora writings for a mainland press.

The multidirectional diaspora writing and publishing ventures, conditioned by their geographically shifting readership, are prone to being nomadic, experimental, and adventurous. The emerging diaspora women writers have passionately responded to the shock waves of their cosmopolitan life. They have tested various rhetorical strategies in their texts to account for everyday confrontations with sexual and cultural identities beyond the narrowly defined national and linguistic boundaries. When we read how one of Hong Ying's female personae, standing on a world map, gets dressed from the innermost layer to the outer shell while conjuring up wild sexual fantasies, we are shaken by the author's audacity in juxtaposing the most intimate experience with the global space ("Dirty Fingers, Bottle Caps"). To further discuss some key features in the women's writings with regard to these global experiences, I will analyze You You's "Xiao Meng's Nirvana" and then end the essay by making references to Liu Sola's "Crowd over Crowd."

In a recent story written in Germany, "Xiao Meng's Nirvana" (*Xiao Meng niepan*, 1995), You You gives the prevalent imagery of haunting dreams a more personified form and situates the feminist character in a wider space collating the subjective dream world and the global experience. The story still contains many themes on the pain of love and the impossibility of marriage, but the multifaceted image of Xiao Meng (which means the Little Dream/er) portrayed in this story emits a liberating energy and the power of fantasy and humor. As an idealized self-liberated "role model," she bring to the "I" character an intense experience of female bonding that borders on erotic attraction. She enlightens her girlfriend, who is torment-ed by love, with pronounced feminist ideas. She proposes to create a "club of fantasy" where they can tell each other ghost stories or extraordinary tales. Xiao Meng comes and goes, leaving no visible traces. When "I" was suffering from aphasia and seemed lost in the deserted emotional world and running madly in the empty city, Xiao Meng suddenly descended, cheering up the sullen friend with wondrous tales of her travels to various places within China, as well as Hong Kong, Japan, Singapore, and Germany. She is engaged in many enterprises, ranging from her own trading business to touring performances. Her cyborg-like appearance is shockingly beau-tiful with shaved head and transparent body, and it is hard to tell if she is really a woman or not. Xiao Meng has become such an integral part in the life of the "I"; when many people including her husband deny Xiao Meng's existence, "I" decides that she is both Xiao Meng and herself: "Perhaps I have become two people at once. I can under any circumstances play on any hands and face anyone with my thousand-sided face—wouldn't that be wonderful?" (98).

Xiao Meng is a city of memory, a women's paradise, and the interstitial space between the self and the Other. Xiao Meng can be infinitely reincar-nated as long as one keeps having dreams, and so her nirvana actually becomes the liberating force that overcomes the atrophy of imagination that so likely befalls the exile. You You cleverly uses the famous "Zhuangzi Dreams the Butterfly" story in which the dreamer and the dreamed are perpetually transpositioned; but she translates the classical allusion about the instability of subject into an open-ended modern myth of female subjectivity. Home and the foreign land, language and desire—these categories can no longer be easily found in a fixed location in a world with multiple, shifting horizons conditioned by sophisticated transportation means and mass media. In a sense, the chameleon-like Xiao Meng embodies the transnational feminist subject in the making. Her versatility—as both a performer (rather than a solitary writer) and a successful self-employed entrepreneur (which makes her economically independent)—and her nomadic adaptability not only prepare her for any unforeseen situations but also enable her to inspire her female friends. Traveling at light speed across vast spaces and looking like a cyborg, Xiao Meng may also be seen as the embodiment of the women-friendly technological hybrid. She is both the medium and the message.

As an open-ended conclusion, and instead of linearly projecting the future, I would like to switch the clock back to 1990 when the resumed *Today* published Liu Sola's "Crowd over Crowd" (*Ren dui ren,* 1990), a short story about the ambivalence of multiculturalism and gender consciousness in a multimedia world. The story opens in an apartment complex in central London inhabited by people from all over the world. It is almost like a miniature of the United Nations or an ethnographic museum: "All kinds of creatures from the world are gathered here." A young woman writer from the Mainland is possessed by her "psychological anomalous hatred" toward her multiracial neighbors. She particularly hates the neighbor who every morning loudly plays the same song ("My postcard . . ."—we never learn the rest of the lyric), which unfailingly wakes her up from her dreams about her being together with her mother in China. After getting out of her dark room, however, she befriends her neighbors and grows accustomed to the song, which becomes an intimate daily background sound rather than noise. She also forms a partnership with a cowboy-styled American. They began to cowrite film scripts about China and Native American Indians with a lot of "ethnic" touches. The first script "I" (the first-person narrator) drafted parodies the "land of civility" (*liyi zhi bang*—China) and its "civilized" habits such as spitting and cursing on buses, and bullying tourists from other parts of China. She is asked to revise and make references to the politics in her host country so that British TV would accept it.

But the revision takes much longer because "during those months the whole world underwent countless changes, and the globe almost bounced to the sky. All sensitive Chinese felt depressed." As the story was written in spring 1990, it does not take much speculation to see that the "changes" broadly refer to the earth-shaking events in 1989, both in China and

Europe. Interestingly, it is at this post-1989 conjuncture that the long-unheard record downstairs is being played again, only this time the broken record can only barely play the line "My pos pos pos. . . ." "I" learned that the neighbor was the original composer of the song, which used to be very popular in his own country. He had come to London to compose more popular songs, but no one wanted his work, so he could only listen to his own song until he turned crazy and was sent to an asylum.

The period of her painful revision also coincides with her becoming aware of the troubled position of the woman artist in the transnational space, especially after witnessing her American cowriter taking advantage of women actresses of different national origins. Her first venture into film and television thus turns into a lesson about the complexity of global media as it brings both possibilities and obstacles to women who try to write, perform, or make films on their own terms, instead of being subordinated to the control of global capital and male chauvinism. Liu Sola's bitterly comic story certainly cannot be read apart from her own experience as a multimedia woman artist who has tried, among other things, to hybridize the blues with Chinese music while continuing to write fiction in Chinese. Her story (echoing her other diaspora writings) is a cautionary tale, or a broken "post-song," about the pain involved in living and creating as a woman in the so-called global village. She mocks any naive conception of a utopian "imagined community" under the impact of old and new cultural imperialism, Asian or white male chauvinism. But at the same time, she admits and confronts the multicultural reality as the condition of the horizon of global experiences.

"Crowd over Crowd," written in the immediate aftermath of the events in 1989 that contributed directly to the emergence of a new mainland diaspora and its literature in a dramatically altered global scene, rehearses many themes that appear in various configurations in diasporic women's writing. Their writing is about making a certain "noise of time," just like that broken song about a postcard. Moreover, because the workshop for this enterprise is a global one, permeated with new media possibilities and challenges, it is intimately linked to an emergent diasporic public sphere where women try to define their multifaceted subjectivity. Through experimenting with new languages and writing styles, and the representational spaces beyond the print media, their writings present diverse yet overlapping versions of a world map in which the place of Chinese identity becomes increasingly problematic. Collectively, their shared sensitivity and the desire to represent the female writing subject and its historical trajectory in the past and present have put forth a considerable body of literature, which deserves more attention on and critical study of its potential as well as limitations in the shaping of a tentative feminist public sphere. It is true that they belong to a certain group of privileged transnational subjects, and the diasporic Chinese women's public sphere that I see emerging out of their artistic adventures remains incomplete and insufficient in addressing some fundamental issues regarding nationalism and feminism. Nevertheless, these writers articulate through their writing about living in the diaspora a new powerful sensibility that challenges the identification of Chinese national culture with masculinity. The diasporic experience that they engage and represent in the literature decenters both the literary privileging of China and the centrality of both Chinese and Western male perspectives, revealing alternative conceptions of subjectivity, temporality, and historicity. Where Liu Sola's story ends, the maddening yet intimate noise of "My pos . . ." played out in a miniature postnational global space would begin to haunt the reader in dreaming and waking hours.

NOTES

A Chinese version of the present essay was presented at the occasion of another conference on freedom and writing held at Brown University, Providence, Rhode Island, March 22–23, 1996. The symposium "Writing and Freedom—Chinese Writing and *Fin de Siècle* Anxiety," jointly sponsored by the International Writing Program at Brown University and *Tendency Quarterly* (a diaspora publication), was attended by Chinese writers, poets, and critics from the Mainland, Taiwan, Hong Kong, and the United States. The essay in Chinese has been previously published in *Tendency Quarterly* 7–8 (fall 1996). I wish to thank Mayfair Yang for inviting me to contribute to the volume and for her, Benjamin Lee's and Lydia Liu's helpful comments and suggestions for the revision of this paper. All translations from Chinese in the essay are mine.

1 Wang Dewei, in an article on the state of fin de siècle Chinese literature, outlines the scenario: "Chinese writers are now busily traveling abroad or settling in diaspora. . . . Due to the increasing ease and speed of international transportation or communication, and due to the volatile changes in political climates, writers crossing the [Taiwan] strait or even faring to farther lands have become a new scene in the literary world. Leave-taking and homesickness have always been an important theme in modern Chinese fiction. The experience of such frequent migrations are definitively adding a new dimension to this theme" (Wang 1993: 151).

2 Zha Jianying is the author of *China Pop: How Soap Operas, Tabloids, and Bestsellers Are Transforming a Culture* (1995).

3 Since I am dealing here primarily with literary writings in Chinese published in *Today*, the acclaimed autobiographical writings in English by Anchee Min (Min Anqi) and Jung Chang (Zhang Rong) (*Wild Swans*) are not discussed. I wish to point out that the controversial autobiography *Manhatunde Zhongguo nüren* (A Chinese woman in Manhattan) by Zhou Li, who in the book recounts the story of her success in America, constitutes another aspect of recent diaspora writing by Chinese women.

Zhang Zhen

≈ 334 ≈

4 I do not include poetry here either, although Hong Ying and Xie Ye were first known as poets. As a poet myself I have also published numerous poems in *Today*. Zhai Yongming, an important woman poet, lived in the United States in the early nineties but has since returned to China with her painter husband. As a whole, women poets do not form a diaspora writing as salient as the prose writers, partly due to the small number living outside China. I think it also has to do with the predominance of male poets who are the "original" and present arbiters of *Today* and whose international visibility overshadows women's poetry writing.

5 Hansen critically applies the concept of the "horizon of social experience" coined by the German filmmakers and critics Alexander Kluge and Oskar Negt to her theory of spectatorship in American silent film. She was, however, quick to point out that Kluge and Negt, in their attentiveness to the female dimension of the public sphere, were caught in "their own idealization of a feminine, that is, maternal mode of production." Dana Polan in his essay "The Public's Fear; Or, Media as Monster in Habermas, Negt, and Kluge" argues that despite their professed intention to critique Habermas, Kluge and Negt shared with him a "nostalgia" for a pristine realm before the media explosion (Polan 1993). This nostalgia perhaps to some degree explains the uncritical exaltation of the maternal in their conception of an alternative public sphere.

6 Since the handover of Hong Kong in 1997, the journal has been printed in Taiwan.

7 The Chinese original title *Huntun gale geleng* (1994) is an onomatopoeic compound phrase connoting the original cosmic, undifferentiated (dis)order and has a comic tone to it.

8 Attempts to theorize "female consciousness" are often fraught with danger of derailment, or sliding into the shackles of essentializing the "female." Poststructuralist feminist theories have sent warnings to any hasty conceptualization of "female writing" as a distinctive aesthetic entity. Even critics like Luce Irigaray and Hélène Cixous, who were most vociferous in naming *écriture féminine*, have expressed their hesitation to define what constitutes the very category of women. They are aware that any *exclusive* subjectivity or aesthetics cannot divorce itself from the existing knowledge structures that have permeated and complicated gender formations (Moi 1985).

9 The New Culture movement refers to the large-scale social movement by young modernizers and radical intellectuals that took place in the late 1910s and early 1920s. The two major objectives of the movement were democracy and science (Chow 1967).

10 Here is the whole quotation: "What is realized in my history is not the past definite of what was, since it is no more, or even the present perfect of what has been in what I am, but the future anterior of what I shall have been for what I am in the process of becoming" (Lacan 1977: 86).

Afterword

Mayfair Mei-hui Yang

At the end of a book, there is often a summing up, a reiteration of key points, a resolution of contradictions and debates, and a movement of the discussion to a higher plane of abstraction, generalization, and profundity. Here, I will not attempt any of these moves, because this book is mainly a beginning to an inquiry into the development of a Chinese women's public space and public sphere, and this important subject has by no means been exhausted. The dispersed but increasingly interconnected modern Chinese cultures in which a Chinese women's public sphere is forming at the turn of this century are vast not only in terms of population and geographical space, but also in terms of its internal complexity, due to both the deep historical lineages of this ancient cultural formation as well as the incredible and incessant transformations it has undergone in modernity. Given this vastness and complexity, this afterword will reflect on the areas we were not able to cover in this book, as a way of suggesting fruitful avenues for future research by others.

The examples of women's public expression presented in this volume have mainly been those of professional and intellectual women. There is a vast unexplored area of women's voices coming from the working class, popular culture, and the peasantry. We need to find out if and how women of other social classes have also come to recognize themselves as a gender collectivity, and the forms in which they have organized and represented themselves. What are the forms of women's associations and networks among the working and peasant classes? What forms of expression and which issues of concern emerge for working-class and peasant women? What are the relationships and linkages between professional and intellectual women's public sphere and that of workers and peasants? How do feminist stances get communicated in working-class and peasant cultures?

If print is not the main medium of choice for working-class and peasant women, through which other media or communicative forms do they express their concerns? Since popular culture entails not just the positioning and representation of women by male cultural production (although this is a major part), perhaps we need to examine more closely the influence of the growing realms of popular culture and popular music, which are readily accessible to a mass public through cassette tapes, CDs, film theaters, radio, dance halls, karaoke bars, video parlors, and of course, television. In this endeavor, we must pay more attention to women's reception. The processes of selection, interpretation, and embodiment of styles and attitudinal stances to the world through singing, dancing, and talking about cultural products are all part of the reception of popular culture. What desires for men are young girls expressing when their hearts ache for such Taiwan pop music idols like Liu Dehua and Zhang Guoyou? Thus popular culture reception becomes a form of expression that must not be neglected as a potential women's public space.

Unlike workers and peasants who form the majority of the population, gays and lesbians are a small minority constituency in Chinese culture. In Taiwan and Hong Kong, they have become publicly vocal in the past decade (Zhuang 1991), as Debra Sang's piece in this book shows, and as transnational films such as *The Wedding Banquet* (a Taiwan-U.S. production) by Ang Lee, *Vivre l'Amour* by Ts'ai Ming-liang (Taiwan), Stanley Kwan's *Yang and Yin: Gender in the Chinese Cinema* (Hong Kong), and Wong Kar-wei's *Happy Together* (Hong Kong) exemplify. In the Mainland, gay and lesbian sexual practice has just begun to be publicly recognized and discussed (Zhang 1994) as a possibility in the human sexual repertoire, although few spokespersons have as yet emerged to weather the strong social stigma involved in forming a gay public sphere. Closed off to the outside world for several decades by a state-ordered economy and discourse that seldom spoke of sexuality and knew very little about homosexual practice, mainland China is now an especially relevant site for exploring the relationship between capitalist desiring production and the emergence of gay and lesbian practice and subjectivity. In the emerging gay culture of China's eastern seaboard cities, we can examine what effects gay sexuality may have on the dominant patriarchal sexuality, now strengthened by the strong male business culture and its various forms of sexual entertainment establishments. It would also be worthwhile for future researchers to look at how a Chinese feminist public sphere relates to any gay public sphere that might be established, and whether the relationship would also be one of alliance such as in the West.

In the Hong Kong and Taiwanese gay communities can be seen the beginnings of links being made with gay people in the Mainland. Several investigative reports on gays in the Mainland have been published in recent years in Taiwan and Hong Kong (An 1995; Li and Wang 1991), where the new form of address among gays, "comrades" (*tongzhi*), which borrows irreverently from mainland terminology, is beginning to make its way back to the Mainland. Although Lee Yuan-chen in our book has described some ties between her Awakening Foundation in Taiwan and feminist sisters on the Mainland, such as the 1990 women's conference in Zhengzhou organized by Li Xiaojiang, this collection was not able to present more interconnections between women in the Mainland and in the two Chinese offshoot communities. If Shu-mei Shih's conclusion is right, then this is because male nationalist and political/ideological borders are too strong to allow even feminists to bridge them. However, with the return of Hong Kong to "the Motherland," there will be more financial, political, and cultural flows between these two Chinese entities. It will be very valuable to see what happens to the Hong Kong feminist grassroots organizations that emerged in the 1980s and '90s. Will they continue to exist or will they be replaced by the state Women's Federation of the north? If they are not closed down, will they also start speaking for a larger body of Chinese women north across the border, now that they are incorporated as part of China?

More discussions of interconnections with another community are needed—that is, what are the transnational conjunctions between a Chinese-language women's public sphere with a Chinese American public sphere? The United States is the country with the largest Chinese diasporic population in the West. Although a Chinese American public sphere has formed in the United States in the past two decades, and Chinese American literature, film, and television (Yang 1997) have developed, except for television, most of these forms are in the English language. Thus, Chinese American discourse has mainly engaged in dialogues with other ethnic publics in the States, especially the dominant Euroamerican one, and the links between Chinese American and Chinese publics abroad have been quite limited. With the growing numbers of first-generation Chinese immigrants in America and Chinese transnationals who make two countries their homes, we can look forward to increasing cultural production at the intersection of these two publics.

Finally, we need to look at two new media for public communication in transnational China, the Internet and the video compact disc (VCD). While Internet participation in Taiwan and Hong Kong has drawn a significant proportion of the educated population, in mainland China there were only an estimated 150,000 users in 1997 (Barmé and Sang 1997: 140), although this figure was growing at a rapid rate. Despite the fact that the Internet is heavily state monitored (especially in the Mainland), and very commercialized (filled with mail-order shopping opportunities), and although it is still largely a male arena of discussion, it nevertheless presents new possibilities for locating a transnational Chinese women's public space that would help link up women's discussions in the different Chinese realms, as Tze-lan Deborah Sang's essay here suggests. The VCD offers a new way of storing feature films that has become both popular and pervasive with amazing speed in urban homes in the latter half of the 1990s. Its compact size, portability, and cheaper price compared with the old VHS videotapes means that, besides the usual best-seller or most current popular Chinese films, audiences will be exposed to a larger repertoire of Chinese-language films, including those from the old Shanghai film industry of the 1920s–30s, the Maoist era, and Hong Kong and Taiwan. This larger selection will mean that audiences might be stimulated by the sharp contrasts in gender styles and ideologies of different times and places to reflect on Chinese gender, and they can draw on a wider, more historical repertoire of gender practices with which to ponder and debate gender issues.

This book is offered in the hope that this ongoing project of carving out a space for a Chinese women's public can be expanded and deepened by other women, whether by those from within Chinese culture, or observers from without, who care about the future of Chinese women and Chinese culture.

Bibliography

Ah Cheng. 1992. "Qi Wang" (The chess king). In *Napen lizi, napen yingtao: xungeng xiaoshuo* (That bowl of pears, that bowl of cherries: The roots-searching novel), ed. Liu Zhi. Beijing: Beijing shifan daxue chubanshe.

Abbas, Ackbar. 1997. *Hong Kong: Culture and the Politics of Disappearance.* Minneapolis: University of Minnesota Press.

———. 1994. "Building on Disappearance: Hong Kong Architecture and the City." *Public Culture* 6: 441–59.

———. 1993. "The Last Emporium: Verse and Cultural Space." *positions: east asia cultures critique* 1(1): 1–23.

Abu-Lughod, Lila. 1993. "Editorial Comment: On Screening Politics in a World of Nations." *Public Culture* 5: 465–68.

Afshar, Haleh. 1987. "Women, Marriage and the State in Iran." In *Women, State, and Ideology,* ed. Haleh Afshar. Albany: SUNY Press.

Ai bao (Love journal). 1993 to present.

Alcoff, Linda. 1994. "Cultural Feminism." In *Culture/Power/History,* ed. Nichols B. Dirks, Geoff Eley, and Sherry B. Ortner. Princeton, N.J.: Princeton University Press.

Allison, Anne. 1994. *Nightwork: Sexuality, Pleasure, and Corporate Masculinity in a Tokyo Hostess Club.* Chicago: University of Chicago Press.

An Keqiang. 1996. "Prelude." *G & L: Re'ai zazhi* (G & L: Passion magazine) 1: 8.

———. 1995. *Hong taiyang xia de hei linghun* (Black souls under the red sun). Taipei: Shibao wenhua.

Anagnost, Ann. 1997. *National Past-Times: Narrative, Representation, and Power in Modern China.* Durham: Duke University Press.

Anderson, Barbara Gallatin. 1990. *First Fieldwork: The Misadventures of an Anthropologist.* Prospect Heights, Ill.: Waveland Press.

Anderson, Benedict. 1991. *Imagined Communities.* London: Verso.

Andors, Phyllis. 1983. *The Unfinished Revolution of Chinese Women: 1949–80*. Bloomington: University of Indiana Press.

Anonymous. 1988. *Qiu Ji: Yige shijixing xuanze* (Global citizenship: The choice of the century). Beijing: Baijia chubanshe.

Appadurai, Arjun. 1996. *Modernity at Large: Cultural Dimensions of Globalization*. Minneapolis: University of Minnesota Press.

———. 1993. "Disjuncture and Difference in the Global Cultural Economy." In Robbins 1993, 269–95.

Appadurai, Arjun, and Carol Breckenridge. 1988. "Why Public Culture?" *Public Culture* 1(1): 5–9.

Appelbaum, Richard P., and Jeffrey Henderson, eds. 1992. *States and Development in the Asian Pacific Rim*. Thousand Oaks, Calif.: Sage Publications.

Ash, Robert, and Y. Y. Kueh. 1993. "Economic Integration within Greater China: Trade and Investment Flows between China, Hong Kong and Taiwan." *China Quarterly* 136 (December).

Austin, J. L. 1962. *How to Do Things with Words*. Cambridge: Harvard University Press.

Baker, Houston A. 1994. "Critical Memory and the Black Public Sphere." *Public Culture* 7(1).

Barbin, Herculine. 1980. *Herculine Barbin: Being the Recently Discovered Memoirs of a Nineteenth-Century French Hermaphrodite*, M. Foucault. New York: Pantheon.

Barlow, Tani. 1994a. "Politics and Protocols of *Funü*: (Un)Making National Woman." In Gilmartin et al. 1994, 339–59.

———. 1994b. "Theorizing Woman: *Funü, Guojia, Jiating* (Chinese Woman, Chinese State, Chinese Family)." In *Body, Subject and Power in China*, ed. Angela Zito and Tani E. Barlow, 253–89. Chicago: University of Chicago Press.

———. 1991. "*Zhishifenzi* (Chinese Intellectuals) and Power." *Dialectical Anthropology* 16: 209–32.

———. 1989. "Asian Perspective." *Gender and History* 1(3): 318–29.

Barmé, Geremie R., and Sang Ye. 1997. "The Great Firewall of China." *Wired* 5(6): 138–50, 174–78.

Baudrillard, Jean. 1988. *Selected Writings*, trans. Mark Poster. Stanford, Calif.: Stanford University Press.

———. 1986. "Requiem for the Media." In *Video Culture: A Critical Investigation*, ed. John Hanhardt. Rochester, N.Y.: Visual Studies Workshop Press.

Beahan, Charlotte L. 1981. "In the Public Eye: Women in Early Twentieth-Century China." In *Women in China: Current Directions in Historical Scholarship*. New York: Philo Press.

Beida xuetongshe (Beijing University student news agency). 1985. "Yingle jiu huanying, shule jiu ye huanying" (Popular after winning the ball game, also popular after losing the ball game). November 29.

Belenky, Mary Field, Blythe McVicker Clinchy, Nancy Rule Goldberger, and Jill Mattuck Tarule. 1986. *Women's Ways of Knowing: The Development of Self, Voice and Mind*. New York: Basic Books.

Benjamin, Walter. 1977. *The Origin of German Tragic Drama*. London: Verso.

———. 1970. *Illuminations*, ed. Hannah Arendt. London: Jonathan Cape.

———. 1968. "The Work of Art in the Age of Mechanical Reproduction." In *Illuminations*, ed. Hannah Arendt. New York: Schocken.

Bergstrom, Janet and Mary Ann Doane. 1990. "The Female Spectator: Contexts and Directions," *Camera Obscura* 20–21.

Berry, Chris. 1994. "Neither One Thing nor Another: Toward a Study of the Viewing Subject and Chinese Cinema in the 1980's." In Browne et al. 1994.

———. 1991. "Market Forces: China's 'Fifth Generation' Faces the Bottom Line." In *Perspectives on Chinese Cinema,* ed. Chris Berry. London: British Film Institute.

Bhabha, Homi K. 1994. *The Location of Culture.* New York: Routledge.

———. 1990. *Nation and Narration.* London: Routledge.

Billeter, Jean-Francois. 1985. "The System of 'Class-Status.'" In *The Scope of State Power in China,* ed. Stuart R. Schram. London: School of Oriental and African Studies.

Borneman, John. 1998. "Toward a Theory of Ethnic Cleansing: Territorial Sovreignty, Heterosexuality, and Europe." In *Subversions of International Order.* Albany: State University of New York Press.

Bourdieu, Pierre. 1990. *The Logic of Practice.* Stanford, Calif.: Stanford University Press.

Bowen, Elizabeth Smith (alias Laura Bohannan). 1964. *Return to Laughter: An Anthropological Novel.* New York: Anchor Books/Doubleday.

Bray, Francesca. 1997. *Technology and Gender: Fabrics of Power in Late Imperial China.* Berkeley and Los Angeles: University of California Press.

Brooks, Peter. 1993. *Body Work: Objects of Desire in Modern Narrative.* Cambridge: Harvard University Press.

Brown, Wendy. 1992. "Finding the Man in the State," *Feminist Studies* 18, no. 1.

Browne, Nick. 1994. "Introduction." In Browne et al. 1994, 1–13.

Browne, Nick, Paul Pickowicz, Vivian Sobchack, and Esther Yau, eds. 1994. *New Chinese Cinemas.* Cambridge: Cambridge University Press.

Brownell, Susan. 1996. "Representing Gender in the Chinese Nation: Chinese Sportswomen and Beijing's Bid for the 2000 Olympics." *Identities* 2(3): 223–47.

———. 1995. *Training the Body for China: Sports in the Moral Order of the People's Republic.* Chicago: University of Chicago Press.

Butler, Judith. 1993. *Bodies That Matter: On the Discursive Limits of "Sex."* New York: Routledge.

Calhoun, Craig. 1994. *Neither Gods nor Emperors: Students and the Struggle for Democracy in China.* Berkeley and Los Angeles: University of California Press.

———, ed. 1992. *Habermas and the Public Sphere.* Cambridge, Mass.: MIT Press.

Cao Xiangjun. 1985. *Tiyu Gailun (General theory of physical culture).* Beijing: Beijing Institute of Physical Education Press.

Carlitz, Katherine. 1994. "Desire, Danger and the Body: Stories of Women's Virtue in Late Ming China." In Gilmartin et al. 1994, 101–24.

Castells, Manuel. 1992. "Four Asian Tigers with a Dragon Head: A Comparative Analysis of the State, Economy, and Society in the Asian Pacific." In *States and Development in the Asian Pacific Rim,* ed. Richard P. Appelbaum and Jeffrey Henderson. Thousand Oaks, Calif.: Sage Publications.

Chan, Cecilia L. W., and Nelson W. S. Chow. 1992. *More Welfare after Reform? Welfare Development in the People's Republic of China.* Hong Kong: University of Hong Kong.

Chan, Cindy, and Law Kar. 1996. "Cantonese Movies of the Sixties: An Oral History by Chan Wan." *Hong Kong Urban Council Publications* 107–14.

Chan, Man Joseph. 1987. *Shifting Journalistic Paradigms: Mass Media and Political Transition in*

Hong Kong. Hong Kong: Centre for Hong Kong Studies, Chinese University of Hong Kong.

Chang Won Ho. 1989. *Mass Media in China: The History and the Future.* Ames: Iowa State University Press.

Chang, Jung (Zhang Rong). 1992. *Wild Swans: Three Daughters of China.* New York: Anchor.

Chatterjee, Partha. 1993. *The Nation and Its Fragments: Colonial and Postcolonial Histories.* Princeton, N.J.: Princeton University Press.

Chen Dongyuan. 1928. *Zhongguo funü shenghuo shi* (The history of the lives of Chinese women). Shanghai: Shangwu yinshuguan. Reprinted in 1970, Taipei: Taiwan Shangwu yinshuguan.

———. 1927. "Guanyu 'Guangdong de buluojia he zishu'" (Regarding 'the deferred marriage transfer and spinsterhood in Canton'). *Xin nüxing* (New woman) 2(2): 203–6.

Chen Ran. 1995. "Po kai" (Breaking up). *Hua Chen Review* no. 6.

———. 1993. "Chao xingbie yishi yu wo de chuangzuo" (Gender transcendent consciousness and my creative writing). *Zhong Shan Review* no. 6.

———. 1992a. "Wuchu gaobie" (No place to say goodbye). In *Kua shiji wencong, Zuichen li de yangguang: Chen Ran xiaoshuo xuan* (Fin de Siècle Literary Collection, Sunshine between the Lips: Selected Stories by Chen Ran), ed. Chen Juntao. Beijing: Changjiang wenyi chubanshe.

———. 1992b. "Yuwang shi ganbei" (A toast to the past). In *Kua shiji wencong, Zuichen li de yangguang: Chen Ran xiaoshuo xuan* (Fin de Siècle Literary Collection, Sunshine between the Lips: Selected Stories by Chen Ran), ed. Chen Juntao. Beijing: Changjiang wenyi chubanshe.

Chen, Nancy. 1995. "Urban Spaces and Experiences of Qigong." In *Urban Spaces in Contemporary China,* ed. Deborah Davis et al., 347–61. New York: Cambridge University Press.

Cheng, Lucy, and Ping-chun Hsiung. 1992. "Women, Export-Oriented Growth, and the State: The Case of Taiwan." In *States and Development in the Asia Pacific Rim,* ed. Richard Appelbaum and Jeffrey Henderson. Thousand Oaks, Calif.: Sage Publications.

Cheng Ying. 1995. "The Typology of New Immigrant Faces in Light of 1997" (xinyimin de jiuqi lianpu). *The Nineties* no. 301 (February): 127–31.

Chi Li. 1993. "Ning mou" (Gazing). *Planned Murder: Recent Works by Chi Li.* Beijing: Zhongguo shehui kexue chubanshe.

Chi Zijian. 1995. "Xiangzhe baiye luxing" (A journey into the white night). In *Red Opium Poppy Collection: Selected Stories by Chi Zijian,* ed. Wang Meng. Press Shijiazhuang: Hebei jiayu chubanshe.

Chiao Hsiung-ping [Jiao Xiongping]. 1993. "'Trafficking' in Chinese Films," trans. John Balcom. *Modern Chinese Literature* 7(2): 97–101.

China News Digest (Internet news service). 1995a. "Ma Junren Talks about His Old Army," March 24–25, 5.

———. 1995b. "Global News Briefs" (Xinhua Chinese News Agency). November 22.

China Quarterly. 1993. Special issue on "Greater China." December.

Choi Po-king. 1995. "Identities and Diversities: Hong Kong Women's Movement in 1980's and 1990's." *Hong Kong Cultural Studies Bulletin* 4 (Winter).

———. 1993. "Women." In *The Other Hong Kong Report,* ed. by Choi Po-king and Ho Lok-sang, 370–400. Hong Kong: Chinese University Press.

Chow, Rey. 1993. "Things, Common/Places, Passages of the Port City: On Hong Kong and Hong Kong Author Leung Ping-kwan." *differences* 5(3): 179–204.

———. 1992. "Between Colonizers: Hong Kong's Postcolonial Self-Writing in the 1990's." *Diaspora* 2(2).

———. 1991. *Women and Chinese Modernity*. Minneapolis: University of Minnesota Press.

Chow Tse-tsung. 1967. *The May Fourth Movement: Intellectual Revolution in Modern China*. Stanford, Calif.: Stanford University Press.

Chu Yiu Wai and Wai Man Sin. 1995. "Between Legal and Cultural Colonialism: The Politics of Legitimation of the Cultural Production in Hong Kong." Paper presented at the Seventh Quadrennial International Comparative Literature Conference, Tamsui, Taiwan.

Chun, Allen. 1996. "Discourses of Identity in the Changing Spaces of Public Culture in Taiwan, Hong Kong and Singapore." *Theory, Culture and Society* 13(1).

———. 1994. "From Nationalism to Nationalizing: Cultural Imagination and State Formation in Postwar Taiwan." *Australian Journal of Chinese Affairs* no. 31.

Cixous, Hélène. 1993. "We Who Are Free, Are We Free?" *Critical Inquiry* 19(2): 201–19.

Clark, Constance. Forthcoming. "Migrations, Markets and Marriage: Gender Dilemmas among Shenzhen Youth." In *Ethnographies of the Urban: China in the 1990s*, ed. Nancy Chen, Constance Clark, Virginia Cornue, Suzanne Gottschang, and Lyn Jeffery. Durham, N.C.: Duke University Press.

Clarke, David. 1996. *Art and Place: Essays on Art from a Hong Kong Perspective*. Hong Kong: Hong Kong University Press.

Clifford, James. 1992. "Traveling Cultures." In *Cultural Studies*, ed. Lawrence Grossberg. New York: Routledge.

———. 1988. *The Predicament of Culture*. Cambridge, Mass.: Harvard University Press.

Cohen, Jean, and Andrew Arato. 1992. *Civil Society and Political Theory*. Cambridge, Mass.: MIT Press.

Cohn, Carol. 1987. "Sex and Death in the Rational World of Defense Intellectuals." *Signs* 12(4): 687–718.

Cornue, Virginia. Forthcoming. "Love, Sex and New Social Forms: Producing Identity and Organization in Contemporary Beijing." In *Ethnographies of the Urban: China in the 1990s*, ed. Nancy Chen et al. Durham, N.C.: Duke University Press.

———. 1995. "What in the World Is an NGO? An Organizational Self-Definition Study." Unpublished survey conducted during the UN Fourth World Conference on Women, Beijing, People's Republic of China.

Cornue, Virginia, Joan Boyle, and Christina K. Gilmartin. 1998. "Morals and the Market: Factoring in Gender." In *Ethics and Social Change: Cultural Values in Transition in Late Twentieth-Century China*. Oakdale, N.Y.: Dowling College Press.

Cott, Nancy F. 1987. *The Grounding of Modern Feminism*. New Haven, Conn.: Yale University Press.

Croll, Elizabeth. 1995. *Changing Identities of Chinese Women*. London: Zed Books.

Dai Jinhua. 1995a. "Invisible Women: Contemporary Chinese Cinema and Women's Film," trans. Mayfair Yang, *positions* 3(1): 255–80.

———. 1995b. *Jing yu shisu shenhua* (The mirror and common myths). Beijing: Zhongguo Guangbo dianshi chubanshe.

Dai Jinhua, and Mayfair Yang. 1995. "A Conversation with Huang Shuqin." *positions* 3(3).

Davis, Deborah. 1993. "Urban Households: Supplicants to a Socialist State." In *Chinese*

Families in the Post-Mao Era, ed. Deborah Davis and Stevan Harrell. Berkeley and Los Angeles: University of California Press.

Dean, Kenneth, and Brian Massumi. 1992. *First and Last Emperors: The Absolute State and the Body of the Despot*. Brooklyn, N.Y.: Autonomedia.

Deleuze, Gilles and Félix Guattari. 1983. *Anti-Oedipus: Capitalism and Schizophrenia*, trans. Robert Hurley, Mark Seem, and Helen R. Lane. Minneapolis: University of Minnesota Press.

D'Emilio, John. 1983. *Sexual Politics, Sexual Communities: The Making of a Homosexual Minority in the United States, 1940–1970*. Chicago: University of Chicago Press.

Dikötter, Frank. 1990. "Group Definition and the Idea of 'Race' in Modern China (1793–1949)." *Ethnic and Racial Studies* 13(3): 420–13.

Ding Ling. 1936. *Shujia zhong* (Summer break). In *Ding Ling wenxuan* (Selected writings by Ding Ling). Shanghai: Qizhi shuju, 145–206. Originally published in 1928.

Dissanayake, Wimal, ed. 1994. *Colonialism and Nationalism in Asian Cinema*. Bloomington: Indiana University Press.

Dölling, Irene. 1993. "'But the Pictures Stay the Same . . .' The Image of Women in the Journal *Fur Dich* before and after the 'Turning Point.'" In *Gender Politics and Post-Communism: Reflections from Eastern Europe and the Former Soviet Union*, ed. Nanette Funk and Magda Mueller. New York: Routledge.

Du Yuenji. 1986. *Seventy Years of Chinese Cinema 1904–1972*. Taipei: Zhonghuaminguo dianying tushuguan chubanbu.

Duara, Prasenjit. 1995a. "Of Authenticity and Woman: Personal Narratives of Middle-Class Women in Modern China." Paper prepared for the conference on Becoming Chinese: Passages to Modernity and Beyond, 1900–1950, June 2–4, Berkeley, Calif.

———. 1995b. *Rescuing History from the Nation: Questioning Narratives of Modern China*. Chicago: University of Chicago Press.

Eisenstein, Zillah. 1989. "Reflections on a Politics of Difference." In *Promissory Notes: Women in the Transition to Socialism*, ed. Sonia Kruks, Rayna Rapp, and Marilyn Young. New York: Monthly Review Press.

Eley, Geoff. 1994. "Nations, Publics, and Political Cultures: Placing Habermas in the Nineteenth Century." In *Culture/Power/History* ed. Nicholas Dirks, Sherry Ortner, and Geoff Eley. Princeton, N.J.: Princeton University Press.

———. 1992. "Nations, Publics, and Political Cultures: Placing Habermas in the Nineteenth Century." In Calhoun 1992, 289–339.

Ellis, Havelock. 1944. *The Psychology of Sex: A Manual for Students*. 2nd ed. New York: Emerson Books.

———. 1920. "Appendix: The School-Friendships of Girls." In *Sexual Inversion: Studies in the Psychology of Sex, Volume II*. 3rd ed., 368–84. Philadelphia: F. A. Davis.

Elvin, Mark. 1984. "Female Virtue and the State." *China: Past and Present* 104: 111–52.

Encyclopedia of New China. 1987. Beijing: Foreign Languages Press.

Engels, Friedrich. 1975. *Origins of the Family, Private Property, and the State*. New York: Pathfinder Press. Originally published in 1896.

Enloe, Cynthia. 1989. *Bananas, Beaches, and Bases: Making Feminist Sense of International Politics*. Berkeley and Los Angeles: University of California Press.

Enzensberger, Hans M. 1986. "Constitutents of a Theory of Media." In *Video Culture: A Critical Investigation*, ed. John Hanhardt. Rochester, N.Y.: Visual Studies Workshop Press.

Erwin, Kathleen. 1998. "Liberating Sex, Mobilizing Virtue: Cultural Reconstructions of

Gender, Marriage, and Family in Shanghai, China," Ph.D. diss., University of California, Berkeley.

Esmein, Jean. 1973. *The Chinese Cultural Revolution.* Garden City, N.Y.: Anchor Books.

Evans, Harriet. 1995. "Defining Difference: The 'Scientific' Construction of Sexuality and Gender in the People's Republic of China." *Signs* 20(2): 357–94.

Faderman, Lillian. 1981. *Surpassing the Love of Men: Romantic Friendship and Love between Women from the Renaissance to the Present.* New York: William Morrow.

Feng Xiaotian. 1992. *Bianqian zhong de nuxin xinxiang—dui "Zhongguo Funu" zhazhi de neirong fenxi* (Images of women in the midst of change: A content analysis of the journal *Chinese Women*), *Shehui* (Society), no. 90.

Fiske, John. 1987. *Television Culture.* New York: Routledge.

Flax, Jane. 1987. "Postmodernism and Gender Relations in Feminist Theory," *Signs* 12, no. 4.

Fonoroff, Paul. 1988. "A Brief History of Hong Kong Cinema." *Renditions* 29/30: 293–308.

Ford Foundation. 1995. *Reflections and Resonance: Stories of Chinese Women in International Preparatory Activities for the 1995 NGO Forum on Women.* N.l.: Ford Foundation.

Foucault, Michel. 1991. "Governmentality." In *The Foucault Effect: Studies in Governmentality,* ed. G. Burchell, C. Gordon, and P. Miller. Chicago: University of Chicago Press.

———. 1990. *The History of Sexuality. Volume I: An Introduction,* trans. Robert Hurley. New York: Vintage Books.

———. 1989. "Film and Popular Memory." In *Foucault Live: Collected Interviews 1961–1984,* ed. Sylvère Lotringer, trans. Lysa Hochroth and John Johnston, 122–75. New York: Semiotext(e).

———. 1979. *Discipline and Punish: The Birth of the Prison.* New York: Vintage Books.

———. 1975. "Film and Popular Memory." *Radical Philosophy* 11 (Summer): 24–29.

Fraser, Nancy. 1997. "Multiculturalism, Antiessentialism, and Radical Democracy: A Genealogy of the Current Impasse in Feminist Theory." In *Justice Interruptus: Critical Reflections on the "Postsocialist" Condition.* New York: Routledge.

———. 1992. "Rethinking the Public Sphere: A Contribution to the Critique of Actually Existing Democracy." In Calhoun 1992.

———. 1989. *Unruly Practices: Power, Discourse and Gender in Contemporary Social Theory.* Minneapolis, University of Minnesota Press.

Friedman, Edward. 1995. *National Identity and Democratic Prospects in Socialist China.* Armonk, M.E. Sharpe.

Funk, Nanette and Magda Mueller, eds. 1993. *Gender Politics and Post-Communism: Reflections from Eastern Europe and the Former Soviet Union.* New York: Routledge.

Funü Xinzhi Jijinhui (Awakening Foundation). 1994–1995. *Funü xinzhi* (Women's Awakening magazine) nos. 149–163 (September–December).

Furth, Charlotte. 1988. "Androgynous Males and Deficient Females: Biology and Gender Boundaries in Sixteenth- and Seventeenth-Century China." *Late Imperial China* 9(2).

G & L: Re'ai zazhi (G & L: Passion magazine). 1996. nos. 1–2 (June–August).

Gal, Susan. 1994. "Gender in the Post-Socialist Transition: The Abortion Debate in Hungary." *East European Politics and Societies* 8, no. 2 (Spring).

———. 1993. "Gender in the Post-Socialist Debate in Hungary." *East European Politics and Societies* 8(1).

Gao Mingxuan et al., eds. 1989. *Zhongguo xingfa cidian* (A dictionary of the Chinese criminal code). Shanghai: Xuelin chubanshe.

Garber, Marjorie. 1995. *Vice Versa: Bisexuality and the Eroticism of Everyday Life*. New York: Touchstone.

Garnham, Nicholas. 1992. "The Media Public and the Public Sphere." In Calhoun 1992.

Ge Shannan. 1992. "Shanghai jiuming nu gaogong lianming shangshu jujue tuixiou" (Nine senior female engineers in Shanghai jointly file a suit to refuse retirement), *Zhongguo funübao* (Chinese women's newspaper), July 6: 1.

Geertz, Clifford. 1973. *The Interpretation of Cultures: Selected Essays*. New York: Basic Books.

Gibson-Graham, J. K. 1996. *The End of Capitalism: A Feminist Critique of Political Economy*. Oxford: Blackwell.

Giddens, Anthony. 1990. *The Consequences of Modernity*. Stanford, Calif.: Stanford University Press.

Gilligan, Carol. 1982. *In a Different Voice: Psychological Theory and Women's Development*. Cambridge, Mass.: Harvard University Press.

Gilmartin, Christina K. 1995. *Engendering the Chinese Revolution: Radical Women, Communist Politics, and Mass Movement in the 1920s*. Berkeley and Los Angeles: University of California Press.

Gilmartin, Christina K., Gail Hershatter, Lisa Rofel, and Tyrene White, eds. 1994. *Engendering China: Women, Culture and the State*. Cambridge, Mass.: Harvard University Press.

Global Citizenship: The Choice of the Century. 1988. Beijing: Baijia Press.

Gold, Thomas B. 1995. "Go with Your Feelings: Hong Kong and Taiwan Popular Culture in Greater China." In *Greater China: The Next Superpower?* ed. David Shambaugh, 255–73. New York: Oxford University Press.

———. 1986. *State and Society in the Taiwan Miracle*. Armonk, N.Y.: M. E. Sharpe.

Golde, Peggy. 1986. *Women in the Field: Anthropological Experiences*. Berkeley and Los Angeles: University of California Press.

Goodman, David S. G. 1981. *Beijing Street Voices: The Poetry and Politics of China's Democracy Movement*. London: Marion Boyars.

Goven, Joanna. 1993. "Gender Politics in Hungary: Autonomy and Anti-Feminism" in *Gender Politics and Post-Communism: Reflections from Eastern Europe and the Former Soviet Union*. Nanette Funk, ed. New York: Routledge.

Gramsci, Antonio. 1971. *Selections from the Prison Notebooks*, trans. and ed. Quintin Hoare and Geoffrey N. Smith. New York: International Publishers.

Grewal, Inderpal, and Caren Kaplan. 1994. *Scattered Hegemonies: Postmodernity and Transnational Feminist Practices*. Minneapolis: University of Minnesota Press.

Gu Mingjun. 1995. "Kanjian he banzhuang zhi wai, nüxing zhuyi zhe daodi neng zuo sheme?" (What can feminists do besides "seeing" and "crossdressing"?). *Funü xinzhi* 159: 8–11.

Guo Lianghui. 1987. *Liangzhong yiwai de* (Beyond two kinds). Taipei: Hanlin.

Gupta, Akhil, and James Ferguson. 1997. "Beyond 'Culture': Space, Identity, and the Politics of Culture." In *Culture, Power, Place: Explorations in Critical Anthropology*. Durham, N.C.: Duke University Press.

Habermas, Jürgen. 1996. "The European Nation-State—Its Achievements and Its Limits. On the Past and Future of Sovereignty and Citizenship." In *Mapping the Nation*, ed. Gopal Balakrishnan. London: Verso, 282.

————. 1992. "Further Reflections on the Public Sphere." In Calhoun 1992.

————. 1989. *The Structural Transformation of the Public Sphere: An Inquiry into a Category of Bourgeois Society*, trans. Thomas Burger. Cambridge, Mass.: MIT Press.

————. 1987a. "Modernity's Consciousness of Time and Its Need for Self-Reassurance." In *The Philosophical Discourse of Modernity*, trans. Frederick G. Lawrence, 1–22. Cambridge, Mass.: MIT Press.

————. 1987b. *The Theory of Communicative Action*. Vol. 2: Lifeworld and System, trans. Thomas McCarthy. Boston: Beacon Press.

————. 1984. *The Theory of Communicative Action*. Vol. 1. Boston: Beacon Press.

Han Shaogong. 1992. "Ba ba ba" (Father, father, father). In *Napen lizi, napen yingtao: xungeng xiaoshuo* (That bowl of pears, that bowl of cherries: The roots-searching novel), ed. Liu Zhi. Beijing: Beijing Shifan daxue chubanshe.

————. 1985. "Wenxue de geng" (The 'roots' of literature). *Zuojia* (The writer), no. 4.

Hansen, Miriam. 1993a. "Foreword." In Negt and Kluge 1993.

————. 1993b. "Unstable Mixtures, Dilated Spheres: Negt and Kluge's *The Public Sphere and Experience*, Twenty Years Later." *Public Culture* 5(2): 179–212.

————. 1991. *Babel and Babylon: Spectatorship in American Silent Film*. Cambridge, Mass.: Harvard University Press.

————. 1990a. Special Issue on Female Spectators, *Camera Obscura*, no. 20–21.

————. 1990b. "Adventures of Goldilocks: Spectatorship, Consumerism and Public Life," *Camera Obscura*, no. 22.

Haraway, Donna. 1991. "A Cyborg Manifesto: Science, Technology, and Socialist Feminism in the Late Twentieth Century" in *Simians, Cyborgs, and Women: The Reinvention of Nature*. New York: Routledge.

————. 1985. "Teddy Bear Patriarchy: Taxidermy in the Garden of Eden, New York City, 1908–36." *Social Text* 11: 20–64.

Harding, Harry. 1995. "The Concept of 'Greater China': Themes, Variations, and Reservations." In *Greater China: The Next Superpower?* ed. David Shambaugh, 8–34. New York: Oxford University Press.

Harvey, David. 1989. *The Condition of Post-Modernity*. London: Basil Blackwell.

Hatem, Mervat. 1992. "Economic and Political Liberation in Egypt and the Demise of State Feminism," *International Journal of Middle East Studies*, no. 4.

Hau Si Kit. 1980. "Ann Hui Playing Hide and Seek with the Audience." *Film Bi-Monthly* 35: 22–24.

Hay, John. 1994. "The Body Invisible in Chinese Art?" In *Body, Subject and Power in China*, ed. Angela Zito and Tani Barlow. Chicago: University of Chicago Press.

Heng, Geraldine, and Janadas Devan. 1992. "State Fatherhood: The Politics of Nationalism, Sexuality and Race in Singapore." In *Nationalisms and Sexualities*, ed. Andrew Parker, Mary Russo, Doris Sommer, and Patricia Yaeger. New York: Routledge.

Herdt, Gilbert. 1994. "Introduction: Third Sexes and Third Genders." In *Third Sex, Third Gender: Sexual Dimorphism in Culture and History*. Cambridge: Zone Books.

Hershatter, Gail. 1996. "Sexing Modern China." In *Remapping China: Fissures in Historical Terrain*, ed. Gail Hershatter, 77–93. Stanford, Calif.: Stanford University Press.

————. 1992. "Courtesans and Streetwalkers: The Changing Discourses on Shanghai Prostitution, 1890–1949." *Journal of the History of Sexuality* 3(2): 245–69.

Hinsch, Bret. 1990. *Passions of the Cut Sleeve: The Male Homosexual Tradition in China*. Berkeley and Los Angeles: University of California Press.

Ho, Elaine Yee Lin. 1995. "Women in Exile: A Study of Hong Kong Fiction." In *Culture and Society in Hong Kong*, ed. Elizabeth Sinn, 133–59. Hong Kong: Centre of Asian Studies, University of Hong Kong.

Hong Kong Association for the Advancement of Feminism. 1993. *The Hong Kong Women's File*. Hong Kong: Association for the Advancement of Feminism.

———. 1992. *The Other Half of the Sky: Women's Movement in Hong Kong since the Post-War Years*. Hong Kong: Association for the Advancement of Feminism.

Hong Kong Cultural Studies Bulletin. 1995. Special Issue on "Northward Imaginary." No. 3 (August). Published by Hong Kong Cultural Studies Program at the Chinese University of Hong Kong.

Hong Kong Government. 1964. *Television Ordinance*. Subsidiary legislation.

Hong Ying. 1994a. "Dirty Fingers, Bottle Caps." *Today* 1: 81.

———. 1994b. "Recent Studies on Yu Hong" (Jinnian Yu Hong yanjiu). *Today* 3: 70–83.

———. 1993. "Fingernail" (Zhijia). *Today* 1: 89–90.

Honig, Emily. 1992. *Creating Chinese Ethnicity: Subei People in Shanghai, 1850–1980*. New Haven, Conn.: Yale University Press.

Honig, Emily, and Gail Hershatter. 1988. *Personal Voices: Chinese Women in the 1980's*. Stanford, Calif.: Stanford University Press.

Hook, Brian, ed. 1991. *The Cambridge Encyclopedia of China*. Cambridge: Cambridge University Press.

hooks, bell. 1984. *Feminist Theory from Margin to Center*. Boston: South End Press.

Horkheimer, Max, and Theodor Adorno. 1968. "The Culture Industry: Enlightenment as Mass Deception." In *Dialectic of Enlightenment*, trans. John Cumming. New York: Continuum. Originally published in 1944.

Hou Zhijin. 1996. "The Social Support Function of the Women's Hotline and Advantages and Disadvantages Operating the Hotline with Volunteers." Paper presented at 1996 New York Annual Regional Meetings of the Association for Asian Studies, Dowling College, Long Island, New York.

Hsiao, Hsin-huang Michael. 1992. "The Rise of Social Movements and Civil Protests." In *Political Change in Taiwan*, ed. T. J. Cheng and Stephan Haggard. Boulder, Colo.: Lynne Rienner.

Hsu Chieh-lin, Li Wen-chih, and Shiao Chyuan-jeng. 1991. *Taiwan's Asia Pacific Strategy* (Taiwan de yatai zhanlue). Taipei: Institute of National Policy Research.

Hu Shuwen. 1995a. "Yi nü chu gui" (Heterosexual women come out). *Funü xinzhi* 158.

———. 1995b. "Zhuti zao yi miandui nimen, zhishi nimen kanbujian" (The subjectivity did exist: It's you who didn't see it). *Funü xinzhi* 163: 14.

Hu Shuwen et al. 1995. "Nü tongzhi yundong chu gui" (Lesbian feminists come out—a talk). *Funü xinzhi* 161: 9–15; 162: 1–7.

Huang Manying et al. 1991. "Tansuo nanren zhibu de shijie" (Exploring a world that shuts men out). *Shibao zhoukan* (Times Weekly) 697: 32–45.

Hui On-wah Ann. 1972. "The Phases of Alain Robbe-Grillet." M.A. thesis, University of Hong Kong.

Hunan sheng fulian funü ganbu xuexiao, Hunan shengwei dangxiao funü lilun jiaoyanshi, eds. (Hunan Women's Federation Cadre School and Hunan Province Party School, Research Group on Women's Theory, eds.). 1987. *Funüxue gailun* (*Overview of Women's Studies*). Jilin: Beifang funu ertong chubanshe.

Ifumi, Arai. 1995. "Suzie Wong's China" (Susi Huang de zhongguo). *The Nineties* 302 (March): 20–21.

Irigaray, Luce. 1985. *This Sex Which Is Not One*. Ithaca, N.Y.: Cornell University Press.

Jameson, Fredric. 1986. "Third-World Literature in the Era of Multinational Capital." *Social Text* 15: 65–88.

Janeway, Elizabeth. 1980. *The Powers of the Weak*. New York: Alfred A. Knopf.

Jayawardena, Kumari. 1986. *Feminism and Nationalism in the Third World*. London: Zed Books.

Ji Dawei et al. 1995. "Xiaoyuan tongxinglian ri" (Gay and lesbian Awakening Day on campus). *Funü xinzhi* 158: 22–28.

Jia Pingwa. 1993. *Feidu* (*Abandoned City*). Beijing: Beijing chubanshe.

Jiang Anguo (Chiang An-kuo). 1994. "A Feminist Study of the News Media Surrounding the Teng Ju-wen Incident." Presented at the Conference on Women and the News Media, Taipei, December 9, 1994.

Jiang Jingfang (Chiang Ching-fang). 1994. "Eighteen Changes in the 'Home Life Section' of Newspapers after the End of Censorship." Presented at the Conference on Women and the News Media, Taipei, December 9, 1994.

Jiang Zidan. 1995. "Sang yan wei shei er shengqi" (For whom does the mulberry smoke rise?) in *Red Opium Poppy Collection: Selected Stories by Jiang Zidan*, ed. Wang Meng. Shijiazhuang: Hebei jiaoyu chubanshe.

Jing Shenghong. 1995. *Minchu nüquan yundong gaishu* (An overview of the early Republican feminist movement), *Minguo chunqiu* (Spring and autumn in the Republican period), no. 3.

Jones, Andrew. 1992. *Like a Knife: Ideology and Genre in Contemporary Chinese Popular Music*. Ithaca, N.Y.: Cornell University East Asia Program.

Judge, Joan. 1996. *Print and Politics: 'Shibao' and the Culture of Reform in Late Qing China*. Stanford, Calif.: Stanford University Press.

Kandiyoti, Deniz. 1994. "Identity and Its Discontents." In *Colonial Discourse and Post-Colonial Theory*, ed. Patrick Williams and Laura Chrisman, 376–91. New York: Columbia University Press.

Kaplan, Ann E. 1989. "Problematizing Cross-Cultural Analysis: The Case of Women in the Recent Chinese Cinema." *Wide Angle* 11(2).

Keller, Evelyn Fox. 1987. *Gender and Science*. Boston: Basic Books.

Kelly, William. 1990. "Japanese No-Noh: The Crosstalk of Public Culture in a Rural Festivity." *Public Culture* 2(2): 65–81.

Kluge, Alexander. 1981. "On Film and the Public Sphere." In *New German Critique* no. 24–25.

Kristeva, Julia. 1991. *Strangers to Ourselves*, trans. Leon S. Roudiez. New York: Columbia University Press.

———. 1986. "Women's Time." In *The Kristeva Reader*, ed. Toril Moi, 187–213. New York: Columbia University Press.

———. 1984. *The Revolution in Poetic Language*, trans. Margaret Waller. New York: Columbia University Press.

———. 1982. *Powers of Horror: An Essay in Abjection*, trans. Leon S. Roudiez. New York: Columbia University Press.

Kruks, Sonia, Rayna Rapp, and Marilyn B. Young, eds. 1989. *Promissory Notes: Women in the Transition to Socialism*. New York: Monthly Review Press.

Ku Yen-lin. 1989. "The Feminist Movement in Taiwan, 1972–87." *Bulletin of Concerned Asian Scholars* 21(1).

Kubin, Wolfgang. 1988. "Writing with Your Body: Literature as a Wound—Remarks on the Poetry of Shu Ting." *Modern Chinese Literature* 4: 149–61.

Kung, James, and Zhang Yueai. 1984. "Hong Kong Cinema and Television in the 1970s: A Perspective." *Hong Kong Urban Council Publication*, 10–14.

Lacan, Jacques. 1977. "The Function and Field of Speech and Language in Psychoanalysis." In *Écrits: A Selection*, trans. Alan Sheridan, 30–113. New York and London: W.W. Norton.

Lai Kit. 1982. "Cantonese Cinema in the 1960s: A New Perspective." *Hong Kong Urban Council Publications*, 25–31.

Lam, Perry. 1991. "Women Shoot in a New Direction." *Sunday Morning Post Guide*, July 31, 6, Hong Kong edition.

Lamphere, Louise. 1993. "The Domestic Sphere of Women and the Public World of Men: The Strengths and Limitations of an Anthropological Dichotomy." In *Gender in Cross-Cultural Perspective*, ed. Caroline B. Brettell and Carolyn F. Sargent. Englewood Cliffs, N.J.: Prentice-Hall.

Lampland, Martha. 1989. "Biographies of Liberation: Testimonials to Labor in Socialist Hungary." In Kruks et al. 1989.

Landes, Joan B. 1988. *Women and the Public Sphere in the Age of the French Revolution*. Ithaca, N.Y.: Cornell University Press.

———. 1984. "Women and the Public Sphere: A Modern Perspective." *Social Analysis* 15 (August): 20–31.

Larson, James F., and Heung-Soo Park. 1993. *Global Television and the Politics of the Seoul Olympics*. Boulder, Colo.: Westview Press.

Larson, Wendy. 1993. "Female Subjectivity and Gender Relations: The Early Stories of Lu Yin and Bing Xin." In *Politics, Ideology, and Literary Discourse in Modern China*, ed. Liu Kang and Xiaobing Tang. Durham, N.C.: Duke University Press.

Lavie, Smadar. 1990. *The Poetics of Military Occupation*. Berkeley and Los Angeles: University of California Press.

Law Kar. 1984. "The 'Shaolin Temple' of the New Hong Kong Cinema." *Hong Kong Urban Council Publications*, 110–14.

Leacock, Eleanor. 1978. "Women's Status in Egalitarian Society: Implications for Social Evolution." *Current Anthropology* 199(2).

Lee, Benjamin. 1993. "Going Public." *Public Culture* 5(2): 165–78.

Lee, Leo Ou-fan. 1995. "Xianggang wenhua de bianyuanxing chutan" (Preliminary observations on the marginality of Hong Kong culture). *Jintian* (Today) 1 (28).

———. 1994. "Two Films from Hong Kong: Parody and Allegory." In Browne et al. 1994.

Lee, Quentin. 1994. "Delineating Asian (Hong Kong) Intellectuals: Speculations on Intellectual Problematics and Post/Coloniality." *Third Text* 26 (Spring): 11–23.

Lee Yuan-chen. 1995. *Nüren shi yan* (Women's poetic eye). Taipei: Taibei xianli wenhua zhongxin.

———. 1990. *Liberate Love and Beauty*, ed. Cheng Chih-hui. Taipei: Women's Awakening Foundation.

———. 1988. *Nüren kaibu zou* (Women boldly striding forward). Taipei: Women's Awakening Foundation.

————. 1986. *Funü yundong de huigu yu zhanwang* (A retrospective and prospective view of the women's movement), *Funü xinzhi zazhi* (Women's Awakening Journal), no. 53.

Lefebvre, Henri. 1991. *The Production of Space*, trans. Donald Nicholson-Smith. Oxford: Blackwell.

Lei Feng. 1968. *The Diary of Lei Feng* (Lei Feng riji), ed. Memorial to Lei Feng, Chairman Mao's Good Soldier.

Leung, Ping-kwan. 1995. *Hong Kong Culture*. Hong Kong: Hong Kong Arts Centre.

Li Cheuk-to. 1994. "The Return of the Father: Hong Kong New Wave and Its Chinese Context in the 1980's." In Browne et al. 1994.

————. 1993. *Viewing the Rebels: An Anthology*. Hong Kong: Qiwenhuatang.

————. 1982. "Survival Is the Most Important: An Interview with Ann Hui." *Film Bi-Monthly* 96: 19–23.

Li Xiaojiang. 1996. *Tiaozhan yü Huiying* (Challenge and response). Zhengzhou: Henan People's Press.

————. 1995. *Shehui yanjiu* (Sociological research), no. 1.

————. 1994a. "Economic Reform and the Awakening of Chinese Women's Collective Consciousness." In Gilmartin et al. 1994.

————. 1994b. "Introduction." In *I Wish I Was a Wolf: The New Voice in Chinese Women's Literature*, ed. and trans. Diana B. Kingsbury. Beijing: New World Press.

————. 1994c. *Sex and China*. Beijing: Sanlian Press.

————. 1992. *Women, a Distant Beautiful Legend* (Nuren: Yige youyuan meili de chuanshuo). Taipei: Women's Awakening Foundation.

————. 1990. "Zouxiang nüren" (Toward woman). In Gu Yanling, *Cong "ren" dao "nüren"* (From person to woman). *Nüxingren* 4(9).

————. 1988a. *Xiawa de Tansuo* (Explorations of Eve). Zhengzhou: Henan People's Press.

————. 1988b. "Gaige he Zhongguo Nüxing qunti yishi de juexing "(Economic Reform and the Awakening of Chinese Women's Collective Consciousness). *Shehui Kexue Zhanxian* (Social science battlefront) 4: 300–10.

Li Xiaojiang and Tan Shen, eds. 1991a. *Zhongguo Funü Fenceng Yanjiu* (Research on Chinese women). Zhengzhou: Henan People's Press.

————. 1991b. *Funü Yanjiu Zai Zhongguo* (Women's Research in China). Zhengzhou: Henan People's Press.

Li Xiaojiang and Xiaodan Zhang. 1994. "Creating a Space for Women: Women's Studies in China in the 1980's." *Signs* 20, no. 1 (Autumn).

Li Yinhe. 1997. '*Lao san jie*' *nuxing de qingchunqi* (The sexual life of female youth of the 'three graduating classes' of the Cultural Revolution), in *Ershiyi Shiji* (Twenty-First Century), no. 39 (February).

Li Yinhe and Wang Xiaobo. 1991. *Tamen de shijie: Zhongguo nan tongxinglian qunluo toushi* (Their world: Revelations of the Chinese gay community). Hong Kong: Cosmos Books (*Tiandi tushu*).

Li Yu. 1990. "Lian xiang ban" (Pity the fragrant companion). In *Li Yu quanji* (The complete works of Li Yu), ed. Xiao Xinqiao et al. 20 vols. Hangzhou: Zhejiang guji chubanshe, 4: 3–110.

Li Yu-ning, ed. 1992. *Chinese Women through Chinese Eyes*. New York: East Gate.

Li Ziyun. 1994. "Women's Consciousness and Women's Writing." In *Engendering China: Women, Culture, and the State*, ed. Christina Gilmartin, Gail Hershatter, Lisa Rofel, Tyrene White. Cambridge: Harvard University Press.

Liang Hu Xueji. 1995. "Valentine's Day: Red Rose and White Rose" (qing'renjie: hongmeigui yu baimeigui). *The Nineties* 302 (March): 10–11.

Liebman, Stuart. 1988a. "Why Kluge?" *October* no. 46–47.

———. 1988b. "On New German Cinema, Art, Enlightenment, and the Public Sphere: An Interview with Alexander Kluge." *October* no. 46–47.

Lin Bai. 1992. "Yige ren de zhanzheng" (One person's war). *Hua Cheng Review* no. 4.

———. 1995a. "Huilang zhi yi" (The chair in the winding corridor). In *Red Opium Poppies Collection. The Chair in the Winding Corridor: Selected works by Lin Bai*, ed. Wang Meng. Shijiazhang: Hebei jiaoyu chubanshe.

———. 1995b. "Ping zhong zhi shui" (Water in the bottle). In *Red Opium Poppies Collection. The Chair in the Winding Corridor: Selected works by Lin Bai*, ed. Wang Meng. Shijiazhang: Hebei jiaoyu chubanshe.

Lin, Fangmei. 1994a. *Shida qiangbao yi-an baoshi baodao fenxi: shei shi jia hai zhe? Shei shi shou hai zhen?* (Who is the victimizer? Who is the victim? An analysis of the Normal University rape incident). Taipei: Political University Journalism Institute.

———. 1994b. *Shehui wenti de jiangou yu quanshi: funu tuanti ruhe chenwei xiaoxi laiyuan* (The construction and interpretation of social problems: How women's organizations have become sources of social information). In *Xinwenxue yu xueshu de duihua* (Dialogues between journalism and academia), ed. Zang Guoren (Tsang Kuo-jen). Taipei: Political University Journalism Institute.

Lin Nien-tung. 1982. "Cantonese Cinema in the 1960s: Some Observations." *Hong Kong Urban Council Publications*, 32–40.

Lin Tongqi, Henry Rosemont Jr., and Roger T. Ames. 1996. "Chinese Philosophy: A Philosophical Essay on the 'State-of-the-Art.'" *Journal of Asian Studies* 54 (3): 727–58.

Ling Shuhua. 1984. *Ling Shuhua xiaoshuo ji* (Collected short stories by Ling Shuhua). 2 vols. Taipei: Hongfan shudian. Originally published in 1926.

Liu Dalin et al. 1992. *Zhongguo dangdai xing wenhua* (Sexual behavior in modern China). Shanghai: Sanlian shudian.

Liu Fuchu. 1991. *Zhongguo xingfa shiyong daquan* (A complete and practical guide to the Chinese criminal code). Hebei: Falü chubanshe.

Liu, Lydia. 1995a. *Translingual Practice: Literature, National Culture and Translated Modernity*. Stanford, Calif.: Stanford University Press.

———. 1995b. "Disjuncture of Theory: Transnationals, (Im)migrants and/or Diaspora?" Presented at the conference Mass Media, Gender and a Chinese Public: Mainland, Taiwan, Hong Kong. University of California, Santa Barbara, April 1–3.

———. 1994. "The Female Body and Nationalist Discourse: Manchuria in Xiao Hong's 'Field of Life and Death.'" In *Body, Subject, and Power in China*, ed. Angela Zito and Tani E. Barlow, 157–77. Chicago: University of Chicago Press.

———. 1991. "The Female Tradition in Modern Chinese Literature: Negotiating Feminisms across East/West Boundaries." *Genders* 12 (Winter): 22–44.

Liu Sola. 1994. *Chaos and All That*, trans. Richard King. Honolulu: University of Hawaii Press.

———. 1991. *Huntun gale geleng*. Hong Kong: Tupo chubanshe.

———. 1990. "Ren dui ren" (Crowd over crowd). *Today* 1: 19–25.

Liu Xin. 1997. "Space, Mobility and Flexibility: Chinese Villagers and Scholars Negotiate Power at Home and Abroad." In Ong and Nonini 1997, 91–114.

———. 1995. "Hong Kong Files" (xianggang dang'an). *The Nineties* 302 (March): 78–79.

Liu Zhi, ed. 1992. *Napen lizi, napen yingtao: Xungeng xiaoshuo* (That bowl of pears, that bowl of cherries: The roots-searching novel). Beijing: Beijing Shifan daxue chubanshe.

Louie, Kam. 1991. "The Macho Eunuch: The Politics of Masculinity in Jia Pingwa's 'Human Extremities.'" *Modern China* 117, no. 2: 163–87.

Lu Hanchao. 1995. "Away from Nanking Road: Small Stores and Neighborhood Life in Modern Shanghai." *Journal of Asian Studies* 54(1): 92–123.

Lü Meiyi and Zheng Yongfu. 1990. *Zhongguo Funü Yundong—1840–1921* (The Chinese women's movement—1840–1921). Zhengzhou: Henan People's Press.

Lu Tonglin. 1993. "Can Xue: What Is So Paranoid in Her Writings?" In *Gender and Sexuality in Twentieth-Century Chinese Literature and Society*, ed. Lu Tonglin, 175–204. Albany: State University of New York Press.

Lu Yin. 1985. *Lu Yin xuan ji* (Selected works of Lu Yin), ed. Qian Hong. Fuzhou: Fujian renmin chubanshe. Originally published in 1923.

Lui Tai-lok. 1988. "Home at Hong Kong." *Hong Kong Urban Council Publications*, 88–93.

Lui, Terry T. 1995. "Political Participation." In Pearson and Leung, 1995, 133–66.

Lull, James. 1991. *China Turned On: Television, Reform, and Resistance.* New York: Routledge.

Luo Canying (Luo Ts'an-ying). 1994. "*Shushi*" *qiangbao de meiti jiangou* (The media construction of 'rape between familiars'). Presented at the Conference on Women and the News Media, Taipei, December 9, 1994.

Luo Qiong. 1986. *The Basic Knowledge of Women's Liberation.* Beijing: People's Press.

Ma, Teresa. 1988. "Chronicles of Change: 1960s–1980s." *Hong Kong Urban Council Publications*, 77–80.

MacAloon, John. 1984. "Olympic Games and the Theory of Spectacle in Modern Societies." In *Rite, Drama, Festival, Spectacle: Rehearsals Toward a Theory of Cultural Performance*, ed. John MacAloon, 241–80. Philadelphia: Institute for the Study of Human Issues.

Madsen, Richard. 1993. "The Public Sphere, Civil Society, and Moral Community: A Research Agenda for Contemporary Chinese Studies." *Modern China* 19(2): 183–98.

Mao Shi-an et al. 1989. *Dazhong chuanbo zhong de nüxin xinxiang* (Female images in the mass media), *Shanghai Wenlun* (Shanghai Literary Forum), no. 2.

Mao Zedong. 1986. "Hunan nongmin yundong kaocha baogao" (An investigative report of the Hunan peasants' movement). In *Mao Zedong Wenji* (Selected works of Mao Zedong). Beijing: Renmin chubanshe.

Martin, Emily. 1987. *The Woman in the Body.* Boston: Beacon Press.

Massey, Doreen. 1994. *Space, Place, and Gender.* Minneapolis: University of Minnesota Press.

Meng Hui. 1994. "Meng Hui xiaoji" (Selected stories by Meng Hui). *Zhong Shan Review* no. 3.

Meng Yue. 1993. "Female Images and National Myth." In *Gender Politics in Modern China*, ed. Tani E. Barlow, 118–36. Durham, N.C.: Duke University Press.

———. 1992. "Zhongguo wenxue 'xiandaixing' yu Zhang Ailing" (The "modernity" of Chinese literature and Zhang Ailing). *Today* 3: 176–92.

Meng Yue and Dai Jinhua. 1988. *Fuchu lishi dibiao* (Emerging from the horizon of history: Modern Chinese women's literature). Zhengzhou: Henan Renmin Chubanshe.

Meyer, Alfred G. 1985. "Feminism, Socialism and Nationalism in Eastern Europe." In *Women, State, and Party in Eastern Europe*, ed. Sharon L. Wolchik and Alfred G. Meyer. Durham, N.C.: Duke University Press.

Miao Hui. 1987. "Bushi jinpai shengguo jinpai" (It wasn't gold medals surpassing gold medals). *Tiyu bao* (Sports news), 4 December.

Min, Anchee. 1994. *Red Azalea*. New York: Pantheon.

Mo Yan. 1996. *Feng ru fei tun* (Full breasts and wide bottoms). Beijing: Zuojia chubanshe.

———. 1993. *Red Sorghum*. New York: Viking Press.

———. 1992. "Hong gaoliang" (Red sorghum). In *Napen lizi, napen yingtao: xungeng xiaoshuo* (That bowl of pears, that bowl of cherries: The roots-searching novel), ed. Liu Zhi. Beijing: Beijing Shifan daxue chubanshe.

Modern China. 1993. Special issue on the question of public sphere in China. 19(2).

Mohanty, Chandra. 1988. "Under Western Eyes: Feminist Scholarship and Colonial Discourses." *Feminist Review* 30: 61–88.

Mohanty, Chandra, Anne Russo, and Lourdes Torres, eds. 1991. *Third World Women and the Politics of Feminism*. Bloomington: Indiana University Press.

Moi, Toril. 1986. "Introduction." *The Kristeva Reader*, ed. Toril Moi. New York: Columbia University Press.

———. 1985. *Sexual/Textual Politics*. New York: Routledge.

Moore, Henrietta L. 1994. *A Passion for Difference: Essays in Anthropology and Gender*. Bloomington: Indiana University Press.

Morrison, Toni, ed. 1992. *Race-ing Justice, En-gendering Power: Essays on Anita Hill, Clarence Thomas, and the Construction of Social Reality*. New York: Pantheon Books.

Mulvey, Laura. 1986. "Visual Pleasure and Narrative Cinema." In *Narrative, Apparatus, Ideology*, ed. Philip Rosen. New York: Columbia University Press.

———. 1990. "British Feminist Film Theory's Female Spectators: Presence and Absence," *Camera Obscura* 20–21.

Nanda, Serena. 1990. *Neither Man nor Woman: The Hijras of India*. Belmont, Calif.: Wadsworth Publishing.

Negt, Oskar, and Alexander Kluge, eds. 1993. *Public Sphere and Experience: Toward an Analysis of the Bourgeois and Proletarian Public Sphere*. Minneapolis: University of Minnesota Press.

New Women's Promotion Association (xin funü xiejinhui). 1995. *Services for Women in Hong Kong* (xianggang funü fuwu). Hong Kong: New Women's Promotion Association.

Newton, Esther. 1984. "The Mythic Mannish Lesbian: Radclyffe Hall and the New Woman." *Signs* 9(4): 557–75.

———. 1972. *MotherCamp*. Chicago: University of Chicago Press.

Ng Chun-hung. 1995. "Bringing Women Back In: Family Change in Hong Kong." In Pearson and Leung 1995.

Nonini, Donald. 1997. "Shifting Identities, Positioned Imaginaries: Transnational Traversals and Reversals by Malaysian Chinese." In Ong and Nonini 1997, 203–27.

Nonini, Donald, and Aihwa Ong. 1997. "Introduction: Chinese Transnationalism as an Alternative Modernity." In Ong and Nonini 1997, 3–35.

Notar, Beth. 1994. "Of Labor and Liberation: Images of Women in Current Chinese Television Advertising," *Visual Anthropology Review* 10, no. 2.

Nü pengyou (Girlfriend). August 1994–present.

Ong, Aihwa. 1997. "Chinese Modernities: Narratives of Nation and of Capitalism." In Ong and Nonini 1997, 171–201.

———. 1996. "Strategic Sisterhood or Sister in Solidarity? Questions of Communitarianism and Citizenship in Asia." *Global Legal Studies Journal* 4.

————. 1995. "Women out of China: Traveling Tales and Traveling Theories in Post-colonial Feminism." In *Women Writing Culture*, ed. R. Behar and D. Gordon, 350–72. Berkeley and Los Angeles: University of California Press.

————. 1993. "On the Edge of Empires: Flexible Citizenship among Chinese in Diaspora." *positions* 1(3): 743–78.

Ong, Aihwa, and Don Nonini, eds. 1997. *Ungrounded Empires: The Cultural Politics of Modern Chinese Transnationalism*. New York: Routledge.

Ong Xiuqi (Ong Hsiu-ch'i). 1994a. *Woguo funü yundong de meijie zhenshi he "shehui zhenshi"* (Media reality and social reality in our country's women's movement), *Xinwenxue yanjiu* (Studies in journalism), no. 48 (January).

————. 1994b. *Funü yundong yu xinwen baodao zhi yanjiu* (A study of the women's movement and its news reporting: A source analysis of *China Times* and *United Daily News* reporting of how the women's movement mobilized the redrafting of the Kinship Section of the Civil Code). Presented at the Conference on Women and the News Media, Taipei, December 9, 1994.

Ono, Kazuko. 1989. *Chinese Women in a Century of Revolution, 1850–1950*. Stanford, Calif.: Stanford University Press.

Orr, John. 1993. *Cinema and Modernity*. London: Polity Press.

Ortner, Sherry. 1996. "The Problem of Women as an Analytic Category." In *Making Gender: The Politics and Erotics of Culture*. Boston: Beacon Press.

Pan Guangdan, trans. 1946. *Xing xinlixue* (The psychology of sex), Havelock Ellis. Beijing: Sanlian shudian, 1987. Reprint.

Pan Suiming. 1987. *Nüxing xingquanli de lishi mingyun* (The historical fate of women's sexual rights), *Zhongguo funü* (Chinese women), no. 12.

Pan Yuan and Pan Jie. 1985. "The Non-Official Magazine *Today* and the Younger Generation's Ideals for a New Literature." In *After Mao: Chinese Literature and Society 1978–1981*, ed. Jeffrey Kinkley. Cambridge, Mass.: Harvard University Press.

Parker, Andrew, Mary Russo, Doris Sommer, and Patricia Yaeger, eds. 1992. *Nationalisms and Sexualities*. New York: Routledge.

Pateman, Carole. 1989a. *The Disorder of Women*. Stanford, Calif.: Stanford University Press.

————. 1989b. "Feminist Critiques of the Public/Private Dichotomy." In Pateman 1989a.

Pearson, Veronica, and Benjamin K. P. Leung, eds. 1995. *Women in Hong Kong*. Hong Kong: Oxford University Press.

Pellow, Deborah. 1993. "No Place to Live, No Place to Love: Coping in Shanghai." In *Urban Anthropology in China*, ed. G. Guldin and A. Southall, 396–424. New York: E. J. Brill.

Peterson, V. Spike, ed. 1992. *Gendered States: Feminist (Re)Visions of International Relations Theory*. Boulder, Colo.: Lynne Rienner.

Pickowicz, Paul. 1995. "Velvet Prisons and the Political Economy of Chinese Film-making." In *Urban Spaces in Contemporary China: The Potential for Autonomy and Community in Post-Mao China*, ed. Deborah Davis et al. New York: Cambridge University Press.

Polan, Dana. 1993. "The Public's Fear; Or, Media as Monster in Habermas, Negt, and Kluge." In Robbins 1993, 33–41.

Poster, Mark. 1995. *The Second Media Age*. Cambridge: Polity Press.

Public Culture. 1988. "Editor's Comments." 1(1).

Qiu Zhang and Lin Cuifen. 1994. *One Country, Two Wives* (Yiguo liangqi). Taipei: Jingmei chubanshe.

Rabinow, Paul. 1989. *French Modern: Norms and Forms of the Social Environment.* Cambridge, Mass.: MIT Press.

Radicalesbians. 1988. "The Woman-Identified Woman." In Hoagland and Penelope 1988, 17–21.

Rankin, Mary. 1993. "Some Observations on a Chinese Public Sphere." *Modern China,* 19(2).

Read, Richard. 1993. "Satisfying Two Thousand Million Spectators." In *Olympic Review.* Lausanne: International Olympic Committee, 508–10.

Riordan, James, and Dong Jinxia. 1996. "Chinese Women and Sport: Success, Sexuality and Suspicion." *China Quarterly* 145 (March): 130–52.

Robbins, Bruce, ed. 1993. *The Phantom Public Sphere.* Minneapolis: University of Minnesota Press.

Rofel, Lisa. Forthcoming. *Modern Imaginaries and "Other" Modernities.* Berkeley and Los Angeles: University of California Press.

———. 1994a. "Liberation Nostalgia and a Yearning for Modernity." In Gilmartin et al. 1994.

———. 1994b. "'Yearnings': Televisual Love and Melodramatic Politics in Contemporary China." *American Ethnologist* 21, no. 4.

Rong Gaotang et al., eds. 1984. *Dangdai Zhongguo tiyu* (Contemporary Chinese sports). Beijing: Chinese Social Sciences Press.

Rosaldo, Michelle. 1974. "Women, Culture and Society: a Theoretical Overview." In *Woman, Culture and Society,* ed. Michelle Rosaldo and Louise Lamphere. Stanford, Calif.: Stanford University Press.

———. 1980. "The Uses and Abuses of Anthropology," *Signs* 5, no. 3.

Roscoe, Will. 1991. *The Zuni Man-Woman.* Albuquerque: University of New Mexico Press.

Rosen, Stanley. 1994. "Chinese Women in the 1990s: Images and Roles in Contention." In *China Review 1994,* ed. Maurice Brosseau and Lo Chi Kin. Hong Kong: Chinese University of Hong Kong Press.

Rosenfeld, Marthe. 1988. "Splits in French Feminism/Lesbianism." In Hoagland and Penelope 1988, 457–66.

Rowe, William T. 1993. "The Problem of 'Civil Society' in Late Imperial China." *Modern China* 19(2).

———. 1990. "The Public Sphere in Modern China" in *Modern China,* vol. 16, no. 3, July.

Rubin, Gayle (with Judith Butler). 1994. "Sexual Traffic: An Interview" in *differences,* vol. 6, no. 2-3.

———. 1984. "The Traffic in Women: Notes on the 'Political Economy' of Sex." In *Feminist Frameworks,* ed. Alison M. Jagger and Paula S. Rothenberg, 155–71. New York: McGraw-Hill.

Ryan, Mary P. 1992. "Gender and Public Access: Women's Politics in Nineteenth-Century America." In Calhoun 1992.

———. 1990. *Women in the Public: Between Banners and Ballots, 1825–1880.* Baltimore: Johns Hopkins University Press.

Said, Edward. 1978. *Orientalism.* New York: Vintage Press.

Salaff, Janet W. 1981. *Working Daughters of Hong Kong*, reprinted 1995. New York: Columbia University Press.

Sandoval, Chela. 1991. "U.S. Third World Feminism: The Theory and Method of Oppositional Consciousness in the Postmodern World" in *Genders*, no. 10.

Sang, Tze-lan D. 1996. "The Emerging Lesbian: Female Same-Sex Desire in Modern Chinese Literature and Culture," Ph.D. diss., University of California, Berkeley.

Schein, Louisa. 1997a. "Gender and Internal Orientalism in China," *Modern China* 23, no. 1: 69–98.

————. 1997b. "Urbanity, Cosmopolitanism, Consumption." In *Ethnographies of the Urban: China in the 1990s*, ed. Nancy Chen, Constance Clark, Virginia Cornue, Suzanne Gottschang, and Lyn Jeffery. Durham, N.C.: Duke University Press.

————. 1994. "The Consumption of Color and the Politics of White Skin in Post-Mao China." *Social Text* 41 (Winter): 141–64.

————. 1992. "Reconfiguring the Dominant: Multidimensionality in the Manufacture of the Miao." Presented at the American Anthropological Association meeting, San Francisco, November.

Schell, Orville. 1985. *To Get Rich Is Glorious: China in the 80's*. New York: New American Library.

Schlupmann, Heidi. 1990. "Femininity as Productive Force: Kluge and Critical Theory." *New German Critique* 49 (Winter).

Shambaugh, David, ed. 1993. Special Issue on Greater China. *China Quarterly*, no. 136 (December).

Shan Zai. 1911. "Funü tongxing zhi aiqing" (Same-sex erotic love between women). *Funü shibao* (Women's times) [Shanghai] 1(7): 36–38.

Shih, Shu-mei. 1997. "Problems of the 'Northward Imaginary': Cultural Identity Politics in Hong Kong" ("Beijin xiangxiang" de wenti: Xianggang wenhua rentong zhengzhi zhi wojian). In *Northward Imaginary*, ed. Stephen Chan. Hong Kong. Oxford University Press.

————. 1996a. "Gender, Race, and Semicolonialism: Liu Na'ou's Urban Shanghai Landscape." *Journal of Asian Studies* 55(4): 934–56.

————. 1996b. Interview with Alfred Cheung. Santa Monica, Calif., March. Transcript.

————. 1995. "The Trope of 'Mainland China' in Taiwan's Media." *positions* 3(1).

Shu Kei. 1987. "We Didn't Wait in Vain." *Film Bi-Monthly* 219: 4–5; 220: 5–6.

Shue, Vivienne. 1994. "Philanthropic Ventures: Problems of Charity and Social Welfare." Prepared for presentation at the Columbia University Modern China Seminar, May 12.

Silber, Cathy. 1994. "From Daughter to Daughter-in-Law in the Women's Script of Southern Hunan." In Gilmartin et al. 1994, 47–68.

Sinn, Elizabeth, ed. 1995. *Culture and Society in Hong Kong*. Hong Kong: Centre of Asian Studies, University of Hong Kong.

Sivin, Nathan, Frances Wood, Penny Brooke, and Colin Ronan. 1988. *The Contemporary Atlas of China*. London: Weidenfeld and Nicolson.

Sommer, Mathew. 1994. "Sex, Law and Society in Late Imperial China." Ph.D. diss., University of California, Los Angeles.

Spivak, Gayatri Chakravorty. 1988a. "Can the Subaltern Speak?" In *Marxism and the Interpretation of Culture*, ed. Cary Nelson. Chicago: University of Chicago Press.

Spivak, Gayatri Chakravorty. 1988b. "Subaltern Studies: Deconstructing Historiography."

In *Selected Subaltern Studies*, ed. Ranajit Guha and Gayatri C. Spivak. New York: Oxford University Press.

————. 1987. *In Other Worlds: Essays in Cultural Politics*. New York: Routledge.

Stewart, Susan. 1993. *On Longing: Narratives of the Miniature, the Gigantic, the Souvenir, the Collection*. Durham, N.C.: Duke University Press.

Stoler, Ann Laura. 1991. "Carnal Knowledge and Imperial Power: Gender, Race and Morality in Colonial Asia." In *Gender at the Crossroads of Knowledge: Feminist Anthropology in the Postmodern Era*, ed. M. DiLeonardo, 51–101. Berkeley and Los Angeles: University of California Press.

Su Tong. 1993a. "Lihun zhinan" (A guide for divorce). In *A Guide for Divorce and Other Stories*. Beijing: Hua Yi chubanshe.

————. 1993b. "Ling yizhong funü shenghuo" (Another kind of woman's life). In *Kua shiji wencong, Su Tong xiaoshuo xuan* (Fin de siècle literary collection: Selected novels by Su Tong, ed. Chen Juntao. Beijing: Changjiang wenyi chubanshe.

————. 1993c. "Yihun Nanren Yang Bo" (The married man Yang Bo). In *A Guide for Divorce and Other Stories*. Beijing: Hua Yi chubanshe.

————. 1992a. "Hong Fen" (Rouge powder). In *Kua shiji wencong: Su Tong xiaoshuo xuan* (Fin de siècle literary collection: Selected novels by Su Tong), ed. Chen Juntao. Beijing: Changjiang wenyi chubanshe.

————. 1992b. "Qiqie chengqun" (Wives and concubines). In *Raise the Red Lantern: Selected Novels of Su Tong*. Guangdong: Hua Chenchubanshe.

————. 1992c. "Yingsu zhi jia" (The poppy family). In *Kua shiji wencong, Su Tong xiaoshuo xuan* (Fin de siècle literary collection: Selected novels by Su Tong), ed. Chen Juntao. Beijing: Changjiang wenyi chubanshe.

Su Xiaokang and Wang Luxiang. 1991. *Deathsong of a River: A Reader's Guide to the Chinese TV Series Heshang*, trans. Richard W. Bodman and Piu P. Wan. Ithaca, N.Y.: Cornell East Asia Program.

Su Yaping et al. 1991. "Nü tongxinglian zhe xing'ai biantai da jiemi" (Revealing a hundred secrets in female homosexuals' sex and love). *Dujia baodao* (Exclusive reports) 139: 25–38.

Sui, Bobby. 1981. *Women of China: Imperialism and Women's Resistance 1900–1949*. London: Zed Books.

Sutton, Constance, ed. 1995. *Feminism, Nationalism, and Militarism*. Arlington: Association for Feminist Anthropology/American Anthropological Association.

Taida Lambda (Taida nü tongxinglian wenhua yanjiushe). 1995. *Women shi nü tongxinglian* (We are lesbians). Taipei: Shuoren chuban.

Taipei Golden Horse Film Festival. 1994. "'Division' and 'Reunion': A Perspective of Chinese Cinemas of the 90s" ("Duanlie" yu "fuhe": Zhanwang jiushi niandai zhongguo dianying).

Taussig, Michael. 1993. *Mimesis and Alterity: A Particular History of the Senses*. New York: Routledge.

Tie Ning. 1989. *Meigui men* (The rose gate). Beijing: Zuojia chubanshe.

Time. 1985. "Old Wounds." December 2, 50.

Track and Field News. 1995. "Ma's Army Disbands." April: 58–59.

Tsing, Anna. 1993. *In the Realm of the Diamond Queen*. Princeton, N.J.: Princeton University Press.

Tu Weiming. 1991. "Cultural China: The Periphery as Center." *Daedalus* 120 (2).

Turner, Matthew. 1995. "Hong Kong Sixties/Nineties: Dissolving the People." In *Hong Kong Sixties: Designing Identity*, ed. Matthew Turner and Irene Ngan, 13–34. Hong Kong: Hong Kong Arts Centre.

Turner, Matthew, and Irene Ngan, eds. 1995. *Hong Kong Sixties: Designing Identity*. Hong Kong: Hong Kong Arts Centre.

Ueno, Chizuko. 1997. "Interview." In *Broken Silence: Voices of Japanese Feminism*, ed. Sandra Buckley. Berkeley and Los Angeles: University of California Press.

Urla, Jacqueline. 1995. "Outlaw Language: Creating Alternative Public Spheres in Basque Free Radio." *Pragmatics* (June).

Verdery, Katherine. 1994. "From Parent-State to Family Patriarchs: Gender and Nation in Contemporary Eastern Europe," *East European Politics and Societies* 8, no. 2.

Vitiello, Giovanni. 1994. "Exemplary Sodomites: Male Homosexuality in Late Ming Fiction." Ph.D. diss. University of California, Berkeley.

Wakeman, Frederic. 1993. "The Civil Society and Public Sphere Debate: Western Reflections on Chinese Political Culture." *Modern China* 19(2).

Wakeman, Frederic, and Wen-hsin Yeh, eds. 1992. *Shanghai Sojourners*. Berkeley: Institute of East Asian Studies, University of California.

Walden, Margie Joy. 1995. "Exclusion of Taiwan Activists Diminishes Impact of the U.N. Fourth World Conference on Women." *Bulletin of Concerned Asian Scholars* 27, no. 3.

Wang Anyi. 1996. *Chang Hen Ge* (The long ode of lost love). Beijing: Zuojia chubanshe.

———. 1991. "Shushu de gushi" (My uncle's story"). In *The Sacred Altar: Selected Stories by Wang An-yi*. Shanghai: Renmin wenxue chubanshe.

———. 1990. *Liu Shui Sanshi zhang* (The thirty chapters of the flowing stream). In *Xiaoshuo jie wenku* (The treasury of novels). Shanghai: Shanghai Wenyi chubanshe.

———. 1987. "Jinxiugu zhi lian" (Love in brocade valley), *Zhongshan*, no. 1.

———. 1986a. *Xiao Bao Zhuang*. (Xiao Bao village). Shanghai: Shanghai Wenyi chubanshe.

———. 1986b. "Xiaocheng zhi lian" (Love in a small town), *Shanghai wenxue* (Shanghai Literature), no. 8.

———. 1986c. "Huangshan zhi lian" (Love in a wild mountain), *Shi yue* (October), no. 2.

Wang Benhu. 1991. *Amoi Bride* (Xiamen xinniang). Taizhong: chenxing chubanshe.

Wang Dewei. 1993. "Shijimode zhongwen xiaoshuo: yuyan size" (Fin de siècle Chinese fiction: Four predictions). *Today*. 2: 150–65.

Wang Shaoguang. 1995. "The Politics of Private Time: Changing Leisure Patterns in Urban China." In *Urban Spaces in Contemporary China: The Potential for Autonomy and Community in Post-Mao China*, ed. Deborah Davis et al., 149–72. New York: Cambridge University Press.

Wang Shuo. 1992. "Guoba yin jiu si" (Die but after the throw). In *Collected Works of Wang Shuo*. Vol. 1. Beijing: Hua Yi chubanshe.

Wang Yeujin. 1991. "Red Sorghum: Mixing Memory and Desire." In *Perspectives on Chinese Cinema*, ed. Chris Berry. London: British Film Institute, 80–103.

Wang Zheng. 1995. *The Ascent of Women: Contemporary Feminist Movement in the U.S.* Beijing: Dangdai Press.

Watson, Rubie. 1991. "Wives, Concubines and Maids: Servitude and Kinship in the Hong Kong Region 1900–1940" in *Marriage and Inequality in Chinese Society*. Rubie Watson and Patricia Buckley Ebrey, eds. Berkeley: University of California Press.

Wei Xuan and Lao Min Sheng. 1990. "Interview with Ann Hui." *FB* 289: 12–17.

Weng Ouhong, and Ah Jia. 1965. *Red Lantern* (Hongdengji). Beijing: Zhongguo xiju chubanshe. Adapted.

Whitehead, Harriet. 1981. "The Bow and the Burden Strap: A New Look at Institutionalized Homosexuality in Native North America." In *Sexual Meanings: the Cultural Construction of Gender and Sexuality*, ed. Sherry Ortner and Harriet Whitehead. Cambridge: Cambridge University Press.

Williams, Linda. 1989. *Hardcore: Power, Pleasure and the Frenzy of the Visible*. Berkeley and Los Angeles: University of California Press.

Williams, Raymond. 1973. "Base and Superstructure in Marxist Cultural Theory." *New Left Review* 82 (November–December): 31–56.

Wilton, Tamsin. 1995. *Lesbian Studies: Setting an Agenda*. New York: Routledge.

Wolchik, Sharon L., and Alfred G. Meyer, eds. 1985. *Women, State, and Party in Eastern Europe*. Durham, N.C.: Duke University Press.

Wolf, Margery. 1985. *Revolution Postponed: Women in Contemporary China*. Stanford, Calif.: Stanford University Press.

———. 1972. *Women and the Family in Rural Taiwan*. Stanford, Calif.: Stanford University Press.

Wood, Robin. 1977. "Ideology, Genre, Auteur." *Film Comment* 13(1): 46–51.

WRI (Women's Research Institute). 1995. Organizational Brochure. Beijing: WRI.

———. 1994a. "The Perplexed State of Women in Contemporary PRC: Statistical Data of Women's Hotline." Beijing: WRI.

———. 1994b. "What Progress We Have Made." Annual Report. Beijing: WRI.

———. N.d. "Hot Line for Women/Specialists' Hot Line for Women." Beijing: WRI.

Wu, Rose. 1995. "Women." In *The Other Hong Kong Report*, ed. Stephen M. H. Sze. Hong Kong: Chinese University of Hong Kong Press, 122–56.

Wu Wenxin (Wu Wen-hsin). 1988. *Riju shiqui Taiwan de fangzu duanfa yundong*. (The anti-footbinding and hair-cutting movement in Taiwan during the Japanese occupation). In *Zhongguo funü shilun wenji* (Collected essays on the history of Chinese women). Vol. 2, ed. Li You-ning, Zhang Yufa (Chang Yu-fa). Taipei: Shangwu Publishers, 465–510.

Xiandai hanyu cidian (The dictionary of the modern Chinese language). 1973. Beijing: Shangwu.

Xiao Mingxiong. 1984. *Zhongguo tongxing'ai shilu* (The history of homosexuality in China). Hong Kong: Fenhong sanjiao chubanshe.

Xie Se, trans. 1927. "Nü xuesheng de tongxing ai" (The school-friendship of girls), Havelock Ellis. *Xin wenhua* (New culture) [Shanghai] 6: 57–74.

Xie Ye. 1993a. "Huangxi huxi" (In a trance). *Today* 2: 35–49.

———. 1993b. "Nide minzi jiao Mu'er" (Your name is Samuel). *Today* 4: 1–12.

Xie Zhimin. 1991. *Jiangyong "Nüshu" Zhi Mi* (Enigmas of the Jiangyong "women's script"). Zhengzhou: Henan People's Press.

Xin Tiyu (New sports). 1981. "Kan nüpai duo kui huaxu" (Tidbits from watching women's volleyball seize supremacy). *Xin Tiyu* December, 22.

Xinzhi gongzuoshi. 1995. "Chai jie hunyin shenhua" (Dismantle the marriage myth). *Funü xinzhi* 158: 10–12.

Xu Kun. 1995. "Congci yuelai yue mingliang" (Brighter and brighter from now on). In *Beijing Wenxue* (Beijing literature) no. 11.

Xu Lan. 1995. "Xu Lan xiaoshuo xuan" (Selected stories of Xu Lan). In *Xiaoshuo jie wenku* (The treasury of the World of Novels). Shanghai: Shanghai wenyi chubanshe.

Xu Xiaobin. 1995. "Shuang yu xingzuo" (The double fish constellation). In *Mi huan huayuan* (The garden of illusion: Selected works by Xu Xiao-bin), ed. Chen Xiaoming. Beijing: Hua Yi chubanshe.

Xuan Xiaofo. 1990. *Yuan zhi wai* (Outside the circle), 2nd ed. Taipei: Wansheng chuban.

Yan Renghua. 1988. "Jinguo bu rang xumei" (The women don't yield to the men). *Tiyu bao* (Sports news), March 9.

Yang Cui (Yang Ts'ui). 1993. *Riju shiqi Taiwan funü jiefang yundong* (The women's movement in Taiwan during the Japanese occupation). Taipei: Times Cultural Publishing.

Yang, Mayfair Mei-hui. 1997. "Mass Media and Transnational Subjectivity in Shanghai: Notes on (Re)cosmopolitanism in a Chinese Metropolis." In Ong and Nonini, 1997, 287–319.

Yang, Mayfair. 1996a. "Tradition, Traveling Anthropology, and the Discourse of Modernity in China." In *The Future of Anthropological Knowledge*, ed. Henrietta Moore. New York: Routledge.

———. 1996b. "Sacrifice and Sexuality: Female Media Icons and the Changing Relationship between Domestic and Public/State Spheres in China." Presented at the American Anthropological Association meetings, San Francisco, November.

———. 1994a. "State Discourse or a Plebeian Public Sphere? Film Discussion Groups in China." *Visual Anthropology Review* 10(1).

———. 1994b. *Gifts, Favors, and Banquets: The Art of Social Relationships in China*. Ithaca, N.Y.: Cornell University Press.

———. 1993. "Of Gender, State Censorship and Overseas Capital: An Interview with Chinese Director Zhang Yimou." *Public Culture* 5(2): 1–17.

Yao, Esther. 1994. "Border Crossing: Mainland China's Presence in Hong Kong Cinema." In Browne et al. 1994, 180–201.

Ye Shaojun (Ye Shengtao). 1987. *Ye Shengtao ji* (Works by Ye Shengtao), eds. Ye Shishan et al. 4 vols. Jiangsu: Jiaoyu chubanshe. 287–95. Originally published in 1922.

Ye Zhaoyan. 1992. "Zaoshu de gushi" (The story of the date tree). In *Kua shiji wencong: Ye Zhaoyan xiaoshuo xuan* (Fin de siècle literary collection: Selected novels by Ye Zhaoyan), ed. Chen Juntao. Beijing: Changjiang wenyi chubanshe.

You You. 1995. "Xiao Meng's Nirvana" (Xiao Meng niepan). *Today* 4: 69–98.

———. 1993. "The Screaming Wood." *Today* 1: 114–19.

Yu Mo-wan. 1982. "A Study of Zhong Lian Film Company." *Hong Kong Urban Council Publications*, 41–50.

Yuan Weimin. 1988. *Wode zhijiao zhi dao* (My way of teaching). Beijing: Renmin tiyu chubanshe.

Yuxuan Aji. 1995a. "Jiehun quan yu bu jiehun quan" (The right of marriage and the right not to marry). *Nü pengyou* 3: 16–17.

———. 1995b. "Xishou zhi qian, fenli, you qi biyao" (Before holding hands, it is necessary to break up). *Funü xinzhi* 161: 16–18.

Zha Jianying. 1995. *China Pop: How Soap Operas, Tabloids, and Bestsellers Are Transforming a Culture*. New York: New Press.

———. 1990. "Jiemu" (Program). *Today* 1: 10–18.

Zhang Beichuan. 1994. *Tongxingai* (Homosexuality). Jinan: Shandong Kexue Jishu chubanshe.

Zhang Jie. 1989. *Zhiyou yige taiyang* (There is only one sun). Beijing: Zuojia chubanshe.
————. 1986. *Love Must Not Be Forgotten*. Beijing: Panda Books.
Zhang Yingjin. 1994. "Engendering Chinese Filmic Discourse on the 1930s: Configurations of Modern Women in Shanghai in Three Silent Films." *positions* 2(3): 603–28.
————. 1990. "Ideology of the Body in 'Red Sorghum': National Allegory, National Roots, and Third Cinema," *East-West Film Journal* 4, no. 2 (June): 38–53.
Zhao Yu. 1988. "Qiangguo meng" (Superpower dream). *Dangdai* (Contemporary times): February.
Zheng Langping. 1994. *August, 1995* (yijiujiuwu runbayue). Taibei: shangzhou wenhua gufen youxian gongsi.
Zheng Xian. 1994. "Wei wanchengde pianzhang: Wei jinian *Jintian* shiwu zhounian erzuo" (The incomplete chapter: Commemorating the fifteenth anniversary of *Today*). *Today* 1: 1–17.
Zheng Yefu. 1995. *Daijia lun: yige shehuixue de xin shidian* (On paying a price: A new perspective from sociology). Beijing: Sanlian shudian.
Zheng Yi. 1989. *Old Well*. San Francisco: China Books and Periodicals.
Zhong Xueping. 1994. "Male Suffering and Male Desire: The Politics of Reading *Half of Man Is Woman*." In Gilmartin et al. 1994, 175–94.
————. 1989. "Why Do Chinese Women Look For 'Real Men'?" Presented at the annual conference of the Association of Chinese Historians in the United States, Los Angeles, August 1989.
Zhou Huashan. 1996. *Beijing tongzhi gushi* (Stories of Beijing queers). Hong Kong: Xianggang tongzhi yanjiushe.
Zhou Huashan and Zhao Wenzong. 1995. *Yigui xingshi* (The history of the sexual closet). Hong Kong: Xianggang tongzhi yanjiushe.
Zhuang Huiqiu. 1991. *Zhongguoren de tongxinglian* (Chinese homosexuality). Taipei: Zhang Laoshi chubanshe.

Contributors

SUSAN BROWNELL received national media coverage as "the American girl who won glory for Beijing University" when she won a gold medal for Beijing City in the 1986 National College Games during a year of language study at Beijing University. She returned to China to study sport theory at Beijing University of Physical Education (1987–88) and is currently associate professor of anthropology at the University of Missouri, St. Louis. Brownell is the author of *Training the Body for China: Sports in the Moral Order of the People's Republic* (1995), as well as several articles on sports television and nationalism in China.

VIRGINIA CORNUE is a doctoral candidate in anthropology at Rutgers University currently completing her dissertation "(Re)Organizing 'Women': Gender, Non-government Organizations, and Contemporary Change in the PRC." She has published several articles on Chinese gender issues and is coeditor of the forthcoming book *Ethics and Social Change: Cultural Values in Transition in Late Twentieth-Century China.*

DAI JINHUA is a feminist scholar of film and literature at the Institute of Comparative Literature at Beijing University and the Beijing Film Academy, where most of China's Fifth and Sixth Generation filmmakers learned their art. She is one of China's outstanding younger scholars who attended college after the Cultural Revolution. Having taught and attended conferences in the United States and France, she is familiar with Western cultural theories while being solidly grounded in the changing dynamics and social issues of contemporary Chinese society, media production, and intellectual culture. She is coauthor with Meng Yue of *Emerging from the Horizon of History* (1988), and author of *Storming the Barricade: Women/Film/ Literature, The Screen and Popular Folklore,* and *A Handbook of Film Theory and Criticism.*

KATHLEEN ERWIN received her doctorate in anthropology at the University of California, Berkeley, in 1998. She first lived in Shanghai in 1984–85 and conducted her fieldwork there in 1993 and 1994–95. She is currently revising her dissertation, "Liberating Sex, Mobilizing Virtue: Cultural Reconstructions of Gender, Marriage, and Family in Shanghai, China" for publication.

ELAINE YEE LIN HO is associate professor in the department of English at the University of Hong Kong. She has published articles on Renaissance literature, postcolonial writing, and Hong Kong fiction, and is currently writing a book on the writer Timothy Mo.

LEE YUAN-CHEN is associate professor in the department of Chinese literature at Tamkang University, Taipei, Taiwan. She has played an integral role in the leadership of the women's movement in Taiwan since 1982 and has also written numerous poems, works of fiction, and literary criticism. Her publications include *Women Boldly Striding Forward* (1988), *Liberate Love and Beauty* (1990), and *Women's Poetic Eye* (1995). She is currently working on a book on feminist poetics and continuing her feminist political activism in Taiwan.

LI XIAOJIANG is a well-known and influential feminist intellectual in China. She teaches Chinese and Western literature and is based at Zhengzhou University in the city of Zhengzhou, as well as the Women's Studies Center at Henan University in the city of Kaifeng, both in Henan Province. In the post-Mao period, she was one of the earliest feminist writers to take an independent feminist position in a different register from that of official feminism. She was perhaps the most important person behind the launching of women's studies programs at research institutions throughout the country in the 1980s, and she is the editor-in-chief of the path-breaking *Women's Studies Series.* Her many publications include *Explorations of Eve* (1988) and *Women, a Distant Beautiful Legend* (1992).

LISA ROFEL is associate professor of anthropology at the University of California, Santa Cruz. She is the author of the forthcoming book *Other Modernities: Gendered Yearnings in China after Socialism.*

TZE-LAN DEBORAH SANG is assistant professor in East Asian languages and literatures at the University of Oregon. Born and educated in Taiwan, she received her doctorate in comparative literature from the University of California, Berkeley, in 1996. Sang is the author of the forthcoming book *The Emerging Lesbian: Female Same-Sex Desire in Modern Chinese Literature and Culture* and is developing a manuscript on transnational Chinese cinema.

SHU-MEI SHIH is assistant professor of comparative literature, Asian American studies, and East Asian languages and cultures at the University of California, Los Angeles. She has published articles in journals in the United States (*Journal of Asian Studies, Signs, positions: east asia cultures critique*), Taiwan (*Con-temporary, Unitas, Chung-Wai Literary Monthly*), China (*The Scholars*), and Hong Kong (*Twenty-First Century*), as well as in various anthologies. Shih has just completed a manuscript titled "The Lure of the Modern: Writing Modernism in Semicolonial China, 1917–1937."

MAYFAIR MEI-HUI YANG is associate professor of anthropology at the University of California, Santa Barbara. She is the author of *Gifts, Banquets, and Favors: The Art of Social Relationships in China*, and numerous works on state power in China, the construction of "tradition" in Chinese modernity, and Chinese mass-media development. Yang has also made the documentary videos *Through Chinese Women's Eyes* (1997) and *Public and Private Realms in Rural Wenzhou, China* (1994).

ZHANG ZHEN completed her Ph.D. in Chinese film and literature at the University of Chicago. She is currently an Andrew W. Mellon postdoctoral fellow in the humanities and visiting assistant professor in the Asia languages department at Stanford University. She will assume an assistant professor post in the department of cinema studies at New York University in 1999. She is a widely published poet in China and the diaspora.

Index

consciousness, 273
consumer culture. *See* capitalist culture
core-periphery relations, 9
Cott, Nancy, 25
cultural China, 6, 303
  Confucian heritage, 6
  critique of, 7
  as site of Chinese public sphere, 303
  undermining hegemonic statism, 303
cultural destabilization, 172
cultural feminism, 69–70, 89n5, 91n17
  Alcoff, Linda, 69
  as women's space, 70
cultural logic, 16, 209
cultural production
  commercialization of, 21
  discourse, 5, 167
  ownership of, 11
  representational spaces, 5, 119–20

Dai Jinhua, 35, 58
decentering the West, 23
  gendered and sexualized discourse of,
    238, 242–43
  reversal of West-Other relations, 9, 238
  sinicization, 250–51
Deleuze, Gilles, and Félix Guattari, 61,
  278
deterritorialization, 280, 292, 302
development model, East Asian, 10
diaspora, Chinese 282–83, 309
  as cultural dislocation, 312
  haiwai (beyond the ocean), 309
  literature (*haiwai wenxue*), 309, 315
  qiaoju taxiang (residing in other coun-
    tries), 309
Ding Ling, 324
discourse, 262–63, 268
  choosing, 29, 262
  construction of history, 264
  Enlightenment, 266–67
  feminist, 35–39, 56, 83, 268
  life experience as, 272
  male discourse, 264
  socialist, 266–67
  as tool of ideology, 265–57
  West Wind, 266

East Asian development model, 10
Engels, Friedrich, 37
Enzensberger, Hans M., 23, 151
equality, 274

familiarity shock, 73
feminism and discourse (Chinese), 35–39,
  56, 83
  consciousness of sexuality and desire,
    61–63, 143, 204
  gender as a category, 36, 39, 47, 58,
    126, 144
  goals of, 103
  nüxingxue discourse, 84
  postcolonial feminist theory, 35, 36,
    56
  postmodern feminist theory, 36
  and nationalism, 59, 292
  sports, 219
  and state feminism, 57, 82, 84, 88, 203
  transnationalism, 59, 107, 110, 112
  trope of, 81–82
  and Western feminism, 59, 275
  women as social category (*nüxing*), 81,
    83, 128–29, 272, 277
  See also state feminism
Fifth Generation films, 21, 28, 191, 205n1
film and cinema
  as critical practice, 163–64, 167, 182
  New Wave, 15, 28, 163–66, 183n3
  Through Chinese Women's Eyes, 21
Foucault, Michel
  biopower (of the state), 62
  governmentalization, 25
  on homosexuality, 132
  memory, 186n17, 292
  power, 87, 118
  repressive hypothesis, 44
Frankfurt School. *See* Theodor Adorno
Fraser, Nancy, 79, 85, 314

gender binary, 36, 39, 47, 305n5
gender as a category, 36, 39, 47, 58, 126,
  144
gender erasure (*xingbue muosha*), 40–47,
  215–16, 218
  desexualization, 41, 44

queer theory and identity, 140, 147

race, and gender, 200
resistance, 175–76
reterritorialization, 292
Ryan, Mary P., 85

self-Orientalizing, 192–93, 195, 198–202
Shanghai, as metaphor, 240
Sino-British Joint Declaration, 14, 172
sisterhood, 276
spatialization, 3
state, the
  absorption of public and private
    spheres, 26
  as cultural force, 9, 210
  developmental vs. revolutionary, 10
  disciplinary power, 229
  discourse of, 28
  gender of (male), 45–46, 64, 227
  governmentalization of family, 25, 46
  as mode of production, 9
  modernist projects of, 80–81
state Confucianism, 25, 46
state feminism, 12, 57, 82, 84, 88, 203
  decline of, 52–54
  erasure of gender, 11, 37–38, 42–43, 46,
    268–71
  gender division of labor, 11, 53
  incorporation (limited) of women into
    public sphere, 46
  and the law, 37
  nationalism of, 40, 80
  new forms of, 73–74
state nationalism, 40, 210, 215, 226
  gender erasure in, 215–18, 221
  male subject-position of, 221, 227
state patriarchy, 9, 26, 37, 112
Su Tong, 198
subaltern perspective, 228, 235
subaltern publics, 5
subjectivity, 35, 186n21
  constituted by language, 317
  constituted by time, 323
  and love and sexuality, 35, 78
  male, 50, 154, 229–30
  modern, 324

  See also gendered subjectivity
subject-positions, 36
  consumer nationalist, 36
  feminist or women's, 36, 272
  male, 221, 223, 225, 227, 228, 231
  Maoist state, 36, 45

Taiwan, 12–13
  and cultural hegemony of Mainland, 12
  fear of takeover by Mainland, 285–86
  feminism, 12, 100–107, 112, 291
  immigration of mainland Chinese to,
    284, 286
  Martial Law, 12, 101
  state patriarchy, 12
telecommunications, 74, 76
television
  importance of, 20, 22
  coverage of feminism in Taiwan,
    98–100, 101–4
  in Hong Kong, 164
  national and transnational subjectivity,
    210, 233–34
  sports coverage in China, 210–12
  and state, 235
Today (journal) (*Jintian*), 315–16
traffic in women, 29, 99, 111, 233, 239,
  284
transnational capital, 9
transnational China, 3, 7–8, 279, 303
  capitalism of, 19, 280
  through Chinese-language media, 8
  vs. cultural China, 6
  cultural and material flows, 7, 8, 279
  cultural zones of, 10
  vs. Greater China, 6
  as network, 7
  and state, 9, 303
transnational Chinese identity, 232, 248,
  253
  expunging feminized nation, 243
  masculine identity, 241, 243, 249–50
  masculinist narratives of, 233, 235, 238,
    243, 248, 252–53
  model femininity, 249–50, 253
  and modernity, 233, 236–37, 239–42,
    249